HIDDEN ACADEMICS: CONTRACT FACULTY IN CANADIAN UNIVERSITIES

Over the past two decades, continual government cutbacks to higher education have forced universities to become increasingly dependent on full- and part-time contract faculty. This situation has reinforced the functional split in the academic labour force, a split that has resulted in dramatic differences in status, compensation, career opportunities, and professional development between faculty members.

In *Hidden Academics*, Indhu Rajagopal examines the multiple ways in which contract faculty have emerged as an underclass in academia. She explores the identity of the part-time faculty, the nature of their work, and their feelings about their status within the university. Central to these discussions is an analysis of occupational segregation and the feminization of the part-time workforce. In the course of the study, Rajagopal also looks at full-time faculty and their perceptions of part-timers, academic administrators' reasons for hiring part-timers, and the future of the university in this context.

INDHU RAJAGOPAL is an Associate Professor of Social Science at York University.

HIDDEN ACADEMICS

CONTRACT FACULTY
IN CANADIAN UNIVERSITIES

Indhu Rajagopal

UNIVERSITY OF TORONTO PRESS
Toronto Buffalo London

© University of Toronto Press Incorporated 2002
Toronto Buffalo London
Printed in Canada

ISBN 0-8020-4258-9 (cloth)
ISBN 0-8020-8098-7 (paper)

Printed on acid-free paper

National Library of Canada Cataloguing in Publication Data

Rajagopal, Indhu, 1938–
    Hidden academics : contract faculty in Canadian universities

    Includes bibliographical references and index.
    ISBN 0-8020-4258-9 (bound). ISBN 0-8020-8098-7 (pbk.)

    1. College teachers, Part-time – Canada.   2. Universities and
    colleges – Canada – Faculty.   3. Part-time employment – Canada.
    I. Title.

    LB2331.74.C3R34 2002   378.1′22   C2002-900799-2

This book has been published with the help of a grant from the Humanities
and Social Sciences Federation of Canada, using funds provided by the
Social Sciences and Humanities Research Council of Canada.

The University of Toronto Press acknowledges the financial assistance to its
publishing program of the Canada Council for the Arts and the Ontario
Arts Council.

University of Toronto Press acknowledges the financial support for its
publishing activities of the Government of Canada through the Book
Publishing Industry Development Program (BPIDP).

For Amba, Raj, Arun, and Anil
without whose inspiration, generosity, and love,
this book would not have been possible

Contents

viii Contents

Tables and Figures

Tables

Figures

Preface

When I completed *Tyranny of Caste* (Rajagopal 1985), in which I examined caste politics and hierarchical power in India, I became keenly interested, as a political economist, in studying power structures in Canada. I grew up in India in a family that was politically conscious. Many of my relatives – the generation that participated in India's struggle for freedom – were socio-political leaders advocating the dismantling of caste hierarchy in southern India. My ancestral home in Madras, south India, has been the venue of many revolutionary speeches, events, and conflicts. On occasion my grandfather, as an officer of the Order of British India (OBI), quite dramatically, would symbolically brandish his First World War general's sword against social injustices. Those were times when caste powerfully shaped both social mores and political power. However, all his grandchildren learned not to observe caste traditions and discriminate against lower castes but to respect everyone as an individual.

When I left India in the late 1960s as a young student bound for the University of Toronto, I envisaged Canada as a young and attractive nation, not overburdened with the political rifts and social hierarchies that the long, tortured history of a nation may engender. When I earned my doctorate in the 1970s and started looking for academic positions, however, I found myself in a 'lost generation of scholars.' At that time, I could not understand why the Canadian immigration attaché had told me that educationally qualified people were what Canada needed.

When I was a part-timer in academe, no one inducted me into the pathways and problems of getting a 'full-time appointment' – I simply believed that everyone with merit would earn such a position. After many years, in the late 1980s York University gradually began to consider competitively qualified candidates from among its large pool of part-timers for full-time positions. The Canadian Union of Education Workers, representing part-timers, bargained for and won a collective agreement by which every year a few – two or three – long-service part-timers would be candidates for what was called as 'affirmative action' for part-timers. Certain disciplinary areas and fields where part-timers had been teaching for a long time would create full-time positions for competition among the university's internal candidates. This was a hard-fought struggle, not far different from deconstructing and resisting the caste system.

As a child, I was socialized to question and examine this system. Similarly as a young, idealistic, new arrival in Canada, I had the privileged view of one 'looking in from outside.' I was jolted by what I saw as the politics of academic hierarchy – not always merit based but often rank based. While a part-timer, I began to explore the feelings of others in a similar situation. As a tenured full-timer from the late 1980s on, my experiences broadened, enabling me, I believe, to look at matters from all sides. These perceptions inform the writing of this book.

Acknowledgments

A number of people provided information and helped in the collection of data on part-time faculty. Without their support and kindness, I could not have accomplished my work.

First and foremost, my sincere gratitude to the staff at various levels in universities across Canada; without their time and interest in processing the surveys I could not have made any headway in this project. I am most indebted to the senior administrators in each university – the presidents and vice-presidents – for their permission to conduct the surveys and their cooperation in many other ways. Their administrative staff were very prompt in distributing the surveys to the part-time faculty and also were generous with their time and personal commitment throughout the processing of many surveys and follow-ups. The survey respondents were generous with their time in answering my surveys, especially with their rich and incisive comments.

An equally crucial role was played by two successive vice-presidents (finance and administration) at York University, Bill Farr, who was actively involved in the survey stage, and Sheldon Levy, who continued to support my work. Their long-term interest, knowledge, and resourcefulness helped to ensure depth in the information sought through the questionnaires. They understood the real dimensions of the situation of part-timers, and I cannot express adequately my gratitude to them for their support.

Enormous thanks go to David Northrop and John Pollard of the Institute of Social Research (ISR). They brought professional strength to this project, and their warmth was a constant throughout the project. David Northrop was committed to accomplishing every detail of my exceptionally complex and voluminous surveys. John Pollard, sincere and gentle, guided me through the entire process; he was a dream-come-true project director. Overall, I am grateful to all the many people in ISR who have been involved in this project, from the survey stage to data processing. I could not have chosen a better academic home than the ISR and feel enormously fortunate.

I extend special gratitude to my colleague, distinguished researcher Michael Ornstein, whose advice on revisions, editing, and the shaping of the surveys made them less intimidating to the respondents and able to yield rich data. Also, I am thankful to Paul Axelrod, Gordon Darroch, Lillian Lerman, and Arthur Siegel, colleagues whose advice and support were invaluable.

I also wish to acknowledge the help of many other colleagues, administrative staff, officers of part-timers' unions, and friends, who made implementation of this project less onerous. Gary Brewer, Noli Swatman, James Brown, Judy Horwood, and Gladys Strangways, to name a few special people at York University, were warm and generous with their time and unwavering support.

My research assistants were superb. Zeng Lin prepared the survey data and processed them for analysis. His sensitivity to the statistical data and his background knowledge on many issues in higher education were invaluable for this project. Maher Wehbe assisted me for many years in library research. Although he has taken up a full-time career elsewhere, he continues to provide research support whenever I need it. He loves libraries and, given a chance, he would probably live in one.

The staff at the University of Toronto Press, especially Virgil Duff, deserve my special thanks for their encouragement and hard work in successfully bringing the project to completion. John Parry and Catherine Frost superbly edited the book and brought their magical touch to shaping the manuscript and sharpening its focus. Their intense involvement and creative suggestions have made the final product more satisfying for me. I also appreciate the enormous care and insight with which the two anonymous reviewers commented on the manuscript.

The Social Sciences and Humanities Research Council (SSHRC) of Canada gave me a research grant for the project, which enabled me to establish a national database on part-time and limited-term faculty in Canada. The Aid to Scholarly Publishing Program (ASPP) of the Humanities and Social Science Research Federation of Canada supported the publication of the book.

Finally, and most centrally, my family's constant support, unwavering confidence, and deep understanding made this book possible. My greatest debt goes to my late mother, whose endless love, continuous care, and constant inspiration nurtured my love of learning. To my daughter, Sudha Rajagopal, and my husband, Raj, who understood my time commitments, encouraged my research, and stood by me, and my two angels, Arun and Anil, who had to forgo much of my time with them – I owe everything I can think of.

Abbreviations

AAUP	American Association of University Professors
AUCC	Association of Universities and Colleges of Canada
AUT	Association of University Teachers, United Kingdom
CAUT	Canadian Association of University Teachers
COU	Council of Ontario Universities
CAUBO	Canadian Association of University Business Officers
FTE	Full-time equivalent
LTFT	Limited-term, full-time faculty
NATFHE	National Association of Teachers in Further and Higher Education, United Kingdom
NCES	National Center for Education Statistics, United States
NCSCBHEP	National Center for the Study of Collective Bargaining in Higher Education and the Professions, United States
NEA	National Education Association, United States
NP	Never part-time
NSOPF	National Survey of Post-Secondary Faculty, United States
OCUFA	Ontario Confederation of University Faculty Associations
OECD	Organization for Economic Cooperation and Development
PP	Previously part-time
UTFA	University of Toronto Faculty Association
YUFA	York University Faculty Association

HIDDEN ACADEMICS:
CONTRACT FACULTY IN
CANADIAN UNIVERSITIES

Introduction
'Changing Times and Changing Mission'

'Professors Ripped Off: Part-Time Faculty at Poverty Level,' read a headline in the *Halifax Chronicle-Herald* (Erskin, 1997), capturing the continuing malaise brought on by misplaced political and administrative priorities in academe undertaken in the name of financial efficiency. The harm caused by these policies is most severe for marginalized groups, that is, contract faculty. Canadian higher education faces an ominous situation. There is an increasing tendency to look at universities as corporate businesses and at education as a commodity for profit. John Ralston Saul warns us about the all-encompassing influence of corporatism in western civilization:

> Our civilization [is] locked in the grip of an ideology – corporatism, an ideology that denies and undermines the legitimacy of the individual as the citizen in a democracy. The particular imbalance of this ideology leads to a worship of self-interest and a denial of public good .While corporatism limits society to self-interest, it is far more than that. The origin of corporatism in the second half of the nineteenth century lay in two things – the rejection of citizen based democracy and the desire to react in a stable way to the industrial revolution. These original motives would evolve into the desire for a stable managerial, hierarchical society .Democracy is weakening .Corporatism is strengthening .Certainly corporatism is creating a conformist society .An expected development in a corporatist society [is that] the larger picture, the longer term, is lost in the incremental details of specialization, and .fact collecting stretches deep into our universities. (1995: 191, 90, 94, 106)

Governments in Canada, as the major sources of public funding for universities, have moved towards an ideological stance that focuses on privatization and corporatization. Those who argue that higher education is a business insist that there is no need to provide universities with huge research grants and that these institutions should be required to return a profit on the capital invested by the provinces.[1] In contrast to views that became popular in the 1960s, that education is a public good, governments in the 1990s pushed hard for job-market-oriented education and research that further corporate interest. 'Universities which are financed like private corporations also tend to be managed like private corporations and to generate corporate cultures' (Graham, 1998: 4).[2] The consequences of this approach are all too evident: 'Administrations, looking for cost savings, are resisting salary increases, trying to limit benefits, and demanding greater workloads. Limited term faculty with little security are being used in greater numbers. University administrations are replacing the traditional collegial approach of self-governance with private sector managerial models' (Flynn, 1998: 9).[3]

In contrast to declining academic budgets, non-academic salaries in Canadian universities have been increasing: 'In many institutions, savings from faculty salaries were spent on technology .This is the university of the future; it seems more administration, more technology, fewer teachers' (Melchers, 1998: 10).[4] Many administrators hoped that universities could cut costs by replacing faculty members with technology or by turning universities into business enterprises. Universities tend to look for ways of increasing their financial autonomy and reducing their current dependence on uncertain government funding (figure 0.1). In May 2000 the Council of Ontario Universities (COU) released statistics showing the decline in university operating grants from provincial governments and widening gaps between provinces in their funding levels. During the period 1996–2000, while funding for Canadian universities declined drastically, state funding for U.S. universities grew by 28 per cent on average. Ontario, the richest province in Canada, ranked second to last among the ten provinces and fifty U.S. states in government spending on universities (figure 0.2). Also, faculty numbers in Ontario universities declined by 10 per cent between 1988–7 and 1998–9. Since 1991–2 faculty and staff salary and benefit costs declined by about 12 per cent in Ontario (CAUT, June 2000). In the 1970s, as Janice Newson[5] points out, Canadian universities responded to 'the shift in higher education funding policy from expansion to contraction' by rationalizing budgets, and academic

FIGURE 0.1
University revenues by source, 1997–8

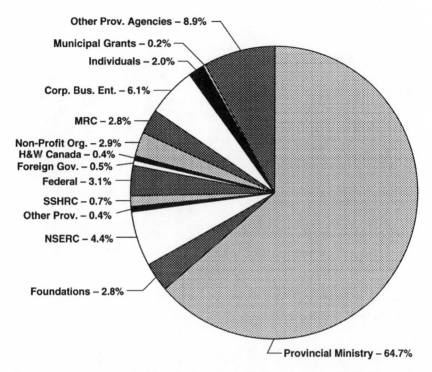

Revenue sources are: provincial ministries responsible for universities; Medical Research Council (MRC); Natural Sciences and Engineering Research Council (NSERC); Health and Welfare Canada; Social Sciences and Humanities Research Council (SSHRC); federal funding; foreign governments; other provinces; non-profit organizations; foundations; corporate business enterprises; individuals; municipal grants and contracts; other provincial ministries and agencies; Canadian Association of University Business Officers (CAUBO).
Sources: *CAUT Bulletin* (Dec. 1999); data from Statistics Canada and CAUBO

workers reacted to this situation through collective bargaining and other structural changes in the academic workplace (2000: 9). A significant development from budget rationalization was the creation of a cadre of part-time members of faculty. At the same time there was, and still is, a lurking fear among university administrators that their entrepreneurial role may compromise the university's quality and effective-

FIGURE 0.2
University operating grants per capita, Canada, 1999–2000

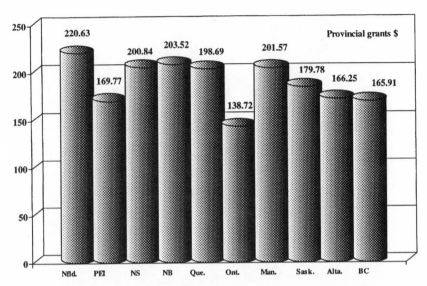

Canada's provinces: Newfoundland, Prince Edward Island, Nova Scotia, New
Brunswick, Quebec, Ontario, Manitoba, Saskatchewan, Alberta, British Columbia
Source: *CAUT Bulletin* (June 2000)

ness as an educator (Lewington, 1997). Patricia Gumport's warning
about U.S. universities has a clear resonance in Canada: 'While the
public universities and colleges have increasingly come to rely on market discourse and managerial approaches in order to demonstrate
responsiveness to economic exigencies, they may end up losing legitimacy as they move away from their historical character, functions and
accumulated heritage as educational institutions' ((2000: 67).

In an international survey Altbach and Lewis[6] found that fewer than
10 per cent of the faculty respondents in 1991–2 felt that they contributed to key academic policies of university governance. Clearly, most
felt alienated from the senior central administration. They distrusted
top-level administrators and had doubts about their management of
finances. In eight countries, a majority expressed negative feelings
about academic administrators, whom they find autocratic (1995: 55).

Under the pretext of preventing financial crises, administrations
across North America are introducing broader structural changes,

without necessarily examining the longer-term implications. The administrators are quite pragmatic in their strategies. Shapiro notes that Donald Kennedy, president of Stanford University (1980–92) during the burgeoning years of part-time appointments, in his book *Academic Duty* (1998) does not address the probability that many new scholars who graduate might not get to teach. Some of their teachers and mentors, like Kennedy, continue to work after age sixty-five, effectively blocking the younger generation from advancing. Shapiro warns that in the absence of any U.S. commitment to replace all retirees by tenure stream young scholars, administrators will continue to terminate faculty positions or replace full-timers with part-timers. 'The danger today is that the administrations that now set policy at most universities are increasingly tempted to act as if they are running a business – letting profit motive drive educational policy. In such a climate, revenue generating programs and inexpensive part-time professors are winning out over a committed faculty, good libraries, and small classes' (1998: 18).

Before I explain the surveys and data that ground this book, I wish to introduce the more general context in which the crisis in Canadian universities that led to the establishing of 'permanent temps' has emerged, namely, the commodification of labour, the development of academic capitalism, and the emergence of non-traditional work.

Commodification of Labour and Academic Capitalism

International institutions and agreements that emerged after the First World War brought fundamental ideological changes to how labour was characterized and how workers were treated in the labour market. Labour harnessed to produce commodities is social labour. A commodity producer engages other human beings for their labour in commodity production. This labour appears to commodity producers as their private labour – that is, they own the workers – and as a part of the impersonal market forces. Thus emerges a fundamental contradiction of the commodity form in the context of labour. If production owners see labour as a commodity, they consider the relations to workers as 'relations to things,' not as 'relations between people.' In *Capital* (I, chaps 6 and 19), Karl Marx splits the concept of labour into the pair 'labour and labour power' – labour meaning the 'activity' of a worker and labour power representing her/his 'capacity' to do useful work that adds measurable value to other commodities. Workers exchange their labour power for money wages. Thus, labour power appears in the market as a commodity, although this power is embodied in the worker and is not produced as a commodity. In the context of capitalism and the market economy, securing and harnessing labour power are at the command of the owners of production (Foley, 1983). Ideology serves to achieve the exploitation of labour as a commodity. The functions of ideology, Althusser explains, are to achieve social cohesion and secure class domination. To the extent that an ideology provides a camouflage or 'imaginary relationship of individuals to the real condition of existence,' it can effectively perform these functions (Althusser, 1971: 153).

After the First World War the International Labour Organization (ILO), in its founding constitution of 1919, affirmed that 'labour is not a commodity' and stated that workers have certain fundamental rights. These provisions, entrenched in ILO conventions,[7] theoretically regulated the labour market in Canada until 1997. In that year the ILO abandoned its original position advocating advancing full-time regular employment for workers, regulating labour market fee-charging intermediary agencies, and endorsing worker benefits and securities. This reversal legitimized the use of temporary workers and worker-supplier agencies that mediated between the market and production firms and made the labour market as flexible as industries and businesses wanted (Vosko, 2000: 3–45).

In 1919, in order to control high unemployment and to prohibit intermediary employment agencies' abuse of the labour market, the ILO introduced conventions regulating the use of temporary labour. In 1944, at the International Labour Conference, member nations of the ILO reaffirmed their commitment to the constitution of the ILO and its cornerstone premise that labour was not a 'commodity.' They endorsed provisions to bring about a welfare state: full employment and rising standards of living, social security, medical care, nutrition, housing, recreation, culture, education, child welfare, and maternity benefits. In response, during the post-war era countries took different paths in dealing with these provisions: prohibition, regulation, or non-regulation of temporary labour. Although many continental European countries – France, Greece, Italy, Spain, and West Germany – moved towards regulatory regimes, the United States, Canada, and Great Britain chose not to firm up the regulatory rules except for an informal commitment to monitor the labour market (Vosko, 2000: 105–13).

Guy Standing notes that 'flexibilization' of the labour market is an integral facet of 'the rolling back of public sector ... as part of "privatization" initiatives and as a result of ... outsourcing public service functions' (1999: 593–4). From the 1970s to the early 1990s a growing trend to a flexible labour market in Canada became more prominent. Vosko refers to four features of the deregulated labour market that became increasingly entrenched in Canada: between 1980 and 1990, for the first time in seven decades, a decline of wages; growing 'casualization' of work; deregulation of workers' benefits and declining work-related social programs; and stagnation of the rate of unionization as unionized jobs declined with the contraction of the public sector (2000: 162).

Instead of regulating all types of workers – temporary or regular – in the labour market, current trends in industrialized countries are to replace regular workers with temporary labour in order to reduce costs of providing job security, protections, and benefits for workers. In support of this trend, a new convention, adopted in 1997, reversed the ILO's original position against intermediary agencies between the employer and workers and its delegitimization of non-standard forms of employment. This convention recognized temporary-help agencies as legitimate employers in 1997, thus affirming their role in the labour market. By the mid-1990s, these agencies had gained such legitimacy that temporary-help intermediaries were effectively deregulated, leaving non-standard forms of employment outside the purview of labour regulations in Canada except in Quebec (Vosko, 2000: 200–9). Vosko emphasizes: 'The need to adapt the system of collective bargaining in Canada to accommodate the growing pluralism in employment relationships ... is particularly pressing ... to protect rights for *all* workers in Canada' (228); (emphasis added).

As we move from workers in the marketplace to workers in the ivory tower, we find a parallel situation. When government underfunding led to declining revenues for Canadian universities, the latter began to look for new funding sources, especially partnerships between higher education and business. Conservative governments tied research and development (R&D) funding to corporate contributions to universities. Just as the temporary-help industry was an intermediary between workers and the firms that hired them, corporations providing funding became the intermediary in research innovations and lured universities to perform research under their control. Many Canadian universities established 'centres of excellence' and 'research parks' to promote industry-university partnerships. Canadian academics, perhaps, have been able substantially to resist government and business pressures to heed to corporate interests, however, because Canada has a tradition of less government intervention for a mostly publicly funded higher education system than is the case in Australia, Britain, or the United States (Slaughter and Leslie, 1997: 52–63; Skolnik, 1990; Jones and Skolnik, 1992). For instance, as Skolnik points out, in the United States state budgetary allocations tie funding to universities' performance and their accountability for students' learning outcomes. Commonly, universities undergo periodic reviews of their performance by state legislators. In contrast, provincial governments in Canada do not conduct such reviews of universities or their programs; and reviews, if any – for instance, graduate or professional programs – are done by universities themselves. Funding accountability is not measured in terms of learning outcomes. Skolnik argues: 'In Canada ... where the number of institutions is strictly limited, where competition is constrained, where institutions collectively and co-operatively police themselves, quality is more likely to be assured, and hence there is less pressure for accountability ... public universities in Canada are in many respects treated by governments more like private concerns (or ... crown corporations), while public universities in the United States are treated as an extension of the public service, for example ... even legislative intervention [occurs] with regard to university curriculum requirements' (1990: 90–2). However, Canadian universities are finding it increasingly difficult to resist the ever-increasing government demand for profit-yielding cost–benefit analyses.

In *Campus, Inc.* Ronnie Dugger comments: 'As corporations conquer the universities too, they attempt to turn students into consumers, education into training for jobs, professors into hired-out consultants and researchers, and campuses into corporate research and profit centres. All this is done on premises and through employees who are maintained at the public expense' (2000: 21). Clear trends of corporate encroachment on academic freedom and faculty members' diminishing right to tenure, show that the higher-education sector is also increasingly becoming deregulated. University administrators assuming the role of chief executive officers (CEOs) make cost–benefit calculations and find contract or part-time faculty members good value for the money. Many members of faculty, themselves, often guided by a notion of 'professionalism' and by the conventional (albeit no longer true) thought that academics control their universities, think unionization is irrelevant (Huber, 2000: 123–5).

Another significant variable is the interaction between the world of work and higher education. Kivinen and Ahola note: 'As individuals stay longer and longer in school, and with available jobs scarce, the warehouse function of education becomes more important. The human capital ideology interprets prolonged schooling as a means to keep the worker reserve "up to date" and in "good moral shape." However, in the reality of risking available jobs, young people with lower qualifications usually prefer work, although the present system seems unable to place them either in education, or in employment' (1999: 194). In this context, temporary workers, such as part-timers and contractees, are easily available for hire, camouflaged as 'professionals in reserve.'

In parallel, other processes are under way. The weakening of tenure and the increasing number of part-time and contract hirees have deprofessionalized the faculty. Turning away from the time-tested values of higher education, universities have altered curricula to meet the needs of the job market and workplace. Government keenly enforce the rules of business accountability while decreasing their funding for universities. Government approaches of offering to university administrators the carrot of managerial control and the stick of funding cuts have turned them into 'fiscal-efficiency' managers and CEOs of the university (Cutright, 2000: 490).

In the context of the rising trend of temporary workers in the overall labour force discussed above, it is easy to understand the emergence of contract faculty in Canadian academe. From this general labour trend, universities seem to gain legitimacy for policies designed to meet their need for more faculty by hiring contractees. As the shortage of full-time tenure-stream academic jobs becomes more pronounced, these contractees are more acutely aware of their plight.

Emergence of Non-Traditional Workers in Industrialized Economies

Trends in the general labour force provide us with a wider perspective and context for understanding the increase of part-time faculty in higher education. Growth in numbers of part-time workers across the labour force is clearly identifiable in the 1980s and 1990s, both nationally and internationally. International trends show that their numbers in industrial market economies grew by about 30 per cent during 1980–9 (ILO: 1989; Krahn: 1992). In most advanced industrial economies (OECD countries), the proportion of employees who work part time continued to rise during the 1990s from 13.4 per cent of the labour force in 1990 to 14.3 per cent in 1998. In most countries, increasing numbers of workers, male and female, are now more likely to work part time than they did in 1990. In Australia, 14.4 per cent of male workers held part-time jobs in 1998, compared with 11.3 per cent in 1990. Second to Australia, in Japan, the proportion of men among part-time workers increased from 9.5 per cent (1990) to 12.9 per cent in 1998 (*Economist*, 1999: 118). In 1999 in the Netherlands, part-time workers accounted for 30 per cent of the labour force, the highest proportion among industrialized countries. The labour force in Belgium has shown a remarkable increase in its part-time component from 16.3 per cent (1998–9) of jobs to 19.9 per cent (1999–2000). During the same period, in OECD countries as a whole, numbers of part-timers as a proportion of all workers rose from 14.3 per cent to 15.8 per cent. From 1990 to 1999 the European Union (EU) average in part-time work also increased from 13.3 per cent to 16.4 per cent (*Economist*, 2000). In 2000 part-timers constituted one in six workers in OECD countries. Although women dominated the part-time workforce, in some countries, for example, Britain, men's share increased from 15 per cent in 1990 to 20 per cent in 2000 (*Economist*, 2001).

Among part-time workers in OECD countries, however, a greater proportion are far more likely to be women than men. In 1998 women comprised 97 per cent of part-timers in Sweden, 84 per cent in Germany, 83 per cent in Switzerland, 82 per cent in Belgium, 80 per cent in Britain – on average 82 per cent in the EU and 74 per cent in the OECD. Of all industrialized countries, the lowest level occurred in Finland (63 per cent). In 1999 there was little change in the preponderance of women among part-time workers. High proportions of women continued as part-time workers in major economies: Austria (87 per cent), Germany (84 per cent), Switzerland (83 per cent), Britain (80 per cent), France (79 per cent), Canada (70 per cent), and the United States (69 per cent). Overall, in the EU, women constituted 79 per cent of the total workforce, and the average female component in the OECD workforce was 72 per cent (*Economist*, 2000).

Part-time workers are but one component of a much larger group of 'non-standard' or 'contingent' workers.[8] Similarly, there are temporary workers who hold multiple jobs and others who describe themselves as self-employed. During the 1980s and 1990s non-standard work – part-time, contract, multiple-job, and contingent – has increased in Canada and other OECD economies (Krahn, 1992: 19; Krahn and Lowe, 1998: 80). More than 750,000 Canadian workers – that is, 8 per cent of all workers – had only temporary jobs – that is, jobs with a specific end date. Similar proportions prevailed in other industrialized countries, for example, 5 per cent in France, 6 per cent to 7 per cent in Britain, 8 per cent in Germany, more than 10 per cent in Japan, and more than 12 per cent in Denmark (Krahn, 1992: 61).

In 1999 among young people (age 15–24) in Canada's workforce 52.1 per cent of females and 37.6 per cent of males were more likely to have non-standard jobs. Also, among all older workers (age 55–64), a greater proportion of females (31.4 per cent) than males (10.2 per cent) were in the contingent workforce (Statistics Canada, 2000b: 123–5). Women are almost three times more likely than men to be working part time – that is, work fewer than thirty hours per week in their main job – in Canada. In 1994 those involved in non-standard work rose from 28 per cent (1989) to 33 per cent of all Canadian workers age 15–64 (Krahn and Lowe, 1998: 81). In 1996, 18.9 per cent, or 2.6 million Canadian workers were part-timers. Preponderant were women (76 per cent) among adult part-time workers (more than 24 years old). One in four adult women in the labour force is a part-timer. In 1995 involuntary part-time workers constituted 31 per cent of the more than 2.5 million part-time workers in Canada – a steep rise from 11 per cent of 1 million part-timers in 1975 (Krahn and Lowe, 1998: 84–6). Women part-time workers were 28 per cent of all women working (versus 10 per cent male part-timers among all men working) in the Canadian Labour force. Since the mid-1970s seven in ten of all part-time workers have been women (Statistics Canada 2000b: 103).

In Canada, from 1975 to 1985, involuntary part-time employment grew by 375.4 per cent and voluntary part-time employment by 41 per cent. In the same period, full-time employment increased by 15.2 per cent. Involuntary part-time workers increased in number from 109,000 (1975) to more than 500,000 (1985). The ratio of workers who reported themselves as involuntary part-timers rose from 1 in 100 in 1975 to 1 in 20 in 1985. Married women constituted more than a third (37.6 per cent) of involuntary part-timers in 1985. The severe economic recession of the 1980s, the increasing significance of the service sector, and growing numbers of women entering the workforce all contributed to an expansion of involuntary part-time employment during that decade (Akyeampong, 1986). Among those on the margins of the labour force in 1986, a greater percentage of them were women (63 per cent versus 43 per cent of all workers) (Akyeampong, 1987)

Canada, whose part-time workforce grew from 15.2 per cent in 1989 (ILO, 1989)[9] to 18.9 per cent in 1998 (*Economist*, 1999: 118), was one such country. In Canada, from 1989 to 1998, part-time work grew by 24.4 per cent, whereas full-time work increased by only 8 per cent. This trend is not moderating, since the growth of part-time work continued to be strong between 1997 and 1998 (an increase of 5.3 per cent), compared with that of full-time jobs (an increase of 2.7 per cent) during the same period. In 1997 women were the largest group of involuntary part-timers. Of women working part time, 34 per cent (390,000), preferred full-time hours, although in 1998 there seemed to be a gender shift in involuntary part-time workers, since 44 per cent of adult men wanted to work full time but could find only part-time work (Statistics Canada, 1999a, c).

A Lost Generation?

Universities in Canada altered considerably with 'changing times and changing mission' during the 1980s and 1990s (Levin, Perkins, and Clowes, 1992). Have we come to 'the end of the Ivory Tower'? (Wachman, 1994).[10] Faced with governments' financial restraints since the 1970s, universities in Canada responded in various ways. Their strategies created tensions and conflicts, segmenting the faculty into groups with conflicting interests. Political pressures, manifested in a discourse over 'tenure' and 'control over curriculum,' threatened to strip away full-timers' hard-won rights of academic freedom. Administrators had two choices: either cut salaries and hire cheaper teaching resources to handle enrolment bulges, or retrench tenured faculty (Hardy, 1992).[11] Full-time faculty's efforts to preserve academic freedom and curricular control led to the emergence and accommodation of part-timers with no full-time jobs elsewhere ('Contemporaries')[12] and full-timers' assumption of a managerial role vis-à-vis part-timers.

Robert Bellah[13] describes the push of the market forces: 'The tyranny of the bottom line drives academic decisions in several ways. When the university is seen simply as a part of the economy then ... pressures for market efficiency set in ... In academy, downsizing takes a subtle form. It is difficult to cut the number of instructors, since a certain number of classes must be taught ... Many more institutions, however, have reduced the percentage of faculty who are tenured or on the tenure-track, and increased the number of part-time and temporary instructors, at considerable savings in their salaries' (1999: 19). The dramatic increase in the numbers of 'temporary adjuncts' that started in the mid-1970s has changed academe. A tenured, full-time faculty member of a major university writes about how universities began creating contract appointments (although these are not part time) instead of regular tenure-track faculty appointments:[14] 'More than 15 years ago, in order to take advantage of an oversupplied academic job market, the university underhandedly created a new job category, the exploitive nature of which it tried to cover up by giving it the prestigious British title of TUTOR. So, the university placed a number of individuals, whose superior capacities it had recognized, in a position to have their heads cut off whenever it would deem convenient. Why is this so unethical? Simply because it is clear to any honest person that these terminated individuals, generally in their 50s, stand almost no chance of continuing to practice their profession with dignity, largely because of the very conditions of employment under which they have served this institution' (UTFA, 1991: 12).

A Continuing Crisis?

The analysis of part-timers in this book rests on data that I collected in 1991–2, but the findings are as relevant today as they were then. The continuing trends of cutbacks, increasing corporatization of universities, and growing labour strife on campuses show that conditions have not changed for the better. The surplus value that part-timers create is critical to the stability of universities and allows them to operate with reduced resources. Statistics Canada's (2000a) recent report on the increased hiring of part-timers, shrinking full-time faculty positions, and diminishing public funding reveals the continuation of the situation of 1991–2. The 'temps,' as part-timers are known, continue to work and live under the conditions that unfold in the following chapters and have been too marginalized for their situation to get any worse. The following comment from a part-timer today tells us that conditions for part-time faculty in Canadian universities have not changed much since 1991–2, the year I surveyed part-timers: 'My advice to other part-time instructors in Canada is to take the bull by the horns and organize now ... the difference between the treatment of contract faculty and that of the regular faculty has reached absurd and scandalous proportions' (Thomas Hood, quoted in *CAUT Bulletin*, March 2000: 1).[15] Part-timers' conditions and relationship with university administrations seem to have worsened, if we judge by the increasing number of strikes. In fact, in a recent preliminary report from Statistics Canada it is noted that part-timers' numbers have increased and their workloads have intensified: 'Universities are relying more on their part-time faculty to deliver their educational programs.' Part-timers increased 6 per cent between 1992–3 and 1997–8, and the greatest increase (13.8 per cent) occurred in Atlantic Canada, where part-timers were teaching more hours (an increase of 20.9 per cent) measured in 'full-time teaching equivalents' (FTEs).[16] In western Canada, also, the number of part-timers rose by 13.5 per cent and their teaching hours, measured in FTEs, increased sharply (by 43.7 per cent) (Statistics Canada, 2000a).

A part-timer's experiences become indelibly etched in his or her memory – waiting for next year's appointment, long hours of work, heavy course loads, and the research work through sleepless nights – as standard work patterns. When I was a part-timer, my deep interest (as a political economist) was to find out why highly qualified people were stuck in part-time academic work for years. Many were getting older and had no pensions or benefits from the workplace. Coincidentally, in 1990, when the Tripartite Task Force on Academic Resource Planning with a mandate to inquire into the problem of faculty shortage was appointed in Ontario, I started to look into the large pools of part-timers as sources of supply.

Establishing Data

It was not easy for me to get information on contract faculty, since universities are not required to collect data on them as they do on full-time faculty. I understood that without the cooperation of central administrators in all the Canadian universities, collecting data on part-timers would be well-nigh impossible. Therefore, I sought help from York University's senior central administrators, Bill Farr and, later, Sheldon Levy. I asked Bill Farr to be my associate in survey administration and data collection.[17] Without his knowledge about finances and faculty, his personal contacts with central administrations of many universities, and his interest in and countless hours spent on this project amid his heavy workload as vice-president of finance and administration, I could not have accomplished this task. His successor, Sheldon Levy, who believes in the usefulness of data, was and is always ready to help.

There are no institutional data on the contract (part-time) faculty in Canada as there are in the United States, whose National Survey of Post-Secondary Faculty is periodically updated. Even in the United States, David Leslie observes: 'The data from [the National Survey of

Post-Secondary Faculty conducted by the National Center for Education Statistics (NCES) in 1992] were gathered (at this writing) nearly six years ago ... Although a new survey is due to be distributed in the Fall of 1998, publication of the results will lag, perhaps by years ... The other principal issue in analyzing faculty work, jobs, and careers is to find the appropriate level of disaggregation [based on disciplines, institutional types, and so on] ... The availability of ... data from the NCES surveys will be helpful ... but ... qualitative studies may even be more fruitful in yielding up more textured and grounded understandings about who the faculty are, what they do, and how their work lives are connected to and play out in varied institutional and disciplinary contexts' (1998: 96–7).

The data presented in this book, on faculties, disciplines, regions, and institutional types of Canadian universities, yield such a 'textured and grounded understanding,' although it has taken many years to establish and to process them. A rush to finish the job would not have done justice to their richness. My database on contract faculty (both part time and limited term) and their interrelationships with tenured faculty and academic administrators required four years (1992–5) to assemble and disaggregate. Despite my undertaking other research projects and teaching, this project – analysis of many surveys, breadth of qualitative information, and reviews of literature presented in this book – easily absorbed most of my research time in the years that followed. An understanding of contract faculty in Canadian universities has advanced considerably through these databases. In this book I describe not simply a group of workers, but how they became indispensable for the operation of universities as we know them. There is little doubt that the conditions that created a new academic workforce in the 1970s and the rationale for its continuing use have not changed. Not only teaching but also the very financial viability of universities depends very much on their flexibility in hiring and firing contract faculty.

The financial allocations for higher education in provincial budgets are shrinking. A systemic response to this trend is to hire the most 'temps' at the least cost (see below, chapter one). In order to survive the repeated cutbacks and to find teachers to conduct classes, universities argue that they must resort to desperate measures. A consistent trend of budget cuts and funding crises in U.S. higher education has led to shifting patterns of jobs and careers in academe. Participants in the Sloan conference of 1997 identify a 'new majority' of non-tenure-track temporary academics (Leslie, 1998). David Leslie observes how this trend, in turn, led to the development of an academic hierarchy in the United States: 'As higher education has expanded ... the definition of faculty [is] beginning to change ... marking the subfaculty as a growing part of the academic workforce ... faculty work and faculty roles may be evolving through a sort of vertical differentiation' (ibid.: 95). In British Columbia, at the college level, there has been a recent move to some regularization of temporary members of faculty. 'Job security for temps in BC,' reads a caption in *CAUT Bulletin*, reporting that instructors 'who work at least 50 per cent of a fulltime workload for two consecutive years where the workload is expected to continue in the third year will now be converted to regular faculty members with salary, health and welfare benefits, and other rights and benefits of the collective agreement based on equity with the full-time regular faculty' (October 2000b: A4). In reality, the number of such conversions is an open question.

Such changes are not in the air in universities.[18] The plight of part-timers has pushed them to organize themselves or to press to join full-time faculty unions. A full-timer notes: 'We're aware that part-time faculty members in Nipissing [University] ... have been abused in the past ... By bringing them into the union, we're not only attempting to secure ... the same rights we enjoy as full-time faculty, we're recognizing the important role they play in our community ... With the double cohort [of students] coming [in 2003–4], part-time faculty will become an even more integral part of ... universities' (*CAUT Bulletin*, October 2000a: A1). At Bishop's University in Lennoxville, Quebec, a veteran part-timer points out the reasons for colleagues' turning to unionization: 'People have been so frustrated, not just with the low pay but also with the sense that we've been invisible, even to our colleagues ... Because we don't have offices, email, phone numbers, or a listing in the faculty directory, we don't really feel connected. Now that we're part of APBU [Association of Professors of Bishop's University], we have an opportunity to be taken seriously, to be involved.' Instances of this part-timer's (non)-status situation are typical of conditions in many universities.

Identifying the dissonance between the university and part-timers – who constituted more than a third of the total faculty in the early 1990s – part-timers have narrated their paradoxical experiences: 'I feel totally disconnected to the university, but very connected to students.' And, 'The conditions related to the esteem and recognition of my work – recognized as excellent by my students – are contradictory to the menial terms in which university administration has framed my work.' Fragmentation within academe is clearly evident from discussions in the popular press about the plight of part-timers. Universities' financial problems over the years have created a palpable conflict of interests along lines of faculty status, gender, and decision-making powers. In 1992 two articles in *Monday Magazine* in Victoria, BC, drew a barrage of comments. The sessionals (part-timers) are, one said: 'the worker bees, the sled dogs, the slaves of the system, the people who do much of the teaching at UVic, maybe for a third of the pay, and none of the perks or security' (Tafler, 1992a). A part-timer said: 'Being a Sessional is like being an illegal immigrant worker' (Tafler, 1992b). The university president tried to rebut Tafler's portrayal of the faculty and the sessionals. He emphasized that the university had significantly improved part-timers' salaries and benefits and extended full benefits to those teaching half time or more. He added that the amount of credit-course teaching by 'short-term' or part-time appointees had remained more or less stable: 21 per cent in 1977–8 and 24 per cent in 1990–1. Policies were also in place to ensure that all its teaching members were treated equitably and with respect (Strong, 1992). About the Atlantic region in Canada, we read in the press: 'Part-time faculty at three Halifax universities are living at poverty level ... some of [them] ... have to go to food banks to make ends meet ... [They] make $5,000/full 8 month course compared to $10,600 at York University in Toronto' (Erskin, 1997).

Part-timers, themselves, are clearly aware of their position:

I fully recognize that much of the problem is rooted in the underfunding of the universities. I fear that my generation of Ph.D.s is indeed turning into the *lost generation*, at a time when the federal government is insisting we need to be better educated to meet the challenges of global competition.

I work in a field very sensitive to budget restrictions. I once worked 24 hours classroom contact for 1/2 salary of full timers (9 hours classroom contact). I have often seen in the past the most energetic, imaginative, resourceful, creative, generous teaching from part-timers. However, these impulses are quashed by the despair of being forever part-time, which means work more for less pay. It is difficult to offer good teaching when faced with such a bleak future.

Some describe the distress that financial constraints create:

> I have gone through the pressures and poverty of graduate school in the process of getting my PhD. Now I am 36 and jobless, except for this part-time teaching position. I have spent in vain endless hours looking for full-time academic positions. It troubles me when I hear about cutbacks in university funding and how they are worsening. Often I feel that I am lost in a dark era of joblessness. My family is quite stressed as a result of my job uncertainties. Sometimes I cannot sleep and tears well up when I think about my children caught in this tentative situation.

> I am very distressed that government and university administration feel compelled to suppress funding for full-time positions. Surely they must realize part-time employees (instructors, et al.) cannot afford to be completely, or even semi loyal to the institution due to income decisions. It used to be that part-time faculty were specialists with full-time jobs in business (non-academic). Now they may be under-qualified, quasi-specialists with two, or three jobs apart from the school. It's a shame!

Another part-timer comments on the nature of work:

> Part-time teaching is becoming very onerous and unrewarding due to the increasing class sizes and lack of support and resources for doing a good job. Part-timers become very demoralized as this factory approach to education is intensified. Instead of gaining expertise and experience over time one feels increasingly ghettoized and alienated from one's work. The fact that one must continue all research on one's own time and the fact that this research is unrecognized and unrewarded adds to the growing cynicism of part-timers toward the universities that employ them. It is a terrible double standard that full-time faculty are highly rewarded for research while it is totally ignored for part-timers. The insecurity of part-time contracts also puts a terrible strain on those who live entirely off of these earnings. We must work toward instituting a disincentive for universities to continue expanding the part-time pool of labour at the expense of full-time jobs.

The above vignettes show how part-timers feel as a 'lost generation of scholars'[19] during what may be labelled as 'the faculty crisis.'

Surveys on Part-Timers

Turning to the part-timer situation in Canadian universities, I gathered direct information on part-timers and other groups that interact with them, through surveys. In total, I conducted six national surveys during 1990–2:

- National institutional pre-survey, 1990
- National institutional survey, 1990
- National survey: part-time faculty in Canada: 1991–2
- National survey: full-time faculty in Canada: 1991–2
- National survey: academic administrator in Canada 1991–2
- National survey: limited-term, full-time faculty (LTFTs) in Canada 1991–2.

The last four were direct surveys addressed to the respective populations of part-timers, full-timers (tenured or tenure stream), academic administrators, and LTFTs. Surveys of part-timers and LTFTs address issues of work life; surveys of full-timers and academic administrators elicit information on their views on and interactions with part-timers and LTFTs. Full details of survey criteria, definition of terms, and procedures for survey administration are provided in the appendix. Hence, I will limit the discussion here to my general approach to the surveys and data.

The analysis in the chapters that follow is grounded in two broad factors – the population surveyed, and types of universities. Data aggregated on the basis of direct respondents – part-timers, full-timers, limited-term full-timers, and academic administrators – provide the resources for discussing the various aspects of academe or administration, as the case may be, such as their work, attitudes, and interactions and relationships with each other. Part-timers are differentiated by university types and by demographic variables, in both chapters two and three. In chapter four focus is on the differentiation between those I refer to as Classics (who have full-time non-academic jobs) and those referred to as Contemporaries (who have only part-time academic employment or academic as well as non-academic jobs). In chapter five, I analyse full-time faculty responses, differentiating them by rank, sex, discipline, length of service, career path, and university types. In chapter six, I tabulate academic administrators by their university types, by academic ranks (full professor, associate and assistant professor) as well as by their administrative ranks (vice-president, dean, department chair, and program director). For clustering the various universities as types in order to examine differences between them, I use certain characteristics specific to Canada and Canadian higher education – geography, language, size of student population, range of Faculties, research funding, unionization, and intensity of part-time use – both at the stage of selecting universities to survey, as well as to disaggregate survey responses on the basis of those characteristics. In the text, I have rounded off 0.5 per cent or over to their nearest full percentage point; in the tables, however, I have provided the actual percentage to one decimal point.

The definition of part-timers was, indeed, the hardest task. This burden was lightened, however, by the National Institutional Pre-Survey and the university administrators' clarifications of terminologies provided subsequently. It allowed me to see the variations across universities and to develop consistent definitions for both types of contract faculty, namely, the part-timers and the LTFTs (see appendix).

Starting with the well-established U.S. surveys on part-timers as a model, I decided to go further in gathering more qualitative and attitudinal responses from each of the four populations: part-timers, fulltimers, limited-term full-timers, and academic administrators. I felt that these responses were essential to an understanding of the relationships within the university between the various segments in academe and to a comprehensive overview on how each type of universities (based on the criteria discussed above and given in the appendix) functioned with the unique interrelationships between academic workers. The respondents rewarded this approach doubly, first, by answering the attitudinal questions to fullest, and then by perceptively complementing the responses with their own reflections on the various issues of importance to them. Most of their narratives as well as the survey data depict not merely the work and situation of academics and administrators, but also the life and times of Canadian universities.

Outline of Chapters

First and foremost, I wish to explain why I decided to write this book in the present tense, although it is based on my 1991–2 surveys. First, the situation of part-timers has not changed to any considerable extent since I surveyed them. The universities' reliance on this group of academics has remained stable, and universities have come to acknowledge that their presence is indispensable to maintain a full curriculum and lower student-faculty ratio. Therefore, the issues that we discuss here are of current relevance, not to be relegated to the annals of history. As a result, I felt that it was necessary to address the issues and underscore their relevance to the present.

How part-timers, who were hired initially by the universities because of their financial shortfalls, became a permanent workforce and emerged as an underclass is the focus in chapter one. In chapter two the identity of the part-time faculty, the nature of their work, and their feelings about their status in the university are explained. The feminization of part-timers, the work and status of women part-timers, and their marginality in the workplace are the focus of chapter three. Two types of part-timers, whom I label 'Classics' and 'Contemporaries' in order to uncover the hopes and ambitions of the career-oriented part-timers, are compared in chapter four. In chapter five I examine the relationship between the full-time faculty and part-timers and full-timers' perceptions of part-timers. An analysis of academic administrators' reasons for hiring part-timers and their perceptions of the latter are provided in chapter six. In chapter seven the major theoretical understandings of this contract faculty's work and status, which our empirical finding fleshed out in earlier chapters are outlined. In the epilogue I speculate on the future of the university and the situation of the contract faculty. In the appendix I explain the methodologies of my surveys and the process of gathering the data.

Terminology

The terms 'contract' and 'part-time' faculty (or 'part-timers') refer to those members of faculty who work part time in academe, but they do not include graduate assistants or full-timers teaching courses on overload. Among part-timers, there are two segments – 'Classics' (who hold, as well, full-time non-academic jobs) and 'Contemporaries' (who mainly teach part-time in academe and sometimes also hold non-academic jobs to make ends meet) – a classification that helps to differentiate their interests. 'Full-time faculty' members (or 'full-timers') hold full-time tenured or tenure-track appointments. I call 'Insiders' those full-timers who have held part-time academic appointments prior to becoming full-timers, and 'Outsiders' those who have no such experience, in order to differentiate their perspectives on part-timers.

Among decision-makers, there are two groups – 'university central administrators' and 'academic administrators' – that have different roles and functions. In reference to academic administrators, I differentiate between two variables: administrative rank and academic rank. The main administrative rank groups are vice-presidents, deans, chairs, and program directors. Professors, associate professors, assistant professors, lecturers, and instructors delineate the academic rank. I grouped universities by size, region, research or teaching orientation, range of programs, language, and unionization and call the groupings 'university types' so that I could compare them. I use the terms 'francophone part-timers' and 'anglophone part-timers' to refer to those in francophone or anglophone universities; the terms are not restricted to those whose mother tongue is French or English.

As universities may differ in their structures (their administrative and academic governing bodies), I use terms and definitions in their most common form and in their broadest sense. Generally, a university's central administration consists of the bureaucratic and business management wings. Internally, its hierarchical tiers are top, middle, and lower. Often, academics may also be found among the central administrators; for instance, a professor might be appointed as vice-president of administration. Presidents of universities, more often than not, are academics. Academic administrators – the academic vice-president and his or her associates, 'Faculty' deans, chairs and heads of departments, and program directors – represent faculty and academe in general. Commonly, a university senate consists of central administrators, academic administrators, representatives of different 'Faculties,' and students elected by their respective constituencies. Some institutions have a unicameral governing body, which combines within its structure what are 'senate' and 'board of governors' in other institutions. The terms 'Faculty' or 'Faculties,' as distinct from 'faculty' (referring to faculty members) are used in this book to refer to disciplinary groupings under rubrics such as arts, pure and applied sciences, fine arts, medical, engineering, law, and so on. These units – for example, 'Faculty of Arts' or 'Faculty of Sciences' – have governing bodies usually called Faculty councils made up of faculty members and students from the Faculty. The university senate (or the senior representative decision-making body) consists of high-level administrators of the bureaucratic wing, academic administrators, and representatives from Faculties and student bodies, all elected by their respective constituencies.

Part One

THE CONTRACT FACULTY

Chapter One

Permanent 'Temps' and Surplus Value

*I worked as a part-time teacher only one semester, but I do not intend to do it
again. Part time is an inexcusable way for the university to get a cheap labour
force. I'd rather work at McDonald's.*

The comment above illustrates the frustrations expressed by part-
timers in their open-ended responses to my survey.[1] In the introduction I discussed the faculty crisis in Canadian universities, which
began in the 1970s, and its formative role in part-timers' discontent. In
contrast to the 1970s, however, 'the 1960s were a "golden era" for
[U.S.] education in general, as well as for the academic profession'
(Bowen and Sosa, 1989: 147).[2] In Canada, too, there was a parallel
strengthening of the academic profession, but increased rates of inflation and a decline in public funding in the 1970s and 1980s translated
into a tightening labour market and the emergence of a part-time academic workforce in Canadian universities. Provincial underfunding of
universities in Ontario, for instance, resulted in an institutional search
for efforts to achieve a built-in flexibility to handle uncertain finances
(Rajagopal and Farr, 1989: 268–9). The growing belief that education is
a privately marketable commodity rather than a public good encouraged this process. Full-time faculty appointments could not keep pace
with growth in enrolment because of cutbacks, and part-timers were
hired to help. As these funding and staffing patterns continued,
employing part-timers became a standard strategy for handling
increasing enrolments while maintaining acceptable levels in student–
faculty ratios (figure 1.1).

While shifting the blame to the financial shortfalls, in order to extract

FIGURE 1.1

Ratio of FTE students to faculty in Canadian universities, 1978–94

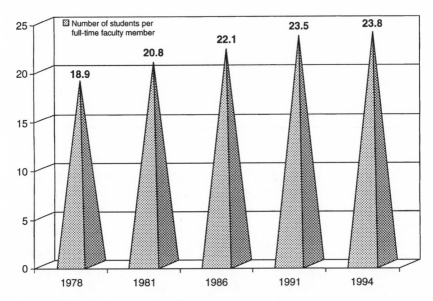

Source: AUCC databases sent to author

surplus value, central administrations in universities have effectively stratified the academic workforce. In this process, they have sharpened the contradiction between the rhetoric of accommodating motivated, career-oriented, and highly skilled part-timers and the realities of their low pay and status. This theme is explained in the chapter's four sections: events that led to part-timers' emergence, their entrenchment in academe, the expansion of the corps of part-timers as (funding) dollars vanished, and the surplus value created for universities by part-timers' low wages.

Emergence

Since the Second World War, three key forces – enrolment, size of faculty, and funding – have been central to the dynamics of universities, shaping the mandate for mass higher education and access. During the last four decades, enrolment and faculty numbers have expanded, making the part-time faculty a large but marginalized segment of the

Canadian academic workforce. After the war, Canadian universities assumed the responsibility for educating a much broader portion of society than they ever had done before. An influx of veterans doubled enrolment in years 1945–8. In 1951 the authors of the *Massey Report* urged the federal government to offer financial support to Canadian universities to fulfil a mandate of mass education. The expansion of higher education continued to ride the country's wave of economic growth, prosperity, and conspicuous consumption.

Faith in the economic value of higher education and confidence that it would repay an investment of large-scale public funding continued generally firm into the 1960s.[3] In 1965 the Economic Council of Canada identified education as crucial for economic growth and for raising living standards (Economic Council of Canada, 1965: 71). Full-time enrolment in Ontario rose from 32,000 in 1960 to 120,000 in 1970 and the full-time faculty from 2,555 to 9,335 (Neatby, 1985: 14). Governments made immense investments of capital and created new, major spending programs to sustain the operating budgets of the new 'instant university systems.' Academic careers, although still not as lucrative as other professions, became attractive, and enrolments in graduate schools flourished. Much in demand, the full-time faculty was able to strengthen its position and consolidate its status as the essence of the university community. Neatby reflects: 'It happened so quickly, and with so little resistance, that most of us never noticed that we were living through a revolution' (ibid.: 13). This 'Academic Revolution' (Jencks and Riesman, 1968: 1–27), altered the power structures within the university and entrenched the ability of the faculty collegium, to 'collectively ... determine what shall be taught, how it shall be taught, and who shall be qualified to receive the teaching. In a word, they should be self-governing, as are the members of other learned professions' (Neatby, 1985: 14).[4]

In the 1970s, although enrolments continued to increase until mid-decade, funding levelled off or declined in many jurisdictions, as did the gains of the academic profession. Both government and corporate leaders continued to worry about the large-scale operating costs of the institutions that they had helped to build and called for economy measures to reduce duplication and produce 'more scholar for the dollar' (Axelrod, 1982: 141–78, 183). The underemployment of graduates in the 1970s created a dilemma; among those who had aspired to academic positions, frustration and disappointment replaced the success of graduates of 1960s.[5]

In the United States, by the end of 1970s the job crisis for graduates in the humanities showed no sign of abating and demoralized the new entrants to graduate studies. David Riesman's consternation that graduate studies in sociology could no longer tempt his brightest students was not a lone complaint in academe.[6] The professoriate in humanities has aptly called the 1970s and 1980s graduates in humanities a 'lost generation of scholars.' Riesman compared them to the victims of China's Cultural Revolution. Not everyone got lost as a 'gypsy scholar' or the 'ubiquitous taxi-driving humanist'; some got jobs as 'applied humanists' in corporations and some worked in museums and archives (Jones, 1990). In his preface to *Managing Finances in Community Colleges*, Lombardi (1973) pointed out that public education was in the midst of a financial crisis in the United States. Levin, Perkins, and Clowes (1992) elaborated on the effects of reductions in state funding on patterns of spending among institutions within the Virginia Community College System. For instance, to deal with a 55 per cent system-wide increase (1981–91) in the ratio of instructional and general expenditures to full-time equivalent students (FTES), college presidents cut academic costs of various types, for example, expenditures on hiring regular faculty members to meet increasing enrolments. Instead of hiring tenure-track faculty, they increased the number of part-timers and also increased the ratio of students to faculty to keep the instructional expenditures relatively constant. Since salaries account for a large proportion of any university's budget, university central administrators cut down on full-time faculty numbers while increasing short-term or part-time contracts. Part-timers would help to teach larger numbers of students.

In Ontario, by the end of the 1970s many of the PhD graduates of that decade continued to occupy the 'room at the bottom' of the academic workforce, not having given up 'the dream of a permanent academic position' (Moffat, 1980: 22). When the financial crisis hit the university and threatened the earlier gains of 'the academic revolution' of the 1960s, the professoriate 'closed ranks to defend their gains' (Neatby, 1985: 15). Few full-time tenure-track academics lost their jobs; instead, their universities used limited-term contracts and part-timers in large numbers – employees easily redeployed or terminated in response to enrolment shifts or financial constraints. The larger this buffer zone of 'flexibility,' the greater was the insulation protecting the full-time faculty. From the mid-1970s through to the mid-1980s the academic job market remained shrunken and limited generally to intermittent, short-term, non-tenure-stream, or part-time positions. The COU, which had first addressed this problem in *Academic Career Planning* (1976), reported almost a decade later in *Bottoming Out* that the situation remained desperate: 'Because of chronic under-funding ... Ontario universities have had recourse increasingly to sessional, non-tenure track appointments, in essence, short-term contracts for one or two years, many of them part-time, and for teaching only, as opposed to the earlier practice of multiyear probationary appointments leading to tenure, contingent on a positive performance review as both teacher and researcher. Holders of such short-term appointments have been called "gypsy scholars" ... Some of these academics hold concurrent part-timer appointments at several institutions, or combine academic duties with their employment in their efforts to stitch together an adequate income. The real academic concern is that their scholarship tends to suffer' (1985: 16). In many Ontario universities, the number of part-timers hired and their ratio to full-timers increased considerably after the early 1970s.[7] Despite a lamentable lack of nation-wide, regularly updated data, my own surveys show that universities have used the hiring of part-timers to help to manage their fiscal problems.[8]

This strategy of employing part-time or full-time contract faculty inevitably but imperceptibly erodes the tenure system. A policy statement issued by the Canadian Association of University Teachers (CAUT) calls for restricted use of contract faculty to fill temporary vacancies. Many academics see expansion of such temporary appointments as an ongoing process intended to circumvent the tenure system, rather than as an outright abrogation of the system. The 'misuse and abuse of sessional appointments' (Banks, 1995: 3) not only reduce the number of new tenure-track appointments but also lower the regular faculty's average salaries and their standard of living. Further, the practice equips management with a bargaining weapon against the demands of full-time faculty. The university's central administrators could easily threaten to meet fluctuations in enrolment by hiring low-paid, temporary sessionals instead of acceding to full-timers' demands. Misuse of part-time appointments, however, 'poses a number of threats to the quality of university education' (ibid.). It dilutes academic freedom, subverts the tenure system, and forces talented but frustrated teaching candidates to leave academe.

FIGURE 1.2

Faculty, enrolment, and expenses in Ontario universities, 1977–89

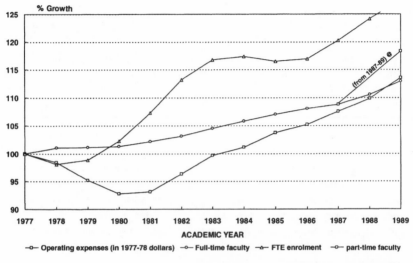

% Growth

-○- Operating expenses (in 1977-78 dollars)   -○- Full-time faculty   -△- FTE enrolment   -○- part-time faculty

⊕: Actual numbers from surveys: COU (1988) and National Institutional (1990)

Sources: Council of Ontario Universities (COU) financial reports, Ontario universities 1977–90; Rajagopal and Farr (1988), COU survey, and National Institutional Survey; Ministry of Colleges and Universities' (MCU) statistical summaries 1986–8; Statistics Canada, Cat. No. 81-258

Entrenchment

The impact of cutbacks beginning in the 1970s continued to create a ripple effect in the 1990s. Edward Renner, a consultant on higher education and author of *New Agenda For Higher Education* (1995), reported that Canadian universities had hired a third of their current teaching staff from the late 1980s through the mid-1990s. These additions, however, were not young, new graduates: their average age was forty-four. Although there was no dearth of new doctoral graduates, some of them interested in academic jobs 'still cannot get' them. Renner's analysis shows that by the mid-1990s only 6 per cent of university faculty members were under thirty-five, whereas in the 1970s, when the cutback started, the figure was 36 per cent. He added that more than half the faculty members were over fifty, compared with only 15 per cent in

1971: 'Those from Generation X who have pursued advanced degrees at great personal and financial expense are still waiting in line behind the baby boomers' (Shegda, 1996).

Financial restraint has been the order of the day. By the mid-1990s the first batch of the academic age bulge had reached age 55, and universities began to offer them early-retirement incentives as a cost-cutting measure. Continuing cutbacks, however, led universities to freeze the hiring of full-time replacements. Iris Shegda, communications officer for the Ontario Confederation of University Faculty Associations (OCUFA) observed that a cut of $400 million from the university system from 1995 to mid-1996 produced 'an enormous and constant drain ... Anyone born after the baby boom is still on the outside looking in ... By the time a full-time position opens up, a PhD graduate has had to do post-doctorate work as well as contract work for years, so they are a lot older ... That's the difference from the [early] '70s when [universities] were grabbing them before they finished their PhD theses, because there was a need for faculty' (Shegda, 1996).

According to the Association of Universities and Colleges of Canada (AUCC), in the 1970s provinces began to shift funding away from education. From 27.3 per cent of their total budgets net of debt, during 1965–78, their allocation for education declined to 21 per cent in the 1990s. Since 1993 governments have reduced their support in real dollars by 20 per cent (AUCC, 1999: 21–4). A direct result has been declining faculty numbers, down 11 per cent in 1999 from 1992 levels (ibid.: 40). In its seventh annual ranking of universities, *Maclean's* magazine[9] found that the 'battle to preserve excellence in Canadian universities has never been more critical,' especially under shrinking budgets: 44 per cent of the universities reported a drop in their operating budgets; and 56 per cent had increased class sizes. In 49 per cent of the universities, tenured faculty members taught fewer first year classes (1997: 30).[10]

The Ontario Confederation of University Faculty Associations (OCUFA), which represents about 11,000 faculty members and librarians, reported in spring 1998 that Ontario's universities, the largest aggregate in Canada, would have fewer teachers but more administrators and more technology. In Ontario, faculty numbers declined by nearly 9 per cent from 1994–5 to 1996–7, shrinking expenditure on faculty salaries from 37.5 per cent of total general operating expenditures in 1994–5 to 35.1 per cent in 1996–7. Social Contract[11] policies cut some $53 million from academic salaries during 1994–7. Coincident with the resumption of collective bargaining in 1997, faculty numbers declined rapidly because of early retirements. Instead of transferring the savings accruing from early retirements back to academic budgets, university administrations diverted the largest share to other expenditures. Non-academic salaries and technology-related expenditures rose from 27.5 per cent in 1994–5 to 28.7 per cent in 1996–7 (Melchers, 1998: 10).

According to Deborah Flynn (1998), president of OCUFA, not only have universities adopted the business-competition paradigm for funding and enrolments, but also greater cutbacks from the mid-1990s on have resulted in fluctuating enrolments. On average, 35–50 per cent of the money for academic programs is derived from tuition fees, which makes universities quite vulnerable to volatile enrolments in times of lower government support. Not only is the Ontario government directing more funds to areas such as science and technology, but it is also indirectly forcing universities to reduce numbers of tenured faculty members and replace them with temporary instructors or technology. Sid Gilbert cautions that in the political economy of 'performance indicators' (PIs), under the pretext of ensuring 'public accountability,' PIs could be misused 'if [they are] externally imposed and often meaningless, statistical comparisons masquerading as performance indicators.' He quotes Bill Graham's critique in the *Toronto Star*: the new design of higher education has 'students as "clients"' and the bottom line as the ultimate objective' (1999: 19).

This scenario continues. OCUFA's media release on 2 May 2000 is titled 'Budget Ignores Critical Shortage of University Faculty' (YUFA, 2000). It is noted that in budget after budget of provincial Tory governments higher education and its value as a public good is de-emphasized in favour of tax cuts. Deborah Flynn examines the faculty shortage: 'The Ontario government has once again ignored the impending critical shortage of university faculty in today's budget. While some money has been set aside for additional university buildings, nothing was done to provide the resources required to hire the professors and librarians to teach in them. A number of recent studies conclude that nearly 13,000 new faculty will have to be hired over the next few years ... This is the number necessary to replace retiring faculty and to meet the demand of an additional 90,000 students expected in the next few years' (ibid.). Are the governments expecting full-time faculty members to carry a greater workload, or are they trying to encourage the hiring of 'temps,' that is, part-timers, and non-tenure-track full-timers on short-term contracts? Governments' sparse funding encourages universities to hire part-timers and sessionals instead of committing moneys for tenure-track appointments. Referring to Statistics Canada's analysis of part-time faculty budgets, the AUCC identifies a parallel growth of 30 per cent in part-timers and full-timers, but deep cuts in budgets between 1992 and 1995 led to dropping of vulnerable part-timers. Since 1996, however, there has been an increase in the salary budgets allocated to part-time faculty, perhaps, as suggested in *Trends*, indicating a resurgence in their numbers (1999: 47).

According to the Canadian Union of Public Employees (CUPE),[12] which represents part-timers in twelve unionized universities, part-timers' numbers increased in 1999. In 1990 fifty-nine universities[13] that responded to my institutional survey had 18,652 part-time faculty members.[14] It is difficult to get current numbers on all part-timers (using my definition of 'part-time faculty') without conducting a repeat survey. If we take Statistics Canada's (2000a) preliminary figures, in 1998–9 there were 27,983 part-timers.[15] Statistics Canada's definition of part-timers includes instructional staff with part-time appointments, those with a full-time appointment of less than twelve months, and full-timers teaching overload hours. This definition is broader than the one I have used in my surveys. As we saw in the introductory chapter, however, Statistics Canada's own figures for 1992–3 and 1997–8 show that part-timers in Canadian universities increased and that most of this growth has been in universities in the Atlantic (13.8 per cent increase to 2,858 part-timers) and western Canada (13.5 per cent to 6,062). In many Ontario universities that had a high ratio of part- to full-timers, part-timers have slightly declined by 6 per cent from 9,209 in 1992–3 to 8,655 in 1998–9.[16] One reason may be that those who had higher ratios of part-timers seem to have curtailed their hiring – for instance, by changing program structures and course requirements for degrees,[17] increasing the enrolment of graduates and using them as teaching assistants, increasing class sizes and student-faculty ratios – to reduce their need for hiring part-timers. Such strategies helped to reduce their hiring when 'cheap skilled temporary workers' began to turn into entrenched 'permanent temps,' and in unionized universities, during part-timers' contract negotiations, administrators felt encumbered, or became overloaded with part-timers' grievances. However, non-unionized universities have few such concerns.

In contrast to the increase in total part-timers, the number of full-timers in Canadian universities has gone down by 9.7 per cent; some

3,600 full-time positions have been lost between 1992–3 and 1998–9, while enrolments declined only by 1.4 per cent of FTEs. The largest declines were in Newfoundland (–18.6 per cent), in Manitoba (–15.9 per cent), and in Ontario (–11.7 per cent). The entrance positions – assistant professors, lecturers, and so on – fell by 20.5 per cent (Statistics Canada, 2000a). A recent study, 'Voices from the Classroom: The Ontario Colleges and the Question of Quality,'[18] funded by York University's Centre for Research on Work and Society (CRWS), the Social Science Research Council of Canada (SSHRC), and the Ontario Public Service Employees Union (OPSEU) examined the quality of post-secondary education, especially in Ontario community colleges (*York Gazette*, 2000). The intense concerns of 81 per cent of the faculty members about the repercussions of a decade of government funding cuts were reported. Universities' hiring fewer full-time faculty, replacing them with instructors and technicians, and requiring students to work independently in 'self-taught classes,' have, they believe, seriously harmed the quality of education. Full-time faculty's heavier workloads, reduced time for contact with students outside the classroom, increased stress, and declining morale have hurt students' work and the quality of teaching. Drummond (2000) noted that the COU and OCUFA also have reported a decade of steady decline in numbers in the tenure-stream faculty, a direct result of decreasing government funding for hiring new people or for replacing retirees. The detrimental impact on the quality of university education and research is imponderable.

According to the AUCC, 'universities are doing 'less with less.' Reductions in faculty numbers have led to shifts in workload of faculty who remain on campus as they increase the amount of their teaching time to make up for gaps' (1999: 40). Full-time faculty numbers in Canadian universities have declined by 11 per cent since 1992. In the United States, the *Digest of Education Statistics, 1998* shows an increase in part-timers from 36.4 per cent (300,000) in 1989 to 40.9 per cent (381,000) in 1995 (NCES, 1999: 254, table 255). Meanwhile, the total instructional faculty (full and part time) grew by 13 per cent. However, full-time faculty increased by only 5.3 per cent (from 524,000 to 552,000) and part-timers by 27 per cent.

This trend is not unique to North America. In Australia and Germany, too, numbers of part-time faculty have increased, while those of full-time faculty have declined. During the last two years in Australia, there has been a decline of about 6 per cent in numbers of full-timers, whereas those of part-timers have increased by more than 10 per cent. In Australia's thirty-seven public universities, 40 per cent of 80,000 faculty and staff are on contract and are not eligible for tenure (Maslen, 1998). In fifteen universities across five states, Australian faculty's job satisfaction with job security has dropped from 52 per cent in 1993 to 43 per cent in 1999 (*CAUT Bulletin*, September 2000: A9).[19] In Germany, from 1992 to 1997, full-time faculty members declined by 1 per cent, while part-timers mushroomed by 21 per cent. In France, however, the part-time faculty's share of teaching and growth has not been a critical factor, since they constitute only 2 per cent of the total (AUCC, 1999: 47).

The presence of part-time faculty in British universities is becoming noticeable. During the ten years between 1981 and 1991, the Association of University Teachers (AUT) reports in *Part-Time, Poor Deal* (1993), in the older, long-established universities part-time faculty increased in numbers by 160 per cent from 1,738 to 4,549 and full-time faculty by just above 20 per cent. In the newer universities, women accounted for half of the part-timers but only 24 per cent of the full-timers (National Association of Teachers in Further and Higher Education, 1993). Women part-timers' increases are in arts Faculties, a traditionally female enclave. Most post-retirement full-timers teaching part time are men. The AUT concludes that part-time faculty are 'grossly exploited' in terms not so much of pay but of hours worked. British part-timers describe their work situation: 'It is the *au pair* job of the department. You do all the unwanted work and get no recognition.' '[I am] unlikely to have any say in what I teach and the days I teach. It seems very much in the lap of [the] gods. You never know whether the set texts will be ones you know' (*Times Higher Education*, 1994: 15–16). The AUT suggests that the trend towards casualization of teaching was being halted in the 1990s. Since 1992 numbers of part-timers (13 per cent of all faculty) have increased by only 8 per cent, compared with 23 per cent growth among full-timers (AUCC, 1999: 47). This 'underclass' of British part-timers was created as 'a response to funding pressures ... to the 13 per cent cut in governmental grants in 1981–82 ... The universities in the U.K. are merely passing on structural job insecurity to their hapless employees to deal with as best they can.' In *Part-Time, Poor Deal* it is pointed out that part-timers offer universities an inexpensive way of subsidizing teaching by keeping them on short contracts at low pay. Extracting cheap labour from part-timers to run a 'flexible university' during the periods and in disciplinary areas where institutions are over-enrolled keeps them quite cost efficient (Fosh and Husbands, 1993: 15, 13).[20]

International trends show that part-time workers as a proportion of the whole labour force in industrial market economies grew, on average, by about 30 per cent during 1980–90. We saw in the introductory chapter how part-time work rapidly increased in Canada and how this trend in the general labour force in the long run could have implications for education workers. Beck (1993) argues that the education sector is larger than the mining, forestry, food, beverage, rubber, plastics, and clothing industries combined. In 1992 the education sector accounted for almost 6 per cent of gross domestic product (GDP), and in the 1990s this sector was expanding. It created employment for one in ten Canadians and contributed significantly to the economy of the province and of the region (ibid.). In 1992 universities created and maintained over 182,000 'person years' of employment. They contributed $9 billion to the gross provincial product in Ontario (Kubursi, 1994). It appears as a rebuke that their direct contributions to the economy were rewarded with reduced funding for operating and revitalizing universities. Annette Kolodny, a professor of comparative cultural and literacy studies and a former dean at the University of Arizona, warns in *Failing the Future* about the disastrous impact of cutting educational funding (1998; quoted in Limerick, 1998). Yet people refer to her call for increasing finances for education as 'science fiction.' Limerick comments that it may not be 'science fiction' but a sort of 'inspirational literature.'

Expansion

In Ontario, the interrelations of enrolments, numbers of full-time faculty, and operating expenses suggest the reasons for increasing use of part-time faculty. During the period 1977–88 enrolment grew by 20.2 per cent and constant dollar operating expenses by only 7.5 per cent (figure 1.2), the consequence of continued government underfunding. Increases in both full-time faculty numbers and their salary total exceeded the rise in operating expenses, but their numbers fell well short of enrolment growth. Universities did not add full-time faculty as quickly as they added students. Part-timers represented a cheap way to keep the ratio of students to faculty low.[21] Since 1978 full-time equivalent (FTE) enrolments in Ontario have increased by 29.1 per cent and full-time faculty by only 13.2 per cent. The ratio of students to full-

FIGURE 1.3

Ratio of FTE students to faculty in Ontario universities, 1988–9

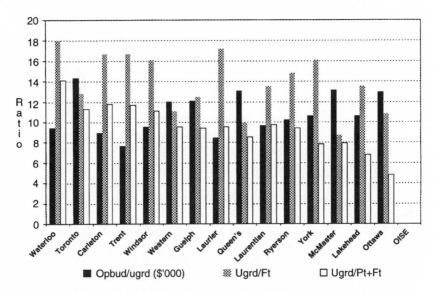

Notes: Ft: full-time faculty; Opbud: operating budget in $'000; Ugrd: undergraduate students; Pt: part-time faculty. No undergraduate students at OISE
Source: See figure 1.2.

time faculty, 18:1 in 1977–8, had increased to 20:1 by 1989–90, and dropped to 16:1 overall only if one added in part-timers (COU: 1990). Figure 1.3 presents the situation in 1988–9.

In Quebec, at many institutions 'non-traditional' students, usually part-time and/or off-campus students, frequently are taught largely by part-time faculty (Conseil, 1989: 40–1). Universities have found this strategy feasible, since governments only marginally fund the teaching of part-time students, and full-time faculty resist the increasing workload. Universities also have found it convenient and 'surplus generating' to employ independent practitioners to instruct part-time students in professional certification courses (for example, teacher education, accounting).

This scenario continued in the 1990s. In 2001, as funding declines, enrolments increase and universities are still struggling to fill classes with instructors. Inadequate financial resources push universities to hire more part-timers instead of new full-time faculty. In January 2001 a North American conference, Coalition on Contingent Academic Labour (COCAL), of part-timers representing higher education faculty in sixteen U.S. states and four Canadian provinces condemned the increasing use of marginalized academics on temporary assignments to meet the increasing enrolments in universities as inequitable and exploitive (*CAUT Bulletin*, February 2001).

Analogous to Braverman's corporations and their bureaucracies, underfunding drives the universities to organize their production in new ways and 'battle to realize values, to turn them into cash' (Braverman, 1974: 302). They seek to extract greater value from the efficient labour needed to teach the undergraduates 'productively,' while maintaining pedagogic standards and a complete curriculum.

Part-Time Faculty and Surplus Value

Universities could easily measure the success of their strategy in using part-timers by calculating how many part-timers they could hire for an average full-time salary. Part-time stipends per full course in 1987–8 ranged between $4,000 and $7,800, with a median of about $5,400; the 1989–90 range was $4,100 to $9,141, with a median of $6,300. My estimate of the total for Ontario's part-time faculty salary in 1987–8 is about $53 million, compared with full-time salaries of about $651 million. Part-time salaries, therefore, represented about 7.6 per cent of the total, even though part-timers represented 32.4 per cent of total faculty members and performed a fifth of the total teaching. For a single 'average full-time salary' most universities could acquire teaching from part-timers equivalent to that which would require four or more full-timers. Further, the costs of salaries, benefits, and professional development for part-timers are disproportionately lower than those for full-time faculty. In 1987–8, fringe benefits amounted to 4.5 per cent of part-time salaries, in contrast to 12–13 per cent for full-timers. Currently, health benefits, such as supplementary health, disability insurance, vision care, dental plans, and group life insurance, are only minimally or rarely available to part-timers. They rarely receive other full-timer benefits, such as sick leave, maternity leave, and paid vacation.

The 'temporary' label pinned on part-timers has also been used to legitimize the neglect of their professional development that many full-timers consider to be related to merit, specialization, and quality of academic work. Commodification of part-time academic work inevitably leads to an almost total absence of opportunities for career development, reinforcing their treatment as pieceworkers and in stark contrast to the opportunities provided to full-timers. My survey also revealed that even where institutional policy does not explicitly exclude part-timers from developmental support, in practice, the actual levels lie far below. Only 6 per cent of responding universities reported that they provide 'sabbatical or research leave' for part-timers or offer professional retraining. At 10 per cent of universities, part-timers were eligible for training in research skills, yet such leave or training was 'rarely given.' Remarkably, even in teaching, for which the universities hired the part-timers, only 35 per cent of institutions provided opportunities for training in instruction, and only a sixth of these actually delivered such training. Some made travel expenses to attend conferences available to part-timers; at 38 per cent of universities, part-timers were eligible, but only 18 per cent extended actual support heavily or moderately.

Although universities commonly express commitment to the quality of their faculty and to excellence in teaching, my survey responses contradict the rhetoric. Even though part-timers perform a substantial portion of undergraduate instruction, they are considered marginal to the academic enterprise. They are excluded almost entirely from even rudimentary training in the work that they do and *totally* from the professional development that full-timers deem essential for a healthy academic life and effectiveness in the classroom. Parallel savings in cost of service support relative to those provided to full-timers further augmented the surplus value accruing to the university from the use of part-timers (Rajagopal and Farr, 1988, 1990). Where support services to part-timers represented direct incremental costs to the university – for example, telephones, offices, and secretarial support – hardly any were provided.

Part-timers, therefore, are clearly a relatively less expensive teaching resource, in terms of not only their salaries, but also their claim on space and support services. They are an obvious resource in times of financial stringency, but they are also one of the expenditures most easily reduced in those very circumstances. Full-timers' costs are effectively locked-in expenditures; part-timers, who lack job security, are highly vulnerable, despite their relatively low marginal costs. When universities find themselves in a tight corner, forced to cut where they can, they reduce that 'flexible' workforce.

FIGURE 1.4
Creating an underclass in Canadian universities: a conceptual model

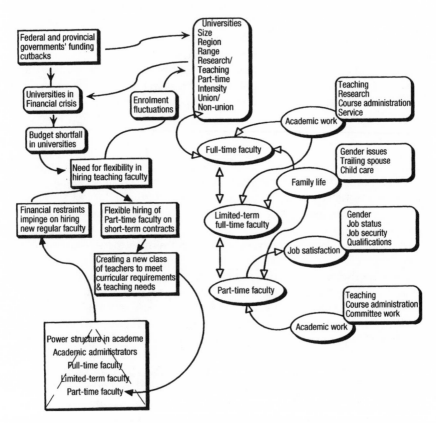

The part-time faculty does most of the teaching work that goes unrewarded. As an underclass, it is entrusted with the more routine and less exciting jobs of grading, marking, and labour-intensive teaching (figure 1.4). A part-timer writes about academic stratification of work – research versus teaching: 'At universities there are full-time positions for professors who only do research so why would there not be full-time positions for professors who only teach? Universities seem to value only research, and teaching is not a qualification required for getting a full-time position. You could be an excellent researcher but useless in terms of pedagogy and the university will open wide its doors for you. On the contrary, if you excel in teaching (contact with students, pedagogic approaches, being available to students, profound knowl-

FIGURE 1.5
Ratio of FTE students to full-time faculty, 1997–8

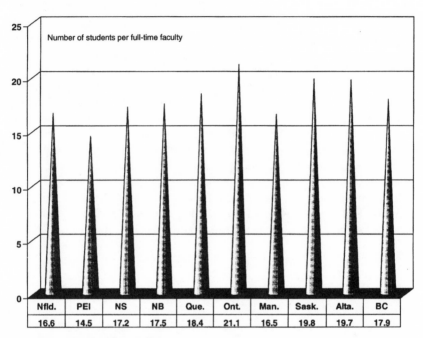

Nfld.	PEI	NS	NB	Que.	Ont.	Man.	Sask.	Alta.	BC
16.6	14.5	17.2	17.5	18.4	21.1	16.5	19.8	19.7	17.9

Source: *CAUT Bulletin* (June 2000)

edge in your discipline, etc.) but don't do research, you cannot get a full time position.' Yet part-timers strive to be far from 'underclass' in their work: 'As ... teachers, part-time or otherwise, our primary responsibility is to educate the students. The only way to do this is to constantly evaluate, refresh, and upgrade our courses. No matter how good they are they can always be better. A bonus to this approach is that we ourselves stay fresh and interested.' However, they are disillusioned by the lack of prospects: 'Fluctuating budgets cause a very uncertain situation for part-time / short-contract staff. It makes it impossible to plan your courses in a rational and sensible manner. 'And, I think one has to be really enthusiastic about any university-related employment (research and/or teaching) to stay in this field. I have almost lost hope after 3 years at this university.' And, 'I sometimes felt like a visitor or intruder rather than someone who was teaching 40 students.'

The financial prospects for Canada's universities seem no better for the coming decade than they were for the last. Universities' budgets get tighter and tighter, and if the past proves any guide for the future, they will respond by expanding class size, increasing full-timers' workload, and shifting ever-growing proportions of their teaching towards part-timers. Despite the fact that this faculty resource is helping universities to manage their financial strains, these institutions have identified employment of part-time academics as an aberration in higher education (FNEEQ, 1990: 4, 6). Of all the provinces, the highest student-faculty ratio for 1997–8 was in Ontario, followed by Alberta – two of the affluent provinces – mainly because of declining government funding (figure 1.5). Continued financial cutbacks have forced university administrations to extract surplus value from temporary academics. In injecting the 'temps' into the collegium, they have effectively stratified the academic workforce.

In the next chapter, focusing on my direct survey of part-timers, we turn to a more detailed analysis of their situation and a selection of their discerning and sensitive comments.

Chapter Two

Hidden Academics

While I appreciate the income and the opportunity to practise my chosen profession, although in a limited fashion, the life of a part-time academic is not one I would wish on a dog. University departments impose a form of academic apartheid [on part-timers] ... constantly one is made to feel the third-class status.

The above quotation encapsulates the experiences of many qualified academics working as part-timers and frustrated by their job search. University central administration and full-time faculty are often in the dark about part-timers' career aspirations, their motivations, and other aspects of their work life, although they are visibly working among, and along with, them in academe. It is obvious that the full-time faculty do not share a similar plight in job search and work status, but this is only part of the reason why their interests have diverged from those of part-timers.

As we saw in chapter one, universities' financial shortfalls drive them to hire contract and part-time faculty instead of tenure-streamers in order to create surplus value. Such value ensues from the relationship between wages and value of their labour, that is, money gained from part-timers' increasing workloads and money saved from their low wages. The process of exploitation leads to the realization of surplus value when the university gains more value than it pays part-timers in wages. As a consequence of commodification of part-time academic work – that is, when academic work is deemed a commodity and the part-timer is separated from her or his work – exploitation occurs. Through marginal pay, temporary hiring, heavier teaching loads, and neglect of professional development and career mobility of part-timers, universities extract surplus value. The 'temporary' label pinned on part-timers serves to legitimize universities' obliviousness to part-timers' professionalism, merit, specialization, and quality of academic work. Further, the marginalized position of part-timers in decision-making bodies denies them the opportunity to influence policies to advance their interests. This conceptual framework is fleshed out in the chapter's subsequent three sections; I explain why part-timers are invisible or hidden by looking at, in turn, who they are, their work, their aspirations, and their influence. In the first section I examine their low status, their increasing work but its declining rewards, and their inadequate pay and lack of job security. In the second section I focus on their hopes of career mobility: their aspirations for academic careers, the barriers to full-time academic jobs, the difficulties of research, and lack of professional development. The influence of part-timers in academe, their marginality in decision-making, and the resulting non-participation are considered in the third section.

Who Are the Part-Time Faculty?

There are more men (54 per cent) than women (46 per cent) part-timers, including those with full-time jobs elsewhere (table 2.1). Women part-timers (age 43 on average) are almost the same age as or perhaps slightly younger than men (age 44). A majority of part-timers live with spouses/partners; compared with women who are single (26 per cent), however, fewer men (15 per cent) are in that category. A majority of part-timers have dependent children. Half the part-timers have a master's degree, while a fourth have a doctorate (table 2.1a). More men (32 per cent versus 21 per cent women) hold a doctoral degree. The comparable part-timers' qualifications reported in U.S. higher education in 1992 were 16 per cent with a doctorate and 76 per cent with an advanced degree ('Statement from the Conference,' 1998: 55).

Part-time faculty women's personal incomes are far lower than those of men. Half of the women earn less than $30,000, and more men than women earn an upper-level income. Half of the women (men 32 per cent) are clearly dependent on academic part-time jobs for more than 30 per cent of their personal income. Although two-thirds of all part-timers make their part-time income from one university, three in four women have only part-time jobs, academic or non-academic, and earn their total incomes from part-time work; if part-timers have a partner

TABLE 2.1
Part-time faculty in Canadian universities: demographic profile and
discipline, by gender

		Men %	Women %	Overall total %	Overall total no.
	Total %	54.1	45.9	100.0	2,208
Faculty or discipline where they teach***	Education	11.9	19.0	15.2	335
	Fine and applied arts	7.6	10.0	8.5	187
	Humanities	17.8	27.8	22.2	490
	Social Sciences	40.0	29.8	35.2	777
	Science and applied arts	22.7	14.6	18.9	419
	Total %	100.0	100.0	100.0	2,208
Age, years %*	<30	5.4	7.6	6.4	141
	<40	34.9	32.0	33.6	742
	<50	34.7	38.1	36.2	799
	50+	25.0	22.3	23.8	526
	Total %	100.0	100.0	100.0	2,208
Family status***	Spouse	85.3	74.0	80.1	1,769
	Single	14.7	26.0	19.9	439
	Total %	100.0	100.0	100.0	2,208
No. of dependent children**	0	41.3	46.7	43.8	967
	1	58.7	53.3	56.2	1,241
	Total %	100.0	100.0	100.0	2,208
Birthplace (n.s.)	West	89.2	90.1	88.8	1,961
	Non-west	10.8	9.9	11.2	247
	Total %	100.0	100.0	100.0	2,208

Notes: Significance: p = *<.05; **<.01; ***<.001. All are significant unless indicated non-significant (n.s.).
Source: Rajagopal, Part-Time Faculty Survey (1991–2)

TABLE 2.1a
Part-timers: education and income, by gender

		Part-timers			
		Men %	Women %	Overall total %	Overall total no.
Hold 'full-time non-academic job' versus 'only part-time' job (%)	Classic	43.0	24.0	34.5	762
	Contemporary	56.7	76.0	65.5	1,446
	Total %	100.0	100.0	100.0	2,208
Degree (%)	<Master's	20.7	22.9	21.7	479
	Master's	47.5	56.4	51.5	1,137
	Doctorate	31.9	20.8	26.8	592
	Total %	100.0	100.0	100.0	2,208
Part-time income	Mean $	11,948	12,767	12,320	
Part-time academic income (%)	<30 (%)	68.0	47.2	58.5	1,291
	>30 (%)	32.0	52.8	41.5	918
	Total %	100.0	100.0	100.0	2,208
Part-time income from one university (%)	<50 (%)	23.8	22.6	21.3	470
	>50<100 (%)	6.2	9.8	7.9	174
	100 (%)	69.9	67.6	68.9	1,521
	Total %	100.0	100.0	100.0	2,208
Personal income $ ($ 000)	<30	22.8	49.9	35.4	781
	>30 and <60	37.1	35.5	36.4	803
	60+	40.1	14.6	28.3	625
	Total %	100.0	100.0	100.0	2,208
Household income $ ($ 000) (n.s.)	<30	11.3	12.5	11.8	260
	>30 and <60	26.8	24.7	25.9	572
	60+	61.9	62.9	62.3	1,326
	Total %	100.0	100.0	100.0	2,208

Note: Differences are significant at p = <.001 unless indicated not significant (n.s.).
Source: See table 2.1.

with an income, however, gender differences in their average household incomes seem to fade. The 1996 survey of non-tenure-track faculty members at McGill University identifies more women than men in a precarious situation, regarding both their career paths and their earnings, since women rely more heavily on non-tenure-track jobs (Cumming Speirs et al., 1998).

Since there is little gender-differentiated data on part-timers' wages, to understand women's situation in hiring, promotion, and salary differentials in general, we may briefly look at the gender gap among full-time faculty both in the United States and in Canada. In the United States, Marcia Bellas's (1993) study, which employs national data from the 1984 Carnegie survey of faculty, identifies a persistent gender-based wage gap, reflecting discrepancies between men and women in reward structures. Even after one controls the data for differences between women and men in education levels, professional achievement, and other standard predictors of faculty salaries, 'sex continued to exert a strong independent effect on salary. Even at equivalent standing, women received salaries 6.6 per cent lower than men's average' (ibid.: 73). Further, Ernst Benjamin (1999) reports on gender disparities in salaries in relation to academic women's relegation to less remunerative and lower-rank or part-time appointments in U.S. institutions. Even if they attain higher ranks, they cluster in associate professor rank, a result of the 'glass ceiling.' In Canada, Ornstein and Stewart (1996) have done a statistical analysis of faculty pay, based on Lennards's Canadian full-time faculty survey conducted in 1986 (see Lennards, 1988). This analysis shows that the overall gender gap in pay was about $8,500 per year. Even after one allows for male faculty members' older average age and for level of highest degrees, the estimated gender gap in salaries was about $4,910 per year. The authors conclude that gender-based discriminatory practices in promotion account for much of this difference. Further, productivity in research does not seem to influence the pay or the gender gap. The gap is also much wider at higher ranks, that is, greater for women at the full-professor level than for women at lower ranks. A survey done at a small university in Atlantic Canada of how it deals with gender issues as an employer also shows that women in each employee group, academic and non-academic, earn much less than their male counterparts, even after rank/grade, job type, seniority, and education are controlled for (Looker, 1993).

In my Institutional Survey in 1990 I collected data on the actual number of part-timers as a group in all Canadian universities.[1] Men constitute a majority (59 per cent versus women 41 per cent) of part-timers. Two-thirds of part-timers work in arts (65 per cent) and much smaller percentages in business administration and law (16 per cent) or in pure, applied, and health (excluding medical) sciences (19 per cent). Within those universities that report the disciplinary breakdown of part-timers in arts, a fifth of the faculty work in the social sciences (20 per cent), about another fifth in education (19 per cent), and far fewer in humanities (12 per cent). More than half are women in health (excluding medical) sciences (59 per cent), in humanities (53 per cent), and in education (50 per cent). Four in ten women work in fine and applied arts (43 per cent) and more than a third in the social sciences (38 per cent). In the pure sciences (28 per cent), in law (25 per cent), and in business administration (24 per cent), about a fourth are women. Proportionately fewer part-timers are women (19 per cent) in applied sciences, and 39 per cent are women among those who do not fit into any of these disciplines.

My survey of part-time faculty, 1991–2,[2] indicates that almost half of the part-timers (48 per cent) received their highest degree in the 1980s – the era of the 'lost generation of scholars.' One in two part-timers in education, fine and applied arts, and humanities are women; they constitute only a third of those in social sciences and sciences (table 2.2). In age, one in seven part-timers in social sciences and fine and applied arts is over 50, whereas one in four is in the over-50 group in sciences, humanities, and education. Of those who were born in non-western countries, more of them are found in sciences and humanities. In both humanities and social sciences, more than half of the part-timers have only a master's degree; only about three in ten have a doctorate (table 2.2a). In education, most have a master's degree or less, and only a tenth (10 per cent) have doctorates. About one-third in sciences (36 per cent) and humanities (34 per cent) have doctorates, which is the highest proportion of doctorate holders in all the disciplines. Compared with part-timers in humanities (14 per cent), however, more than a quarter in pure and applied sciences (29 per cent) have less than a master's degree, but only 38 per cent in sciences (humanities 77 per cent; social sciences 70 per cent) are pursuing a doctorate. Overall 21 per cent of part-timers are working on a higher degree; a comparable proportion of pure and applied sciences (19 per cent) and arts (21 per cent) part-timers were in a similar pursuit.

Anglophone[3] and francophone part-timers present contrasting pictures in age, education, and income (table 2.3). Closer to half of the

TABLE 2.2
Part-timers: demographic profile by discipline

		Education	Fine and applied arts	Humanities	Social sciences	Sciences	Overall total %	Overall total no.
Sex (%)	Male	42.9	48.8	44.1	61.6	65.1	54.1	1,194
	Female	57.1	51.2	55.9	38.4	34.9	45.9	1,014
	Total %	100.0	100.0	100.0	100.0	100.0	100.0	2,208
Age, years (%)	<30	3.7	4.3	5.8	8.3	6.8	6.4	141
	<40	27.0	48.2	29.0	36.4	35.8	33.6	742
	<50	39.5	31.7	40.2	35.7	31.7	36.2	799
	50+	29.7	15.9	25.0	19.6	25.7	23.8	526
	Total %	100.0	100.0	100.0	100.0	100.0	100.0	2,208
Family status (%) (n.s.)	Spouse	79.7	78.9	78.6	81.7	81.2	80.1	1,769
	Single	20.3	21.1	21.4	18.3	18.8	19.9	439
	Total %	100.0	100.0	100.0	100.0	100.0	100.0	2,208
Dependent children (%)*	0	42.9	48.8	47.7	39.7	45.1	43.8	967
	1+	57.1	51.2	52.3	60.3	54.9	56.2	1,241
	Total %	100.0	100.0	100.0	100.0	100.0	100.0	2,208
Birthplace (%)	West	94.0	94.0	87.0	91.3	84.9	88.8	1,961
	Non-west	6.0	6.0	12.8	8.7	15.1	11.2	247
	Total %	100.0	100.0	100.0	100.0	100.0	100.0	2,208

Notes: Significance: p = * <.05; ** <.01; *** <.001. All are significant at p = *** <.001 unless otherwise indicated. (n.s.): not significant.
Source: See table 2.1.

TABLE 2.2a
Part-timers: education and income by discipline

		Education	Fine and applied arts	Humanities	Social sciences	Sciences	Overall total %	Overall total no.
Degree held	<Master's	20.5	35.5	13.5	18.9	28.9	21.7	479
	Master's	69.1	48.8	52.8	52.7	35.1	51.5	1,137
	Doctorate	10.4	15.7	33.7	28.3	35.9	26.8	592
	Total %	100.0	100.0	100.0	100.0	100.0	100.0	2,208
Degree pursued	<Master's	6.2	10.0	3.9	3.9	9.7	6.3	35
	Master's	37.0	40.0	19.6	26.6	52.8	33.9	162
	Doctorate	56.8	50.0	76.5	69.5	37.5	59.8	286
	Total %	100.0	100.0	100.0	100.0	100.0	100.0	483
Personal income ($'000)	<$30	24.0	54.9	52.0	24.6	33.6	35.4	771
	>$30 to <$60	44.6	37.0	32.9	37.3	33.6	36.4	810
	$60+	31.4	8.0	15.1	38.1	32.8	28.3	627
	Total %	100.0	100.0	100.0	100.0	100.0	100.0	2,208
Part-time income	Mean $	12,043	10,776	15,125	11,784	11,622	12,450	
Part-time income from	One university	65.6	53.5	66.8	70.7	77.0	68.8	1,519
	More universities +non-academic	34.4	46.5	33.2	29.3	33.0	31.2	689
	Total %	100.0	100.0	100.0	100.0	100.0	100.0	2,208

Note: Differences are significant at p = ***<.001.
Source: See table 2.1.

TABLE 2.3
Part-timers: demographic profile by language

		Anglo-phone	Franco-phone	Overall total %	Overall total no.
Sex (n.s.)	Men	53.6	56.2	54.1	1.194
	Women	46.4	43.8	45.9	1,014
	Total %	100.0	100.0	100.0	2,208
Faculty or discipline	Education	13.9	19.5	15.2	335
where they teach***	Fine and applied arts	9.7	4.7	8.5	187
	Humanities	22.3	21.7	22.2	490
	Social sciences	35.0	35.3	35.2	777
	Science and applied arts	19.0	18.8	18.9	419
	Total %	100.0	100.0	100.0	2,208
Age, years %***	<30	5.8	8.1	6.4	141
	<40	31.9	38.8	33.6	742
	<50	36.4	35.8	36.2	799
	50+	25.8	17.3	23.8	526
	Total %	100.0	100.0	100.0	2,208
Family status	Spouse	81.0	77.4	80.1	1,769
(n.s.)	Single	19.0	22.6	19.9	439
	Total %	100.0	100.0	100.0	2,208
No. of dependent	0	44.1	42.9	43.8	967
children (n.s.)	1	55.9	57.1	56.2	1,241
	Total %	100.0	100.0	100.0	2,208
Birthplace*	West	87.9	91.6	88.8	1,961
	Non-west	12.1	8.4	11.2	247
	Total %	100.0	100.0	100.0	2,208

Notes: Significance: p = *<.05; **<.01; ***<.001. All are significant unless indicated non-significant (n.s.).
Source: See table 2.1.

TABLE 2.3a
Part-timers: Education and income by language

		Anglo-phone	Franco-phone	Overall total %	Overall total no.
Degree held	<Master's	21.4	20.7	21.7	479
	Master's	47.8	65.2	51.5	1,137
	Doctorate	30.7	14.1	26.8	592
	Total %	100.0	100.0	100.0	2,208
Degree pursued*	<Master's	5.0	7.8	6.3	35
	Master's	35.9	24.1	33.9	162
	Doctorate	59.1	68.1	59.8	286
	Total %	100.0	100.0	100.0	483
Personal income ($'000)	<$30	37.3	29.4	35.4	771
	>$30 to <$60	33.1	46.6	36.4	810
	$60+	29.6	24.0	28.3	627
	Total %	100.0	100.0	100.0	2,208
Part-time income*	Mean $	12,135	13,442	12,450	

Notes: Significance: p = *<.05; **<.01; ***<.001. All are significant at p = ***<.001 unless otherwise indicated.
Source: See table 2.1.

francophone part-timers are less than age 40, compared with more than half of anglophones (over age 40). Although twice as many anglophone part-timers (31 per cent versus francophone 14 per cent) have doctorates, more of them (37 per cent versus francophone 29 per cent) earn less than $30,000, while more francophone (47 per cent versus anglophone 33 per cent) earn $30,000 to $59,000 in personal income (table 2.3a). Of all part-timers, those with a master's degree are in a majority, about two-thirds of the francophones and nearly half of the Anglophones. More francophone than anglophone part-timers are in education, and twice as many anglophone than francophone part-timers are in fine and applied arts.

Work

The status and conditions of part-timers' teaching in academe, their increasing workload and its diminishing worth, and their pay and job security are examined in this section.

Teaching

Why do part-timers want to work in academe, enduring a role and a status that are deliberately and consciously devalued in their workplace? Part-time teaching is generally not regarded as professional work. Gary Rhoades (1996) examined references to part-timers' work in faculty contracts that would give them professional credit. He found that more than a fourth of contracts that referred to part-timers had negative references, which emphasized that faculty members should not be given time credit for teaching part time. Less than a third of the contracts credited part-time teaching 'experience' in calculating eligibility for professional rewards and advancement, that is, salary scale, time towards sabbatical (ibid.: 648). Shelly Park (1996) concluded that teaching itself is stereotyped as mere 'dissemination' of knowledge and as 'women's work.' On the contrary, she argues, it should be regarded as an important and difficult task of 'reproducing (and empowering) knowers. Thus, an institution that acknowledged the scholarship of teaching could no longer trivialize this facet of academic "women's work"' (1996: 77).

Although part-timers are aware that their work is mostly taken for granted and goes unrecognized, and although they are poorly supported with services, they continue to teach in this marginalized environment. Their two foremost reasons for choosing a teaching job are personal satisfaction and enjoyment of contact with students. A woman part-timer observes: 'Engaging in part-time teaching on a full-time basis is an experience quite different from [doing] other part-time jobs. If we spend a lot of time in contact with students we could gain an insight into their thinking patterns, patterns of difficulty they encounter. Also, we get an opportunity to experiment with teaching techniques we possibly could not have if we spent only a limited time transmitting information.' Another woman part-timer, however, who also loves teaching rather than research, rings a note of warning. She cautions that 'teaching-only' would downgrade one's status in academe: 'I want to teach and not do research. For this reason, a part-time position is more suitable than a full-time position. I don't want to spend my time on committees and in doing research. I want to work with students. But I am penalized for this orientation instead of respected for it, since as a part-time worker I get poor benefits and salary.' Most part-timers love to teach, and the sense of fulfilment seems to compensate them for their low status: 'I enjoy teaching. When students evaluate my teaching as excellent, it is indeed an encouragement to return to the campus next year, although once again, as part-time faculty. The precarious status of being part-time disappears for a moment and my primary interest in teaching and helping students appear more real. That is the way it should be.'

It is also clear from part-timers' responses that they logically differentiate between their 'extrinsic' and 'intrinsic' rewards of teaching (Pucel et al., 1992).[4] Pucel et al. found that a fresh entrant into part-time teaching is more interested in the intrinsic gratification of teaching: seeking and sharing knowledge, career mobility, and collegiality. Lundy and Warme (1989)[5] arrived at similar conclusions: many part-timers in a Canadian university felt rewarded when their students rated their competence slightly above that of full-timers. However, students' ratings of part-timers versus full-timers do not show any perceptible differences in teaching abilities (Abel, 1984; Leslie, Kellams, and Gunne, 1982; Lundy and Warme, 1989). Such 'intrinsic' gratification seems to compensate initially for part-timers' otherwise poor conditions as 'temporary' workers. The passage of time can alter this attitude: continuing to teach part time (with no other full-time job) for a few years, despite their love of teaching many of them become concerned about their economic and job security as well as their working conditions: salary, benefits, workload, and adequate time to work with students. We saw, above, that a critical reason for the increase in part-timers in Canadian universities in the 1980s was the shortage of full-time jobs relative to graduates aspiring to jobs in academe. A majority (53.9 per cent) of part-timers are aware of the job shortage in academe. Most (82.7 per cent) use the situation as an opportunity to keep up with new knowledge in their fields of specialization. All fondly hope, however, that the shortage of full-time positions will only be temporary: 'Although I feel that part-time Sessionals are underpaid and overworked at [this university], I appreciate the opportunity to gain teaching experience while I wait for a full-time position in my field.' And, 'I hold an academic [research] position in a medical school. I primarily do research. I teach part-time for the contact with undergraduates. I would like a full-time [teaching] appointment but have not been able to get one ... but I would like to continue teaching so that I may keep abreast of new research in my field.' Most part-timers opt for teaching part-time in order to get an income in the interim – before securing full-time positions – to support their families. Many have dependent children or a spouse/partner.

A gender gap is evident from their explanations for being stuck in part-time work. Women (70.4 per cent versus men 49.3 per cent) give flexible work schedules as an important reason and argue that flexibility in working part time would be advantageous not only to women but also to the university: 'There has to be a way of making it possible for people who wish to work half or two-thirds time, whether it is for child raising, or due to retiring. If they feel that they could make, and in fact are now making a valuable academic contribution, options should be open to them. They could be paid according to the level of their contributions so that it reflects what they are worth.' And, 'Flextime people usually are less interested in financial rewards and more interested in self-actualization and putting something back into the system. Not everyone needs the benefits and/or large salaries. So this may be less problematic then we think.' An American study by Carol Muller on the relationship between academic careers and family responsibilities found increasing flexibility within individual career patterns. Women in academe are using ' "hidden passages" – either professionally acceptable variations in career patterns, such as visiting or postdoctoral positions or variations invisible on the résumé, such as part-time work – to accommodate families and careers' (1990: 20). Whereas such variations were not professionally acceptable in the 1950s, we now find women who have gone through 'hidden passages' in tenured or tenure-track jobs. Canadian academic experience, however, does not indicate that professionally acceptable variations in career paths are widespread, or that the pursuit of 'hidden passages' would probably be rewarded at the end of the process. Many women part-timers in my survey criticize universities' inflexible policies on job sharing and notice the inequity inherent in the fact that women with young children end up in part-time positions with no benefits: 'Is it possible [for the university] to recognize that one can be equally responsible to family and career and still be considered a valuable contributor to a program? If so, then why does [the department] not introduce floating or flex time positions and job sharing opportunities when it advertises for new faculty? I suspect there will be a positive response.' And, 'There are many part-time faculty who wish to continue teaching although part time, as it allows for flexibility to fulfil other family responsibilities, e.g., childcare.'

Part-timers with a doctoral degree strongly prefer a full-time academic job, but there are some who are voluntary part-timers: 'They [universities] seem to assume that a part-timer has his/her eyes fixed on a full-time academic position and that a part-timer would necessarily want to "upgrade" him/herself to full time. This is not necessarily the case. I personally like the flexibility, which I did not have in my earlier full-time job.' Although many women who possess a doctorate would like to find full-time academic positions, they are unable to do so for various reasons. More women than men part-timers (65.6 per cent versus men 51.2 per cent) say that they cannot move to another city for a full-time job because of family demands. So they are looking for a full-time position in the city where their family is located because of their partner's job, or to avail themselves of family support, or to accommodate their children's schooling: 'Personal circumstances make it impossible to move elsewhere to accept a full time position. It is a difficult decision to give up such a chance. But as my husband has a good job here, it is not likely that we would move to a new location.' And, 'As a single parent, I need my family's support to care for my young children when I am working. My mother and sisters help me with my child-care, which I will lose if I were to move to a distant location.'

Increasing Workload and Declining Rewards

Across Canada, part-timers uniformly express their discontent with the value, both monetary and non-monetary, that universities attribute to their work. A woman reflects: 'We [part-timers] cannot escape the awareness that we are thought of as just satisfying the department's work requirements. Our creative work is not considered or appreciated beyond that. I can think of no solution to this problem, but feel quite despondent. Sooner or later, this attitude must affect individual self-evaluation and in turn their quality of teaching.' An artificial split, that is, teaching versus research, legitimizes part-timers' low pay and job status. Degradation of teaching in contrast to research and the definition of part-timers' work as 'teaching-only' strongly reinforce this dichotomy. Not only does it serve as a justification for the claim that the role of part-timers should be limited to teaching, which also merely supplements the work of full-timers, but also it effectively deprofessionalizes their other academic contributions to the university. Rhoades notes: 'Part-timers' work responsibilities are delimited more narrowly than those of full-timers. As increasing numbers of part-timers are hired, the faculty workforce is being deskilled, in terms not only of certification, but also of the nature of work being performed. Part-time faculty simply deliver instruction ... Such a pattern offers little room for professional growth and development. It offers a direct contrast to the literature that calls for the integration of part-time faculty members into the academic life of the unit in which they work' (1996: 648).

There is evidence that part-timers do perceive themselves as 'academics.' They find that this image conflicts with the degraded reflection seen by university decision-makers, that of an underclass in the faculty hierarchy with radically different definitions of work and allocations of rewards. The university's bureaucracy rationalizes this process as a temporary means of solving fluctuating enrolments and teaching workload, but an artificial split is thereby created between teaching and research within academic work. A part-timer describes how similar the work is to that of full-timer, although it is labelled differently: 'Most of us are part-time in name only; many of us teach more than a standard full-time course load ... We participate in and organize conferences, contribute articles and reviews, and vet papers for scholarly journals ... We enrich the Department with skills acquired in teaching in other [departments and disciplines] by the necessity to teach various courses beyond our specialization.' Part-timers are well aware of how artful the university is in labelling their workload 'part time,' even though it is often equal to a full-time load: 'Although I hold no full-time faculty position and am called "part-time," I have put together five part-time teaching positions. I do much more teaching than a full-time faculty member would. My average weekly teaching load is 33 hours in the classroom, 13 hours in telephone tutoring and 18 hours marking assignments.'

Part-timers also appear frustrated with their lack of control over course assignment. A woman part-timer expresses her dismay at the disproportionate amount of work that she does in developing new courses, knowing full well that she may teach the course once or twice at most. The department has the power to ask her to teach a new course, according to its needs: 'In order to maintain the curriculum, my university uses part-timers like me only to fill in courses and areas where no full-timers are interested. I am asked to create new courses and establish new resources for students both for the library and for class use. Many times over this has to be done since I may be assigned a new course next time around. Our Department gives very little thought or direction to such curricular work I do. The task of taking on course-development is enormous since you may prepare a course but never use it again.'

In a recent international survey involving fourteen countries across the globe, Altbach and Lewis (1995) asked faculty about their satisfaction with teaching. Respondents expressed general dissatisfaction with their workload, particularly given their fewer facilities. While demands for teaching have increased, fewer resources are available. This fact could help to explain the growing tendency towards more teaching for the least cost and with fewer personnel.

Half of all part-timers (54 per cent) teach two or more full-year courses, and one in three (29 per cent) has a load of three courses or more (table 2.4). In Quebec, 75 per cent of part-timers teach more than two courses. Nearly half of Quebec's part-timers (49 per cent) teach three courses or more. Part-timers' course loads are heavier in universities that are large, do intensive research, and offer a full range of programs (see the appendix for university types); in these institutions one in three part-timers teaches three courses or more. In small universities a majority of part-timers teaches less than two courses; in contrast, in large and mid-size universities one in two teach more than two courses. This discrepancy perhaps indicates the smaller number of total courses for which smaller universities have to hire part-timers. Enrolments being higher and more fluctuating in larger universities, it is likely that more courses need one in two part-timers to cover them. Universities with a wide range of programs show a similar pattern: one in two part-timers teaches two courses, in such universities. In teaching universities, one in two part-timers teaches fewer than two courses, and, in contrast, one in two teaches more than two courses in research universities. It is interesting to note that in universities that have high part-time intensity – that is, the ratio of part-timers to all faculty – one in two part-timers teaches more than two courses. This finding would suggest that such universities perhaps hire fewer part-timers than the number of courses that cannot be covered by regular faculty.

A report by the U.S. National Center for Education Statistics indicates that a third of part-timers in U.S. institutions of higher education carry a heavy load of fifty students, similar to that of two-thirds of full-timers (NCES online, March 1999: 188). Nearly a fifth of U.S. part-timers (18 per cent) teach ten hours per week, which is almost half the

TABLE 2.4
Number of courses taught by part-timers in twelve months, by university type

Number of full-year courses taught	Part-timers		Size***			Region***				Research/ Teaching***		Part-time intensity***	
	Total no.	Total %	Large	Mid	Small	West	Ontario	Quebec	Atlantic	Research	Teaching	Higher	Lower
<.5	282	13.1	12.3	13.7	16.7	19.4	13.4	4.5	14.5	10.7	15.1	10.7	16.4
<2	706	32.7	32.2	30.3	44.6	32.0	38.6	20.5	35.5	28.9	35.9	31.3	34.8
<3	537	25.0	24.0	27.9	21.5	24.5	24.3	26.4	26.6	24.8	25.1	24.1	26.1
3+	632	29.2	31.5	28.1	17.2	24.1	23.7	48.6	23.4	35.7	23.9	33.9	22.6
Total %	100.0	100.0	100.0	100.0	100.0	100.0	100.0	100.0	100.0	100.0	100.0	100.0	100.0
Total no.	2,157		1,330	640	187	569	990	470	125	45.3	54.7	58.7	41.3

Note: Differences are significant at p = *** <.001.
Source: See table 2.1.

number of full-timers' hours. Closer to a fifth of them (18 per cent) also have a full-time load of three course or more, similar to that of 61 per cent of full-timers. In many situations, universities apparently give part-timers full loads (as many courses and students as full-timers handle) or too many courses, in order to meet enrolment bulges and provide teaching for more students at lower costs; these loads do not reflect part-timers' desire to earn more. Two-thirds of part-timers (66 per cent) do not wish a larger workload, despite a commonly held belief to the contrary. Many part-timers believe that carrying a full load without either pay or faculty rights comparable to those of full-timers' is inequitable: 'I feel that anything over 2 courses constitutes a full-time commitment. It is a commitment, which Sessionals are too poorly paid to make. It is not worthwhile to take on responsibilities without rights and rewards associated with a full-time position.'

Many part-timers work year round. Most of them teach during autumn/winter sessions, on average about two courses that are day-time/weekday courses and one and a half evening/weekend courses. Normally, the unpopular and inconvenient class times and sessions are left to part-timers. Many find that, if they need a teaching job, they must be ready to take on any session available, which is most likely to be in the summer or during evenings or weekends. Although many complain about this situation, only those with a full-time job elsewhere could afford to object: 'The major dissatisfaction with my part-time teaching is that we have no option but to teach in the evenings or weekends. Universities should make arrangements, particularly with larger business employers, to allow their staff to have some daytime hours off work, so that they may have the opportunity to teach in the daytime and meet other faculty in the department.'

Part-timers must also be prepared to teach in a variety of campus locations. Although part-timers on average teach more than two courses per year on universities' main campuses, they are given 'left-over' courses and times that full-timers do not want. Full-timers can generally get teaching schedules and campus locations that suit them. Part-timers are more likely to get off-campus assignments: 'I often get asked to do off campus courses because few like to go out of town. There were no questions asked about getting off-campus courses ... Only part-time people like me would pick up these courses.' The practice of hiring part-timers to teach off-campus courses seems to be more prevalent in Quebec and the Atlantic region (more than two such courses) than in other regions of Canada (average 1.7 courses).

To maintain the required curriculum in departments and to offer programs at all course levels, universities often hire part-timers because of the flexibility that this practice brings. A part-timer notes: 'Part-time faculty plays a major role in teaching, especially in fulfilling all course requirements in the undergraduate curriculum. We teach an increasing number of courses both at the introductory level, as well as at the second, third and fourth year levels.' Part-timers' teaching is well integrated into the departmental curricula, especially at the undergraduate level. Some 34 per cent of part-timers teach all of their courses at the first-year undergraduate level and 55 per cent of them teach all of their courses at the undergraduate upper level. Only 11 per cent of part-timers teach all their courses at the graduate level. Although a number of part-timers (22 per cent) teach courses at both undergraduate and graduate levels, part-time teaching seems to be indispensable for undergraduate programs. However, the universities' rhetoric is inconsistent with the reality: 'In this department, the policy is that senior faculty should teach especially freshmen and women. Senior professors should teach first-year students so that their introduction to their departments would be through renowned scholars in the field. Such a policy is admirable if indeed full-professors teach first-year students. But, in ... [my department], this is not the reality as we can see from the report recently issued. It indicates that a disproportionate number of course directorships are held by part-timers. Instead of acknowledging the situation and recognizing their work, part-timers are made to feel out of place here. This is hardly our fault!'

Many part-timers feel strongly that the university should realize that part-timers are not a temporary phenomenon: 'Given that full-time appointments are not available for the next several years, it is time for the Department to come to terms with the fact that part-time faculty are going to continue to do a substantial proportion of teaching.' Most part-timers (76.4 per cent) carry full responsibilities as course directors: they direct, administer, and teach the courses assigned. Only a fifth of part-timers (21.9 per cent) are hired to teach tutorials only. Universities depend on part-timers to staff high-enrolment sessions or mandatory courses. Part-timers with doctorates question why universities should be exploiting them instead of creating new faculty positions to meet curricular demands: 'Departments have policies that suggest that the part-time faculty should not teach the same courses year after year, but may be used to replace full-time faculty on leave or to deal with enrolment increases. In fact, however, part-time faculty repeatedly are hired to teach the same courses year after year, at all course levels. The departments could strengthen their demand for more full-time appointments by pointing out the gaps in curricular areas that cannot be taught by the existing full-time faculty ... By using the part-time faculty's areas of expertise as ammunition, departments could ask for new positions in such areas.'

Part-time faculty spend almost as much time as full-time faculty do in performing their academic work. In addition to class contact hours, part-timers work thirty-five hours per week on average, which is more than the average of twenty-seven hours reported by full-time faculty (Lennards, 1988).[6] Most part-timers find course development, lecture preparation, marking and grade reporting, and administrative duties as course director too demanding and time-consuming to allow any time left for their own research. A woman part-timer describes the responsibilities and pressures: 'We are constantly working up new courses, a time consuming process, which interferes with our own research. I recall attending a Departmental meeting in 1989, and learning that faculty working up a new course had their load cut from three courses to two, how nice it was, and how they could do a better job. As a part-timer, I was teaching four courses during the regular session, including working up two new full courses at ... [one university] and two half courses at ... [another university] ... and I received excellent student evaluations! By adding on a Spring Session that year, I think I earned as much as the lowest paid tenured faculty member. I once had a full-time sessional appointment, but I was paid only for the months I was actually teaching, not for the full year.' Another part-timer describes the increasing workload and declining rewards: 'We perform many duties, which are not within our job descriptions, for which we are not remunerated, and which we cannot count toward promotion and tenure as full-time faculty do. Many part-timers contribute time, energy and expertise to the university community. None of us hesitate when asked to serve on departmental or university committees, as advisors for first-year entrants, to write department review reports, etc.' Depending on the pedagogical component of a course, part-timers' workload may vary: 'This is a technical course and both teaching the course, and assessing students' progress [are] very time consuming ... During an academic year, I assign ... weekly homework. It takes me about an hour to set each problem-set and about five hours to correct each set. I also give four in-class tests during the year. It takes me about two or two and a half-hours to set each test, and seven to ten hours to mark each of the tests. Setting the final exam takes about three to four hours. From last year's experience in marking the three-hour final exam, I can say that, marking the final exam and assigning the final grades will take about 30–40 hours.'

Shelly M. Park discusses the impact of pedagogical style and goals on workload. For instance, not only do women tend to spend more time on teaching and related activities, but they also use different pedagogical styles related to distinctive goals. While men are more interested in developing students' ability to 'think' clearly, women faculty encourage the whole gamut of development – from personal to social – of their students. Park points out that these gender differences are more likely to increase women's workload (1996: 58).

Part-timers' work extends beyond their classrooms: 'Our contributions to the university and to the Department are not limited to the duties specified in our teaching contracts. Part-time faculty [serve] ... as second readers for theses and ... [supervise] upper [level] undergraduate or graduate level directed reading courses ... Some of our students have won university prizes for the work done in our courses.'

Most part-timers do not get teaching or grading assistance, but many of them help individual students and try to be sensitive to their needs: 'Throughout the years of teaching I found out that the students in large courses ... with 100 plus enrollment and where no Teaching Assistants are assigned ... are rather reluctant to approach the professor for academic help. Therefore in this course ... before every weekly homework assignment, and each of the four tests during the year, I spend a minimum of four hours per assignment or test, with students who come for help.' In the business world time means money, but in academe part-timers cannot be calculating returns based on time spent. Yet many find the extra, unpaid hours: 'Other than academic supervision regarding this course, I counsel students regarding jobs in these fields I teach ... and in advanced studies they may wish to pursue in these fields ... I find it very difficult to break down my advising time involved into measurable hours. It seems to depend on how long the students want to consult, not on my allocation of time for each consultation. This, of course, is entirely different from the business world.' Many part-timers write letters of reference for students – another contribution that goes largely unrecognized: 'This year I would have spent close to ten hours writing recommendation letters for students. Students do not care whether you are part-time faculty or full-time ... They come to you requesting letters. They say that I know their work, and that they have done well in my courses. But ... it is a pity that we have specially to request the staff for university letterheads for writing these letters of reference ... could some stationary materials not be supplied to us at the beginning of the year?' Part-time faculty often spend time with students who seek their advice on general non-academic problems: 'Apart from academic counseling, I find that more and more women students are approaching me for advice on all kinds of problems. Although I always encourage these students to make use of the available services on the campus, I feel a responsibility to follow up on how these students are doing.' Given their workload, it is hardly surprising that a majority of part-timers – those who like to teach the same number of or fewer courses (63.5 per cent versus 34.4 per cent who wish to teach more courses) – sooner or later seem to reach the point of diminishing returns. A few part-timers (6.8 per cent) would actually like to teach less.

Pay and Security

In 1991–2, part-timers' average annual income from teaching in Canadian universities surveyed was $12,421. A part-timer speculates on the origins of their low pay: 'There are distinct disadvantages to teaching part-time. First, the pay is woefully inadequate. The stipends were devised when tenured faculty taught additional courses as extra load, and the payment proportional to regular salary has not changed. As part-timers, we are told that the ridiculously low stipend is justified as we only teach, while tenured faculty are expected to do research, publish, and serve on committees.' Part-timers are paid on a per course basis, and the rate may vary within an institution, depending on the discipline, years of service, and qualifications, or it may be a single rate across the university. Although some institutions recognize seniority or qualifications, these factors do not carry as much weight as they do in determining full-time faculty salaries (Biles and Tuckman, 1986: 38). Part-timers' rates of pay also vary substantially among institutions, depending on local circumstances; in such cases, unionization appears to help. However, most institutions reduce costs of instruction by employing part-timers rather than full-timers. Faced with a need to increase revenue and balance the budget, many have expanded their enrolments, yet kept down operating costs by using more part-timers.

An instance in point is York University's situation in 1988–9 (for which data on expenditure on part-timers are available). York paid the highest rates in Ontario for part-time teaching,[7] but it was just above the midpoint in its salaries for full-time faculty. Thus, savings from using part-timers ought to have been relatively less than those of other universities where part-time pay was lower. Yet York's direct savings were still substantial. When York was spending approximately $12 million per year on part-time teaching, at $7,300 per full-year course, the cost of that amount of teaching time at the average rate per teaching hour of assistant professors in the Faculty of Arts would have been an additional $5,675,000. Its cost at the university's overall average rate per hour for full-timers would have been an additional $12,757,000. A similar U.S. situation confirms the savings from hiring part-timers. A comparison of salaries in California's community colleges in 1993–4 reveals that full-timers earned more than twice as much as part-timers on a contact-hour basis, even after one adjusts for full-timers' advising and counselling work (California State Postsecondary Education Commission, 1994). In another study of U.S. community colleges it was estimated that a full-time teaching load would cost from $35,000 to $40,000 per year, whereas its part-time replacement would cost $15,000 ('Statement ...' *Academe*, 1998).

Savings in teaching costs represent only one facet of the budget equation. Vis-à-vis part-timers, there is no obligation to provide sabbaticals, office space, tuition waivers for dependants, computer time, secretarial services beyond those directly related to courses, or much in the way of research/conference funding. The savings on space also are significant. Housing only half the number of full-timers that would be needed to absorb York's part-time hours at even a twelve-hour-per-week teaching load would require 116 additional faculty offices and offices for 25 support services. The capital cost for those offices would be nearly $4 million, with additional operating costs of $150,000 per annum for maintenance and heating/cooling. York's financial circumstances from the mid-1970s to the end of the 1980s simply would not have allowed such expenditures.[8] Nor could it have afforded institutional benefits in the form of higher enrolment and revenues, larger increases in the salary for full-timers, and smaller classes.

Part-timers are often frustrated about their job insecurity and low pay, and they worry that they might miss the few full-time opportunities that might arise: 'The major problem is a lack of security and benefits. We [the family] will not undertake any large expenditure, and we operate only on cash basis, as we do not know what my income will be session to session. My income tax is wild, because I have small contracts and it is difficult to estimate how much tax should be deducted.' And, 'One of the most frustrating aspects of part-time teaching is the uncertainty. We cannot plan in advance as three weeks before classes begin I will be phoned that enrollment has gone through the ceiling again, and the administration has finally come through with the money to pay me. We need the money, I want to keep working, and so I don't want to turn down any opportunities to teach. I also want to keep in touch, to be on site, so I will know if anything is coming up.' Their pay, as we saw above, is based neither on qualifications nor on experience: 'Although I am now "part-time faculty," my teaching duties are the same as when I was a full-time graduate student with a T.A.-ship. I teach the same courses, but am now paid less per hour as "part-time faculty!"' And, 'In this university, you get the same pay whether you're teaching a course for the 1st time or the 10th time, whether you are perceived by students to be fair or excellent, whether you teach 25 students or 100. I don't think this is fair.'

Rhoades has examined U.S. faculty contracts that refer to part-time faculty: 'In sum, one powerful indicator of part-time faculty's professional position is the extent to which conditions of employment are undefined for *any* category of part-timers, despite the inclusion of at least some part-time faculty in 118 contracts. Managerial discretion is extensive because few professional constraints are built into the contracts. Further, part-time faculty's conditions of employment make for a significant contrast with the conditions that attach to full-time faculty's employment. Finally, the rights/perquisites and duties clauses, in particular, point to divisions and gradations among part-timers' (1996: 650). The Canadian situation is not very different.

Career Mobility

In this section I focus on part-timers' career aspirations, the barriers to full-time appointments, the place of research in their work, and at the possibilities for professional development.

Aspirations for an Academic Career

Although some Canadian part-timers have other full-time careers (I call them 'Classics': 34.5 per cent), two-thirds have only part-time jobs (I call them 'Contemporaries': 65.5 per cent). Of the Contemporaries, a majority (60 per cent) want a full-time academic job and declare their career as academic. If the university took their interests and concerns seriously, it would treat them as a potential pool of full-timers. In reality, however, part-timers are on a different footing altogether in terms of credit gained in teaching and research experience through their work. In the United States, also, full-timers' terms of employment are not qualitatively on the same footing as those of part-timers. Full-timers take priority over part-timers in the ownership of courses and curricula as well as in other work-related matters (Rhoades, 1996: 649–50). Part-timers' professional identity is in question. Lorena Stookey, a part-timer, is highly critical of the working conditions that 'undervalue [their] professionalism'; she notes, 'when an institution calls [some] of its employees a "Permanent Temp," it is having its cake and devouring it too' (1994: 30). The only way to secure their professional identity would seem to be to give them a contract or an agreement that addressed them as full professionals.

More than a third of the Classics (37 per cent) also wish to switch to academe. A majority of part-timers (53 per cent) want a full-time academic position, and many of them feel quite hopeful about getting one within three years (table 2.5). Most Contemporaries (74 per cent) identify themselves with a teaching and research career. If they could start over again, 83 per cent say that they would still choose an academic career, and 91 per cent would pursue their present discipline. Observers often assume that part-time work is a last resort that provides an income supplement in a situation where there are no jobs. Among these Contemporaries, however, only a minority (39 per cent) report that they work part time only for the income.

Two-thirds of part-timers with doctorates want a full-time faculty position but find it difficult to get one: 'My preference is a full-time position, and I have applied for positions repeatedly. I have not confined my search just to teaching positions; I have also applied for positions as a course developer. I have even been interviewed – and then informed that the university decided not to fill the position.' Many are quite frustrated with their search and are quite aware that this experience is widespread: 'I suspect you will find [through this survey] that most of us are diligently looking for full time positions, and we are becoming increasingly despairing of ever finding one of these privileged positions.' And, 'While working part-time is alright for me, I am uneasy about the large number of capable part-time sessional staff in our department who would like to work full time but cannot.'

TABLE 2.5
Part-timers' career aspirations

	Total no.	Total %	Sex %		Degree holders %			Job status %	
			Men	Women	<Master's	>Master's	Doctorate	Classics	Contem-poraries
Want full-time academic job	1,150	53.0	51.4 (n.s.)	55.5	32.0	55.1	66.3	37.4	60.3
Actively seeking academic full-time job	495	23.0	22.5 (n.s.)	23.6	8.0	21.3	39.0	10.0	30.2
Not sure	524	24.0	26.1	20.9	60.0	23.6	5.3	52.6	9.5
Total %		100.0	100.0	100.0	100.0	100.0	100.0	100.0	100.0
Chances for academic job in next 3 years (%) 0%	878	40.5	40**	41.1	55.1	39.7	29.8	46.2	37.7
<50%	686	31.6	34.5**	28.4	28.9	32.6	31.6	35.7	29.2
>50%	605	27.9	25.5**	30.6	16.0	27.7	38.6	18.0	33.1
Total %		100.0	100.0	100.0	100.0	100.0	100.0	100.0	100.0
Total no.	2,169		1,174	995	467	1,111	576	743	1,405

Notes: Significance: p = *<.05; **<.01; ***<.001. All are significant at p = ***<.001 unless otherwise indicated. (n.s.): not significant.
Source: See table 2.1.

Barriers to Full-Time Academic Jobs

Part-timers confront three barriers in their quest for full-time jobs: *university policies*, their *own limited academic records*, and *discriminatory treatment in the workplace*. Many part-timers (57 per cent) are highly critical of universities' ineptitude in managing university budgets and their shortsighted policies, which limit full-time, tenure-stream appointments. A woman part-timer explains her anomalous position: 'I teach a full course load of a full-timer. I have all the necessary qualifications, a good academic record, and also the highest ratings from students evaluating my teaching – several times higher than some full time faculty. But, every year I am told that lack of financial resources is the reason for not hiring me as regular stream.'

Most part-timers, especially those with doctoral degrees, are extremely critical of the hiring process that favours candidates from highly reputed universities: 'The last time I applied for a tenure-track job (2 years ago), I was told that my articles [publications] are not the right kind ... Some of the full-time faculty in my department sabotaged even my application for a post-doctoral fellowship ... and they hired a Harvard PhD for a job for which I was more qualified.' Part-timers regard their academic qualifications as their true strength, one that increases their chances of being hired. Most of them (83 per cent) see themselves as 'real' faculty member with a good teaching record. They do concede, however, that their lack of control over what they teach and how many hours they need to work to earn a livelihood often leaves them with little time for engaging in and keeping up the pace of research. A part-timer who feels trapped says: 'I am told my chances of receiving a full-time appointment would be enhanced by more research and publications. Yet my other part-time job, as a high school teacher ... deprives me of the time and energy needed to do research and scholarly publications. Only a full time academic appointment would give me the time and funding for research ... It seems to be a vicious circle.'

In most Canadian universities, part-timers have little access to faculty funding or time-release for their own research and publishing. Half of them (51 per cent) believe that their research record would increase their prospects for a full-time academic position. A majority of those with doctoral qualifications (63 per cent versus 48 per cent with a master's degree) and a majority of Contemporaries (54 per cent versus 46 per cent Classics) rely on their research and publication record when applying for full-time positions. Although part-timers with a research record view it as a credit to get full-time positions, they must still confront the competition from younger graduates or those with more recent doctorates. Based on criteria established by full-timers, part-timers may be deemed less productive because of their age and years since graduation. The professoriate holds the power to hire and decide on the hiring criteria. It has usually looked unfavourably on long-time part-timers. Full-timers perpetuate the status quo through such 'gatekeeping' and thereby legitimize the stratification of power within the university.

Most part-timers (83 per cent) regard their teaching skills as the best qualification they can offer, but they feel betrayed when universities devalue teaching-only work: 'There are no rewards for good teaching for part-time instructors. We may individually be evaluated as the best among all faculty, but only full-time professors, and even graduate assistants are given merit points. This is a pity!'

Most part-timers (72 per cent) have quite a positive view of their past service as part-timers in their quest to move up the career ladder. They hope that service and loyalty to the university will be recognized and rewarded in hiring. Many (67 per cent) also believe that their professional standing outside the university should help them to obtain a full-time academic career. Nearly two-thirds (63 per cent) sincerely feel that they will get full-timers' personal support in their search for full-time positions.

In their open-ended comments to our survey, some part-timers have articulated another barrier: the likelihood of a bias against particular sexual preferences or orientations. A part-timer complains: 'As a lesbian part-timer, I have encountered repeated discrimination in hiring processes established for full-time jobs. It is quite subtle ... my scholarship is in [the] women studies area, and some of my research publications are on gays and lesbians. This becomes a barrier in my interviews for full-time positions. The university where I work certainly does not have employment procedures that would control such biases.' Some are critical of the convention in academe that values certain kinds of research subjects and publications and devalues others. Research on women's issues and in women studies has long been discounted. Similarly, some part-timers with a non-mainstream sexual orientation feel that most hiring authorities in universities have not been sensitized to gay and lesbian issues and therefore lack standards to evaluate scholarship in such studies or related publications. As a result, research in this area has not been treated as mainstream: 'I am frustrated that my

FIGURE 2.1

Part-time faculty and influences of gender and ethnicity in obtaining full-time academic jobs: women versus men

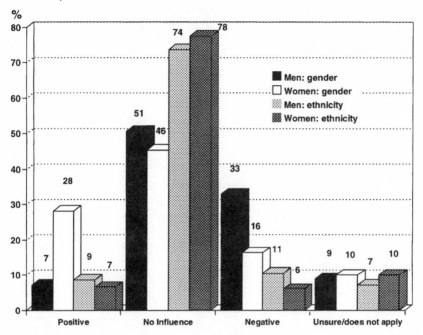

Source: Rajagopal, Part-Time Faculty Survey (1991–2)

research and fiction relating to lesbian issues are unlikely to advance my academic career.'

The literature on higher education indicates a deep-seated prejudice in academe against women with children. Part-time women with children feel that they are not perceived as professionals, and as a result they do not feel encouraged to compete for full-time positions. For instance, when positions open up and for family reasons they find it difficult to relocate, universities assume that they are 'available' and often exploit this predicament (Bottiani, 1994).[9] Therefore, for women part-timers with children, it becomes a double whammy on account of both their gender and their part-time status within academe.

One in four part-timers in our survey thinks that gender bias (figure 2.1) is present: 'There is a strong anti-feminine bias in the discipline [of my specialization]. But that department, because of its strong gender bias against hiring women, did not hire me. I am working in another department where no such anti-feminine bias is evident. However, with a Ph.D. in [one language], it is not easy to obtain a full-time position in [another].' Men (33 per cent) more than women (16 per cent), seem to feel that their gender would be a negative factor in getting full-time positions, and some male part-timers feel that there is reverse discrimination:

> I work in a medical school affiliated to the university. I hold an academic position that primarily involves research. I teach part-time in the university for the extra money and contact with undergraduates. I would like a full-time appointment. But I have been discriminated against because I'm a male and White.

> White, European males are facing discrimination because of affirmative action policies aimed at repairing past injustices of WASP men against women, visible minorities, people with disabilities, and aboriginal peoples. I am stuck in part-time teaching positions because I cannot be hired on a full-time basis. Positions are reserved for women and other oppressed peoples although these groups are not qualified or do not want to teach courses offered in my area of specialization. Thus, I am kept on as a part-time instructor, while the university attempts to find a representative of one of these oppressed groups to teach my courses on a full-time basis.

Very few part-timers belong to visible minorities (5 per cent) or are aboriginal Canadians (0.6 per cent). A part-timer explains: 'I have a non-Canadian Ph.D. in [sciences] and my teaching experience abroad is not counted as relevant to get a full-time teaching job in Canada. Although I have retrained and upgraded my qualifications in Canada, I had to settle for a part-time job. Although my past work experience related to more advanced levels in [sciences] than what is currently taught here in Canada, it is not recognized but discounted. I face a double jeopardy: I am looked upon as an older person, but one with no Canadian experience to his credit. This is unfair.'

Far-flung campus locations and year-long terms may hamper research (see below, table 4.5). Of the Contemporaries, some teach in only one university ('Rooted' 49 per cent), whereas others teach in several universities ('Gypsy Scholars'[10] or 'Freeway Fliers' 20 per cent). A third group ('Straddlers' 31 per cent) hold part-time jobs in both academic and non-academic sectors. Both the Rooted and Freeway Fliers

FIGURE 2.2
Academic and non-academic part-time jobs held by part-time faculty: women
versus men

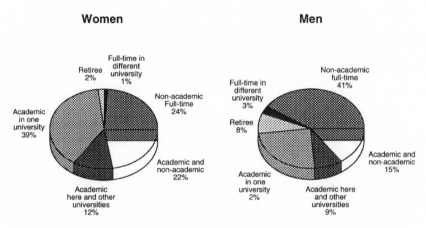

Women **Men**

Source: See figure 2.1.

(69 per cent) work only in academe. Although a majority of the Rooted
hold a doctorate (55 per cent), all work only part time in academe and
are more numerous in the humanities. Figure 2.2 shows the gender
ratios of these groups. More women are in academic jobs, whether as
'Rooted' or as 'Freeway Fliers,' while more men are in non-academic
sectors. Two part-timers in ten are Freeway Fliers. University hopping
is their way of life. In order to earn an adequate income, they teach on
various campuses or in nearby cities that are at driving or flying distance. More Freeway Fliers are found in Quebec universities. A woman
part-timer explains her work life as a Freeway Flier: 'One university ...
appointment was out of town. It entailed an overnight stay, returning
the following morning in time to teach at this university ... then an
evening class at ... my third university. I barely finished marking the
finals for those three courses in time to begin Spring Session at ... this
university. I know I am not alone in carrying virtually a full time teaching load of three courses, but in various universities, for less than half
the salary.' Several other part-timers echo these words: 'I work
part-time for three academic institutions. It is often wrongly assumed
that part-timers worked only in one university.' And, 'I have been
employed every year since graduating, but frankly I feel like a Ping-

Pong ball. Perhaps there is an advantage to my location in [this prov-ince], as there are three universities here. I bounce back and forth between them. This may keep me employed, but given the stipends I am paid, I'm fortunate to have a husband with a reliable income to support our youngest daughter, an engineering student, and me.'

The Straddlers constitute almost a third of all part-timers; four in ten have less than a master's degree and are in fine and applied arts. Obvi-ously, Straddlers and Freeway Fliers have difficulty finding any time at all for research or for advancing their academic careers (see table 4.5).

To sum up, not only recognizing the career ambitions of part-timers but also acknowledging them as academic professionals would go a long way towards enhancing their career mobility. A few Canadian universities accord such recognition by allowing part-timers an equal chance as outside applicants to compete for newly created positions or by filling new positions through a special process of closed competi-tion, based on merit, among internal candidates.

Research

Many part-timers have done scholarly research and have refereed publications, although these tasks are not deemed part of their job responsibility. The university's definition of the role and functions of its faculty expects research and publications of full-timers but not of part-timers. Although some full-timers (33.4 per cent)[11] may be more involved in and inclined towards teaching than research, research is nonetheless expected of them. In contrast, part-timers' work is clearly seen as 'teaching only,' and they have little access to funding for research. Even if they wish to pursue research of their own volition and at their own expense, they can rarely find time. A woman part-timer explains: 'I've prepared so many new courses and am always looking for jobs [and due to] that I am left with no time for my own research or publishing. Talk about Catch 22! After 7 years of teaching part-time on one-year appointments, numerous new courses and many new loca-tions, I need a break. But, sabbaticals are not available to us. The whole system is geared toward full-time positions, which are rare to find. And the only two available faculty appointments, part-time or limited term, are not treated as alternate academic career possibilities. This needs to be re-evaluated.' Part-timers frequently feel marginalized: 'All of my research is directed toward preparing my classes and improving my teaching. I have lost confidence in my ability to write scholarly papers,

FIGURE 2.3

Percentage of part-timers with scholarly publications

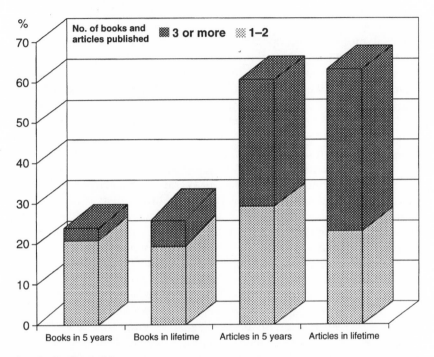

Source: See figure 2.1.

partly because of my marginal position and insecurity.' Financial stresses complicate the issue and create a dilemma: 'University funding is often restricted to tenured faculty. Part-time faculty need funding for both research and conferences, and we can hardly afford to provide our own funding for these "luxuries" from our meager stipends. If we do earn a reasonable amount to live on, it is only by taking on so many extra contracts that we don't have the time or energy on top of it, for doing research. Financial support for part timers' research and educational leave for research are essential.'

Many part-timers actively pursue research and produce scholarly publications (figure 2.3). In the last five years, a majority of part-timers (61 per cent versus 67 per cent of full-timers) have published one to three refereed scholarly articles or chapters, and one-fourth of them (24 per cent) have published one to three scholarly books. Most (77 per cent) spend, on average, ten hours (full-timers average thirteen hours) per week on scholarly research but want to spend more time (table 2.6). Ten per cent more part-timers in francophone than in anglophone universities have published at least one to two books; in contrast, 10 per cent more anglophone than francophone university part-timers report no scholarly publication in their whole career at the time of this survey. Most part-timers with doctorates are active in research. Half of them have published more than three refereed articles in the last five years. Although they publish more articles and chapters than whole books, they come close to full-time faculty's average record of publications. Lennards's 1986 survey shows that 43 per cent of full-time faculty are inclined more towards research than teaching and 24 per cent are involved equally in both. During the three-year period preceding the survey, full-timers published on average 3.96 refereed and 1.67 non-refereed scholarly articles or chapters. During their lifetime, they have published on average 0.52 scholarly single-authored books or have been involved in 1.92 inventions (Lennards, 1988).

Lewis and Altbach's international survey depicts the continuing emphasis in academe on research productivity (1996: 31). The percentage of faculty members leaning towards or primarily involved in research in the top three countries is reported as 76 per cent in Netherlands, 72 per cent in Japan, and 67 per cent in Sweden. In a majority of countries surveyed, faculty members acknowledge that it would be difficult for someone to achieve tenure without publications (Altbach and Lewis, 1995: 54). Therefore, it could be expected that Contemporaries with aspirations for a full-time academic job would feel that full-timers' notion of part-timers' work as 'teaching only' hurts their professional standing in academe.

Professional Development

Despite rhetoric on improving teaching quality in general, universities have paid little attention to professional development for part-timers. Both TAs (Shannon et al., 1998) and part-timers report that they need pedagogical training. Such programs are readily available to full-timers – but not to part-timers. Candice Johnson notes that this disparity – not the increased hiring of part-timers – is likely to threaten the quality of programs: 'A self-fulfilling prophecy goes into effect when part-time faculty are made to feel like second-class citizens ... Providing a professional atmosphere to all faculty rather than reserv-

TABLE 2.6
Part-timers' research and publications

Research and publications	No. of hours	Degree holders %				Part-timer type %	
		Total %	< Master's	> Master's	Doctorate	Classics	Contem-poraries
Part-timers total no.			479	1,137	592	762	1,446
No. of hours/week spent on research	<11	77.8	85.8	79.5	66.1	86.0	72.1
	<21	11.6	7.5	11.6	14.9	6.5	14.4
	21+	11.5	6.7	8.9	19.1	7.6	13.5
No. of hours/week they would like to spend on research	<11	56.4	70.8	61.0	36.7	68.9	49.6
	<21	23.6	16.7	23.0	30.4	18.7	26.2
	21+	20.1	12.6	16.1	32.9	5.1	13.1
	No. of publications						
No. of scholarly books published in last 5 years	0	76.2	85.4	79.3	69.7	85.5	70.9
	1–2	20.7	11.9	17.5	30.9	12.7	25.3
	3+	3.2	2.6	3.2	3.5	1.8	3.8
No. of books published during whole career	0	72.3	84.8	76.0	58.3	80.1	67.8
	1–2	19.4	9.3	16.9	30.0	16.2	21.3
	3+	8.3	6.0	7.0	11.7	3.7	10.9
No. of scholarly papers published in refereed journals in last 5 years	0	39.5	65.0	47.0	19.3	47.7	35.1
	1–2	29.2	20.9	31.8	29.5	23.2	32.3
	3+	31.3	14.1	21.1	51.2	29.1	32.6
No. of scholarly papers published in refereed journals during whole career	0	36.7	65.0	44.0	15.1	41.7*	33.9*
	1–2	23.3	17.2	26.7	21.7	20.3	25.0
	3+	40.0	17.8	29.2	63.2	38.1	41.1

Notes: Significance: p = *<.05; **<.01; ***<.001. All are significant at p = ***<.001 unless otherwise indicated.
Source: See table 2.1.

ing such treatment for full-time, tenure track members is a vital step in decreasing the threat to the quality of programs and teaching' (1993: 43). Much of the literature is focused on the absence of professional development programs for part-time faculty (Greenwood, 1980; Parsons, 1980; Albert and Watson, 1980; Biles and Tuckman, 1986; Lampignano, 1990; Eggers, 1990; Hall and Atnip, 1992; Faulkner et al., 1992; Gappa and Leslie, 1993; Lankard, 1993; McGuire, 1993; Johnson, 1993; Kamps, 1996).[12] McGuire argues: 'Part-time faculty are a problem only if they are relegated to the margins of the institution and treated with respect usually reserved for the skeletons in the collective [academic] closet. In fact, a good case can be made that part-time faculty bring important benefits ... if care is taken for their professional development and integration into the mainstream of the institution. Part-time faculty can be key assets in the delivery of quality, up-to-date instructional programs ... More likely, the biggest problem appears to be institutional neglect of part-time faculty, who are routinely treated as second-class citizens – the 'neglected majority' (1993: 2). Professional development programs for adjunct or part-time faculty in a few colleges in California and New York have proved quite successful in promoting good teaching practices. Participants adopted many of the best practices, which encouraged student involvement in learning (Kelly, 1992; Mattice and Richardson, 1993; Yantz and Brechtold, 1994).

Four reasons for scarcity of such programs are identified in the literature: historical assumptions, institutional neglect, a policy vacuum, and part-timers' academic isolation. For a long time, universities have been in denial about part-timers. They have not responded to part-timers' needs and their requests for professional development programs. Stanley and Lumpkins, in their study of U.S. universities and colleges, attribute part-timers' sense of isolation and neglect in the workplace to the lack of appropriate teaching support: 'The part-time faculty use less [sic] instructional media, are less aware of campus events, have less choice in the selection of course materials, and are less likely to have access to instructional support services'; the authors warn: 'Continued use of part-time faculty ... without providing an adequate support program may have serious deleterious effects on the college community' (1992: 62–3, 68).[13]

My surveys show that 'institutional passivity' (Stanley and Lumpkins, 1992: 65) has left part-timers academically isolated. Indeed, in many universities and colleges, faculty development programs and the officers who implement them receive lower priority than full-time faculty engaged in research, innovation, and productivity. Myrna Smith et al. note: 'Faculty Development Officers could be called the "Woody Allens" of the academic world – isolated, disempowered figures, serving outside the chain of command' (1992: 167). Universities using full-time faculty as their model, assume that part-timers must take the initiative to equip themselves with professional skills needed for their job. They hire full-time faculty for their professional contributions and standing in the university and therefore assume that they possess appropriate work skills. Full-timers, however, have plenty of instructional resources and research funds at their disposal if they need them. Part-timers, in contrast, have little or no access to such resources.

Power and Influence

In this section I consider part-timers' role in decision-making and how it affects their level of participation.

Place in Decision-Making

Parsons and Platt characterized university faculty as denoting a 'basic equality of colleagues' (1973: 159). This is, indeed, a highly idealized picture, as my survey responses show. In practice, academe is hierarchically stratified. Tenured full-timers at the top exercise hierarchical line authority over part-timers, who are at the bottom. The main academic decision-making councils of the university essentially comprise full-time faculty. Generally, full-timers form the core of the academic senate (or unicameral governing bodies in some universities) in Canadian universities. Part-timers are occasionally eligible for membership in a senate, but this is a token membership. A similar pattern holds for governing councils of Faculties. Part-timers have little, if any, say in the departments' decisions, although many of them have the right to attend meetings. Analogous to 'minority' full-time faculty perceptions part-timers find themselves segmented within the university and excluded from decision-making (Aguirre, Martinez, and Hernandez, 1993).[14] This situation reinforces their perception that they are marginal to decision-making within the university, Faculty, or department. Part-timers' experiences reveal that their treatment as 'marginalized outsiders' silences them and privileges the speech of others at the centre as powerful. Those who learn to live with their inequities tend to internalize the notion that they do not know enough to be able to speak with any authority (Cayton, 1991).[15] My survey found part-timers only minimally involved in decision-making – either because they are excluded from these bodies or because they doubt that their views would be listened to. Exclusion from even department-level decision-making bodies, which actually determine their work, strains the relationship between part- and full-timers. In their survey responses, part-time faculty often denounce this situation as undemocratic: 'Many of us would like to be able to participate more actively in department affairs. Although we are entitled to attend department meetings, many of us do not, because we have no vote and are not eligible to sit on department committees. In departments, governance is described as democratic ... all policy decisions are collegially made by full-time members meeting as a council. Since full-time faculty do not constitute all faculty, this is an extremely imperfect form of democracy.'

How open do part-timers find collegial bodies? A majority of respondents (61 per cent) report that they have access to department-level meetings (table 2.7). Part-timers in Quebec universities have the least; 41 per cent of them can attend. A higher percentage of part-timers have access in universities in the west (part-timers 72 per cent), as well as in small size (65 per cent), limited range (65 per cent), teaching-oriented (65 per cent), lower intensity (70 per cent), and non-unionized (72 per cent) universities. A francophone part-timer explains why it is easy to exclude them from decision-making bodies: 'Many of us carry full course loads equal to full-time faculty's. We have also been here for many years. But, our problems or concerns are not a part of faculty issues ever discussed in my department meetings. We are not expected to express our ideas on teaching or students in any forum. Our ideas on academic issues even if we are so bold as to discuss them with full-timers, are marginalized and no change is made to remedy the problem.' Echoing this feeling, an anglophone reports: 'While our presence and even our voices may be tolerated at department meetings, we have no real standing there, and our concerns seem to be of little interest to full-time faculty. In fact ... our presence ... [is characterized] as an obstruction to long range curricular planning.' In Quebec universities, 18 per cent of part-timers are eligible to sit in the senate (Ontario 24 per cent, Atlantic 20 per cent, and west 19 per cent), and in Quebec, part-timers are least aware of their eligibility or ineligibility for such a seat. The exclusion and absence of a majority of Quebec part-timers from both senate and department-level decision-making may suggest that they have to look elsewhere to

TABLE 2.7
Part-timers' participation in academic decision-making, by university type

Decision-making level	Eligible Participate	Total %	Region***				Unionization***	
			West	Ontario	Quebec	Atlantic	Union	Non-union
Dept. meeting	Eligible	61.2	72.4	64.8	40.5	57.4	57.4	71.8
	Participate	34.9	47.8	33.9	20.1	37.2	30.9	46.7
Dept. committees	Eligible	44.3	50.5	47.3	32.6	41.0	41.9	51.1
	Participate	17.5	24.4	16.3	11.2	18.9	5.5	23.6
Faculty councils	Eligible	30.2	25.9*	33.8*	28.2*	36.0*	30.8 (n.s.)	28.6(n.s.)
	Participate	6.3	7.1	6.5	3.3	12.2	5.5**	8.6**
Faculty committee	Eligible	31.9	30.0 (n.s.)	33.5	30.4	36.0	31.3 (n.s.)	33.3(n.s.)
	Participate	6.5	8.7**	6.0**	4.2**	9.8**	5.7**	9.2**
Senate	Eligible	20.6	19.0 (n.s.)	24.0 (n.s.)	17.5 (n.s.)	20.0 (n.s.)	21.6 (n.s.)	17.7 (n.s.)
	Participate	2.1	3.4*	2.0*	0.7*	2.4*	1.9 (n.s.)	2.7(n.s.)
Senate committees	Eligible	19.5	14.8*	22.5*	21.1*	13.8*	21.5(n.s.)	13.4(n.s.)
	Participate	2.6	2 (n.s.)	2.3 (n.s.)	3.7 (n.s.)	3.3 (n.s.)	2.7 (n.s.)	2.1(n.s.)
Overall total no.		2,177	585	999	471	122	1,636	541

Notes: 'Don't know' responses constitute the balance of 100% for each question. Significance: p = * <.05; ** <.01; *** <.001. All are significant at p = *** <.001 unless otherwise indicated. (n.s.): not significant.
Source: See table 2.1.

influence policy that could affect their jobs and work. Either this is the reason for strong unionization of part-time faculty in the Quebec system of universities, or their strong union representation is forcing universities to keep them off the collegial bodies. It is quite plausible that their exclusion from decision-making bodies has encouraged part-timers to strengthen their unions.

Part-timers in western Canadian universities do not fare much better than part-timers at both Faculty councils and senates in Quebec. Three-quarters of part-timers in the west (the highest figure in Canada) are formally excluded from their Faculty councils. Relatively few universities in the west have unions for part-timers, and most part-timers do not have representation through their inclusion in a full-timers' faculty union or association, or in other collective organizations.

Non-unionized part-timers have greater formal representation in departmental decision-making bodies. In non-unionized universities, most part-timers (72 per cent versus 57 per cent in unionized universities) are included in departmental meetings, and a majority of them (51 per cent versus 42 per cent in unionized universities) are eligible to serve on departmental committees. Yet there is no difference at higher levels, that is, in Faculty councils or in the senate. Two-thirds of part-timers are ineligible or unaware of their right to sit in Faculty councils, and most part-timers (unionized part-timers 78 per cent and non-unionized part-timers 82 per cent) are excluded from senates in both types of universities.

Janice Newson refers to institutional changes that are rapidly marginalizing the collective academic interests of tenured faculty in the decision-making process. Financial shortages and inadequate funding of higher education in Canada have reduced the representation of tenured faculty at all levels to a formality, leaving them little power to shape or control academic policies. Financial experts and technical writers of 'five year plans, mission statements, and collective agreements' have hijacked the influence and power of the formal institutions. Newson emphasizes that 'these documents don't only define but they actually constitute the relationships that exist among the various *units* of the university'; part-time faculty, with their tenuous links to the university, constitute one of these *units* hired or fired as finances dictate, and excluded from this 'documentary form of decision-making' (1990: 8, 9).[16] For tenured faculty who confront their own marginalization resulting from such a decision-making process, adding part-timers to their representative strength would not do much –

it would add merely another set of demands. Tenured faculty, them-selves, are increasingly turning to their own unions, rather than to their senate or other faculty councils, to resolve policy or jurisdictional conflicts with their universities' central administration.

In this context, one can see that part-timers would naturally turn to their collective representation in unions or associations if they have any. However, many part-timers still continue to demand representa-tion on faculty bodies and their decision-making processes. They are aware that their tenured 'bosses' have the power to make regulations that affect their jobs and work and feel that collective organization could not balance their lack of representation.

Part-timers feel strongly that they should be included in department meetings and asked to contribute their views even if they cannot attend (Roderer and Weissbecker, 1990). Many part-timers in my sur-vey see it as illogical and undemocratic for universities to exclude their participation in making decisions related to teaching and curriculum. They feel that the university should see these decisions as concerns of mutual relevance to the university and to part-timers: 'We need a voice in department decisions that directly affect our working conditions and we feel that we could make valuable contributions to the curricu-lum and teaching issues. The area of curriculum is of particular interest to us. Those who teach the same courses year after year would have some insights for improving reading lists to suit the needs of students, as well as to keep it up-to-date ... Many of us have designed courses at the department's request, especially at upper levels, and would appre-ciate the opportunity to propose courses in our own areas of interest.' But membership in the collegial bodies is not easy to achieve. To be included in these bodies, one has to be defined as part of the 'real fac-ulty.' A woman part-timer comments: 'Most of us are here year after year. But we are not expected to voice our views in my department, as we are not included as voting members. Only real "faculty" voices will be heard. We may listen to discussions or respond, but our voices do not count. But if the department wishes, it is within its rights to define the collegium as it sees fit. *How unlikely that the part-time faculty, identi-fied in the department planning documents as an "embarrassment" will be included!* (emphasis added). There are no policies or principles that guide departments in integrating courses developed (at the request of departments) by part-timers into their curricular objectives. Part-timers are left with the inescapable feeling that they are being taken for granted and treated as temporary workers. A part-timer ponders: 'Is there any Department policy on the proposal of courses by part-time faculty? Would the Department be interested in developing such a policy?'

Participation

Most part-timers see collegial bodies as blocking them from helping to make decisions related to the workplace. Feeling thoroughly alienated, most part-timers do not participate even in bodies from which they are not excluded. Those who participate (35 per cent) do so only at the grass-roots, departmental level – at universities in the west (48 per cent of part-timers); and in limited range (40 per cent), lower-intensity (44 per cent), and non-unionized (47 per cent) universities. Beyond the department level, however, the predominant pattern is one of exclusion, non-recognition, and non-participation of part-timers. Many part-timers express their discontent with the central and departmental administrators for ignoring their 'voices' when they speak in these assemblies. A woman part-timer explains: 'Many of us would like to participate more actively. However, it is not encouraging merely to attend department meetings where you have no real say. Many of us do not attend because we have no vote and are not eligible to sit on department committees.' In particular, most Contemporaries who aspire to a full-time academic position are quite bitter about their exclusion, and they comment profusely in their responses about the way their departments deny them rights but demand their duties. Further, they are also highly frustrated by the difficulty of finding time to attend meetings and by the indifference of full-timers to their views. They are often told that it is not necessary for them to attend departmental meetings or serve on committees because their job does not require it. A Contemporary part-timer comments: 'When the full-time faculty seem generously to exempt us from committee work or from other service, are they doing us a favor? Or, are they circumscribing the collegium as a way of excluding us from any share in the department's decision-making power? ... Are we not expected to attend meetings? Are we allowed to participate in the decision-making process involving our professional lives?'

In Canada, government policy generally supports public sector unionization and protects unions during a period of organizing and negotiating a first agreement (Rogow and Birch, 1984).[17] As a result, at many campuses part-timers and teaching assistants have built up reasónable bargaining power through their union affiliation. Most part-timers in my survey (78.2 per cent) turn to their own unions or associations to represent them. They believe that these organizations are more effective in presenting their views than the universities' decision-making bodies. Almost all part-timers (93 per cent) believe that their unions or associations offer effective protection against arbitrary treatment, and most of them (87.8 per cent) definitely rely on their organization to represent their interests in the university. Most part-timers actively support their unions or associations. Women part-timers (68 per cent versus 53 per cent of men) and Contemporaries (64 per cent versus 52 per cent of Classics), in particular, rely heavily on them. There are, however, a few part-timers who generally oppose unions: 'I prefer to contract for myself, without a union. Once I sign a contract, I consider it my moral responsibility to fulfil the terms to which I freely agreed. In other words, don't bother me with strikes, etc.' And, 'Appointments to part-time positions should be made on the basis of professional reputation and expertise. The current system mandated by a union in [this] university is demeaning and insulting – a bricklayer approach to the training of educators.' At the other end of the spectrum, some have given up their research time and used it, instead, to build up their union: 'Since ... 1987, I have devoted a lot of my time to forming a union of part-time lecturers, serving on the executive, and on the negotiating team for our first contract. This meant sacrificing all the time that I would have spent on research and writing academic articles.' Particularly in universities that exclude part-timers from formal decision-making bodies – for example, Quebec universities – part-timers turn to unionization. Elsewhere, in the absence of a union or association, they seek informal means. For all part-timers, personal influence (89 per cent) or reliance on their personal relationships with the full-timers seem to add to their bargaining strength, formal or informal: 'I believe the part-time union is necessary to represent my interests. But ... I have always had much better success dealing with administrators at the departmental and faculty levels than in dealing with either the union executive or the higher levels of university administration, largely because both seem to be governed more by ideology than common sense.'

In summary, part-timers' feelings of marginality are powerfully conveyed in their survey responses. In a job that they love, they face obstacles in their day-to-day work that threaten to weaken their spirit and proficiency. They are exasperated that the university denies their continuing presence. They feel that it ignores their perspectives – their reasons for teaching part time, their aspirations, their attitude towards their work, their role in the universities, and their place in the collegium.

Chapter Three

Invisible Women

Unlike their full-time counterparts, part-time faculty women are not statistically reported on. Although more numerous proportionally than women full-timers, women part-timers are less visible. Full-time faculty women are significantly fewer than full-time men. Compared with part-time faculty women, however, full-time faculty women are far more visible and are recognized both as individuals and as a group. In this chapter I will examine women part-timers' situation: who they are, the rhetoric of women's work as voluntary, the realities of their work, and their influence.

Who They Are

Historically, the proportion of women among full-time faculty in Canadian universities has been abysmally low, but from 1976 to 1992 there was an upturn. Numbers of women full-time faculty doubled from 4,000 to nearly 8,000, while those of men increased from 25,000 to slightly more than 29,000. Women's numbers increased from 14 per cent of full-timers in 1976 to 25 per cent in 1997 (AUCC, 1999: 44) to 26.2 per cent in 1998–9 (*CAUT Bulletin* Insert, April 2000).[1] From 1992 to 1997, however, total numbers of both men and women declined by 11 per cent and new hirings of women dropped from 900 in 1989 to 500 in 1996. In contrast, in the United States, full-time faculty increased by 5 per cent from 1991 to 1997 and women constituted a third of all full-timers (AUCC, 1999: 45), a figure that is up from 27.1 per cent in 1992 (AAUP, 1992: 41). In Britain in 1992 only 20 per cent of full-time academics were women (ibid., 1).

Since Statistics Canada does not report on numbers of part-time faculty in Canadian universities, in 1990 I organized an institutional survey to collect such information. My institutional survey reveals that in 1989–90 there were 18,652 part-time faculty members, 40.8 per cent of them women. More important, my direct survey on part-time faculty (1991–2) shows that women constitute 53 per cent of Contemporaries (versus 32 per cent of Classics), while the breakdown for men is Contemporaries 47 per cent versus Classics 68 per cent (see chapter two, p. 68, for definitions). The statistics for Ontario, which has one of the largest systems of higher education in Canada, show the feminization of the part-time faculty. The proportion of full-time faculty women in Ontario universities is on the rise. In a decade and a half, it went from 12 per cent in 1971–2 to 17 per cent in 1987–8. Two years later it reached 20 per cent (1989–90). In about a quarter of a century, from 1971 to 1995, it doubled to 25 per cent (1995–6). Of even greater significance, women part-timers outnumber women full-timers. Women part-timers increased in number from 1,743 (38 per cent) in 1987–8 to 2,335 (44 per cent) in 1989–90. In nearly two-thirds of the institutions that reported in 1990, women part-timers' increasing presence suggests a rapid escalation (17 per cent rate) in the two years (1988–90) in the feminization process of an already female-intensive (cf. full-timers) faculty.

As we saw in chapter one, according to the 1999 report of the U.S. national survey, the proportion of part-timers increased from 36 per cent (300,000) of all faculty members in 1989 to 41 per cent (381,000) in 1995 (NCES, 1999: 254, table 225). The proportion of women is on the rise. It remained at about 44 per cent from 1988 to 1992 but then climbed from 168,000 women (45 per cent) in 1992 to 178,141 (47 per cent) in 1995 (ibid.: tables 223, 227, 228, 230). In the 1990 report of the U.S. survey (completed in 1988) it was stated that women part-timers earned less than their male counterparts and spent more time teaching than the men. Fewer women than men expressed satisfaction with their work, salary, benefits, participation in decision-making, and opportunities for advancement (NCES, 1990b: 23, 58). Proportionally more men than women held 'regular' employment outside academe, according to both the U.S. and the Quebec studies. The survey taken by the Conseil des universités, Québec, of part-timers in Quebec identifies women as preponderant in two groups: those dependent upon the university for a major share of their income (58 per cent of all part-timers) and those teaching part time without other significant outside employment (55 per cent). In contrast, of the 'traditional' part-timers with regular, full-time, non-university employment 76 per cent are

FIGURE 3.1

Part-time faculty: gender and academic Faculties

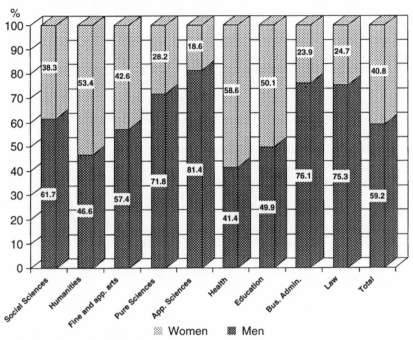

Source: Rajagopal, National Institutional Survey (1990–1)

men (Conseil, 1989: 51). As a consequence of feminization of the academic profession, a majority of women who choose academic employment receive low wages in 'dead-end' jobs.

According to my institutional survey (respondent institutions reported their actual numbers of part-timers), the disciplinary profile of women part-timers in Canadian universities (1989–90) that reported their gender breakdown[2] revealed that women are proportionally more numerous in health sciences (women 59 per cent versus men 41 per cent), and in humanities (women 53 per cent versus men 47 per cent). Far fewer women were in applied sciences (women 19 per cent versus men 81 per cent). In business administration, law, and pure sciences, only one in four part-timers was a woman. As for gender ratios among part-timers across disciplines, more women (27 per cent) taught in arts than in sciences (14 per cent versus men 28 per cent) (figure 3.1).

In Ontario, the disciplinary profile paralleled all-Canada figures. It showed that the largest group of women part-timers taught in the fine arts and humanities. The next-largest group taught in health studies and education, with substantial representation at seven of the reporting universities. The numbers and proportions represented in pure and applied science, business, and law were relatively low. In Ontario universities as a whole, women constituted 46 per cent of part-timers in the arts, humanities, and social sciences in 1989–90. The proportion was even higher in health and education, at 54 per cent. In pure and applied sciences, in contrast, only 20 per cent of part-timers were women, and in business and law 28 per cent. These proportions mirrored findings for Quebec (Conseil, 1989: 32).

The academic labour force is therefore marked not only by differences in compensation, career opportunities, and professional development, but also by increasing feminization and occupational segregation. In academe, as in other job-segregated labour markets, the marginalized sector experiences entrenched pay differentials, absence of career mobility, and lack of power to make decisions in the workplace. With increasing feminization, this trend will probably continue and the gap between full-time and part-time academics widen.

Demographic Profile

My survey of part-timers in 1991–2 shows that the age profile of men (average age 44 years) and women (average age 43 years) part-timers is broadly similar. Women full-timers are, on average, ten to twelve years younger than men (Berkowitz, 1996). This may be a result of the recent hiring of new women graduates by universities with affirmative action hiring policies. More men part-timers (85 per cent versus women 74 per cent) live with a spouse or partner. While a majority of men (59 per cent) as well as women (53 per cent) have financially dependent children, slightly more women (47 per cent versus men 41 per cent) have no children (table 3.1). Most women part-timers (90 per cent) were born in Canada. Very few part-timers belong to minority groups – that is, visible minorities (4 per cent), aboriginal peoples (0.6 per cent), or disabled people (1.2 per cent).

On average, men have been teaching in academe part time for 6.31 years – a little longer than women (4.58 years). However, women part-timers are not newcomers. Many have taught part time for a considerable period: a third teaching for more than seven years, a quarter for

TABLE 3.1
Demographic profiles of part-time faculty: women versus men

		Women	Men	p value
Average age		42.5	43.7	$p < .01$
Average personal income		$30,000–$39,000	$50,000–$59,000	$p < .001$
		%	%	
Living with a spouse/partner	Yes	74.0	85.3	$p < .001$
	No	26.0	14.7	$x^2 = 43.1$ odds ratio for male = 1.44
	Total no.	998	1,172	
Have dependent child/children	Yes	53.3	58.7	$p < .01$
	No	46.7	41.3	$x^2 = 6.49$ odds ratio for male = 1.13
	Total no.	997	1,172	
Education	Doctorate	20.8	31.9	$p < .01$
	Masters	56.4	47.5	$x^2 = 34.1$
	<Masters	22.9	20.7	
	Total no	992	1,171	
Pursuing a degree	Yes	26.4	17.4	$p < .01$
	No	73.6	82.6	$x^2 = 25.3$ odds ratio for male = 1.31
	Total no.	986	1,165	
Degree pursued	Doctorate	57.6	62.7	(n.s.)
	Masters	34.0	28.4	
	<Masters	8.4	8.8	
	Total no.	262	204	

Note: All differences are significant unless indicated not significant (n.s).
Source: Rajagopal, Part-Time Faculty Survey (1991–2)

four to six years, and a fifth (22 per cent) for ten years. Gender differences are not as clearly reflected in age, family, and teaching experience as in academic qualifications. Fewer women (21 per cent versus men 32 per cent) have a doctoral degree. More than half (56 per cent versus men 48 per cent) have only a master's degree, and more are pursuing a master's degree (34 per cent versus men 28 per cent). More women (26 per cent versus men 17 per cent) are pursuing a degree; of those with a doctorate more women (10 per cent versus men 4 per cent) are working towards a second doctorate.

Women's personal income is considerably lower than that of men. More than twice the percentage of women (50 per cent versus men 23 per cent) earn a total personal income that is less than $30,000 a year, whereas considerably more than twice the percentage of men (40 per cent versus women 15 per cent) earn in excess of $60,000. Twice the percentage of women (20 per cent versus men 9 per cent) are dependent on part-time teaching for their total income, and nearly a third of women (31 per cent versus men 13 per cent) earn low personal incomes (less than $20,000 per year) from all employment sources. When we compare total personal incomes of Contemporaries alone, a majority of women (61 per cent versus men 33 per cent) earn less than $30,000 per year, and a higher proportion of men (28 per cent versus women 9 per cent) earn more than $60,000. Even among Classics, although they have full-time non-academic jobs, more among the women (18 per cent versus men 9 per cent) earn less than $30,000 per year as their total personal income, while a majority of men Classics (56 per cent versus women 30 per cent) earn more than $60,000. This income disparity declines if average household incomes are taken into account.

Feminization of Employment

In the 1980s, as rising unemployment levels constrained the Canadian economy, private sector employers were relentless in urging governments to cut back and privatize services as well as to deregulate universal programs, state education, health and welfare services, and work-related benefits. Squeezed by economic and employment pressures, governments stepped in with wage and cost cuts, reined in the unions, and emphasized debt reduction rather than full employment. The deregulation and financial and service cutbacks marginalized, in particular, women workers who were already at the periphery of the job market, under minimum wages and standards. This situation, as Armstrong and Armstrong point out, accentuated the subordinate status of women in the labour market (1983: 76–103). In addition to deregulation of wages and standards of employment, privatization of public-sector industries aggravated the wage differentials between men and women, since wage differentials were generally higher in private enterprise than in the public sector (ibid., 1988: 77–82).

The above forces – deregulation, privatization, and retrenchment – had a clear structural impact on the labour market. Employment became more flexible, and creating any types of jobs, not necessarily full time, could reduce the widespread clamour for job creation and for expansion of the employment market. Part time work became a practical solution to the need for workers to fill in instantly, on demand (Armstrong and Armstrong, 1988: 80–1). As jobs increased, structuring of employment as part-time or temporary became a deliberate and resilient strategy in the job market. Such work did not carry the norms of a 'good job,' with standards and benefits; as a consequence, it led to the 'gendering of jobs,' or feminization of employment.

In the literature, there are two opposing interpretations of the impact of feminization, but not of the fact of feminization itself. The first is Guy Standing's interpretation of global feminization. Originally Standing (1989) argued that women are appropriating men's jobs; that sex segregation in job markets was declining; and that 'bad jobs' with limited mobility were increasing while 'good jobs' were declining. When Standing recently revisited his thesis, his position seemed to alter. He has identified certain global trends in the feminization of employment continuing from the 1970s; despite this continuation, he has modified considerably his position on their manifestations in the labour market, such as occupational, or job-sector-related sex segregation and women taking away jobs from men (1999: 600). Feminization, according to Standing (1999), has the following characteristics. First, the temporary, insecure, irregular, and low-paid jobs traditionally associated with women are now expanding more than those that are regular, unionized, stable, skilled, and characterized as 'good jobs' stereotypically associated with men. Second, increasing numbers of women are entering and remaining in the workforce. Third, there is a declining trend of men's stable employment in the labour market. Not only do patterns of employment show a decline in stable, secure, and regular jobs, but there is also a general trend towards more flexible, informal, and temporary jobs. More men, therefore, are pushed to the margins of the labour market, whereas more women seem to be in a less informal situation and globally their labour force participation is increasing. Standing affirms, however, that this means not that women are gaining over men in securing good jobs but rather that men's position in the labour market is eroding and more men are entering the expanding flexible and feminized job market.

Challenging Standing's (1989) original description of 'feminization,' Leah Vosko elucidates five features that are integral to the process of 'global feminization of employment': increasing numbers of women are entering the formal labour force, which suggests a shift from informal to formal sectors rather than women's new entry into economic production; the gendered nature of casualization of employment in the labour market – more jobs resemble traditional women's work; women's labour force participation is expanding; sex segregation persists across industrial sectors and job types; and polarization of incomes and occupations has increased between men and women as well as within the two groups (2000: 38–40).

Vosko argues that 'standard employment relations,' or full-time, good jobs, as a normative model of employment in the labour markets of advanced capitalist economies are fast declining; feminization and temporary employment relations are accelerating (2000: 34–44). Empirically, she attributes the feminization of employment norms in the Canadian labour market during the 1970s and the 1980s to four factors. First, jobs in the labour market increasingly resemble those meant for 'secondary breadwinners,' which may therefore be labelled 'women's work,' that is, temporary terms, poorer employment conditions, inadequate wages, few or no benefits, and no security. Second, since the 1950s the temporary-help industry has actively promoted women's participation in the job market to supplement the income of the so-called main (male) breadwinner in the family. This trend continues, with greater structural accommodation in the job market offered for women's social-reproduction functions, such as flexible hours of work and pliable workplace arrangements. Third, the gendered characteristics of casualization, or the gendering of jobs as a result of global restructuring of employment, seem to be clear and predominant in the job market (Armstrong, 1996: 30). It is important to note that jobs are becoming feminized, with the declining of standard jobs that offer security, benefits, and career mobility. Gender composition in different employment sectors and varied occupations is changing to incorporate male workers in 'gendered jobs,' thus increasing the feminized nature of the casualization process. Fourth, because temporary employment is relentlessly replacing standard, full-time, 'good' jobs, the norms have become sex segregation, income disparities, and both inter- and intra-gender occupational rifts (Vosko, 2000: 42–4).

In higher education, a job sector traditionally dominated by men, feminization of employment seems to reflect the general trend in the overall labour market. When governments began to cut funding for higher education in the 1970s, and given enrolment fluctuations, part-time and temporary workers appeared to be the only solution for universities. The jobs were temporary, insecure, and deregulated and existed entirely at the whim of the university administrators who managed money. These jobs were feminized or gendered, whether held by men or by women. The disciplinary areas in which they are predominant – that is, women part-timers in arts and humanities and male part-timers in sciences and professional studies – seem to confirm the occupational segregation of women that Vosko posits. Further, as my figures discussed above show, although the part-time sector is feminized, there is a marked gender gap, and males predominate among full-timers. The gender gap (see chapter 4) between full-time versus part-time job sectors – more men among Classics (those with full-time non-academic jobs) and more women among Contemporaries (those holding mainly academic part-time jobs) – also confirms the patterns of segregation. Thus, women do not seem to shrink job opportunities for men by taking away their jobs, as some observers would suggest.

Women Working: The Rhetoric and the Realities

The Rhetoric of Women 'Voluntarily' Working Part Time

The assumption that Canadian women want to work part time rather than full time is not founded on fact, because there is a steady increase of women in the 'involuntary' labour force. One in ten jobs in the total workforce created 'involuntary' part-time employment in the 1980s, of which more than 80 per cent pertained to women age 25–54 and youth age 15–24 (Veltmeyer and Sacouman, 1998: 128).[3] In two decades (1975–93), women age 15 and over in the workforce increased from 41 per cent of all women to 51 per cent. As a result of the 1993 recession, 34 per cent of women could not find full-time jobs, and another 11 per cent could work only part time because of family responsibilities (Statistics Canada, 1994b: 12–59). The most recent figures on part-time workers available from *Labour Force Update* (Statistics Canada, 1999a) reinforce this pattern and show an increasing proportion of involuntary part-timers among women. Nearly a third (30 per cent) of adult women overtly expressed their 'involuntary' part-timer status, and, in addition, 20 per cent said that they were working part time to take care of children. The latter did not say that they were voluntarily working part time. Perhaps some of them would have preferred full-time work if they had had access to care for their children. Because not enough day-care spaces are available, about three-quarters of all children under 6 remain mostly with women, mothers or relatives, in the unpaid 'household sector' (Statistics Canada, 1994b: 48–50).

By all estimates, women constitute a considerable portion of the workforce that has fewer options than men do for working full time. Statistics Canada (1999c: 19) reports that women are also more likely than men to be concentrated in 'traditional occupational' structures, one of which is education. This is a double whammy for women who are interested in full-time work and advancing their career interests outside the 'glass box,'[4]

According to a study by Tolbert and Oberfield,[5] women encounter hiring barriers in universities with more resources, which can hire higher-priced men. Women do not choose to work in less research-oriented universities, or in lower-paying, part-time, or temporary contract jobs, 'trading off higher compensation for work environments' in order to accommodate their family responsibilities. Further, there is clear evidence that women academics do not consciously seek the less demanding or less time-consuming work (1991: 311–12).

The Delusion of Dismantling Barriers

Discrimination of one form or another against women is present on every university campus. Many studies have shown that degradation of women is a result of male dominance of the academy, sex discrimination, and men's refusal to consider women as their equals (Young, Mackenzie, and Sherif, 1980; Meyer-Renschhausen, 1990; Bagilhole, 1993;[6] Dean, 1995; Melamed, 1995). Women in universities continue to confront barriers arising from gender discrimination (Pleck, 1990). In the United States, there is no evidence to show that universities more heavily dependent on federal funding improved gender equity via affirmative action policies (Kulis and Miller-Loessi, 1992a: 179).[7]

Despite general awareness of the low proportion of women among faculty and the continued administrative and collective interest in some form of affirmative action to advance their hiring, universities seem reluctant to discard the 'merit principle' in hiring. They fear that such hiring might lead to a possible decline in standards. In public discussions on processes to encourage the hiring of women in Canadian universities, the spectre of reverse discrimination against men is often raised. James Butrica writes that 'restrictive search' to restore equity for women would mean that 'simply being a female constitutes a more important qualification than any of those conventionally regarded as important.' This approach would seem, he argues, to skew the issues to dissociate merit from women's qualifications and fairness from hiring (1999: A11).

We need to consider the above criticisms in the context of existing evidence that once a demographic pattern and gender mix is established in academe – for example, if males are in dominant numbers in faculties – the imbalance becomes self-perpetuating (Tolbert and Oberfield, 1991: 313). Kanter (1977) finds that both men and women are inclined to hire or promote colleagues of the same sex. White men blame the women's movement for this situation and 'scapegoat' women – and also the minorities – for their inability to find jobs in a shrinking academic market. When affirmative action emerged, it shifted the 'label of victim' from women and minorities to white males (Freeman, 1977: 185–6).

Much worse than the negative ideological stances against women's efforts to break conventional barriers, other more concrete and visible obstacles also daunt women. Women faculty are likely to hit the 'glass ceiling,' since they teach more hours than men, but research continues to be given more weight in university decisions on tenure and promotion. It is often assumed that women prepare less prestigious research publications. They are also boxed in by traditional assessment criteria that cannot evaluate the newly emerging field of women's journals or, at best, that assess them as substandard. Tenured male faculty members evaluate women's research more harshly, and they unfairly assess women's journals as of secondary significance (Hayes, 1990;[8] Lindsay, 1988). Studies on why fewer new women faculty in the United States sail through the tenure process show that both the university and the faculty member's household or family create structural barriers against their pursuing a career. However, responsibility for creating new barriers or not dismantling existing ones rests squarely with the universities. According to Finkel and Olswang's (1996) study,[9] more women are obstructed in getting tenure by severe impediments in academe rather than by problems in their domestic sphere. They face a chilly climate.[10] As a further aggravation in the work environment, women full-timers are asked to put in too much time on committees (40 per cent), and they lack grant support for advancing their scholarly publications (39.8 per cent). They are excluded from the mainstream (33.9 per cent), face sexism (33.6 per cent), and have too few graduate students (24.3 per cent) to supervise. Departments do not integrate them within their groups (22.5 per cent). Women must deal with a hostile environment (19.3 per cent) and sexual harassment (8.4 per cent). In addition, they face other problems: their partners' career demands (24.6 per cent), time needed for discharging obligations to elders (8.7 per cent), lack of support from their partners (6.2 per cent), and other familial factors that complicate their careers. Women part-timers in my survey also confirm many of these findings.

In 'Education and the "Woman Question"' (1997) Sandra Pyke reported that the largest differentials in terms of declared obstacles between men and women in the university environment are financial. More women (46 per cent versus men 28 per cent) who are either completing their studies or advancing their academic careers say that they have to earn money – through teaching as much as possible or working elsewhere. Other subtle and insidious forms of exclusion keep women from positions of authority, as do systemic practices of disregarding their work, diverting their time, or wearing down their confidence (Caplan, 1993). Reports of women's experiences show that they are more disadvantaged in a system that simply tries to fit them within the existing framework without dealing with the inequities that uniquely apply to women in academe. Dorothy Smith shows that 'the multiple small "incidents" [of perceptions and anecdotes of women students] map into a model of the social relations of gender in educational that is familiar' (1997: 254).

It is clear that the public has become more aware of the 'gender wars' in the 'Ivory Tower.' In 'A Woman Academic Pins Down Exactly What Is at Stake in the Campus "Gender War"' (*Western Report*, 1994) it is emphasized that the real conflict is not between men and women but between those who see the university as an initiator of social change and those who do not.[11] In 'Ivory Towers under Siege' (*Western Report*, 1995) it is suggested that complaining about their condition in academe draws resentment against women as a group.[12] Both student and faculty women are perceived as a group that threatens a rational system based on 'merit' by demanding corrections for inequities. More problems have arisen inside academe that have challenged free thought and speech in the 'sacred grove.' It is concluded in the *Western Report* articles that within the so-called ivory towers faculty women are subjected to various degradations and smears. Bruce Feldthusen describes why men are silent about sexism although they have the power to end the gender wars: 'Men exercise "their" ultimate tool of oppression, their right "not to know"' (1995: 282).

Women faculty and professionals are often reminded in an outrageous fashion that they would 'have to work extra hard to make up for the handicap of being a female.' Although most women do not anticipate this discrimination, since they do not see their workplace or careers as any different from those of men, in reality they experience gender and wage discrimination. In Canada, unionized women earn an average of 83.7 per cent of a man's wage, compared with 69.6 per cent for non-union women. Women are the fastest increasing segment of the North American labour movement and represent the largest potential growth area. In national and international unions in Canada, women hold 25 per cent of executive board seats – well below their union membership level of 39 per cent but more representative than the U.S. figures (Taylor, 1995).[13]

Modes of Marginality

Women's marginalization in academe occurs in various ways and assumes different forms. Three major manifestations are *failure to recognize women as individuals* with characteristics and requirements as academics different from those normally attributed to men; *labelling and straitjacketing women into teaching roles*, which overloads them with student-intensive work; and *exclusion of women and their ideas* in the process of decision-making. The first two are intertwined and reinforce each other.

NEGLECT
There are two opposing forces at work in the ivory tower. Women are readily typecast into 'female roles' in the division of labour (Krefting and Berger, 1979). Of the types, the relevant ones for our discussion are those of women as 'teachers' and men as 'researchers.' Yet women are expected to fit themselves into the system, shaped by the male-

dominated hierarchy, as merely another hiree no different from any other! Women's differences from men spring from their roles in the household. Integrating their personal life and their work role has long been a practice with men. Faculty men have enjoyed housing, recreation, family support, and medical and health benefits. Women, as their spouses or 'appendages,' indeed may have benefited from these perquisites, but faculty women's needs are hardly recognized or considered, even in universities that genuinely try to integrate them. Many studies have shown that women and men prioritize differently the personal characteristics that enhance or deter their work and productivity (Freeman, 1977; Teevan, Pepper, and Pellizzari, 1992; Lane, 1993; Park, 1996; Tsai and Schwindt, 1996; Norrell and Norrell, 1996; Didion, 1996; Finkel and Olswang, 1996). Since women academics emphasize family responsibilities and household needs and constraints more strongly than men do, it is necessary to address their needs in these areas through a different, specially designed, female-centred framework (Rothblum: 1988). Such a framework would deviate totally from conventional wisdom regarding family and work. Traditionally, men and women are expected to separate and balance the family sphere of activities and work, but women with high research productivity seem to merge their personal and work lives in a way that enhances their productivity (Bielby and Bielby, 1988; Toren, 1991; Creamer, 1996).

The situation of women part-timers is far worse than that of women full-timers. While women full-timers do occupy the lower levels of the academic hierarchy, part-timers are deemed interlopers. Thus, their voices are not heard in the hallowed halls if and when they speak of their heavy workloads. A survey of American full-timers and part-timers reports that women are overburdened with work. They are expected to meet family obligations as well as job requirements. As a result, faculty women at all levels find themselves hemmed in by structures and situations where they are less likely to do research or attain high academic rank. Trapped in their gender role, most women are unable to relocate to advance their career without regard to their spouse's employment situation (Watkins et al., 1996). Part-timers who work only in academe carry heavier burdens of work; 'part-time' is a misnomer, because many carry a full load. Most women part-timers carry a double burden, working more hours both at the university and at home. Although we would expect job insecurity or job inequity to be top-level stresses, women rank job load and job demands highest (Tsai and Schwindt, 1996).[14] The onerous workload as well as the demanding variety of jobs inevitably lead to stress.

LABELLING

Along with this double burden, academic images of women are structured more intensively as teachers and student advisers. This definition of their role has long endured and has created a vertical split between female and male faculty members, the latter being seen primarily as researchers (Kirk and Rosenblatt, 1984; Henry, 1990; Sowers-Hoag and Harrison, 1991; Park, 1996; Sandler, 1996). In resisting these stereotypes and further marginalization, academic women try to excel by publishing and teaching more than their male colleagues do (Henry, 1990: 128).

Full- and part-time women faculty members are most similar in facing almost insurmountable obstacles to their entrance into and working in academe. They are segmented in their interests and efforts at resistance. The existing professoriate is split vertically into males and females. The split between female full-timers and female part-timers further exacerbates divisions within academe. Just as women are more isolated from men in informal collegial contacts and male faculty members communicate more with other males than with women on similar research interests, women's informal contacts are largely restricted to other women of equal or lesser rank (Smith and Hixson, 1987). In reality, women full-timers find little time for or common interest in connecting with women part-timers. Comparing women in the labour market in Britain, France, and Germany, Christel Lane finds that women face vertical and horizontal segregation (1993: 287). Women are ghettoized in a few occupations. Within occupational or organizational hierarchies, they are concentrated in lower-level jobs. Segmentation works against women's efforts to gain equity, especially in the area of pay. Because the fewer women at the higher-end jobs are segregated from the much larger group that is near the bottom, they lack group strength and cohesion. Much worse, they also tend to compete against each other (Henry, 1990).

The male-dominated university administration and its paternalistic assumptions about women perpetuate these divisions among academic women. The origins of the long-enduring 'chilly climate' can be explained by the way in which women were treated from the earliest days of their entrance into academe (Lee, 1990). Ascribed characteristics of age, sex, colour, or race influence decision-making in academe (Stiver

Lie and O'Leary, 1990; J. Cole, 1979; S. Cole, 1979). Until the 1960s the systematic exclusion of women and Blacks was not even discussed in the United States. Faculty hiring and career advancement are also informally influenced by idiosyncratic factors like sponsorship by 'the powerful professor' (Goyder, 1992).[15] Further, women's role as academic mentor is weak and insecure because of the systemic discrimination against women mentors. As a result, women confront what is called the 'Matthew effect'[16] or the 'Salieri phenomenon'[17] (Clark and Corcoran, 1993: 401–2), which worsens inequalities. Segregation of women in academe, irrespective of their rank and status, makes it difficult for women to resist these trends and make gains in their careers.

EXCLUSION
From the experiences of women full-timers we can see how, and to what extent, women in academe are devalued. Although women are increasing in numbers both in student body and in faculty, they are not generally present in higher levels of authority and are segregated across departments (Toren and Kraus, 1987). Gender gap and inequality in Canadian higher education and its replication in many countries throughout the world are evident from the unequal distribution of wealth, rank, and power based on the ascribed characteristics of gender (Lie, Malik, and Harris, 1994). Rossiter (1995) finds fewer women in the higher ranks in academic administration. Women are eased into positions analogous to their ascribed gender role, for example, 'advisers' to students rather than academic deans (Eisenmann, 1996: 868). We might add to this group women appointed as 'academic colleagues' or as 'advisers' to the president rather than as vice-presidents, thus enabling the university to count them as women in top-level positions. Parallel conditions prevail within the part-time faculty, only more intensely so. Already at the bottom of the hierarchy, women part-timers have little say in decision-making. Their sense of powerlessness is a fundamental problem for them (Speer, 1992). They are made to feel like aliens in the collegium or as newcomers and outsiders in the male-dominated professoriate. If allowed into representative committees of departments, they tend to be seen and treated as token rather than full members.

The Fact of Feminization

Feminization of the part-time academic workforce has further lowered the status of part-timers. Elaborating on Braverman's account of the degradation of clerical workers, Graham Lowe discovers a critical variable – 'the centrality of gender' – at work in early-twentieth-century Canada. In the process of bureaucratic rationalization of offices, he identifies a correlation between the deterioration of clerical wages and working conditions and the dramatic shift from a male to a female labour supply in a changing labour market. Lowe argues that the split in relative pay and job characteristics was related directly to increasing recruitment of women into clerical ranks, which became a 'major female job ghetto' (1982: 16). Similar trends also appeared in higher education, since the part-time faculty has a greater proportion of females than the full-time faculty.

Feminization has directly reinforced the stereotype that part-timers are, by and large, 'temporary' and work for pin money. Nonetheless, this academic part-time employment is the principal source of income for many, and for a considerable length of time (Sherwood, 1993). As part-time women are labelled 'home-workers,' they receive little by way of benefits, service support, or career development, and no job security. A further, and more insidious, consequence of feminization has been the absence of basic statistical data on part-timers. Administrations are presumably reluctant to maintain such data or other systematic documentation on supposedly tentative operations. Since part-timers constitute a 'contingent' labour force, and women part-timers among them are seen as visitors to academe from the household, their presence goes unrecorded and cannot become an authoritative 'textual reality' (Smith, 1990: 70–1). Universities have refused to recognize women part-timers as legitimate because of the dominant assumption, also made elsewhere about women workers in general (Lowe, 1982: 11–15), that they are economically dependent on the household, not on the workplace.

Such assumptions do not merely predetermine intellectual discourse; more directly, they inform the methods of creating and organizing accounts of the world. Dorothy Smith identifies them as ideological practices or procedures – methods of reasoning that 'confine us to the conceptual level, suppressing the presence and workings of the underlying relations they express.' Smith's analytical structures of 'ideologies of expression, evaluation, and theory, and the ideologies of organized action' expose the argument of women's incremental participation in academe:[18] 'The forms of thought and images we use do not arise directly or spontaneously out of people's everyday lived relationships. Rather, they are the product of the work of specialists occupying influential positions in the ideological apparatus (the educational system, communication, etc.). Our culture ... is manufactured' (Smith, 1990: 37, 19).

Women have been excluded from the work of producing the forms of thought and the images and symbols in which thought is expressed and ordered (Smith, 1990: 18). Smith argues: 'The closer the positions come to policy-making or innovation in ideological forms, the smaller the proportion of women ... The closer the ideological forms are to the conceptual and symbolic forms in which power is exercised, the less likely women are to be found in the relevant professional educational structures' (Smith, 1975: 362). Knowledge creation and innovation in scientific enquiry, in originating critical concepts, and in the organizing action of commerce and law shape dominant ideologies and power relations in society. In contrast, ideologies of expression and theory as represented in the arts, education, nursing, and other health studies, suggest training and distribution of forms of thought that originate elsewhere.

Work

In the Canadian economy as a whole, feminization of part-time workers has continued speedily in the 1980s and 1990s with the rapid increase in proportion of part-time to full-time jobs. From 1989 to 1998 part-time jobs increased by 24.4 per cent but full-time jobs increased by only 8 per cent. It seems to be a long-term trend affecting both youth and adult women. Examination of the current age and gender profile of all Canadian workers shows that, of the youth (age 18–24), 57.2 per cent are female and, of the adults (age 25 or older), 76.3 per cent are women working part time (Statistics Canada, 1999c). Statistics Canada's classification of women 'voluntary' part-time workers (70.3 per cent versus men 56.3 per cent) may indicate the reasons for their working in this way, but it does not acknowledge why they must do so. If the existing system could accommodate and transform itself to meet women's requirements as they enter the workforce – for example, allow full child care or relief from other so-called women's work both at home or in the labour force – perhaps a truer picture of involuntary part-timers could emerge.

Women themselves may wish to work part time in jobs that are conducive to their roles as a spouse or as a mother. Looking at women's reasons for working part time, we find that there are many strikingly gender-specific reasons for, and therefore differences between, the choices of men and women, and these choices rarely involve the status of voluntary career or job. Some women have left a full-time academic job as a 'trailing spouse' (6 per cent versus men 2 per cent). Most prefer a flexible work schedule (70 per cent versus men 49 per cent.) Despite the social conditions that deter them, women Contemporaries are as strongly inclined as men, or even slightly more inclined (77 per cent versus men 71 per cent), to pursue teaching and research as their main career, and they therefore regard part-time academic work merely as a foot in the door (see table 3.2). Obviously, their career paths are different. A third of the women, in contrast to very few men (10 per cent), report that they teach part time because they need extra time to raise their families. Although they cannot accommodate a full-time job at present, many (women 80 per cent versus men 69 per cent) would definitely want one in the future. Most women Contemporaries report that, if they were asked to choose again, they would still pick their current discipline (see table 3.2).

Many of the above themes are illustrated by women Contemporaries' additional comments on their career interests and life situations: 'Unfortunately financial restraints imposed by the inadequate funding from the government ripples down to affect the lives of people. Being a single parent with a sparse income may have limited my ambitions to pursue my master's and beyond, but it has not crippled my desire to remain in academe, and find my way through my chosen path. I enjoy teaching and will surely continue to proceed with my education, despite financial constraints.' Another woman with family and child-care responsibilities states: 'Part-time teaching exactly suits my needs at this time in my life. I have not yet decided if I will pursue a full-time academic career if offered a position now. But, I get the feeling that if I do not actively seek academics full-time, and accept it if one were available, I will soon no longer be able to work part-time and remain in academe.'

If a full-time position became available elsewhere, would women move to another city? A third of the women (34 per cent versus men 49 per cent) are ready to do so. This is particularly significant for women part-time workers who are trapped in social and familial obligations; it also perhaps reaffirms their interest in and commitment to, an academic career. A positive experience was narrated by a woman part-timer: 'Although it is difficult for us to move to a different city now that my husband has found a good job, we will still consider moving

TABLE 3.2
Career interests of Contemporaries, by gender and education

Contemporary part-timers say that they teach part-time %	Total %	Sex %		Degrees held %		
		Men	Women	<Master's	Master's>	Doctorate
Because teaching and research is their career, although they have no full-time academic position	73.9	70.7**	76.8**	57.6	72.2	87.4
But they would move to another city for a full-time academic job	40.8	48.8	34.4	24.5	42.4	49.6
But they would accept full time even if it meant a drop in income	39.1	39.5 (n.s.)	38.6 (n.s.)	24.2	40.5	48.0
Because they need time to raise family	22.3	9.6	32.5	32.0	22.3	16.0
Because they have no time for full-time job at present	28.2	20.2	34.7	47.6	27.5	20.1
To supplement their income	39.3	39.1	39.2	46.7	39.9	32.8
Because the teaching is related to other part-time professional interests.	85.4	82.2	88.0	90.7	87.6	77.8
But they would consider full-time academic job in the future (if they don't get it now)	75.2	68.8	79.7	73.4*	78.4*	70.4
If starting over again, they would still choose academic career	83.3	81.1*	85.3*	83.1 (n.s.)	84.7 (n.s.)	81.9 (n.s.)
If starting over again, they would still pursue present discipline	91.3	91.6 (n.s.)	91.0 (n.s.)	91.9 (n.s.)	92.2 (n.s.)	89.2 (n.s.)
Total no.	1,422	600	822	237	766	419

Notes: Significance: $p =$ *<.05; **<.01; ***<.001. All are significant at $p =$ ***<.001 unless otherwise indicated. (n.s.): not significant. 'No' response constitutes the balance of 100% in each cell.   Source: See table 3.1.

the family if I am offered a full-time teaching position. My husband is in a field where he could perhaps easily find another position in the job market. He encourages me to apply to various universities, even abroad, so that I will not get stuck in part-time teaching.' In reality, situations are not often so clear-cut and sanguine. A common response is exemplified by one woman: 'My husband has a higher-level technical job in [this city] but I could only get a part-time job in [one of the universities]. If he moves, he will lose all he has built up here as network in his field ... his business contacts and experience will also suffer if we move. Yet I would like to commute if a full-time position becomes available in a nearby city.' Many single women part-timers especially are quite sensitive to child-care problems that they would encounter if they lost the support of their extended family and had to relocate in order to secure a full-time position. Personal and familial stress increases if couples desiring academic careers are relocated apart from each other or from the extended family of origin whose support they have depended on (Norrel and Norrel, 1996).

Working Part Time?

Women, like men, may have several simultaneous part-time jobs, in order to make a living. Less than a third of women part-timers have held or are now holding a full-time non-academic position. Men are nearly 1.5 times more likely than women to have a full-time non-academic job. As we saw above, these women carry a workload that could hardly be called 'part time'. Although women are a majority (55 per cent versus men 46 per cent) among all part-timers who work in only one university (49 per cent), many teach several courses, which could add up to more than a full-time load. Also, more women (23 per cent versus men 20 per cent) are among the (21 per cent) 'Freeway Fliers' teaching in multiple universities (see chapter 2, n.11). Among a third of all part-timers who work part time in both academic and non-academic worlds, 5 per cent more are women (36 per cent versus men 31 per cent).

If many women are working harder piecing together several part-time jobs, then why do they not work full rather than part time? We may find some answers in their reasons for teaching part time (table 3.3). Women invoke family responsibilities to explain their working part time, whereas men assign professional priorities. Most women (70 per cent versus men 49 per cent) value flexibility in the work schedule,

TABLE 3.3
Reasons for teaching part time: women versus men

I teach part-time because		(N: 1194) Men	(N: 1014) Women	
I get personal satisfaction from teaching.	Important Not important	94.4 5.6	96.5 3.5	$p < .05$ $x^2 = 5.3$ odds ratio for women = 1.34
I'd like to enhance my professional reputation.	Important Not important	60.9 39.1	65.5 34.5	$p < .05$ $x^2 = 4.7$ odds ratio for women = 1.12
I'd like to acquire professional experience for a teaching career.	Important Not important	51.2 48.8	59.5 40.5	$p < .01$ $x^2 = 12.9$ odds ratio for women = 1.20
I'd like to acquire professional experience for a career other than teaching.	Important Not important	30.4 69.6	39.9 60.1	$p < .01$ $x^2 = 16.0$ odds ratio for women = 1.26
It provides me income.	Important Not important	67.8 32.2	76.7 23.3	$p < .01$ $x^2 = 20.8$ odds ratio for women = 1.29
I enjoy contact with students.	Important Not important	93.3 6.7	97.3 2.7	$p < .01$ $x^2 = 17.9$ odds ratio for women = 1.81
I enjoy contact with other faculty members.	Important Not important	56.7 43.3	66.3 33.7	$p < .01$ $x^2 = 19.6$ odds ratio for women = 1.26
I need to keep up with knowledge and new developments in my field.	Important Not important	78.4 21.6	87.7 12.3	$p < .01$ $x^2 = 30.9$ odds ratio for women = 1.49
It is difficult to find a full-time academic job.	Important Not important	48.2 51.8	60.1 39.9	$p < .01$ $x^2 = 18.8$ odds ratio for women = 1.29
I prefer flexibility in my work schedule.	Important Not important	49.3 50.7	70.4 29.6	$p < .01$ $x^2 = 77.1$ odds ratio for women = 1.62

Source: See table 3.1.

while over 60 per cent of men emphasize money, personal satisfaction, or professional interests – primarily the complementary nature of their non-academic work that enhances their professional reputation. Analogously, women full-timers' emphasis on family needs and job attrac-

FIGURE 3.2
Job status and job search of part-timers, 1991–2

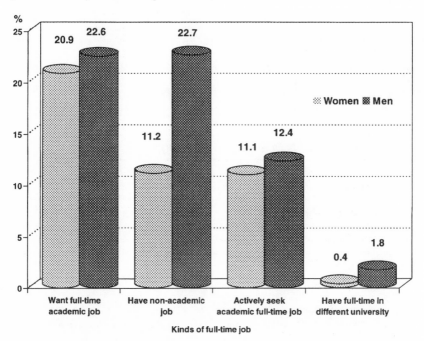

Source: Rajagopal, Part-Time Faculty Survey (1991–2)

tiveness is reiterated in research on women faculty in Canadian universities. In all such studies, recruitment and retention of female faculty are major concerns, and it is evident that these women depend fully on a university climate that is favourable to women. Universities with a 'chilly climate' do not attract women or retain them for long. Women who rejected faculty positions focused on the unattractiveness of the job offer and needs of family members, while men looked at the academic reputation of the department and family needs, including dual-career relationships (Teevan, Pepper, and Pellizzari: 1992).

More women say that they work part time because they could not find full-time academic work (60 per cent), but a majority of men (52 per cent) do not consider this reason. More men are Classics, and their part-time academic earnings supplement the income from their full-time non-academic jobs (figure 3.2). Women (20 per cent versus men 9

TABLE 3.4
Part-timers' teaching, course level and load: women versus men

Yearly load in past five years	(N: 1,155) Men %	(N: 984) Women %	
One half course or less	13.4	12.7	$p < .05$
One course but less than two courses	35.7	29.0	$x^2 = 14.28$
Two courses but less than three courses	24.2	25.7	
Three courses or more	26.8	32.6	

TABLE 3.4a
Part-timers' teaching, graduate courses: women versus men

Teaching graduate courses?	(N: 449) Men %	(N: 356) Women %	
All of my courses are graduate courses	17.1	10.7	$p < .01$
Some of my courses are graduate courses	23.4	20.2	$x^2 = 9.62$
None of my courses are graduate courses	59.5	69.1	

Source: See table 3.1.

per cent) are twice as likely to be dependent on academic part-time work for their sole income or the greater portion of it. As a result, most women indeed carry a heavier course load than men do. A woman Contemporary sums up part-timers' teaching contributions: 'Most of us are part-time in name only; many of us teach more than a standard full-time course load, both in [my] ... Department and in other departments ... of the university. We enrich the Department with skills acquired in teaching in other areas, such as the Writing Workshop, Social Sciences and Humanities. The high volume of teaching [forgoing research time] we do, of course, puts us at a great disadvantage as competitors for full-time appointments. We are in a double-bind position.' A third of the women part-timers (33 per cent versus men 27) teach three or more courses (table 3.4). A quarter of women also teach two or more courses. The workload and, even more, the routinization of their work are quite obvious. Most women (69 per cent versus men 60 per cent) are hired to teach only at undergraduate levels. Fewer women (31 per cent versus men 41 per cent) teach graduate courses, which generally are smaller, more specialized, and central to their discipline and intellectual interests. They also teach more courses than men do in every venue: on universities' main campuses, at off-campus locations, as well as through television. They teach in the autumn session as well as the summer session, and during days or evenings. Although a majority of women (53 per cent versus men 60) consider their course loads adequate, a third of them (37 per cent versus men 32 per cent) wish to teach more courses.

Three Contemporary women describe workload and pay anomalies: 'I work full time [in workload], am responsible for more students than some of the so called salaried full-time faculty, and yet I am paid sessional [part-timer] wages.' And, 'I am a part time faculty member ... yet the teaching, research and administrative load more than equals one full time position. [I perform] these duties and responsibilities ... according to the expectations of my profession and role at a major research university.' 'The part-time designation is problematic. I, like many of my [part-time] ... colleagues teach a higher course load than full-time faculty ... as well as administer a minor program ... thus I am employed more than full-time hours.' A woman Contemporary elaborates: 'My university tends to exploit the spouses of faculty members (low pay, large classes, no decision making power but great responsibility) because it is difficult to commute to other universities for employment. The university makes us feel that they are doing us a favour in giving us a job but without part-time faculty the whole system would crumble. We give fine service and get no credit. Many part-timers have PhDs, but are given the respect of graduate T.A.s. The whole system stinks.'

Studies on U.S. universities show that teaching duties in departments are distributed disproportionately, overloading women with teaching, which leaves them less time for research (Park, 1996; NCES, 1988). For the heavy workload that they carry, women are inadequately compensated. Annual surveys in U.S. universities show little change in the disparity between the earnings of men and women over the years. Men earn more at every rank, and the pay differential is clearly the highest at the levels of full professor and assistant professor and is not comparable to part-timers' lowest pay.

In terms of part-timers' employment histories, more women have worked only part time (in their previous four jobs), whereas more men have moved into full time work. It appears that many women (68 per cent versus men 42) who currently teach part time have not been able to make the transition to other full-time jobs, while many men have begun their careers as part-timers in various jobs but have moved on to other full-time positions. This difference is not surprising, because men are considered breadwinners and are therefore expected to move to full-time jobs; they are generally absorbed faster into the full-time workforce. Further, a review of part-timers' previous five jobs shows that women have moved to higher education from other sectors, while men have gone to jobs elsewhere. With the shrinking of the academic job market, more men have left it to find full-time work elsewhere. Although both sexes have made some zigzag moves in and out of higher education, women's overwhelming presence as academic part-timers is indisputable.

Research

A woman Contemporary sums up part-timers' academic and scholarly contributions: 'The part-time faculty members ... bring with them a substantial body of experience and expertise. Many of us have doctoral degrees and are active scholars – to the extent that our "part-time" schedules permit. We participate in and organize conferences, contribute articles and reviews, and vet papers for scholarly journals.' My survey shows that level of education, more than gender, predicts women's research productivity. Heavier family responsibilities, however, often related to gender roles, surely limit the time available to them to earn a higher degree or to perform research. Many women clearly blame lack of time or of funding, or family constraints that turn them into trailing spouses for interruptions in their careers, yet women are slowly catching up to men's record of published research. In publications during their whole careers, women lag in writing scholarly books (21 per cent versus men 32 per cent), but in recent years, they have narrowed the gap by 5 percentage points (20 per cent versus men 26 per cent). In refereed articles, the record of publication of women (59 per cent versus men 62 per cent) in the previous five years is almost on a par with that of men, although over their whole careers we see a differential of 8 per cent in favour of men (figure 3.3). In recent years, women part-timers with a master's degree have published more scholarly articles or chapters in books that they have edited than have men with similar qualifications. Therefore, research does not seem to be exclusively a male preserve among part-timers. The existing differences in productivity may relate more to women part-timers' late entrance as academic workers or to their need for time to improve their qualifications. A mature woman Contemporary narrates her life and academic pursuits:

FIGURE 3.3

Percentage of women and men part-timers with scholarly publications

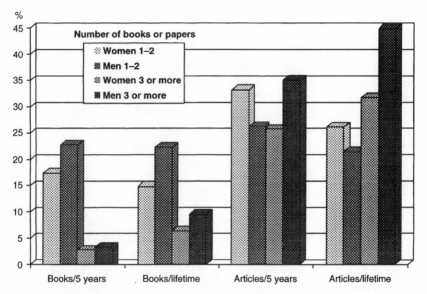

Source: See figure 3.2.

'I returned to university as a mature student, with 6 children ranging in age from 5–16 years of age. I graduated with a PhD in 1986. When I began my studies, employment prospects were reasonably bright. As both universities approached me while I was a graduate student, offering part-time teaching, I didn't even have to apply for a position. Employment opportunities were declining, however, before I had completed my studies. As I went through the last harrowing months of a difficult dissertation, I wasn't sure why I was even bothering to complete the degree. But I couldn't quit, leaving it unfinished ... [Now] prospects for employment and further research have been frustrating.'

Difficulties of bridging the demands of a full-time academic career and of having children and raising a family are described by many part-timers in my survey. Finkel and Olswang's (1996) study echoes their thoughts: half of the women full-timers who have no children and teach in a large U.S. public university have decided to remain childless because they perceive that having a family would take too much time away from the research and publication required to obtain tenure or to continue to fulfil academic expectations. A third of the women (34 per cent) have postponed motherhood, and some (13 per cent) perceive the demands of their career as precluding children. Women part-timers in my survey acknowledge the same conflict: 'The degree to which I am content to be a ... [part-timer] is greatly influenced by the fact that my career has had to [be] *secondary* to that of my husband, and I still do not feel that I can make a heavier commitment in the foreseeable future. I find it very difficult to answer what if questions.' Stories of successful women full-timers show their extraordinary efforts to straddle the two worlds (Cyr and Horner Reich, 1996). A woman part-timer acknowledges similar obstacles: 'My employment prospects are hampered by the need for my family to remain in [this city] where my husband is employed.'

Many women part-timers confront gender biases and other non-academic and irrational barriers: 'Reasons for my failure to obtain a regular faculty appointment after 2 years post-doctoral work and with publications and strong references: 1970s: (1) paucity of academic jobs; (2) discrimination against hiring women, particularly if married. (Men told me this after my being rated 2nd on short lists for jobs at their universities); (3) policies against hiring *couples* as regular faculty members. 1980s: Why pay more for a good thing (i.e., part-time Sessional lecturer acknowledged to be as competent as any regular faculty member) that the department already has [achieved by hiring the spouse].' Universities have "two for one" deal when they hire a male spouse or partner full-time. The female spouse at home works in another dimension of a "double ghetto." For the university, she helps the accrual of value both from her unpaid domestic work and from her academic part-time work. She is the housekeeper and caregiver for the family, a role that is often forgotten in the calculations of material productivity. This is a reality, even for competitively qualified career women academics: 'I have direct experience with [gender and spousal biases] being told that I was a top choice for a term position but the other candidate was a male whose partner was not employed. He got the job. I think women who are known to have an employed partner may be seen as "available" and "only needing" part-time status.'

A woman may encounter a disastrous combination of marriage and expectations of a career or job in the same discipline as that of her spouse or partner: 'I am employed in the same department as my husband who is a full-time faculty member. Part-time positions are at the discretion of the Head of the Department. Should my husband become head this would probably prevent me from being hired for (and accepting) a part-time position!' Phyllis Rose writes: 'The world does not take kindly to a successful collaboration between a married couple' (1984: 132). Studies have shown that marriage could affect a woman's publishing productivity (Fox and Faver, 1985), while it has little effect on that of a man, but positive changes seem to be occurring. Although presence of children might be expected to reduce women's scholarship and publications, studies have reported significant positive effects of having children (Kyvik, 1990; Toren, 1991). In her study of full-timers and women's research productivity, Creamer (1996) points out that women themselves understate the barriers of marriage and family responsibilities. Toren (1991) attributes this phenomenon to their accepting these responsibilities as matters of fact rather than look to other arrangements to share them. Even if women with family responsibilities persevere in doing research, however, commentators often assume that men are principal researchers in collaborations between couples, because they see women with domestic responsibilities as less likely to have taken on research (Ward and Grant, 1996). Women part-timers' comments above illustrate many of these themes.

Many women part-timers (42 per cent) would like to spend more time on research than they (79 per cent) now do – an average of ten hours per week:

> While university departments generally claim to give equal weight to teaching and publication in their hiring decisions, clearly, publication is the privileged term in this binary opposition. As candidates for full-time positions, we are evaluated primarily on our publication records; as candidates for part-time positions, we are evaluated on our seniority as teachers. In order to earn seniority, not to mention make a living, we must do as much teaching as we can, and the time and energy we have available to devote to the scholarly activities we would like to pursue is consequently extremely limited. As members of the profession, then, we face serious constraints in our pursuit of the kind of accomplishment – publication – that is valued, while at the same time, we are valued for the teaching skills that the profession devalues. Nevertheless, we continue to teach, because we are committed to the academy and to our students.

Besides the difficulty in finding time for research, women part-timers confront other barriers. Many (40 per cent versus men 32 per cent) realize that full-timers' support is often necessary if they are to obtain the few available research grants. These women (57 per cent versus men 47 per cent) don't see any opportunity for collaborative research with full-timers. Part-timers in general (women 57 per cent versus men 51 per cent) find that full-timers show little interest in mentoring their careers or in recognizing their (women 62 per cent versus men 56 per cent) research activities in departmental reports. Part-timers (women 60 per cent versus men 57 per cent) are also quite frustrated because their universities provide little or no research funding and do not accord any recognition for part-timers' work. A woman Contemporary could do nothing right to earn her university's attention: 'The conditions related to the esteem and recognition of my work – recognized as excellent by my students – are lousy on the part of the administration at my university.' Two other women Contemporaries write:

> The fact that one must continue all research on one's own time and the fact that this research is unrecognized and unrewarded adds to the growing cynicism of part-timers toward the universities that employ them. It is a terrible double standard that full-time faculty are highly rewarded for research while it is totally ignored for part-timers.

> Part time teaching is becoming very onerous and unrewarding due to the increasing class sizes and lack of support and resources for doing a good job. Part-timers become very demoralized as this factory approach to education is intensified. Instead of gaining expertise and experience over time one feels increasingly ghettoized and alienated from one's work. The insecurity of part-time contracts also puts a terrible strain on those who live entirely off of these earnings. We must work toward instituting a disincentive for universities to continue expanding the part-time pool of labour at the expense of full-time jobs.

Women part-timers' teaching and research areas do not necessarily converge as those of full-timers do. Part-timers' research may be in their own field of specialization, while their teaching (as allocated by departments) might be in other areas not filled by full-timers. A woman Contemporary comments: 'Long-term part-time workers are mainly female and suffer from self-esteem problems. I often feel very schizophrenic because I ... [must] do research in one area (Classical studies) but teach in another (Writing).'

These barriers, however, do not easily discourage women part-timers. Indeed, more women than men apply for (women 45 per cent versus men 34 per cent) and receive (women 54 per cent versus men 41 per cent) funding to attend conferences. More women apply for (22 per cent versus men 14 per cent) and receive (women 26 per cent versus men 18 per cent) funding for organizing academic events or lecture series (see table 2.6). More women (57 per cent versus men 48 per cent) take courses to improve their qualifications and wish to collaborate in research with full-timers (women 23 per cent versus men 17 per cent). More women (39 per cent versus men 33 per cent) train or want to improve their research skills, and more women (women 68 per cent versus men 56 per cent) would like to improve their teaching skills. More women (60 per cent versus men 50 per cent) pursue or plan for higher studies. Yet a majority of all part-timers complain about universities' lack of commitment to their career development, financial support (women 61 per cent and men 59 per cent), and time release (women and men 68 per cent). One response illustrates this point: 'I am interested in returning to do a doctorate but am currently unable [to do so] because of distance ... and I have young children making commuting difficult. One of the biggest difficulties I see about [being part time] is the lack of support for career development (finances for conferences and research) and [lack of] time because we carry such heavy workload to make a reasonable income.'

Place and Influence

Decision-Making

All part-timers, particularly women, feel marginalized in academic decision-making. Two-thirds of all part-timers believe that informal personal influence has more clout than decisions in councils or unions. Most part-timers (90 per cent women and 86 per cent men) have little say and fewer choices than full-timers in the selection of courses or in choosing their (77 per cent women and 74 per cent men) own teaching times. Women, however, feel slightly more aggrieved about lack of power in making decisions that affect their work. A woman Contemporary comments on the exclusion of part-timers: 'Many of us would like to be able to participate more actively in department affairs. Although we are entitled to attend department meetings, many of us do not, because we have no vote and are not eligible to sit on department committees ... Since full time faculty [alone] do not constitute ...

TABLE 3.5
Part-timers' power and participation in decision-making: women versus men

		(N: 1,143) Men %	(N: 967) Women %	
Do you participate in departmental meetings?	Yes	32.5	37.6	p <.05
	No	67.5	62.4	x^2 = 6.20
To what extent can part-timers affect their academic work via part-time faculty union or association?	Effective	75.4	81.4	p <.05
	Not effective	24.6	18.6	x^2 = 5.40

How much influence do part-timers have over the following decision in your department or academic unit?

		(N: 925) Men	(N: 804) Women	
Part-timers' choice of courses to teach	Same as full-timers	14.5	9.9	
	Less than full-timers	45.5	40.8	p <.01
	Little or none	40.0	49.3	x^2 = 17.15
Part-timers' determining their own teaching schedule	Same as full-timers	26.5	23.3	
	Less than full-timers	37.6	33.1	p <.01
	Little or none	35.9	43.7	x^2 = 10.85

Source: See table 3.1.

the department, this is an extremely imperfect form of democracy ... We are accorded at best the status of marginal members of the department. While our presence and even our voices may be tolerated at Department meetings, we have no real standing in the department and our interests seem to be of little interest to full-time faculty ... Is this a way of excluding us from any share in the Department's decision-making power? ... Why are we not ... allowed to participate in the making of decisions that affect our professional lives?'

More women (51 per cent) than men (45 per cent) know the formal rules of eligibility. As most of them feel alienated from the process, they do not go to these meetings (62 per cent versus men 68 per cent), much less participate in the discussions (table 3.5). Most women (74 per cent versus men 68 per cent) feel that they have no say in their work lives because full-timers hold all the powers of hiring, firing, or rehiring of part-timers. Therefore, they must rely on their unions or associations to defend and protect their rights. Among the collectively organized part-timers, slightly more women (81 per cent versus men 75 per cent) seem to be confident about their union's voice in the university and its influence on decisions affecting their jobs.

Women keenly aspire to having a say in the decisions that shape academe, particularly in those regarding faculty hiring, teaching, and salaries. They (67 per cent versus men 61 per cent) wish for a share of decision-making power over the hiring or rehiring of part-timers. They would also like to have the same influence vis-à-vis hiring of new full-timers (women 55 versus men 44 per cent) and over full-timers' tenure and promotion (women 53 per cent versus men 44 per cent). Most part-timers (women 78 per cent and men 72 per cent) want the power to negotiate their own salary. Among part-timers, women more keenly express their belief that part-timers should have control over their own teaching; they would like to have more autonomy in choosing the courses that they teach (women 72 per cent versus men 62 per cent) and in setting up their own teaching schedules (women 65 per cent versus men 54 per cent). One area of exception is decisions about the content of the courses that they teach, over which a majority of part-timers (women 54 per cent versus men 60 per cent) seem to be quite satisfied with their current levels of control and autonomy (table 3.6). Part-timers also resent the absence of democratic decision-making on issues such as their job security and academic work. Their frustrations reduce their motivation to do scholarly research: 'I have lost confidence in my ability to write scholarly papers, partly because of my marginal position and insecurity. All of my research is directed toward preparing my classes and improving my teaching. There are no rewards for good teaching for [part-time] sessional instructors.'

Marginalization

Part-timers' sense of marginality and powerlessness seems to stem from their own perceptions about how full-timers treat them (table 3.7). They know that collegiality does not extend to part-timers, whether Classics or Contemporaries. They are treated always as limited-scope, teaching adjuncts. A majority of women (59 per cent

TABLE 3.6
Part-timers' control over academic work: areas and levels

Would you prefer that the influence of part-time faculty in the following areas:		(N: 961) Men %	(N: 878) Women %	
Part-timers' choice of courses to teach	Be more?	62.0	71.5	$p < .01$
	Stay the same?	37.0	28.4	$x^2 = 21.74$
	Be less?	1.0	0.1	
Part-timers' control of course content	Be more?	39.3	45.8	$p < .01$
	Stay the same?	59.7	54.0	$x^2 = 11.01$
	Be less?	0.9	0.2	
Part-timers' determining their own teaching schedule	Be more?	53.9	64.9	$p < .01$
	Stay the same?	45.1	34.6	$x^2 = 22.30$
	Be less?	1.0	0.5	
The hiring or rehiring of part-time faculty	Be more?	61.1	66.6	$p < .05$
	Stay the same?	37.2	32.8	$x^2 = 7.72$
	Be less?	1.7	0.6	
The hiring of full-time faculty	Be more?	43.9	54.5	$p < .01$
	Stay the same?	54.3	43.2	$x^2 = 15.21$
	Be less?	1.9	2.4	
Tenure and promotion of full-time faculty	Be more?	43.9	53.3	$p < .01$
	Stay the same?	54.1	45.0	$x^2 = 10.70$
	Be less?	2.1	1.7	
Negotiating the part-time faculty salary rate	Be more?	71.5	77.5	$p < .05$
	Stay the same?	28.0	22.2	$x^2 = 8.23$
	Be less?	0.5	0.2	

Source: See table 3.1.

versus men 49 per cent) report that full-timers do not show any collegiality towards them. Part-timers note that they have proved to be a long-term workforce; therefore, they perceive their marginality not only as inequitable but also as a contrived situation that serves the needs of administrative and academic hierarchies. A woman Contemporary suggests that it would benefit the university to see them as an asset rather than as a liability: 'The presence of part-time faculty within the Department and within the University as a whole is not a temporary phenomenon. It is the product of many years of underfunding ... Since part-time faculty are clearly going to continue to be a significant presence within the Department, it would seem wise to adjust departmental policy in order to accommodate [part-timers] and to use our skills to the greatest possible benefit of the Department. We would like to suggest that our presence in the Department should be regarded not as a liability, but as a valuable resource.' Another Contemporary argues for professional self-worth as compensation, even with all the attendant inequalities of part-time status: 'There has to be a way of making people who wish to work 1/2–2/3 time (whether it be due to child raising, retiring, or whatever!), feel like they (can and) are making a valuable academic contribution, and pay them so that this reflects what they are worth. Flex time people usually are less interested in the financial rewards and more interested in self-actualization and putting something back into the system. It is possible to feel equally responsible to family and career and still be considered a valuable contributor.' A woman Contemporary quotes from her department's five-year plan to substantiate her belief that part-timers are not prefabricating their marginality to evoke sympathy and that their perception of their poor treatment is not fictitious: 'The [full-timers] should cease to consider our presence in their midst an embarrassment, as it is characterized repeatedly in the Plan. For example, in the section which deals with Material support, [the Plan reads:] 'The embarrassing disproportion of ... course directorships currently staffed by part-time appointments'. Since objections were raised to the derogatory terms in which an earlier version of the Plan represented part-time faculty, some amendments have been made; however, many of the derogatory implications remain ... There is a perception among us that some full-time faculty members assume that because we are part-time, we are inadequately qualified.'

Academe is no 'ivory tower', particularly for women part-timers. Universities' ad hoc policies of hiring part-timers, from session to session or from year to year, heighten awareness of the university's willingness to compromise academic quality. Most women (70 per cent versus 58 per cent) perceive that universities ignore the need to plan carefully, especially given financial constraints, in order not to neglect academic quality. While class sizes and teaching loads are increasing and new tenure-track positions are declining, universities should rethink their definition of 'regular faculty' and plan to fit in part-timers. Despite their marginal position, part-timers demand recognition rather than indifference; but the system does not heed their demand, and many women (61 per cent versus men 53 per cent) regret that their universities consider employment of part-timers a temporary, money-

TABLE 3.7
Part-timers' perceptions of how full-timers treat them

How do most full-timers consider or treat most part-timers in their departments?		(N: 983) Men %	(N: 840) Women %	
As full-time members of the academic collegium	Agree	31.7	23.3	p <.01
	Neutral	19.0	18.1	x^2 = 18.71
	Disagree	49.3	58.7	
As a welcome source of expertise not otherwise available on the faculty	Agree	51.8	41.7	p <.01
	Neutral	20.7	23.1	x^2 = 19.64
	Disagree	27.6	35.2	

Source: See table 3.1.

saving measure. The realities are, however, that part-timers have been in the system far too long to be regarded as such. Women part-timers see that their personal teaching load has increased over the past five years, and all part-timers find an increase in their class sizes. Women, more so than men, believe that they are still being treated simply as stopgap tools. They suspect that this is one of the ways in which the university maintains full-timers' salaries and working conditions and assigns them a more reasonable course load or class size than finances would otherwise allow.

Part-timers resent this marginalization and express their resistance in rising grievances against university authorities. During five years (preceding the survey), two-thirds of women (67 per cent versus men 50) report laying more grievances against the administration, and a third of them (women 34 per cent versus men 28 per cent) also acknowledge more grievances against full-timers. Most part-timers see that, given increasing teaching loads, it is ideological, not pragmatic, to relegate teaching to the background. This ideological construct clearly permeates the faculty hierarchy. Women warn that such a dichotomy and the weighting of research over teaching hurt academic quality and student interests.

Segmentation

Beyond the gender divide, status segmentation between women part-timers and full-timers is central to their experience within academe.

Although most academic women are aware of the dominant interests of male full-timers and administrators, their own interests are segmented by status. Few opportunities exist for a strong common bond to emerge among women full- and part-time workers marginalized by gender. A woman part-timer observes: 'There is so little interaction with other faculty' that it is difficult to develop common concerns. Three themes could illustrate this segmentation: divided influence, divided collectivity, and divided collegium.

DIVIDED INFLUENCE

Women full-timers clearly note that power is drifting away from the male-dominated full-time faculty to the male-dominated administration. As a part of this scenario, most full-timers consider part-timers to be marginalized by the hierarchy. On all department-level decisions relating to part-timers, such as hiring and salary negotiations, in which the professoriate has autonomy, full-timers know that part-timers have little influence. They are also aware that part-timers have no say in the selection of courses to teach or power to determine their own teaching schedule. Even those full-time women who have been 'insiders' and know from their own experience that part-time women are isolated, however, do not make an effort to establish academic or personal links with part-time women. Although numbers mean strength, women full-timers so far have not taken the initiative to improve their influence for gender equity in the university through collaborative efforts. A Contemporary sums up the situation: 'We, as part-time people, are very much at the mercy of administration. We have little control over staffing, no involvement with full time faculty and no opportunity to access faculty-level professional development. As a graduate student and as a faculty member I felt the impact of an extremely "political" workplace and a total absence of academic freedom.'

DIVIDED COLLECTIVITY

Many women full-timers have experienced as contractees (I call them 'Insiders'), either as part-timers or as LTFTs, the impact of gender on their careers. The career paths of a majority of women have been very different from those of men. Many women began their career as part-timers (56 per cent versus men 39 per cent) and as LTFTs (46 per cent versus men 35 per cent). Although both women and men full-timers (men 50 per cent versus women 43 per cent) acknowledge an increase in the power and influence of their own unions, certainly they do not believe that part-timers' unions have followed suit. Nor do they (women 70 per cent versus men 67 per cent) see part-timers' unions as powerful enough to disrupt academic quality. A small minority of full-timers find that their union has made part-timers' voices heard in the university (men 28 versus women 32 per cent) or has improved their working conditions (men 31 per cent versus women 37 per cent). Perhaps because many women full-timers are Insiders and have first-hand experience, more women than men recognize that unions have slightly improved part-timers' lives. They acknowledge that the unions have helped to increase part-timers' pay (women 52 per cent versus men 43 per cent) and improve their rights and job security by reducing departmental discretion in hiring them (men 32 per cent versus women 44 per cent). Full-timers' and part-timers' unions have conflicting interests. The aim of part-timers is to achieve full-timers rights and status, while full-timers' guard their powers as gatekeepers of the collegium.

DIVIDED COLLEGIUM

The ideal of collegiality in decision-making is central to egalitarian ideals espoused by the professoriate. On the issue of extending some elements of it to part-timers, however, most full-timers (women 68 per cent versus men 74 per cent) clearly reject the idea. They resist equal representation for part-timers in decision-making bodies. A part-timer points out the divide between full-timers and part-timers: 'As part-timers, we often speak about being "used and abused," and a number of us are women ... [On] the information I need about procedure, deadlines, whom to contact, my full-time colleagues are quite useless. Most of all, I am frustrated and even resentful that ideas and suggestions I have, make no impression on my full-time colleagues, but that is a problem not of the departments or the universities making, rather, it is because of their tenured complacency.' Although most full-timers (women 76 per cent versus men 68 per cent) agree that part-timers have a legitimate place in the university, they do not want them in their collegium. Whereas more full-time men (44 per cent versus women 33 per cent) would rather have a separate stream for part-timers, almost half of women (47 per cent versus men 35 per cent) oppose this split and the restrictions on membership. Although most full-timers, both men and women, would reserve decision-making to full-timers, considerably more men (41 per cent versus women 27 per cent) feel strongly that decision-making is their exclusive prerogative. Many men full-timers (45 per cent) seem to have assumed the gatekeeper's role in rejecting the idea that the university has any obligation to offer full-time positions to academically committed long-serving part-timers, whereas a majority of women (53 per cent) welcome it. More full-time women (84 per cent versus men 75 per cent) also would privilege part-timers with a rank and salary structure by replacing the existing flat rank and rate. These differences between women and men full-timers are based not only on gender but also on their different career paths.

A majority of women full-timers are more inclusive and would like to advance long-serving part-timers to full-time positions because they themselves experience the impact of the power structure. Thus, on some issues full-time women are more sensitive to the plight of women part-timers. A woman full-timer acknowledges the dilemmas facing them: 'In our faculty part-time positions are frequently filled by women with young children. Their long-term careers are on hold and this is their way of keeping current. Most are not fully qualified, have potential but are not highly motivated [to advance their degrees, since they cannot find time to continue their studies] while the children are young.' Some women full-timers draw a parallel between the work experiences and career paths of women full-timers and those of male and female part-timers. They warn that the more broadly based concerns of gender, rather than segmentation based on status, elucidate the situation. However, these voices are too few to be heard. A woman LTFT alerts us to the double burden women face: 'Gender is a very central issue here and yet it is not explicit in the questions [the survey has] posed. Women much more often are exploited as part-time faculty ... [If women part-timers] cannot do research because of the heavy teaching requirements ... on top of [family responsibilities], then men are parachuted into the full-time jobs with research time built in.' Ironically, segmentation based more on job status than on gender arises among part-timers themselves, which is the focus of the next chapter.

Chapter Four

Contemporaries and Classics: Segmented Interests

Significantly different profiles of two types of part-timers emerge from my survey. Those who have full-time non-academic jobs I have called 'Classics,' and those who hold mainly academic part-time positions 'Contemporaries' (see chapter 2, p. 68). The two groups have distinct reasons for teaching part time and differing work needs and motivations. Classics and Contemporaries have fundamentally different work, career and decision-making roles within academe. Although both groups are part-timers, most are covered under the same terms and conditions of work, and, where unionized, belong to the same union, they have little in common. Their comments show that they are quite keen on making a clear distinction in their work. A Contemporary notes: 'The greatest concern about "sessionalism," I feel, is the university's inflexibility in recognizing that its Sessionals [part-timers] are not all the same. We may all teach but we do not necessarily feel the same degree of intensity or responsibility – the lawyer or accountant who comes on campus for three hours Tuesday nights and has no office hours has less of a time commitment or a people commitment than do, for example, the Sessionals who teach writing skills in the English department; these folks are here every day for at least 7 hours and often arrange meetings at night as well. Yet the university looks at and treats both Sessionals the same way. There is an injustice here.' A Classic observes: 'There are two categories of part-time faculty. Those who are at the university during the day, are possibly on a full time contract, and therefore have continuing contact with full time faculty and the business of the university. Then there are those of us who work strictly in the evenings and are therefore largely ignored by both the university and the department .Our full time regular employment also imposes limitations on the extent to which we could participate in the university and the department.'

In this chapter I consider, in turn, who the Classics and Contemporary part-timers are, their respective needs and priorities, their work, and their place in academe. The distinction between Classics and Contemporaries is central to our identifying the 'real' part-timers and for grasping their work, interests, and motivations. A logistic regression helps us to identify the factors that differentiate Contemporaries and Classics. The phenomenon of professionals from the non-academic world who drop in to teach one or two courses has been integral to universities since their inception. When universities have needed special expertise to teach new advances in professional and business fields, they have hired non-academic professionals on a part-time basis. Apart from teaching interests that drew them to academe, these professionals have had limited involvement in universities and visited briefly from their varied full-time jobs in non-academic spheres. The contemporary phenomenon of 'part-time only' academics emerged in the 1970s when universities had to manage growing enrolments with shrinking budgets. Increased hiring of Contemporaries continued through the 1980s and 1990s, as universities' financial situations further declined. No specific demarcating policies or rationales emerged either on study areas or on type of teaching positions to which either group was appointed, but the differentiation became inherent in their overall job status. This differentiation could be useful for several reasons. First, their job status – 'full time but non-academic' or 'only part time' – would explain their unique relationships with the university. Second, universities' use of different kinds of part-timers has significantly different implications for policies governing the part-time faculty (Biles and Tuckman, 1986: 10-11; Gappa and Leslie, 1993: 63–4). Finally, an examination of the condition of Contemporaries' marginality in academe may provide insight into their work life and productivity (Scott, 1983: 170–2; Abel, 1984: 225).

In the literature, classifications of part-time faculty have not centred on a dichotomy between Classics and Contemporaries. Part-timer typologies have been based on four demographic or functional criteria: work situations; employment expectations; reasons and motivations for teaching; and preferences and constraints.[1] Contemporaries constitute a much broader category than Howard Tuckman's 'hopeful full-timers,'[2] since they include all those part-timers without a full-time non-academic job, not only the 'Hopefuls.' Nor could we borrow Tuckman's term 'full-mooners' (working full-time elsewhere), because it would cover a broader category than our 'Classics' would allow, which includes only those with non-academic full-time jobs.

In examining the impact of the downturn in the academic labour market – how part-timers' perception of declining numbers of full-time jobs affect their satisfaction level and job commitment – Kuchera and Miller differentiate between two types of adjuncts (1988: 251). One group consists of those who already have, or expect to find, employment outside academe, and the other includes those who wish to find, but are not sure of finding, academic jobs. Gappa and Leslie also differentiate 'professionals' (academic part-timers who have other full-time employment) from 'aspiring academics' (who want participation and rewards equitable to those of full-timers, although their career focus may not necessarily be to teach full time). These authors have emphasized the institutional benefits of recognizing part-timers' contributions in describing part-timers' different motivations and aspirations (1993: 47, 64). Others have examined 'motivations' and job satisfaction in relation to full-time or part-time overall job status (Yang and Zak, 1981; Lundy and Warme, 1990).[3]

No one has attempted an analysis of part-timers' work and career objectives based on job status distinction between Classics and Contemporaries. The distinction becomes significant, given the fact that Contemporaries emerged as the major segment of the part-timers (Rajagopal and Farr, 1992: 319). Fewer academic labour issues have affected career-oriented part-timers as profoundly as labour market fluctuations. Despite their individual achievements, these changes strongly affect their career options (Youn, 1988: 18). As temporary workers, part-timers have no career ladders, tenure, salary progression, promotion opportunities, perks, and benefits (Rajagopal and Farr, 1992: 328; Tuckman and Pickerill, 1988: 109–10). Yet part-timers may continue in academe and foster their careers for personal fulfilment and 'self-actualization' (Leslie, Kellams, and Gunne, 1982: 41–3). Part-timers seem to resolve the inconsistencies between their marginality in the workplace and their career orientation. In *The Theory of Need in Marx* (1976), Agnes Heller identifies a 'new structure of needs' built around activities and human relationships as ends in themselves. Everyday needs for self-realization of the human personality could overcome the constraints of alienating work; if part-timers feel that the academic work life fulfils these needs, fostering their career aspirations could compensate for the marginalizing experiences of part-time work.

Career orientation could be identified as a keen motivation to pursue and derive satisfaction from full- or part-time academic work. To part-timers, it means autonomy in setting objectives, designing methods of achieving them, and attaining goals so set. Some may look keenly for academic full-time positions; some may be freelance academics enjoying the absence of workplace constraints or the demands of a full-time job; some may prefer the virtual anonymity; some may wish to attain professional status in their chosen discipline; and some may find academe convenient for job-sharing (Leslie, Kellams, and Gunne, 1982: 44–5); but all wish to pursue an academic career.

Although part-time teaching does not offer development opportunities or promote autonomy for Contemporaries, it seems to attract them. Despite being considered a 'reserve army of adjuncts' (Scott, 1983: 193), they keep their interest alive in an academic career. My survey data indicate part-timers interested in academic careers among both Contemporaries and Classics. But Contemporaries contain a greater percentage of qualified and trained academics keen on a professorial career. These are, I believe, the 'real' part-time academics.

Who They Are

Contemporaries constitute nearly two-thirds (65.5 per cent) and Classics only a third (34.5 per cent) of part-timers. More than half of U.S. part-timers are Classics. In the U.S. National Survey of Post-Secondary Faculty of 1987 it was reported that of part-timers who constitute 38 per cent of total faculty, 52 per cent had full-time jobs elsewhere (AAUP, 1992: 40). The part-timers' demographic profile, presented in table 4.1, shows that more Contemporaries (27 per cent versus Classics 18 per cent) who are over age 50 are likely to have been trapped in part time. Three-quarters of Classics (76 per cent versus Contemporaries 66 per cent) are in the market-demand years of productivity, age 30 to 49. Slightly fewer Contemporaries (54 per cent versus Classics 61 per cent) have dependent children. More Contemporaries (13 per cent versus Classics 8 per cent) indicate that they were born in non-western countries. Although some Contemporaries have started teaching part time more recently, most have pursued a teaching career for ten years or more. More than a quarter of Contemporaries were hired in the 1990s and half of them in the 1980s. A fifth started teaching before 1980 and had been part-timers for more than ten years when I surveyed them.

TABLE 4.1
Classics and Contemporaries: demographic profile

		Classics %	Contempo-raries %	Total %	Total no.
Sex	Men	68.2	47.0	54.3	1,178
	Women	31.8	53.0	45.7	991
	Total %	100.0	100.0	100.0	2,169
Age, years	<30	5.5	6.9	6.4	139
	<40	37.2	31.7	33.5	726
	<50	38.9	34.6	36.3	787
	50+	18.4	26.8	23.8	516
	Total %	100.0	100.0	100.0	2,169
Family status	Spouse	81.8	79.0	80.2	1,739
(n.s.)	Single	18.2	21.0	19.8	430
	Total %	100.0	100.0	100.0	2,169
Dependent	0	39.2	46.1	43.7	948
children	1 +	60.8	53.9	56.3	1,221
	Total %	100.0	100.0	100.0	2,169
Birthplace	West	91.7	87.4	88.8	1,926
	Non-West	8.3	12.6	11.2	243
	Total %	100.0	100.0	100.0	2,169
Language	Anglophone	76.4	78.6	77.9	1,690
(n.s.)	Francophone	23.6	21.4	22.1	479
	Total %	100.0	100.0	100.0	2,169
Total %		34.5	65.5	100.0	2,169

Notes: Differences are significant at $p = ***<.001$ unless otherwise indicated. (n.s.): not significant.
Source: Rajagopal, Part-Time Faculty Survey (1991–2)

Contemporaries constitute a major proportion of the part-timers in humanities (80 per cent versus Classics 20.4 per cent) and fine and applied arts (78 per cent versus Classics 22 per cent). More Classics (45.5 per cent versus Contemporaries 54.5 per cent) can be found in the social sciences than in education (34 per cent versus Contemporaries

TABLE 4.2
Classics and Contemporaries: discipline in which they teach

	Classics	Contempo- raries	Total %	Total no.
Faculty/discipline				
Education	33.8	66.1	15.0	325
Fine and applied arts	22.3	77.7	8.6	187
Humanities and related	20.4	79.6	22.1	479
Social sciences	45.5	54.5	35.4	768
Pure and applied sciences	37.8	62.2	18.9	410
Total %	100.0	100.0	100.0	2,169
Start teaching part-time				
Before 1980s	17.0	20.0	18.7	406
1980s	59.0	51.0	53.8	1,167
1990s	24.0	29.0	27.5	596
Total %	100.0	100.0	100.0	2,169
Total %	34.5	65.5	100.0	
Total no.	748	1,421		2,169

Note: Differences are significant at $p = ***<.001$.
Source: See table 4.1.

66 per cent) or in sciences (38 per cent versus Contemporaries 62 per cent) (table 4.2).

More Contemporaries than Classics have a doctorate. Fewer Contemporaries have less than a master's degree, and a quarter are pursuing an advanced degree, of whom 64 per cent (Classics 44 per cent) are working on their doctorates and only 29 per cent (Classics 47 per cent) on their master's degree.[4] In general, Classics seem to be less qualified than Contemporaries. Half of the Classics (51 per cent) have a master's degree, and a quarter (27 per cent) have lower degrees. Fewer Classics have a doctorate (23 per cent versus Contemporaries 29 per cent) or are pursuing one (45 per cent versus Contemporaries 65 per cent). Yet Contemporaries earn far less than Classics. A comparison of average personal and household incomes also identifies contrasting income profiles. Nearly half of Contemporaries earn less than $30,000 in personal income, as opposed to half of Classics, who earn at least twice that income. Most Classics (77 per cent versus Contemporaries 54 per

TABLE 4.2a
Classics and Contemporaries: education and income

		Classics %	Contempo-raries %	Total %	Total no.
Degree held	<Master's	26.8	18.8	21.6	469
	Master's	50.7	52.1	51.6	1,119
	Doctorate	22.5	29.1	26.8	581
	Total %	100.0	100.0	100.0	2,169
Degree actively	<Master's	7.6	6.3	6.5	35
pursued	Master's	47.8	29.2	32.9	162
	Doctorate	44.6	64.6	60.6	286
	Total %	100.0	100.0	100.0	483
Personal income	<$30	12.1	47.6	35.4	767
$'000	<$60	40.8	34.0	36.4	788
	$60+	47.1	18.3	28.3	614
	Total %	100.0	100.0	100.0	2,169
Part-time income $	Mean $	$8,539	$14,531		$12,405

Note: Differences are significant at $p =$ ***<.001.
Source: See table 4.1.

cent) have household incomes $60,000 (table 4.3). Academic part-time income figures clearly show that a majority of Contemporaries are dependent on teaching, primarily in one university, for their personal income. The contrast is quite sharp between them and Classics in their total personal incomes (table 4.3).

Thus, several characteristics differentiate the backgrounds of Contemporaries and Classics. What is the relative importance of the characteristics? Are some of them confounded? For instance, since gender is related to both education and age, it is necessary to determine whether it has an independent effect. Therefore, I found a regression model[5] useful for identifying the factors that differentiate between the two groups. Five variables – gender, educational attainment, place of birth, age, and number of dependent children – were entered as independent variables. The model's overall chi-square turned out to be significant ($p < 0.001$), which allowed me to take other characteristics into account. Male rather than female part-timers are more likely to be Classics than Contemporaries. Contemporaries are more qualified

TABLE 4.3
Classics and Contemporaries: academic part-time income and household income

		Classics %	Contempo-raries %	Total %	Total no.
Part-time	30% or less	88.8	43.1	58.4	1,267
academic income	>30%	11.2	57.0	41.6	902
	%Total %	100.0	100.0	100.0	2,169
Part-time	<50%	27.3	21.0	23.3	505
income from one	>50 to <100%	3.6	10.2	7.9	171
university	100%	69.1	68.7	68.9	1,494
	Total %	100.0	100.0	100.0	2,169
Total personal	$30 or less	12.1	47.6	35.4	767
income	>$30 to $60	40.8	34.0	36.4	788
$'000	$60 +	47.1	18.3	28.3	614
	Total %	100.0	100.0	100.0	2,169
Household income	$30 or less	4.7	15.8	12.0	260
$'000	>$30–$60	18.1	30.4	26.1	566
	$60 +	77.3	53.8	62.0	1,345
	Total %	100.0	100.0	100.0	2,169
Total no.		748	1,421		2,169
Total %		34.5	65.5	100.0	

Note: Differences are significant at $p =$ ***<.001.
Source: See table 4.1.

than Classics, with each level of completed education adding to their chances of being a Contemporary. Classics rather than Contemporaries are more likely to have dependent children. Although Classics were somewhat more likely to have been born in the west, when other variables are taken into account, the relation goes in the opposite direction and is no longer significant. Judging by their betas, gender, education, age, and number of dependent children have similar effects of magnitude (table 4.4).

With respect to age, younger part-timers (under 30) are much more likely to be Classics, while the older (over 50) are more often Contemporaries. Those in the age groups between – 30s and 40s – lean in

TABLE 4.4
Logistic regression of the Classic/Contemporary model using gender, education, birthplace, age, and children

Variable		B	S.E.	Sig
Gender		−.4127	.0474	.00
Education	<Master's	−.4437	.0749	.02
	Master's <doctorate	.1390	.0612	.32
Birthplace		.0486	.0491	.32
Age, years	<30	−.4235	.1331	.00
	30–39	−.0092	.0781	.90
	40–49	.0339	.0789	.67
Number of children		.3804	.0550	.00

−2 log likelihood	2695.324	Goodness of fit	2113.902	N = 2,105
	Chi-square:	df		Significance
Model chi-square	222.825	8		.0000
Improvement	222.825	8		.0000

Source: See table 4.1.

neither direction. This may confirm our supposition above that Contemporaries may have grown older without finding a continuing full-time position. In order that we could look at the interaction of age and education, the regression was rerun to examine the contribution of age and education coefficients to its prediction of who is likely to be a Contemporary and who a Classic. Holding a master's degree, but not a doctorate always increases one's chance of being a Contemporary over other education levels (figure 4.1). The interaction effects are particularly true of the under-30s, where those with doctorates are most likely of all age-related education groups to be Classics. This age and education interaction is significant. It is likely that the experience of academic underemployment among contemporaries with doctorates may have had resonance with younger and newer doctoral graduates (among Classics), who perhaps turned to full-time non-academic jobs. This is particularly true of over a quarter of Classics, who would like to have full-time academic jobs.

Contemporaries' average $14,531 per year income from academic part-time work represents half of their total personal income. That proportion is considerably larger than Classics' 17 per cent, based on their

FIGURE 4.1

Contributions of age and education coefficients to logistic regression prediction of Contemporaries versus Classics

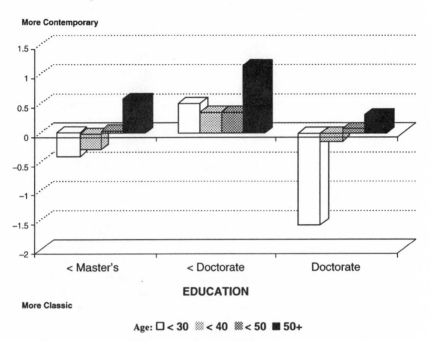

More Contemporary

EDUCATION

More Classic

Age: □ < 30 ▒ < 40 ▓ < 50 ■ 50+

Source: Rajagopal, Part-Time Faculty Survey (1991–2)

$8,539 income mean from part-time teaching. Contemporaries' median personal income from all sources of part-time work ($30,000–$39,999) is far below that of Classics ($50,000–$59,999). In U.S. academe, part-timers on average make U.S.$6,829 per year from academic work. Their overall personal income of U.S.$38,841 (NCES, 1990: 20–1) falls within the Canadian Contemporaries' median range given above. In Canadian universities, Contemporaries' typical course-load is two or more courses (Classics' load is less than two courses). Most Contemporaries (72 per cent) teach in autumn and winter and during daytime and on weekdays; 30 per cent teach in the summer term. A majority of Classics (59 per cent) also teach in autumn/winter but in evenings/on weekends, and a quarter of Classics teach in the summer. While Classics moonlight in academe, half of all Contemporaries depend on one university for their income, nearly a quarter are 'Freeway-Fliers' who rely on several universities, and a third work part time, both in universities and in non-academic jobs.

Needs and Motivations

Comparing the histories of Contemporaries and Classics in terms of job status, sectors, and work responsibilities for four consecutive positions held, including their current jobs, we see different patterns. Over time, nearly a quarter of Contemporaries have shifted from other job sectors into higher education, whereas Classics were moving out of education into other sectors. More Contemporaries have long been working in the education sector; more Classics have worked in the business and government sectors rather than in education.[6]

Part-timers' career orientations express both their extrinsic and their intrinsic needs (Gappa and Leslie, 1993: 36–40). Economic needs, such as the income and benefits of a full-time job, and the intangible aspects of a career, such as professional recognition, status, and perks, are considered 'extrinsic' needs. Other needs, such as career preferences or choice of profession, intellectual satisfaction, and professional interest, are 'intrinsic' in nature. In my survey, Contemporaries and Classics clearly differ in their reasons for teaching part time, which range from income, flexible work schedule, and opportunity for faculty contact to non-availability of academic full-time work and acquiring experience for teaching. Their reasons for teaching reveal that most Contemporaries have chosen an academic career of their own volition, and some Classics might prefer academe if full-time jobs were available (figure 4.2). Most Contemporaries (84 per cent) identify the academic profession as their main choice. Three-quarters consider teaching and research the mainstay of their careers, and a majority regard their academic part-time work as a training ground for an academic career. Working in academe satisfies their professional and intellectual interests. Most of the Contemporaries (76 per cent) want a full-time academic position, and although 79 per cent have to teach part time to earn an income, only a fifth cite financial motivation. Many (63 per cent) seek academic part time work because they do not see in the academic market any possibility of finding a full-time position in their disciplines.

In contrast, most Classics (83 per cent) consider their non-academic professions to be their first choice. Some of them (46 per cent) might

FIGURE 4.2

Reasons for teaching part time: Contemporaries versus Classics

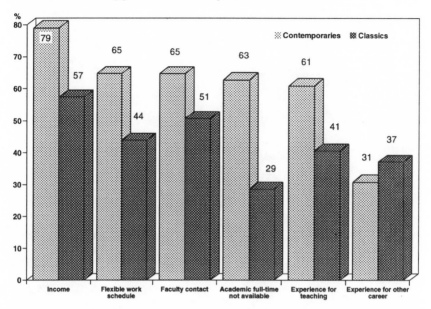

Source: See figure 4.1.

prefer a full-time academic to their non-academic job but early realized that such openings are scarcer; this is particularly true of younger Classics with doctorates. Many of the Classics (85 per cent) are attracted to academe because their teaching areas and interests complement their non-academic professions; they are drawn more by their interest in teaching and by their desire to have contact with faculty (51 per cent) and for extra money than by career motives (figure 4.3). Although 22.5 per cent of Classics have doctorates, fewer than half of them seem to prefer a full-time academic career, and many fewer are actively seeking one.[7] A Classic indicates his motivation: 'Part-time teaching, for me, is "semi-volunteer" [work]. I do it for contact with the faculty. I would appreciate more effort to make me feel included within the academic community, even if salary should decrease. Salary is not important.' Another values factors mutually beneficial both to the university and to Classics: 'Our university makes a practice of employing practitioners in its professional faculties (Law, Dentistry, etc.) The students

FIGURE 4.3

Who is interested in an academic career – Contemporaries or Classics?

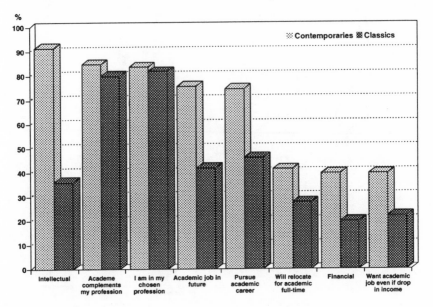

Source: See figure 4.1.

benefit because they learn a practical approach rather than a strictly academic approach. They can hear about what it is like in the "real world"! It offers a good balance for academic approaches they receive from full-time professors. The instructor also benefits because he is forced to re-examine his [area of specialization] in applying the basic academic approach ... it forces him to update the course annually.' Many Classics believe that practical knowledge is indispensable: 'During my years of university studies I deplored the high percentage of full-time professors whose teaching did not include any practical aspects, and was much less pertinent and lacked perspective. Universities are supposed to train young people for integration into society not laboratories.'

Some Classics prefer job-sharing between academe and business world. They also do not seem to understand Contemporaries' emphasis on earning a livelihood from academe: 'I would like to see an increase in Sessionals at universities, if the emphasis were on teaching quality. Too often, Sessionals are just looking at money or experience to get them more money. Universities should be leaders in job-sharing. Perhaps more qualified people would choose a less hectic lifestyle to try to change our present socio-economic system based on capitalism and materialism. When will academics wake up?' Already in full-time jobs, very few Classics (19.7 per cent versus Contemporaries 39.2 per cent) are particularly motivated by the extra income. As a woman Classic explains: 'Part-time teaching is unfair in monetary terms. It takes a lot of prep time since you are always assigned new courses. The pay does not match the effort. I seem to be always busy .With my full-time job elsewhere and teaching here, I have no time to consider the policies and attitudes of my university towards part-timers. In my situation, I look at this teaching opportunity as an incredible way to enhance my career in fine-arts journalism and art curatorship.' A woman Classic reflects on why she pursues a non-academic occupation: 'I have opted not to pursue a PhD degree due to the lack of available opportunities within the Canadian university system. Instead, I have entered a career in filmmaking as a scriptwriter and a filmmaker. Since this is a recent decision, I am required to complete the teaching I have originally accepted. But, I have recently applied for university funding to pursue my artistic research and writing objectives. If I were confident that I could obtain a full time [academic] position I would consider obtaining a PhD. But given the university's lack of commitment to teaching standards and workers in general, I feel it would be a waste of time.'

A notable distinction emerges in career goals. Half of all Contemporaries want a full-time academic career, a desire that is reinforced by their educational readiness. Twice as many Contemporaries (45 per cent) as Classics have or are working on their doctorates. A considerable majority (62 per cent) who have doctorates and 45 per cent who do not yet have them, are actively seeking full-time academic positions, in contrast to 90 per cent of Classics, who seem to be content with their non-academic jobs. Not only do Contemporaries have their minds set on an academic career, but many also wish to find full-time professorships and are hopeful about getting one. A third of Contemporaries – almost double the proportion of Classics – feel that their chance of getting full-time academic jobs is 50 per cent or more. They urge universities to hire long-serving part-timers into regular full-time employement. A majority of them (58 per cent) believe that their universities are obliged to provide full-time appointments to long-service Contemporaries, a prospect that fewer Classics (42 per cent) expect (figure 4.4).

FIGURE 4.4

Want full-time academic job and how to get it: Contemporaries versus Classics

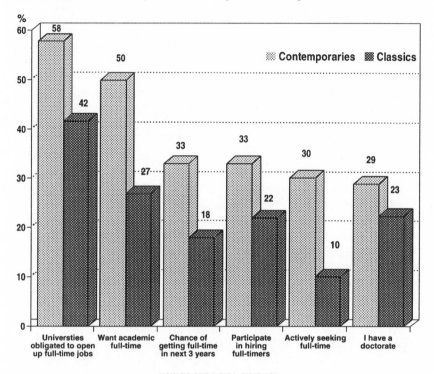

Source: See figure 4.1.

Contemporaries' keenness to pursue academic careers may also be evident from their efforts to advance their own professional skills. More Contemporaries than Classics are engaged in scholarly presentations (Contemporaries 47 per cent versus Classics 37 per cent), training to improve their teaching skills (Contemporaries 44 per cent versus Classics 37 per cent), publishing their own research (Contemporaries 43 per cent versus Classics 34 per cent), and pursuing higher studies (Contemporaries 37 per cent versus Classics 29.5 per cent). Smaller but significant differences emerge between them in efforts such as collaborating with full-timers in research (Contemporaries 27 per cent versus Classics 22 per cent), improving their research skills (Contemporaries

FIGURE 4.5
Why do universities hire part-timers? Who benefits?

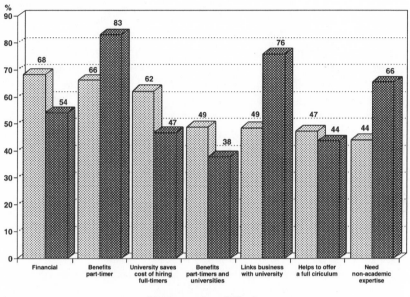

Source: See figure 4.1.

20 per cent versus Classics 16 per cent), and applying for research funding or research leave (Contemporaries 17 per cent versus Classics 12 per cent).

Contemporaries perceive the university as their sole workplace. They do understand why universities use part-timers and fear that academic quality will suffer if staffing with part-timers continues, despite the short-term mutual benefits to both parties. The universities ignore pedagogical issues such as class size, teaching loads, and new tenure-track positions in their calculations. In contrast to Contemporaries' concerns about academic quality, Classics' emphasis is on the benefits to academe from using part-timers like themselves. They believe that universities' financial shortfall may have contributed to a stronger link between academe and outside professions without which expertise from the professions would have been lost to universities (figure 4.5).

Work

The feminized profile of academic part-time-only work – a majority of Contemporaries are women (53 per cent) – mildly echoes the feminization of part-time workers generally (women 70 per cent) in the Canadian labour force (Statistics Canada, 1999c: 33; Best, 1995: 32). Women Classics (32 per cent) are far fewer (see table 4.1). Much like their role in Canadian academe, women constitute 53 per cent of part-timers in British universities (AAUP, 1992: 41). As we saw above (see chapter three) women full-timers in Canada constitute 26.2 per cent of the professoriate (*CAUT Bulletin* Insert, April 2000). Labour force fragmentation, legitimized by degradation of part-time employment as less skilled and low-paid work, and tensions over status between part- and full-timers have facilitated feminization.

Fragmenting the academic work process by splitting it into 'routine' and 'creative' or 'productive' facilitated the hiring of part-timers to do the teaching (Rajagopal and Farr, 1992: 320). Most Contemporaries (82 per cent versus Classics 65 per cent) teach large, first-year, undergraduate courses. As course directors, 73 per cent of them (Classics 82 per cent) handle all associated administrative responsibilities for such courses. Their work involves routinized registering or enrolling of students for over an hour per course (Classics 0.33 hour) per week and supervising teaching assistants for an hour per course (Classics 0.5 hour) per week. Most Contemporaries enjoy teaching, yet they feel stressed. The greater the course load and the more repetitive it is, the greater is the stress. Contemporaries do more teaching and support work – teaching writing skills and tutorials, marking assignments, and preparing grade reports. More than a quarter of their total teaching load (29 per cent versus Classics 16 per cent) consists of teaching writing skills. On marking and grading, Contemporaries spend weekly 6 hours per course (Classics 4.7 hours). The mode for Contemporaries is three full courses, but for Classics it is less than two.

A contrasting pattern also emerges between levels of teaching. Classics come in to fill specific areas of expertise that universities require. A Classic teaches mostly at one level, but more often than not a Contemporary teaches courses at different levels. Both groups find that teaching is not valued as much as research, but feel that it should be if it is to benefit students. A woman Classic regrets this situation: 'From my short time in a part time position I have observed that many university professors are (a) not current in their fields; (b) do what they must to get tenure (c) don't think teaching students is important (d) have an overinflated idea of their own importance. I believe that universities must take a very critical look at their purpose and how they propose to achieve it because the university of today – structured as it is – will not survive. The university can and should make a contribution to our lives and our world. It is too important a vehicle to let die.' Another Classic records the huge workload for poor pay: 'I just wish they would pay me more – it might help justify to my family why the heck I'm doing this! This is the second year I have taught at the university. I kept track of my time in each year on our firm computer. In the first year I spent 6.25 hours preparation for each class. In the second year this dropped to 1.4 hours of preparation for each hour of class. The main reason is the reliance on class notes from the first year. What surprised me was I spent more time preparing and marking the 100 per cent final exam than I did in class (41.2 hours on exam; 34.5 hours in class).'

Contemporaries' workplaces are many. Some teach in only one university (single university part-timers), and others, in many universities (Freeway Fliers). A third group (Straddlers) holds part-time jobs in both academic and non-academic sectors. Nearly half of Contemporaries (49 per cent) teach part time in academe, but in only one university (table 4. 5), and I call them Rooted. A majority of the Rooted (51 per cent) are women. A majority of Contemporaries with doctorates are Rooted. A majority of the Rooted teach in the Atlantic-region (67 per cent) and in the west (52 per cent). More of them are found in mid-size (53 per cent), limited-range (51 per cent), teaching oriented (53 per cent), lower part-time intensity (57 per cent), non-unionized (53 per cent) universities (table 4.6).

Two Contemporaries in ten teach in more than one university – Freeway Fliers – and they declare that their regular work is academic. More of them are women, with a master's or a higher degree, and more of them teach in humanities and in fine and applied arts. More Freeway Fliers (8.6 to 17 per cent more) work at Quebec university campuses. Freeway-flying Contemporaries are more common in large-size, wide-ranging, research-oriented, higher-intensity, and unionized universities. A woman Contemporary explains: 'My one university ... appointments were out of town. It entailed an overnight stay, returning the following morning in time to teach at this university ... then an evening class at ... my third university. I barely finished marking the finals for those three courses in time to begin Spring Session at ... this university.

TABLE 4.5
Contemporaries' sources of part-time work, gender, education, and discipline

	Sex %		Degree %			Faculty %					Total %	Total no.
	Men	Women	<Master's	Master's to higher	Doctorate	Education	Fine arts	Humanities	Social science	Sciences		
Rooted	49.0	50.5	45.5	46.7	55.4	44.6	37.6	54.0	49.3	51.6	49.1	698
Freeway Fliers	20.4	20.0	15.0**	21.5	20.2	23.7	21.8	22.3	18.4	12.1	20.2	287
Straddlers	30.6	29.5	39.5*	31.9	24.4	31.8**	40.6	23.7	32.3	36.3	30.7	436
Total %	100.0	100.0	100.0	100.0	100.0	100.0	100.0	100.0	100.0	100.0	100.0	
Total no.	600	821	237	766	419	182	158	442	406	233		1,421

Notes: Significance: $p = $ *$< .05$; **$< .01$; ***$< .001$. All are significant at $p = $ ***$< .001$ unless otherwise indicated. Rooted: One university, part time as only employment. Freeway Fliers: Only academic part time, but in two or more universities. Straddlers: Academic part time plus non-academic part time.
Source: See table 4.1.

TABLE 4.6
Contemporaries' sources of part-time work, by university type

	Overall total no.	Overall total %	Size %			Region %				Research/ teaching %***		Part-time intensity %	
			Large	Mid	Small	West	Ontario	Quebec	Atlantic	Research	Teaching	Higher	Lower
Rooted	698	49.1	46.5	53.3	41.4	52.2	48.2	40.8	67.1	44.4	53.4	42.9	57.1
Freeway Fliers	287	20.2	22.3	16.9	12.9	13.6	21.2	29.8	12.9	22.8	17.8	25.9	12.4
Straddlers	436	30.7	31.0	29.7	45.7	34.2	30.6	29.4	20.0	32.8	28.8	31.2	30.5
Total no.	1,421	100.0	854	418	149	419	612	298	97	681	740	781	640

Notes: Significance: p = *<.05; **<.01; ***<.001. All are significant at p = ***<.001. unless otherwise indicated.
Source: See table 4.1.

I know I am not alone in carrying virtually a full time teaching load of three courses, but in various universities, for less than half the salary.' Another women Contemporary adds: 'I work part-time for three academic institutions. It is often wrongly assumed that the part-timers worked only in one university.'

Straddlers hold both academic part-time and non-academic jobs, whether inside or outside academe. They make up a third of all Contemporaries. This group contains more Contemporaries who have less than a master's degree, mostly from fine and applied arts. Across Canada, more than the average (30.7 per cent) number of Straddlers are found in universities in the west (34.2 per cent) and in small-size (45.7 per cent), limited-range (33.5 per cent), research-oriented (32.8 per cent), higher-intensity (31.2 per cent), and non-unionized (31.7 per cent) institutions. Many Contemporaries, both male and female, are quite frustrated with their job searches: 'I suspect you will find that most of us are diligently looking for full time positions, and we are becoming increasingly despairing of ever finding one of these privileged positions.' And, 'The prospect of full-time positions opening up in the near future looks bleak. Even full-timers think that their tenure system might be at risk if finances continue to decline.'

In defiance of the relentless routinization of part-timers' work, Contemporaries' interest in research and publication appears to be thriving. It seems as if, in resistance to the degradation of their work, they are keen on research. Despite a lack of time and institutional incentives, over a quarter of Contemporaries (Classics 14.5 per cent) have produced scholarly books within the previous five years, and a third of them (Classics 20 per cent) have done so at some point in their career. They spend 10 hours weekly (Classics 6.4 hours) doing research, but would like to spend more time (16 hours). All this, even though they have little time to engage in research and minimal access to grants. A third of them (37 per cent versus 19 per cent Classics) apply for external grants from the national research granting agencies, and a third of them (Classics 27 per cent) receive such grants.

Contradictions between their career expectations and the realities of workplace marginality contribute to job dissatisfaction among Contemporaries. Two-thirds of Contemporaries (Classics 52 per cent) are dissatisfied that despite their status as 'permanent temporaries' in the university (Lemon, 1994), full-timers could still consider part-time hiring an expedient and temporary solution for underfunding and enrolment pressures. Over five years (1986–91) their grievances against the

TABLE 4.7
Part-time faculty's overall job satisfaction

	Classics	Contemporaries	Total no.
Very satisfied	32.5%	26.1%	576
Somewhat satisfied	60.4%	53.0%	1,130
Somewhat dissatisfied	6.1%	17.5%	277
Very dissatisfied	1.0%	3.4%	53
N	701	1,335	2,036

Note: Gamma = .263; p <.0001
Source: See table 4.1.

administration, class size, and teaching loads increased. Obviously, they are unhappy with their part-time status (table 4.7) and quite dissatisfied with their job security (65 per cent), benefits (57.5 per cent), and salary (51 per cent). A majority of Classics do not worry about internal strains or about a decline in academic quality, however, even when they teach increasingly larger classes. Some Classics (39 per cent) are dissatisfied because there is little time for working with students, and some (20 per cent) regret that their spouses could not find jobs in the region.

Contemporaries, rather than Classics, are disenchanted with their part-time status despite their enjoyment of teaching. A woman Contemporary comments: 'I have difficulty accepting the identity of "part-timer" as a permanent condition.' Another Contemporary remarks: 'I feel totally disconnected to the university – but very connected to the students.' Many Contemporaries also feel that they are marginalized in a number of ways: 'Full-timers are not interested in orienting part-timers in our department. I find that our departmental secretary is invaluable to me. She always can give me the information I need about procedure, deadlines, whom to contact. My full-time colleagues are quite useless in these respects ... I find that, as a part-timer, I simply do not receive enough information about the non-academic aspects of my position and the workings of the university.' And, 'Lack of job security is a disincentive to a personal commitment to the job.' Many Contemporaries are frustrated with the abrupt treatment: 'This year I was not given a teaching assignment for the 92/93 Winter Session, based it seems, on the whim of the person responsible for hiring. I was not offered an explanation for this sudden shock, and have no recourse whatsoever. Needless to say I feel quite bitter after 5 years of dedicated service, but I have support of my students, higher administration and colleagues.' Some Contemporaries reject the notion that financial reasons or ideology should drive the university's objectives: 'Money is not the answer to educational problems. Quality of teachers and their dedication to (1) the discipline (2) the students (3) the taxpayer should be the only criteria. Quotas based on politically correct nonsense are anti-education. Tenure, publish-or-perish are anti-education.' Many career-oriented Contemporaries note the absence of professional development opportunities: '(1) Successful part-timers should be offered, as funds and circumstances warrant, opportunity to increase their course load. (2) Successful part-time faculty should be offered substantial grants to complete advanced degrees and undertake extended research. (3) All' part-time staff should be entitled to participate in some form of a benefits and retirement package.'

Classics, in contrast, seem to be 'willing' part-timers. A woman Classic finds satisfaction in non-monetary factors: 'I work to keep my vision sharp. I do as much or as little as I want. I will continue for as long as (a) I'm enjoying it (b) the students enjoy it and (c) I'm asked. I have a demanding full time job and do not have time for the politics of the university job place. I won't work for nothing, but the salary is not a prime consideration.' And, 'I enjoy the part-time teaching. In my position as special education coordinator of a school board, it provides me with the opportunity of assisting my students (fellow-teachers) in becoming knowledgeable in a field that I take pride in.' However, Classics do feel some dissatisfaction: 'The major dissatisfaction for me is that I have to teach in the evenings. This is an isolating experience. I enjoy interaction with colleagues with similar interests in my field. This is unlikely if I do not teach during daytime when regular faculty members are around.' And, 'The practice of pro-rating salary according to the number of students is, I feel, unjust. Although I am not keen on higher salary, my professional time spent in my class is the same whether it has 10 students or 50 students.'

Place in Academe

Full-timers view and treat Classics and Contemporaries differently. Two types of departments hire part-timers: some hire more Classics; others hire more Contemporaries. I chose the presence of two-thirds or more of Contemporaries or Classics as constituting Contemporary-high or Classic-high, respectively. I assumed that full-timers who hire more Contemporaries are more likely to understand Contemporaries and academic part-timers in general quite differently from those who hire more Classics. Departments differ in their staffing needs. Obviously, fewer full-timers in Contemporary-high (40.8 per cent versus Classic-high 75.1 per cent) departments hire professionals with practical expertise. They (74.9 per cent versus Classic-high 59.6 per cent) hire Contemporaries to lower their student-faculty ratios, and most of them (72 per cent versus Classic-high 62 per cent) see part-time appointments as a temporary solution and would prefer new full-timers.

Full-timers, as gatekeepers of faculty collegium, identify Contemporaries, but not Classics, as intruders and as virtual impostors who aspire to rights similar to those of full-timers. The full-time collegium tends to use its powers of hiring and firing to maintain its exclusiveness and closes its ranks against Contemporaries. A male Contemporary sums up: 'In my opinion Sessionals [Contemporaries] are regarded as a cheap workforce in universities, hired by short contracts. They are ... without any right or appreciation, excluded from the life of the department. Even their research work is neglected. I feel myself exploited, underpaid and discriminated against – a pariah in the academic world – although I edit a book with contributions of eleven committees of two continents. Guidelines policy with respect to employment of Sessionals are inoperative. The present system is a shameful one.'

Exclusion

On all academic matters, full-timers retain their exclusive decision-making powers. In both Contemporary-high (71 per cent) and Classic-high (83 per cent) departments, they refuse to share their power. On non-academic matters such as compensation and service support, however, more full-timers in Contemporary-high (10 per cent more) departments would allow part-timers their own rank and salary structure.

Who is more excluded from the faculty collegium? Full-timers consider Classics outsiders and non-academic. More full-timers (15 per cent more) in Classic-high departments strongly reject proportional representation for part-timers in academic decision-making. They seem to see Contemporaries as more akin to academics but are wary of including even them. A full-timer describes the situation: 'In my department there are two types of part-timers. Some are lawyers, business people, social workers, media and communication professionals, who are teaching a course or giving a few lectures. But there are others who are more numerous working part-time teaching in various courses. All of them would like to have a say in matters that affect their work. But it is not practical to give them powers equal to that of full-time faculty in making departmental decisions because most of them have limited knowledge about department finances, about senate policies, or about matters that affect this university. In any case, many of them do not attend department meetings even though they are eligible to do so and air their ideas.' Full-timers are aware that most Classics (75 per cent versus Contemporaries 60 per cent), since they are employed full time elsewhere, do not have the time to attend faculty meetings. A male full-timer describes the general trend: 'Part-time .faculty play a very useful role but when there are too many of them in a department it places undue stress on the full time faculty members, because the part-time teachers are most of the time not on campus to share with other collegial activities. They are kind of isolated and few of them really participate in social and other activities of the department.'

Part-timers themselves think differently about their input in their departments. Contemporaries, in particular, seem to feel that they are committed to academe and therefore that full-timers should accord them an equitable share of decision-making. Their involvement in universities' decision-making bodies also attests to their career commitment to academe. A third to a half of the Classics are not aware of their rights in their universities' decision-making bodies. Compared with them, 16 per cent more Contemporaries actually participate in departmental meetings, and 7 per cent more are confident that they can use such forums to gain changes in their academic work. Control and influence over their work and salary are very important to Contemporaries. Many want more influence in negotiating their salary (64 per cent), choosing courses to teach (60 per cent), determining their own teaching schedule (53 per cent), hiring part-timers (48 per cent), controlling their own course content (40 per cent), hiring full-timers (33 per cent), and tenuring/promoting full-timers (31 per cent). Not many Classics (8–11 per cent less than Contemporaries) want to be involved in shaping their work in academe. More Contemporaries (64 per cent versus Classics 52 per cent) and women part-timers (68 per cent versus men 54 per cent) always rely on their unions or associations. More Contemporaries (11 per cent more) than Classics always support their unions or associations.

Neglect

Contradictions between full-timers' ideal and actual perceptions of part-timers' career interests, particularly those of Contemporaries, are quite clear in my survey. More full-timers in Contemporary-high departments (44 per cent versus Classic-high 23 per cent) regard part-timers as full members of the academic collegium. Through either formal rules or informal practices, however, they leave them out of most collegial bodies. Most Contemporaries report on this exclusion. More full-timers in Contemporary-high departments (70 per cent versus Classic-high 66 per cent) perceive half or more of part-timers as a necessary expedient. Fewer of them (42 per cent versus Classic-high 61 per cent) view part-timers as a welcome source of expertise. A majority of Contemporaries report that they are treated as junior partners and given limited and specific tasks.

Although most Contemporary-high full-timers (73 per cent versus Classic-high 64 per cent) state that part-timers should belong to the collegium, that inclusion does not happen. These full-timers (52 per cent versus Classic-high 36 per cent) acknowledge an obligation to offer full-time positions based on merit to qualified long-service Contemporaries, but fewer of them (37 per cent versus Classic-high 53 per cent) want to see a separate faculty stream. However, only a few Contemporaries (30 per cent versus Classics 10 per cent) are actively seeking full-time academic positions. Contemporary-high full-timers almost correctly estimate the proportion of part-timers (29 per cent versus Classic-high 8 per cent) likely to be hired through normal competition based on credentials, if positions were available. Yet they are not ready to grant that opportunity. Thus, notwithstanding their rhetoric, full-timers treat part-timers more as an expendable workforce than as one integral to academe.

Devaluation

There are many contradictions between full-timers' rhetoric and their actions vis-à-vis part-timers' work. Most full-timers in Contemporary-high departments affirm that part-timers' work is indispensable. Although more of them (37 per cent versus Classic-high 22 per cent) evaluate part-timers' teaching as being of high quality, many (45 per cent versus Classic-high 39 per cent) worry that such teaching is academically inappropriate. A woman Contemporary comments: 'I have received the highest ratings from student evaluations of my teaching – several times higher than some full time staff. Lack of financial resources is presented as the reason for lack of hiring.'

Many Contemporary-high full-timers also agree (51 per cent versus Classic-high 27 per cent) that part-timers enhance informal social life in their departments, but most of their departments would rather not have them. As well, Contemporary-high full-timers deny them influence in negotiating their pay, although they (80 per cent versus Classic-high 57 per cent) acknowledge that part-timers are underpaid and that their unions have little influence in negotiating pay and benefits. In Quebec, where their unions are more influential, a full-timer complains: 'The part-time faculty union has too much power. It protects the less good and perpetuates their hiring. It's becoming more and more difficult to get those who can bring new ideas because of the union.'

We now turn to Part Two, in which we will examine the forces that fragment academe.

Part Two

FRAGMENTED ACADEME

Chapter Five

Conflicts That Divide: Full-Timers versus Part-Timers

After explaining briefly how I selected full-timers for the survey, in this chapter I present results of regression analyses from the survey of full-timers, isolating areas of conflict between them and part-timers. The two groups are hierarchically organized, each with its own interests and unique demands on the university. Full-timers hire part-timers and regulate their work. There seems to be a marked segmentation of interests among full-timers and also sharp conflicting relations between full- and part-timers. Of all the factors analysed, rank segments full-timers in their attitudes towards part-timers. Rank is a significant predictor in my regression models (discussed below) and explains differences among full-timers in their assessments of part-timers' issues and interests. In the latter half of the chapter I discuss full-timers' perceptions of part-timers' aspirations, work, and status, as indicated in responses to my surveys of full-timers and their views on part-timers and of part-timers.

My survey of full-time faculty represents all full-timers, selected in ratios proportional to part-timers in each department or Faculty (for methodology, see the appendix). The final sample falls under the various disciplines. For each ten full-timers in a department, four are from social sciences, two from humanities, more than two from sciences, and one each from business/administration, law, and education. A quarter are from francophone universities. Six in ten are Canadian born. Their average age is 48. Mirroring the current gender composition of all full-time faculty in Canada, a large majority of full-timers in the survey are men (73.2 per cent). Women full-timers (26.8 per cent) form about one-fourth of those surveyed. In 1998–9 women full-timers constituted 26.2 per cent of all full-timers in Canadian universities.

Full-timers are generally highly qualified: most (81.7 per cent) have doctorates, 16.9 per cent hold a master's or post-graduate professional degree, and a very small number (1.4 per cent) have only a first professional or bachelor's degree.

In academic rank, full professors represent 38 per cent of the full-timers in my survey, 36 per cent are associate professors, 21 per cent are assistant professors/lecturers, and 4 per cent are instructors. Of those full-timers who hold administrative positions, very few surveyed are vice-presidents; more than one in ten are deans, associate deans, and assistant deans; three in ten are department chairs; four in ten are program directors; and two in ten are research unit directors and hold other administrative positions. On average, they have been full-timers for about fifteen years, with a continuing service of twelve or thirteen years in the current university. Six in ten among the full-timers have been on contract as either part-time or limited-term full-time members of faculty. Four in ten have previously been part-timers.

In this chapter I address several questions. Do rank and power divide academe? Is there a split in faculty interests within academe? Is the relationship between the two faculty groups – full time and part time, each situated differently within the power structure of the university – one of conflict or of collegiality? Will the survey findings show that full-timers are segmented along different lines – rank, gender, and university types and so on – or that there is a greater sense of collegiality among tenure streamers? Will they indicate that there are conflicting relations between full- and part-timers? If so, how does a structure of conflicting power relations shape academe?

Segmentation and Conflict

'This growing body of temporary or term employees is our academic underclass. The overclass, of course, are the academic stars, the winners in the academic division of our winner-take-all society ... The academic anxious class are those tenured or tenure-track professors ... who are overburdened with increased teaching loads and unprepared students. Like other members of the anxious class ... even tenure isn't very comforting if their unit, or even their institution is threatened with economic inviability ... [this class] may include most of the faculty. This growing tripartite class division within the university creates major strains on whatever sense of common interest remains making solidarity in defence of academic autonomy increasingly difficult'

(Bellah, 1997: 24–5). Robert Bellah warns that the besieged academic profession in the United States is unable to defend itself because of the intensifying divisions within academe, and class wars within the university. A new class system has emerged that consists of three strata: the underclass of temporary workers (part-timers and teaching assistants), the 'overclass' of academic stars, and the 'anxious class' of tenured or tenure-track faculty. The development and persistence of this new class system threaten the common moral ground that provides the basis of the university's defence against being reduced to an 'education industry' (1997: 22–6).

A decline in the power of and an increase in the fragmentation within the professoriate have been occurring in Canada since the 1970s, when, as Janice Newson observes, the university's 'comparative affluence and expansion' tapered off creating internal institutional changes, which led to a 'decline in collective faculty influence' (1990, 4).[1] In the same vein, Bellah alerts the faculty to the ominous trends of segmentation within U.S. academe: 'After decades of public favor, we are not used to taking a defensive posture. Further, it is not at all obvious that the academic profession is in any position to defend itself because of the growing divisions among us, divisions which are intensifying, both materially and intellectually, all the time. Contention in the university is normal, even desirable, but we have come close to losing the common ground that can be the only basis for self-defence' (1997, 22). In their international survey Altbach and Lewis point to similar trends. Many faculty members in these universities across the globe are dissatisfied with their 'lack of control' over the prevailing conditions and issues in their universities and over future uncertainties. Women faculty more than men are perturbed by these trends in academe. Moreover, a majority of the professoriate surveyed from all countries except the Netherlands feel a loss of the sense of community on campus (1995: 53).

Academe is clearly segmented along lines of job status: tenure stream versus those on contract. In order to cut back on longer-term financial commitments and to reduce costs, universities increasingly tend to hire more contract faculty and reduce hiring in the tenure stream. As a result, there is a general sense of discomfort among full-timers when hiring of part-timers rises. The academic functions of the two groups are further differentiated as teaching versus research. Further, both gender and rank of full-timers significantly divide their interests. A review of studies on women faculty shows that gender invariably differentiates their status and conditions from those of males. Women's presence in the lower ranks is disproportionately high. They get promoted at a slower rate, and fewer are in administrative or governance roles. They have fewer decision-making powers and receive lower pay than equally qualified males (Finkelstein, 1984; Sandler, 1996; Bellas, 1997). Academe has become a hierarchy of ranks, and faculty ranks are associated with research productivity. The greater the university's commitment to research as an institutional mission, the sharper the distinction between ranks as well as genders within the hierarchy (Tien and Blackburn, 1996; Park, 1996).[2]

In Canada, the Status of Women Committee reported 'an ironic consequence of the success of feminism in academic life' (Acker, 1999: 8).[3] With fewer women among full-time faculty on university campuses across the country and disproportionately greater demands on them to be on university committees and mentor women graduate students, women full-timers encounter work overloads heavier than their male counterparts (Acker, 1999). Further, individual grievances by faculty women suppress the commonality of their interests with other women among faculty as a collective. Their complaints get mired in the grievance process, which focuses more on 'personal and professional qualities than on systemic patterns of discrimination' (Abel, 1981: 505).[4] Sharp divisiveness among faculty members spring from differences in their rank. The 'old boys club' continues to be a powerful force among older faculty, although younger colleagues are more pluralistic. This gap continues to divide academe not only along generation lines, but more important, along lines of rank. According to a survey of U.S. universities on the implementation of affirmative action, many faculty members, including departmental chairs, are 'either stereotypically prejudiced or reprehensibly uninformed' about it (Chow, 1996: 32).

The decision-making structures in academe and the roles that faculty members assume exacerbate these divisions. The full-time faculty is further split into two groups with distinct interests and powers. Membership in the senate and appointments as administrators shape the body of full-time faculty and segment its decision-making powers into academic versus administrative. Altbach and Lewis found that administrators are not popular among academics; more than two-thirds of the professoriate from half of the countries surveyed rated the relationship between administration and faculty as fair to poor, not as good or very good (1995: 53).

In my survey, the career paths that faculty members have taken en route to becoming full-timers significantly differentiate their experiences into what we may identify here as those of 'Insiders' and 'Outsiders.'[5] Those who have been contractees (Insiders), either as part-timers or as limited-term full-timers, have different and sometimes strongly adversarial responses against the system, compared with those who have not experienced contract status (Outsiders) – at least on certain matters, such as marginalization of part-timers. Extended comments that full-timers have added to their survey responses clearly bring out these divisions. A male full-timer in the humanities lays the blame squarely on the university's central administration for creating and maintaining the divisive atmosphere: 'In order to save money, university administrators have terminated new or replacement tenure-track positions, and instead are relying more and more on contract appointments, especially part time. While qualified, this faculty is horribly underpaid. Moreover, since new retirees are not replaced with tenure-track positions, both faculty morale and educational quality have been on a downward slope. The faculty association and the faculty bargaining unit are struggling to rectify this state of affairs but the deck is stacked in favour of administrators. And all this, in the face of record enrollments!' Part-timers express a contrary view. Their jobs were stable for a number of years but started declining in the 1990s in universities in central Canada. In securing their own financial interests and academic privileges, many of the tenured full-timers have abandoned the bulk of part-timers to the fluctuations of the day. A part-timer comments on how part-time jobs are disappearing while the faculty union protects those of full-timers: 'I think I have just taught my last course here after 6 years. They asked me to hand in my keys and not to plan to run the course in September due to lack of money. They are planning to teach all the courses without any contract faculty but by using current tenured faculty. When I applied for the two courses that have been taught by me for a long time, I was told that the regular faculty would pick them up. The lack of money is killing part-timers while the strength of the full-time faculty union is able to preserve the interests of tenured members. Such is our academe!'

A full-timer in science, who has no previous contract experience, conveys Outsiders' notions about part-timers. He refuses to accept them as part of regular academe or to extend faculty rights to them because he regards them as 'limited scope teachers': 'Part-timers and limited-term faculty are hired for a specific purpose, for a specified time frame. As long as the job remains to be done, they should be reassigned to continue in their appointments. They would sign a contract for a given salary, but should have no rights in the department other than doing their job well and then leaving for better pastures. If an opening occurs, they should have every right to apply. However, the university has no obligation to hire them.' Obviously, part-timers are not unduly thrilled about the value that full-timers place on teaching. A woman part-timer scoffs at the full-timers' commitment to teaching: 'I find many professors are coasting along with old materials and previous years' notes. They know how to take time off for their own research to the loss of good teaching. They don't think teaching students well is a part of their job. A university that does not care about its students will eventually face the taxpayers' criticism.'

With the increasing need to hire part-timers from year to year in order to deal with fluctuating enrolments, part-timers feel that full-timers have pragmatically segmented their academic functions and because of expediency, have swung either more towards teaching or more towards research. Most part-timers feel deliberately overloaded with teaching but denied the research role, which leaves them 'teaching only.' From the response of an Outsider in science, we can infer the gratuitous assumptions made about part-timers' roles: 'The part-time faculty in [science] ... departments generally teach to gain experience and supplement their income. Only people with adequate teaching skills are hired and they are paid as part-timers *specifically to teach*. Contract faculty members' opinions may be valued in searches for non-academic positions, but will have no influence in department or university affairs. The department view is that students have the right to be instructed by full-time faculty and that part-time or sessional appointments are considered good only for the instructors, not for students or the university' (emphasis added). A tenured full-timer, despite his sympathetic views towards those on contract, rationalizes: 'In our department, year after year, we hire several limited-term full-time and part-time faculty. No permanent full-time positions are being created. But the contract faculty relieves full-timers from the burden of teaching so that they can devote their full attention to "their" research. Part-timers are often among our best teachers. Despite this they are underpaid, have no chance of advancement, and have no future or job security. In our university, and especially in the Faculty of Arts and Sciences, which stresses primarily excellence in research, a permanent professor can succeed very well in doing excellent research while doing very little or no teaching; but an excellent teacher with very little research and publication does not stand a chance.' In sharp contrast, part-timers see themselves as teachers and as researchers as well. They express their keenness and determination to do research despite a heavy teaching load: 'Many part-time faculty members have a heavier teaching load than full-timers; but if we desire an academic career, we must continue with our research publications, secure grants, and spend extra hours on research.' The juxtaposition of these comments of full-timers and part-timers in their survey responses help to contrast their perceptions of and feelings about each other.

Areas of Conflict

Segmentation and conflicts within the university express themselves in various ways in my survey responses from full-timers. I have done six regressions, all of which provide statistically significant models in our analysis of full-timers' evaluations of part-timers' status, academic roles, career options, and influence on decision-making (table 5.1).[6] Six specific questions in the survey asked whether full-timers agree or disagree on various dimensions of part-timers' role and place in academe. Their responses to these six questions constitute dependent variables on part-timers' role, status, and power.

- Should part-timers be represented in proportions equal to those of full-time faculty in academic decision-making bodies of the university (Q17a)?
- Do part-timers have a legitimate place in the university (Q17b)?
- Should the main responsibility for academic collegial decision-making rest with the full-time faculty alone (Q17c)?
- Should part-timers be considered a separate stream of teachers (Q17d)?
- Does the university have an obligation to offer full-time (or equivalent) positions to long-service part-timers who are fully committed to the academic career (18a)?
- Should part-timers have a rank and salary structure that rewards demonstrated quality and length of service (18b)?

Eight factors are independent variables in my regression model: full-timers' discipline, academic rank, past and present administrative rank, years of teaching, year hired as tenure-track faculty, previous contract status as part-timer or limited-term full-timer, gender, and language.

TABLE 5.1
Full-timers' views of part-timers

Variables	B1 17a	B2 17b	B3 17c	B4 17d	B5 18a	B6 18b
Q25 Discipline	.10	.06	−.00	.02	.04	.06
Q26 Academic rank	−.18**	−.16**	.13*	.19**	−.32**	−.11*
Q27 Administrative rank	−.03	−.01	.02	−.03	.08*	−.00
Q28 Total years as full-time faculty	−.01	−.00	.01	.01	.00	.00
Q29 Year hired at this university	.02	.01	−.02*	−.02	.02*	−.00
Q30 Part-time/contract experience	.03	.19**	.00	−.08	.12	.03
Q33 Gender	.16*	.10	−.19*	−.18*	.27**	.23**
Language	.44**	.07	−.55**	.16*	−.57**	−.10
Constant	2.45**	3.78**	3.75**	2.96**	2.84**	3.97**
Multiple R	.22	.16	.26	.17	.29	.15
R^2	.05	.03	.07	.03	.08	.02
F value	8.18	4.11	10.92	4.68	14.20	3.54
Total no.	1253	1253	1253	1253	1253	1253

Notes: p = *<.05; **<.01.
Dummy variables: Q25 'Social sciences' = 1; 'Sciences' = 0
Q30: 'With part-time experience' = 1; 'without part-time experience' = 0
Q33: 'Female' = 1; 'Male' = 0
Language: 'French' = 1; 'English' = 0.
Source: Rajagopal, Full-Time Faculty Survey (1991–2)

The results of the above regressions confirm the segmentation of interests among full-timers and also identify the conflicting relations between full- and part-timers. Of all interests and characteristics, rank incisively divides full-timers in their attitudes and perceptions of part-timers. Rank is a significant predictor in each of the six regression models that have extracted the relative impact of full-timers' characteristics (specified above as independent variables) on their assessments of part-timers' issues and interests.

'Should part-timers be represented in proportions equal to those of full-time faculty in academic decision-making bodies of the university?' (Q17a) Along rank lines, full professors clearly reject the idea (b" –.18). If we add full-timers' gender and language characteristics into the regression, further fragmentation within the full-time collegium emerges. These two factors – gender and language – operate counter to rank and further divide full-timers. In contrast to all full professors (rank factor), full-timers as a group in francophone universities (language factor) strongly approve equal representation for part-timers in academic bodies (b" .44). The addition of gender has a similar impact. Women as distinct from men full-timers also support the equality of part-timers and their inclusion in collegial bodies (b" .16).

'Do part-timers have a legitimate place in the university?' (Q17b) Full professors reject the notion (b" –. 16). But career path – whether a full-timer did or did not have a prior contract – tells a different story. In contrast to full professors as a whole, Insiders who have prior experience on contract, either as part-time or as full-time limited-term faculty, tend far more to acknowledge their place in academe (b" .19). A majority of them are post-Second World War baby boomers whose views tend to be more egalitarian. In contrast, more than half the Outsiders were born before the war and are reluctant to share with part-timers the prerogatives that they have enjoyed exclusively.

'Should the main responsibility for academic collegial decision-making rest with the full-time faculty alone?' (Q17c) Again, full professors see decision-making as exclusively a tenure-track right (b" .13). Language and gender characteristics moderate full professors' views on this issue. Full-timers in francophone universities strongly disapprove of the full professors' claim to exclusive power (b" –.55). Women full-timers (b" –.19) also favour sharing decision-making powers. Full-timers, both men and women, hired more recently (as opposed to long-serving full-timers) join (b"–.02) the women in believing that part-timers should have a say in decisions.

'Should part-timers be considered a separate stream of teachers?' (Q17d) Here again, gender, rank, and language create segmented perceptions. Women full-timers reject the idea of a separate stream, which would effectively degrade part-timers as 'simply a teaching army' (b" –.18). In contrast, full professors (b" .19) as a group and the full-timers in francophone universities (b" .16) favour a separate stream for part-timers. A biology full-timer illustrates the thinking: 'To meet the current demands of heavy teaching load and the extraordinary pressure on faculty to publish, it is becoming more and more evident that it is necessary to separate *career teachers* from *career researchers*. The university will have no choice but to consolidate their resources and create a system that should incorporate both teachers and researchers. But the administrators are responsible for the slow changes as a result of their hyper-conservative and hyper-protective attitude.'

'*Does the university have an obligation to offer full-time (or equivalent) positions to long-service part-timers who are fully committed to the academic career?*' *(18a)* Must a university that has benefited from the long and meritorious contributions of part-timers fulfil this obligation? Once again, full professors (b" –.32), as well as full-timers as a group in francophone universities (b –.57), are obstinate about believing that universities have no such obligation. A gender split is evident on this issue. Women emphasize that universities do have such a moral obligation (b" .27). Full-timers at lower administrative ranks, as opposed to higher-rank administrators agree (b" .08). Also, full-timers hired more recently (in contrast to those who have been around for a long time) believe that universities exploit part-timers and should hire qualified part-timers, based on merit and competition, for filling full-time positions (b" .02). A mathematics full-timer in a francophone university – an Outsider – rejects the possibility of incorporating part-timers into the faculty collegium: 'Part-time teachers represent a bad solution to hiring problems in departments such as Mathematics. It would be better to offer better contracts to our graduate students and give them a larger teaching load. [Otherwise] a part of undergraduate education could eventually be delegated to college instructors who are qualified only with a Masters + degree and this [system] would stabilize itself [as the solution]. It is a serious mistake for the university to hire personnel that do not have a precise career plan that includes a strong component of research. It would be even more serious still to try to stabilize such personnel.'

'*Should part-timers have a rank and salary structure that rewards demonstrated quality and length of service?*' *(18b)* On this issue, also, full-timers are split along academic rank. Full professors, perhaps acutely worried about expanding the academic structure and creating an unnecessary parallel entity or the extra financial demands created, oppose a separate rank and salary structure for part-timers (b" –.11). However, more women (b" .23) than men full-timers are receptive to the idea.

So far, we have seen how full-timers, particularly full professors and higher-rank academic administrators, are not sympathetic towards part-timers and do not wish to integrate them into academe. The professoriate opposes hiring of part-timers as a permanent or long-term solution for handling its financial shortfalls. It argues persuasively that this policy would limit tenure-track hiring. They fear that the results would be the same as those in the United States, where the financial trends are similar. In U.S. higher education, the percentage of teaching done by part-timers has increased (AAUP, 1995: 13), accentuating tensions between the tenured/tenure-track academics and full-time contractees and the so-called readily available pool of part-timers. The professoriate's most powerful reaction is against any decrease in tenure-track appointments and a corresponding increase in part-timers. Herein lies a clear conflict between the vested interests of the two groups – the professoriate and part-timers.

Full-Timers' versus Part-Timers' Perceptions

The two groups are hierarchically organized, each with its own interests and unique demands on the university. Full-timers hire part-timers and regulate their work. Decisions to hire part-timers are always linked to the university's financial situations. As a result, full-timers who argue for increased funding for new tenure-stream positions worry about the increasing availability of part-timers. To understand how full-timers view part-timers and their concerns, we must consider whether full-timers' own departments have part-timers, why they hired them, and whether the part-timers are Classics or Contemporaries.

First, we look at the departmental contexts and reasons for hiring part-timers. Nine full-timers in ten have part-timers in their departments. Full-timers seem to know enough about them to be able to describe their composition accurately: Classics a third and Contemporaries two-thirds of all part-timers. Most full-timers (71.3 per cent) know that the foremost reason for hiring part-timers in their departments is to meet teaching and curricular needs within the strictures of available funding. The second reason they give is that part-timers are needed to replace full-timers who are on leave. A majority of full-timers do not consider other reasons relevant. Low on the list are the following: to fill positions requiring professional expertise from outside academe; to allow full-timers more research time; to deal with shifting enrolments; and to fill positions on an interim basis, while the department looks for qualified candidates.

Second, full-timers dislike their university central administration's strategies of managing faculty resources, particularly in times of enrolment fluctuations and volatility in workloads. In general, they detest enrolment 'bulges' and increases in class size, both of which lead to temporary appointments. In particular, a majority of full professors and associate professors would like to see a decrease in part-time appointments and deny, in principle, the need for flexibility in hiring. In contrast, half of the assistant professors would not like to see any decrease in enrolments because they fear that it would mean 'the last hired would be first fired.' They are more conscious of the direct link between upturns in full-time hiring and increasing enrolments. Every new position created is to be backed by a proportional increase in projected and relatively stable student enrolments. Obviously, a considerable majority of assistant professors (59 per cent versus full professors 47 per cent) would logically resent any likely decease in tenure-track appointments. These segmentations and divisions between tenured and tenure-track full-timers, however, do not prevent them (72 per cent) from coming together as a group to condemn their universities' policies of hiring more part-timers instead of creating full-time positions. Indeed the professoriate, as a whole, wants part-time positions decreased.

The conflicts between full-timers and part-timers are central to the power relations within academe. To flesh out what the above regressions have shown, we now turn to the contrasting perceptions of the two groups about the life and work of part-timers. The first major contrast emerges from their divergent views on part-timers' career aspirations. The second occurs in full-timers' perceptions of what part-timers' academic work should involve. The third is about part-timers' eligibility vis-à-vis decision-making bodies. I draw upon my two surveys (full-timers and part-timers) to illustrate the contrasting images of part-timers – how full-timers see them and how part-timers see themselves – in each of the three areas.

Part-Timers' Aspirations

The first set of contrasting perceptions relates to career aspirations. A career is a general progression of one's working or professional life and 'a profession for which one trains and which is undertaken as a permanent calling.'[7] Many part-time workers tend to believe that they start their careers in workplaces where they accept an appointment. As long as they wish to be academics, working part time does not seem to limit their career orientation: they still aspire to progress in their work life. They want to be in a context that accords them a positive role as a worker and awards due credit for their contributions.

Particularly in 'the professions,' workers seem to be more aware of entering their chosen careers. In academe, careerism is more pronounced because teaching is considered an avocation or a calling. Therefore, it is not surprising that for Contemporaries, and even for some Classics, the academic career starts with their appointment in a university. Three-fourths of Contemporaries affirm that teaching and research are the main planks of their career, despite a lack of full-time academic positions. Even if they were to start their career over again, more than eight part-timers in ten would choose academe. Part-timers feel that their career orientation is being systemically degraded when they find that full-timers and administrators view them as expedient solutions to underfunding or as temporary teachers to fill classes.

Full-timers' comments in response to my survey show how they see part-timers' career issues. Many of them wrote at length, conveying their impressions and reflections. A male professor in history, an Insider, writes about part-timers' dead-end careers: 'My institution has, for the past 15 years or so, been blatantly abusing part-time faculty. Seen as a fruitful source of cheap labour, bright young academics have been hired to teach huge classes without any prospect of tenure or promotion and with no sense of security or commitment. This is all very sad, even though everyone claims that it is the inevitable result of financial expediency.' A male mathematics professor, an Insider (formerly a part-timer), warns against the continual exploitation of part-timers, especially the women: 'Part-time appointments are most often an exploitation of most of the appointees (usually female). Salary and fringe benefits should be comparable to full-time faculty. In many cases, people teach as 'part-timers' with full-time load, the same courses year after year. Such people should be tenured at full-time professor salary if the position is needed for several years and the same person is hired year after year; that is a de facto recognition of competence.'

On the question of hiring for full-time positions, however, full-timers' responses – a greater proportion in francophone universities (francophone 65 per cent versus anglophone 44 per cent) – reject any influence of gender in making such appointments. Francophone full-timers emphasize gender neutrality in hiring part-timers for full-time positions in their departments and deny discrimination in the process against male part-timers (francophone 77 per cent versus anglophone 60 per cent) or against female part-timers (francophone 63 per cent, versus anglophone 49 per cent). Some full-timers of both language groups (anglophone 26 per cent versus francophone 18 per cent) agree, however, that if gender does influence hiring, it could be more negative than positive. Full-timers in anglophone universities (35 per cent versus francophone 19 per cent) say that, in hiring, being male is relatively more negative, whereas being female is more positive (anglophone 45 per cent versus francophone universities 30 per cent) in their universities. These responses might be related to their relative experiences of how effective affirmative action policies have been.

In my data analysis, I looked at gender barriers by grouping universities as research intensive or teaching intensive. From the part-timers survey, we know that part-timers in both research and teaching universities (59 per cent and 40 per cent, respectively) deny that gender has much influence in hiring for full-time positions. Fewer part-timers (14 per cent in research universities versus 21 per cent in teaching universities) feel that their gender might reduce their chances of obtaining a full-time academic position. The full-timers survey presents a somewhat contrasting picture; full-timers in both types of universities declare that gender and visible minority status affect the hiring of part-timers for full-time positions. According to them (48 per cent in teaching universities versus 33 per cent in research universities), women part-timers have slightly better chances of getting full-time positions, particularly in teaching universities. Some full-timers (39 per cent in teaching universities versus 23 per cent in research universities) also believe that men might face a slight gender barrier.

Why, then, do all part-timers not see these barriers? Full-timers' preferences and support, either formal or informal, are crucial in part-time hiring. Since they do have control over hiring, conflicts are latent and are camouflaged by the sympathetic views of some individual full-timers. The following few excerpts show these perspectives. Although he is an Outsider, a male science full-timer understands and appreciates part-timers' contributions. Part-timers' career mobility is dependent on full-timers' support: 'Any success part-time faculty might achieve in their career depends entirely on the open-mindedness and respect of full-time tenured faculty in the department. Too many individuals view part-time faculty as a "purgatory" for Ph.D. waiting to move to the "heaven" of full-time tenure positions. I see part-time staff as playing a vital role in our universities in times of financial restraint. They contribute significantly to student life as well as "fresh blood." I view them as true colleagues.' A male full-timer in fine arts censures the system: 'Part-time faculty has laid the groundwork for the establishment of several departments at this institution, particularly music and fine (visual) arts. Some, who have stayed the course, have been rewarded with full-time tenure-track positions. Many more have left the dept. before their contributions were adequately recognized. Distinctions should be made between sessional faculty who have contributed for many years at full workload (2, 3, or more courses per year), which bespeaks exploitive employment practices, and lecturers, employed in more marginal capacities.' A science full-timer in a francophone university, an Insider (once a part-timer), identifies the kinds of barriers that part-timers, even those with an excellent teaching record, might encounter: 'In our department, we have ... excellent part-timers with exceptional pedagogical talents, teaching university-level courses. They would like to pursue careers exclusively devoted to teaching. But, as part-timers, now they have to teach in three different universities in order to generate sufficient income to support their families. The department is unable to guarantee either a career plan or any long-term employment prospects. The reasons are: they have no research or publication record, but the university hires its tenure track professors only on the basis of their research abilities. Full-time faculty union opposes the hiring of a parallel body of full-time teachers as separate stream; part-timers union does not allow longer term contract for part-timers since it requires that a yearly competition is held for all part-time positions.' From a francophone university, a woman full-timer in sociology, an Outsider, captures the essence of full-timers' ambivalence: 'The question of part-time faculty is a difficult one ... We hire them for teaching, but then criticize them for only doing that, and of remaining uninvolved [in departmental matters]. In my department, part-timers are necessary and often numerous. But we are often ambivalent towards them. They have to replace us, they have to be competent and effective, and must leave when we return ... We often hire them to help us out during a few sessions here and there. In my view, we should also hire them to allow professors to devote more time to research. The compatibility between research and teaching is questionable. The problem of part-time labour is situated in the heart of this debate. The ideal would be to have more full-time positions in order to avoid two categories of teachers.' A male Insider from a francophone university education department talks about how the administrative load of full-timers has increased, and how the university has degraded teaching by virtually turning it into part-time work:

> I hope that this study will denounce the shameful situation, which is becoming firmly rooted in our university environment. Very few full-time professors can say that they are not overburdened with administrative duties. They also teach so much that they have to bend over backwards to do research. At the same time, a professional corps of part-time faculty, maybe with a little less academic qualification (few of them have a Ph.D.), have proved to be effective despite the fact that they are underpaid. For the most part, these part-timers are true intellectuals absorbed in their work ... [We] find that they are more effective and have more time to contribute their knowledge through teaching ... If part-timers became better integrated into our academic structure, university life would be more harmonious and the quality of life in this university would benefit. I was a part-timer for 12 years. During this time I taught many courses and was happy. I have taught full-time for 5 years. I teach fewer and fewer courses and feel less and less cheerful.

Is the empathy for part-timers that some full-timers in francophone universities express more than counterbalanced by discriminatory practices elsewhere against their being hired for full-time work? A majority of full-timers in anglophone universities (64 per cent) and in francophone universities (51 per cent) say that in hiring for full-time posts they do not deliberately discriminate against their own graduates or prefer graduates from prestigious universities to their own part-timers (in anglophone universities 57 per cent versus francophone universities 43 per cent). Part-timers' survey responses, however, contradict those of full-timers. Only some part-timers reject the notion of discrimination against hiring from within the university (francophone 24 per cent versus anglophone 33 per cent), or of preference for graduates from prestigious universities (francophone part-timers 24 per cent versus anglophone 29 per cent). This attitude could be based on part-timers' fear that negative assumptions about them could worsen their chances of being hired for full-time positions. The differences in the two perceptions and assumptions merit further analysis, to which we now turn.

From a francophone university, a male full-timer in history who is an Insider brings out three troubling perceptions. First, it is degrading to view part-timers as a financial expedient. Second, it is gratuitously presumptuous to tantalize part-timers with full-time positions. Third, full-timers should accord legitimacy to part-timers' non-traditional career aspirations instead of regarding them as an aberration in the academy:

> Although [part-time] appointments are typically justified, ad hoc, on grounds of expediency, I regard them as a necessary, permanent and valuable feature of the academic community. My impression is that my view is not widely shared. Certainly, my departmental budgets do not recognize them as I do. It is telling that appointments of this sort are made from 'soft funds' ... highly vulnerable to the vagaries of general funding from fiscal year to fiscal year.

> The presumption underlying this situation – that all [part-timers] wish to have full-time jobs and that they will (soon) receive full-time 'regular' academic appointments – is totally unfounded. This normative view, reflected in budget structures and in the attitudes of tenured/tenurable academics toward such appointees, is inconsistent [with the reality] and demeaning [to part-timers], although, I presume, [such a view] is consistent with the attitude towards all part-time employees throughout the economy.

> Non-traditional career aspirations should be respected. For instance, spousal appointments are made into a 'problem' quite unnecessarily. Some scholars are brilliant researchers, but indifferent teachers and academic administrators. They are highly valuable nonetheless, and not – as the normative view would have it – suspect as 'flawed'. What a 'normal' academic career means needs fundamental reexamination.

An education department full-timer, a male Insider (formerly an LTFT) expresses full-timers' ambivalence. He identifies the impact of financial constraints on the academic workload and resultant utilitarian perceptions that full-timers hold about part-timers' role in the university: 'We "exploit" part-time staff, especially those who hold other full-time positions. Initially, they are flattered to be asked to teach at a university level, but after the third time (usually), the glamour has worn off and they realize they are being underpaid. Central administration sees part-timers as an effective way of handling increased numbers. While the part-timers do "cover the courses," they do nothing towards course development and the committee loads fall to a smaller number to carry out. A love-hate relationship [exists between full-timers and part-timers, that is,] I am afraid. Without them, in today's economy, I would have a significantly higher teaching load. With them, my within-university service load has increased significantly in terms of my time; am I further ahead?' Another comment comes from a science full-timer, an Insider (formerly an LTFT), who blames the faculty for not pulling its weight in the university. The respondent feels strongly that some full-timers overstay in their jobs, even though they are deemed no longer efficient, and that such positions could easily be released and filled by new full-time appointments from the deserving pool of part-timers: 'The Department ... has a miserable record with respect to part-timers, post-docs and research associates who would like to carve out a niche here. Many are very talented who come to us but are disillusioned by internal politics of the ... dead wood in the Department. Other faculty members speak about them but do nothing about this problem.'

Despite empathy from many full-timers, part-timers seem to experience isolation and neglect: 'I personally feel very isolated from the university and have more to do with the Admin/support staff than the academic faculty.' Even a Classic who has a full-time job elsewhere agrees: 'Part-time teaching, for me, is ... for contact with the faculty. I would appreciate more effort to make me feel included within the academic community, even if salary should decrease. Salary is not important.' Many part-timers feel that they are seen as a problem in academe or as a necessary evil: 'Not only are part-time faculty not expected to participate in planning, but the inherent indeterminacy of their appointments constitutes an area in the curriculum in which long-term planning (longer than a year) simply cannot be done.' And, 'I have been teaching part-time for almost 10 years, including since 1986–7 when I received my Ph.D. I love this work and find it incredibly rewarding to teach students with a joy and enthusiasm that they apparently don't receive often from full-time faculty (according to teaching evaluation comments). The only difficult part of the job is being treated as a "necessary evil" by full-time faculty. Their only use for us is in giving them more time to devote to research activities. They clearly regard teaching and students as obstacles to their work at the university.'

Part-timers clearly find the full-timers' utilitarian view of part-timers' role in the university quite untenable. Most part-timers (72 per cent) feel that they are seen as an expedient solution to funding problems. Many (63 per cent) also find that full-timers treat them as limited-scope support staff. Although full-timers agree that part-timers are expected to be a part of academe for the long haul, they grant them very few rights in the workplace. Part-timers feel quite dejected by this kind of treatment; the higher their qualifications are, the greater is their sense of frustration. Most part-timers, particularly in humanities (84 per cent, versus sciences 65 per cent), feel that full-timers in their discipline treat them with great disdain. What, then, is the full-timers' image of the part-time faculty?

First, full-timers see the part-timers' role in quite unflattering terms. 'Part-time faculty member' evokes in full-timers' minds an image of temporary workers, an easy escape for the university's financial problems, and a painless solution to lower student-faculty ratios. Two-thirds of full-timers think that part-time hiring should be a temporary solution, to be used only when universities cannot afford to create full-time positions. They (64 per cent) feel that such appointments should be used mostly for lowering enrolment pressures and student-faculty ratios. More than half of them (56 per cent), however, find that Classics are useful because they bring practical skills and expertise from outside academe.

Second, full-timers exclude part-timers from the academic collegium. A majority of full-timers (62 per cent) would deny full membership to most part-timers. There is clearly an inverse relationship between rank and collegiality. The higher the rank of full-timers, the less their collegiality with part-timers (table 5.2). Assistant professors are slightly more sympathetic to part-timers. More assistant professors (44 per cent versus professors 37 per cent) consider a half of part-timers as full members with full academic commitment. In contrast, many professors (63 per cent) and associate professors (65 per cent) do not regard most of their part-timers[8] as full members of the collegium. A majority of full professors (63 per cent) and associate professors (60 per cent) also consider the part-time faculty to be limited in academic commitment. The survey of part-timers also confirms that they are excluded from full-timers' collegial circles of academic discussions and decision-making. More than half of part-timers (54 per cent), more among women (59 per cent versus men 49 per cent) and those with a master's degree (58 per cent) or a doctorate (50 per cent versus less than master's 48 per cent) are struck by the absence of academic equality or collegiality despite part-timers' substantial level of scholarship and academic interests.

TABLE 5.2
Full-timers' perceptions of part-timers

They treat part-time faculty as	How many part-timers?	Discipline %					Rank %			
		Social sciences	Fine arts/ humanities	Pure sciences	Applied science	Health/ education/ business/ law	Full professor	Associate professor	Assistant professor/ other	Total %
Full members of academic collegium	Many	25.6	36.8	42.4	32.8	35.5	32.5	28.3	33.7	31.4
	Half	6.4	8.4	4.0	7.5	9.7	4.9	7.0	9.9	6.9
	A few	68.1	54.8	54.5	59.7	54.8	62.7	64.6	56.4	61.7
	Total %	100.0	100.0	100.0	100.0	100.0	100.0	100.0	100.0	100.0
Persons with only partial commitment in academe	Many	61.5	54.8	62.4	58.0	57.7	63.3	60.0	51.5	59.5
	Half	7.2	13.8	5.9	10.7	7.9	7.3	9.8	10.2	8.9
	A few	31.2	31.5	31.7	31.3	34.9	29.3	30.2	38.3	31.6
	Total %	100.0	100.0	100.0	100.0	100.0	100.0	100.0	100.0	100.0
Welcome source of expertise not otherwise available	Many	35.7***	39.3***	37.3***	48.5***	46.9***	40.4 (n.s.)	37.8 (n.s.)	38.6 (n.s.)	38.9
	Half	14.6	9.8	6.9	13.2	9.4	11.7	12.2	13.5	12.3
	A few	49.9	50.8	55.8	38.2	43.7	47.9	50.0	47.8	48.8
	Total %	100.0	100.0	100.0	100.0	100.0	100.0	100.0	100.0	100.0
Total no.		563	282	148	188	73	479	453	322	1,254

Notes: Significance: p = *<.05, **<.01; ***<.001. All are significant at p = *<.05 unless otherwise indicated. (n.s.): not significant.
Source: See table 5.1.

Third, full-timers seem disingenuous in their concern to improve part-timers' chances for full-time positions. On the one hand, they consider qualified part-timers as scholars with good research records, teaching effectiveness, professional standing, and fine personal characteristics. They outright reject the notion of any labelling or stereotyping or of gender or ethnic discrimination against part-timers in hiring for full-time positions. On the other hand, their own responses also seem to indicate that there must be some prevalent prejudices or practices that block qualified part-timers. Full-timers state that they are quite pessimistic about part-timers' prospects for full-time academic jobs. Their average estimate is that, even if jobs are available, only 27 per cent of part-timers are likely to get full-time positions through competitive hiring. In contrast, part-timers are quite hopeful about their future prospects. More than half of the part-timers (53 per cent) want an academic full-time job and are confident of getting one in the next three years. Only 41 per cent feel that they have little chance of doing so.

Part-timers' chances of securing full-time positions (if available) clearly appear better in the teaching universities. Research and teaching universities differ sharply in their sense of obligation to their part-timers. A majority of full-timers in the teaching institutions (54 per cent) hold that their universities are obliged to offer full-time positions to long-service part-timers. However, full-timers in research universities (51 per cent) do not agree with this perception. More full-timers in teaching universities (69 per cent versus research universities 60 per cent) regard part-timers as useful in lowering student-faculty ratios and in handling enrolment pressures. More full-timers in research universities (52 per cent versus teaching universities 46.6 per cent) report that they use part-timers to maintain the workload of full-time faculty at an acceptable level. Further, more full-timers in teaching universities (61 per cent versus research universities 50 per cent) feel that part-timers are necessary to cope with an indispensable need for teachers arising from underfunding and enrolment pressures. In contrast, more full-timers in research universities (53 per cent versus teaching universities 49 per cent) regard them merely as fillers in situations demanding professional expertise not otherwise available on the faculty.

Part-Timers' Work

The second set of mutually contrasting perceptions relates to part-timers' academic work and research productivity. Full-timers, as well as university administration, devalue and discount part-timers' work in all three areas: teaching, research, and service. Both full-timers and central administration see a limited scope for part-timers' academic activities. Through their decisions in collegial bodies, full-timers define and circumscribe part-timers' work. University central administration restricts part-timers by limiting them to short-term contracts and by not providing resources and secretarial services to support their teaching. Thus, the university seems to ignore and not acknowledge part-timers' contributions and, by implication, denigrate the work that they do.

First, we turn to part-timers' academic contributions and how they are assessed. A majority of full-timers (56 per cent) acknowledge part-timers' contributions in teaching to be good. In all other aspects, they consider part-timers' work to be quite inconsistent in quality. Full-timers (41 per cent) assign a slightly favourable rating to Classics' professional work external to universities, but they rate as low in quality part-timers' research and scholarship, their contributions to collegial activity, and to the department's informal social life. A male full-timer in management science believes that part-timers' work lowers academic quality: 'Problems with Part-time Faculty (as permanent staff): (1) no pressure to do research so their knowledge quickly becomes outdated. (2) if they do not have the Ph.D. (none of ours has) they have a very narrow non-academic perspective. If budget constraints were not so tight, we should not have any permanent part-timers teaching. They lower academic quality. On the other hand, in a professional school, [it is useful] to have practitioners teach some courses to give students a more practice-orientated view.' A male LTFT in civil engineering expresses a similar view: 'The dominant policy across Canadian universities of not replacing retiring faculty by full-time staff but by part-time faculty is unquestionably leading to an erosion of teaching standards. Just ask any student taught by a part-time member, who has attempted to seek additional help from a faculty member who spends about 3 hrs on campus.' It is not rare to find part-timers denigrated on a basis of personal experiences, often generalized as stereotypes. A male full-timer in the finance department (business faculty) makes a sweeping statement: '80 per cent of part-timers are incompetent!' Another male full-timer in business administration criticizes part-timers' lack of commitment: 'It is this writer's view that the main problem associated with part-time people is their lack of commitment to the academic tasks they are asked to perform by our department.'

In strong contrast, part-timers' own reporting shows that not only are they rated as excellent teachers, but their research productivity is also quite respectable. Despite carrying a heavy teaching load, 24 per cent of part-timers report that they have written at least one scholarly book in the five years prior to the survey. More than 61 per cent say that they have published one or more scholarly chapters or articles in refereed journals in five years; 63 per cent note their publication of three or more scholarly articles or chapters in their whole career. The divergence between full-timers' view and part-timers' own reporting seems to confirm part-timers' sense of full-timers' hostility towards them. Indeed, full-timers themselves (64 per cent) acknowledge that more should be done to integrate part-timers into the formal and informal life of their departments. Yet the fact remains that part-timers are excluded from participation in many collegial bodies.

Second, through their collegial bodies, full-timers define academic work formally through their councils. Informally, through departmental practices, they describe part-timers' roles. A majority of full-timers (64 per cent) feel that part-timers must be restricted to teaching and they should not do research or service (figure 5.1). On the grounds that part-timers should not be overburdened, full-timers view their role as 'teaching only' and exclude them from research as their work responsibility (57 per cent) as well as from service (57 per cent). This attitude effectively degrades part-timers' work and makes them an underclass in academe, where research is highly valued. The role assigned to part-timers excludes them from regular faculty responsibilities, which in turn denies them any claim to parity with full-timers and entrenches the latter as the only 'real' faculty.

Another common practice in universities is to exclude part-timers from certain levels of teaching for specific reasons. Usually, first-year teaching by part-timers, except leading a tutorial, is discouraged: 'As much as possible part-timers are not hired to teach first year law courses because it is assumed that part-timers put less effort into class preparation, are not as available to students, will not be as helpful in integrating students into law school and values of the law.' A woman part-timer in an arts faculty comments: 'A full-time colleague asked me to be an internal reader on a Ph.D. committee in the area of my expertise. Although I have all the qualifications, the Dean of the Faculty objected to it and took me off the committee. The full-time faculty has the confidence in a qualified part-timer to carry other academic responsibilities besides teaching. But administrators would not like to

FIGURE 5.1

Full-time faculty's views on part-timers

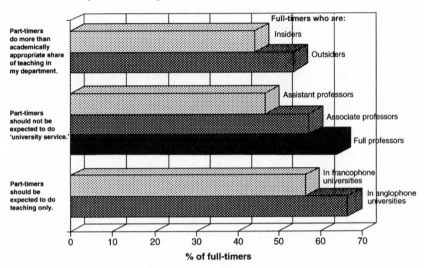

Source: Rajagopal, Full-Time Faculty Survey (1991–2)

extend definition of part-timers as "teaching" support staff. I had no recourse against this action either through my department council or through my union. The collective agreement is written to protect an underclass against administrative excesses, not against its prerogatives.'

Most full-timers (83 per cent) feel that there must be limits on part-timers' teaching loads and restrictions on the number of courses that they can teach in a year. Their rationale is that, to maintain the quality of teaching, the number of courses part-timers can teach should be comparable to the number taught by regular faculty. Four in ten full-timers, however, would like to see a reduction in the number of courses and hours assigned to part-timers. A majority report that part-timers do an inappropriate amount of teaching in their departments. Yet Insiders who formerly were part-timers are less concerned about this issue than Outsiders, perhaps because Insiders themselves have experience, as former contract faculty, with the quality of work that part-timers do (see figure 5.1). In a U.S. study, David Iadevaia (1991) examined whether student success rates were affected by teaching by full-timers versus part-timers and found no differences.[9] In my survey, more full-timers in arts than in sciences believe that their departments would be compromised in academic quality if the share of part-time teaching became disproportionately high. In particular, the full-time faculty in social sciences (46 per cent) and humanities (40.4 per cent) feel this way, since they have to hire more part-timers to deal with their increasing enrolments. Relatively fewer part-timers with responsibility for directing courses are hired in sciences. A female full-timer in education has little confidence in part-timers' ability to develop courses as efficiently as full-timers: 'Usually the course content of part-time faculty does not meet a faculty's integrated program objectives. My concern is also that they generally develop their own course content, which may overlap with full-time [faculty's] course content creating "confusion" for students.'

Full-timers deliberately include in their teaching plans 'part-time' appointments, which they contend are too many and should be reduced. Across all disciplines, full-timers (64 per cent) acknowledge that these appointments lower student-faculty ratios, especially when enrolments fluctuate. Half of all full-timers, especially in departments with huge enrolments and heavier course loads, appreciate part-time appointments, which help to maintain regular faculty's workload at a reasonable level. In contrast, many full-timers also feel that too much teaching by part-timers academically hurts their departments. These apparently self-serving attitudes underlie their ambivalence towards 'the permanent temps,' forced on them by universities' financial straits and administrative decisions. Carolyn Mooney (1993) reports that in the United States the proportion of tenure-stream faculty members has fallen, while the professoriate as a whole has expanded; as a result, about half of the new full-timers are hired on contracts not eligible for tenure. 'Buy-outs' for tenured professors have created another conflict between tenured and other constituencies within the university. It is pointed out that the reason industries, compared with universities, lay off more workers when restructuring is that few workers have job assurance in the industrial sector. In contrast, until recently tenured jobs have been sacrosanct in higher education. Tenure has been preserved during two decades of financial shortfalls through universities' hiring part-time and full-time limited-contract faculty to deliver the curriculum (Mooney, 1993). Leslie, Kellams, and Gunne, in a study done in the heyday of part-time hiring, conclude: 'While it may appear at times as if part-timers are being slipped into the workforce as replacements for full-timers, the evidence suggests just the opposite.

Part-timers are evidently being sacrificed to protect and conserve the jobs of full-time faculty' (1982: 90).

Some full-timers, like this civil engineer, appreciate the contributions of Classics: 'Having been a part-time faculty-member (with full-employment) I favour this status because it allows direct transfer of relevant practical knowledge into teaching.' Others warn about the long-term consequences of a decrease in full-time positions: 'Education of future generations is not a part-time or limited-term process. Even if, and in fact, because the country is experiencing economic problems, our educational system should be strengthened, with both short- and long-term strategies, to better equip our graduates to help the country out of the economic mess. Decreasing full-time tenure track positions in favour of part-time and limited-term faculty is short-sighted and will do more harm to our educational system in the long run.' Some full-timers, however, work for integrating contractees into the system. A female full-timer in sociology argues for accommodating part-timers' career needs: 'I feel strongly that Sessionals [part-timers] should be paid considerably more for teaching courses – most of them are excellent! I would like to see more situations where tenured faculty could share jobs and /or retire early, but teach at half time or 1/3 time at half or 1/3 their salary. We have lost some excellent full time Sessionals because of poor pay and lack of job security. This situation needs to be addressed. Good sessionals in education are hard to find.' A male full-timer in social work, an Insider, agrees: 'Part-time faculty contribute greatly to the richness and effective cooperation of a university – we must develop increasingly formal and universal mechanisms that are more attractive to them to ensure continuous and enthusiastic involvement.'

Part-Timers' Status

Now we turn to the third set of mutually contrasting perceptions, which deals with status and power. As we saw above, full-timers (72 per cent) deny part-timers proportionate representation in academic bodies (table 5.3). They (77 per cent) want responsibility for decision-making to stay with the full-time collegium. Part-timers' marginality results from the hierarchical power-relations within the university. To understand the relations between full-timers and part-timers, we should know how full-timers view the power structure. What do they think of part-timers' unions? Who makes decisions that affect part-timers' work?

TABLE 5.3 Full-timers' views on equitable power and status for part-timers

Part-timers should be/have		Overall total%	Sex %		Rank %		
			Men	Women	Full professor	Associate professor	Assistant professor/ lecturer
Represented in equal proportions to full-timers in academic decision-making bodies	Agree	20.1	18.9	22.6	19.2	15.4	28.1
	Neutral	8.0	7.5	9.6	8.2	8.0	8.2
	Disagree	71.9	73.6	67.8	72.6	76.6	63.7
A legitimate place in the collegium	Agree	69.6	67.8	75.5	64.1	70.9	76.2
	Neutral	14.1	15.2	10.2	18.4	12.0	10.6
	Disagree	16.3	17.0	14.4	17.5	17.0	13.2
Considered a separate stream of teachers	Agree	41.2	44.3	33.0	47.3	42.4	30.9
	Neutral	20.3	20.7	20.1	20.6	17.2	24.4
	Disagree	38.5	35.0	46.8	32.1	40.3	44.6
Rank and salary structure that rewards demonstrated quality and length of service	Agree	77.8	75.4	84.3	75.2*	76.0*	84.5
	Neutral	10.4	11.0	8.5	9.6*	12.0*	8.8
	Disagree	11.8	13.6	9.1	15.0*	12.0*	6.7
No responsibility for collegial decisions, and this responsibility should rest with full-timers	Agree	76.5	78.4	72.0	76.9	80.9	69.9
	Neutral	7.1	6.8	8.0	8.4	5.4	8.0
	Disagree	16.3	14.7	20.1	14.8	13.7	22.1
University's obligation to offer full-time positions to part-timers with academic commitment	Agree	43.6	40.7	52.2	37.0	43.6	53.6
	Neutral	14.3	14.6	13.6	14.7	14.2	13.8
	Disagree	42.1	44.7	34.2	48.3	42.3	32.5
	Total no.	1254	918	336	479	453	322

Notes: Significance: p = *<.05, **<.01; ***<.001. All are significant at p = ***<.001 unless otherwise indicated. Percentages for each question total 100%. Owing to rounding, some may not be exactly 100%. Source: See table 5.1.

FIGURE 5.2

Full-timers' assessment of increase and decrease of influence exerted by
university bodies/groups

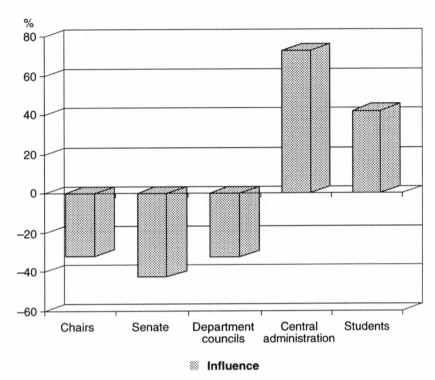

Source: See figure 5.1.

First, let us consider full-timers' views on where power rests in the
university. They report that powers of three groups have increased –
central administration, board of governors or governing councils, and
students. Most full-timers agree that the influence of the university's
central administration has greatly increased (figure 5.2). Strongly critical of the administration's expansion and increasing powers, a male
full-timer in a francophone university writes: 'The "budgetary limitations" imposed by the government acts as the administration's alibi.
The administration never ceases to multiply and expand. Now, it con-
sumes a major part of the budget that would be adequate for hiring
many full-time faculty. It would be interesting to see the statistics on

the rationale for the administration budget and the ratio of administrators to faculty to see clearly where we are in this equation. Are we moving towards a kind of university where faculty would become even more powerless than they were before unionization? Then this is going to be at the cost of the death of the university as we know it. The universities are being eaten away by the cancerous spread of administrators, who dream of only one thing: returning the university to a princely kingdom.' Assessing the relative influence of various groups, most full-timers (73 per cent) clearly identify an increase in the power of the president and vice-presidents (central administration). A relatively smaller proportion of full-timers (48 per cent) note any increase in the influence of faculty associations or unions. Only a few (about 20 per cent) feel that the senate, department chairs, or faculty members have gained power. More than a third believe that the powers of the senate (43 per cent), of department chairs (32 per cent), and of faculty (33 per cent) have actually declined (see figure 5.2). Many full-timers also report a rising influence both at the top and at the bottom of the university's power structure (figure 5.3). Four in ten full-timers (full professors 47 per cent, associate professors 39 per cent, assistant professors 41 per cent) feel that the power and influence of the board of governors or governing councils, as well as of students (full professors 46 per cent, associate professors 39 per cent, assistant professors 39 per cent) have expanded. The lower the rank, the greater the perception of increasing powers in the hands of deans of Faculties (assistant professors 49 per cent, associate professors 42 per cent, professors 44 per cent). Because some full professors are or have been deans, they seem to underplay the dean's power, while more than any other group they assess other bodies as more powerful.

Second, how do full-timers see the role of part-timers' unions and associations? More than half (57 per cent) report that unions or associations represent part-timers in their departments, and some (17 per cent) report that part-timers in their universities are affiliated with full-time faculty unions or associations. According to a quarter of them, in their universities part-timers do not belong to any union. Full-timers as a group see such bodies more as protecting part-timers than as counterbalancing the university's power structures. Full-timers have found that part-timers' unions/associations have increased part-timers' pay, strengthened their voices, improved their working conditions, and reduced departmental discretion in hiring part-timers. Although 53 per cent recognize that part-timers' unions have not blocked full-

FIGURE 5.3
Full-timers' rank-related perceptions of increase in influence of university
bodies/groups

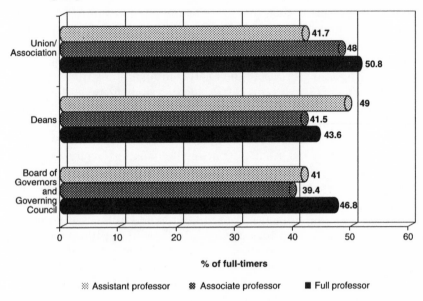

% of full-timers

░ Assistant professor   ✻ Associate professor   ■ Full professor

Source: See figure 5.1.

timers' discretion in assigning courses or other work to part-timers,
half of them (50 per cent) believe that these bodies do not constitute a
positive force in the university. Although 68 per cent acknowledge that
their influence has not compromised academic quality, 31 per cent see
them as a negative development. Full professors, in particular, report
their increasing influence (figure 5.3)

Third, according to full-timers, who are the real decision-makers?
Full-timers are quite sure that power rests in a hierarchy – the board of
governors or the governing council, central administration, senate,
Faculty councils, and deans. They (83 per cent) also know that part-
timers have no say in their own hiring or rehiring, in full-timers' hiring
or tenure, or in negotiating their own pay; but some full-timers (36 per
cent) note that part-timers have as much control as full-timers over
course design.

Part-timers know that they are only as strong as their unions in their
struggle against the arbitrary treatment they receive from universities.

Their eligibility to be represented in collegial bodies is tightly circum-scribed by prevailing rules. A survey of a California college system's part-timers shows that only 15 per cent of them attend their division or department meetings. Most said that these meetings were held during the day, when they were unable to attend. Yet about one in four par-ticipates in committees, and 80 per cent participate in dealing with department affairs and would like to do more (College of the Canyons, 1992). Many full-timers in my survey, however, notice part-timers' absence from meetings or councils, fault them for non-participation and criticize them for their apathy and non-contribution: 'I have great difficulty understanding part-time faculty as they state they want to be involved in activities of curriculum, faculty, creation of job description but few attend meetings or partake in any faculty related activities.' And, '[The part-timers] tend not to serve on committees or on faculty council but could if they wished.'

Not all full-timers see part-timers as virtually powerless; nor do they treat them with the same degree of indifference. A Contemporary woman notes that a few full-timers see them as a potential threat: 'Dis-crimination against part-timers does exist, however, usually among older faculty who seems threatened by the expertise of part-timers, especially the most recent graduates. Perhaps, it is because they have little direct control over them, and cannot delegate committee work to them. Gender bias is also more prevalent in this group. Fortunately they are in the minority and near retirement.' Although these fears are unfounded, many full professors (51 per cent) and associate professors (48 per cent) and fewer assistant professors (42 per cent) worry that unions might affect the existing rank-based balance of power. They do not like to deal with unions that might demand part-timers' rights. A third of full-timers in unionized universities believe that part-timers' unions have disrupted academic quality (figure 5.4).

Some full-timers, both Insiders and Outsiders, however, are positive and indeed generous about part-timers. A female full-timer in history, an Insider, notes: 'Part-timers are the *shadowy people* in our department who work but are rarely seen as equals in social situations. So full-time people don't know them. So, little can be said that is wholly accurate about them.' A male full-timer in education psychology, an Outsider, writes: 'Part-time faculty should be given more access to participating in the faculty decision-making process ... more supportive relation-ships with faculty members should be fostered.' Another full-timer in linguistics, an Insider (formerly an LTFT), urges extension of rights to

FIGURE 5.4
Full-time faculty's views on influence of part-timers' unions or associations

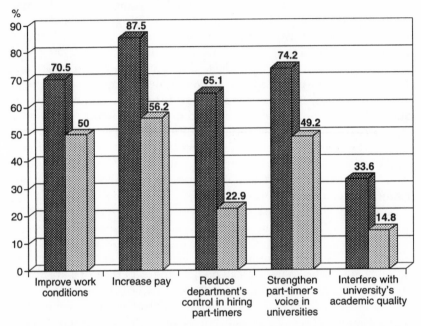

Full-time faculty in universities where ▓ Part-timers unionized ░ Part-timers non-unionized

Source: See figure 5.1.

all part-timers: 'I strongly believe that part time (faculty and other) employment in universities should be encouraged with all rights and duties that full timers have.' In contrast, many full-timers are upset over the likely consequences of an increase in numbers of part-timers and of their unionization. A male full-timer in marketing in a francophone university, though an Insider, feels that his powers are being eroded: 'The part-time union has too much power. The union is protecting those who are not as good and perpetuates their hiring. It's becoming more and more difficult to hire those who can bring new ideas because of this union.' Another francophone professor of science, also an Insider, looks at the issue from a different angle: 'At our university, the part-time faculty collective agreement guarantees academic freedom. This in itself is a good thing. However, as a result it is not possible to regulate part-timers' course content. Thus they can easily avoid teaching materials that are required but difficult to teach. The curriculum is eroded and the situation has become catastrophic with part-timers representing 70 per cent of the teaching body. They are not bad teachers. But they are only inclined to always repeat the same courses in the same manner, without updating the materials, and we have no way of forcing them to do so.' Part-timers feel that the threats seen by full-timers are baseless. A Contemporary part-timer comments: 'For people like me, part-timers, we are discouraged from doing anything of high quality, which would upset the balance of power. Lack of leadership and integrity are serious problems that compromise part-time service in this Faculty.' Faculty members at higher ranks have experience, either as chairs or as course directors, in administering part-timers. As a result, they appear to be somewhat concerned about part-timers' gaining more leverage against academic administrators. However, full professors estimate part-timers' influence as negligible or non-existent. Moreover, the higher the rank, the greater the percentage of full-timers (professors 46 per cent versus assistant professors 36 per cent) inclined to treat part-timers as subordinates. When we review full-timers' observations, we find that they also feel caught in the hierarchy. Most report further bureaucratization and a top-heavy university. Most of them (women 76 per cent and men 72 per cent) see the central administration as gaining power and the full-time faculty as losing its influence.

In the next chapter, we will turn to a special group of full-time faculty, the academic administrators who are responsible for making policies and decisions about all aspects of part-time faculty's work life. A study of their actions and views on part-timers reveals dimensions of full-time faculty interactions with part-timers different from the ones discussed in this chapter.

Chapter Six

Interests That Diverge:
Administrators versus Part-Timers

As things stand we are at the mercy of decision-makers who have an agenda of their own. I often feel that it is the students who end up paying the price.

The administration takes us for granted. They know that working part-time here is the only job many of us have and that we will not leave. We are captive to the system.

To what extent do these comments represent part-timers' experiences in the university? To find out, we need to explore the attitudes of academic administrators and their interactions with part-timers. In the literature, the predominant image of part-timers is one of invisibility and marginality in academe. However, few studies of full-timers or part-timers elaborate on the various factors that shape their situation – the university's mission, full-timers' goals as academic administrators, their perceptions of part-timers, and their treatment of part-timers. Indeed, academic administrators' relationships with part-timers are governed substantially by the complex interactions of these full-timers-cum-administrators with managerial responsibilities as chairs, deans, and vice-presidents. More important, as Baldwin (1982) points out, the administrators have the power to regulate resources that would, if used appropriately, foster the career growth and professional advancement of faculty members. They are in a position to command a sweeping view, identify, determine, and shape where they can, if they choose, all faculty needs in a way that would revitalize and re-energize the professoriate. A supportive and perceptive administrator has the potential to do more than any single academic to benefit both the individuals and the institution. Therefore, we need to examine administrators' attitudes and perceptions, their resource-allocation strategies, and their treatment of part-timers, in order to see how they shape academe.

In a study of administrators' perceptions, several questions arise. How do administrators rate or value part-timers' work? Are they aware of part-timers' career aspirations? Vis-à-vis the university's decision-making processes, do they include or exclude part-timers? Are part-timers empowered or marginalized, or are they mostly isolated, unaffected by administrators' decisions and actions? Do their interests converge or diverge? Answers to these questions might illuminate the relationship between administrators and part-timers. In looking for answers, in this chapter I first examine administrator's reasons for hiring part-timers and the objectives that part-timers are expected to fulfil. Administrators' perceptions about and treatment of part-timers are then studied under the following themes: hiring of part-timers, their (in)visibility, their work, their careers, their power in academe, and their scholarly research. A brief description of the survey respondents (for methodology, see the Appendix) introduces this chapter on administrators and their views of part-timers. Three sections follow, on their hiring of part-timers, on their perceptions of part-timers and of part-timers' work, and on the divergent perceptions of part-timers' place in the university and on the conflicting interests of administrators and part-timers.

Administrators' responses to the survey indicate how they see part-timers as fitting within the university, its faculty, its finances, and its teaching. They rarely raise issues that are at the centre of part-timers' working conditions and interests. According to part-timers, the administrators' perceptions of them spring mainly from their generally utilitarian perspectives. The response of a full-time faculty member identifies the inherent conflict between the raison d'être of administrators and that of part-timers: 'I believe that society has become riddled with people who make careers of paper shuffling [We may find that the bureaucracy has] ... increased ... at most institutions. These people do not understand or care about the operations of the "workers" [whether they are] faculty, or non-academic staff. Increasing amounts of resources are siphoned off from those of us who spend our time in teaching and research. I work seven days a week ... I [would] define these people as parasites ... because they diminish the energy of their hosts.' A full-professor's response – a rare one – shows critical awareness of how underpaid temporary workers perform the regular faculty's labour-intensive task of teaching: 'The university is getting away with spending very little on faculty salaries due to the use of part-timers. If this use were curtailed, the *real* cost of education would, I think, become evident.

New Directions: Academic Administrators as CEOs

Over the last two decades, studies on part-time or contract members of faculty have taken a new direction (see Biles and Tuckman, 1986; Abel, 1984; Scott, 1983; Gappa and Leslie, 1993). The authors no longer discuss the definition and role of this group but suggest, instead, that the university administration and faculty should consider its resilience and its possible integration into the university community. Earlier studies were focused on demographics of part-timers or their plight in a jobless market. Following faculty projections that estimated possible retirements of baby boomers during the early part of the twenty-first century (Bowen and Sosa, 1989; Renner, 1995), authors of more recent studies emphasize labour market structures and the academic job situation (Gappa and Leslie, 1993; Leslie, 1998). They explore universities as institutions, how administrators have shaped academic work, and how to ensure a better workplace for the faculty.

Two theoretical concepts inform the study of the relationship between part-timers and administrators – *ideological practices* that underlie those interrelationships (Smith, 1990) and *the organization of jobs* (Kanter, 1979: 6) and functions within the university.[1] Ideological practices are structures of assumptions and practices that shape relations in institutions. Administrators' decisions and the practices that implement their policies organize the academic work of teaching, research, and decision-making. Unrevealed elements – assumptions that are hidden within views and perspectives – may also affect the worker-management relationship. Therefore, ideological practices form one dimension of the power relations that govern the interactions between part-timers and administrators. These practices, in fact, clearly differentiate part-time academic work from that of the regular faculty. They also segment the workplace and accentuate the status ranking that distinguishes part-timers from full-time faculty and administrators. The organization of jobs[2] – 'the kinds of jobs and how work is structured and located' in the workplace (Kanter, 1979: 6) – shows the other dimension of power relations. Various institutional and structural factors – for instance, the university's language, region, faculty unionization or not, administrators' rank, and their gender – influence the way in which academic work is organized into jobs.

The ideological practices that formulate, legitimize, and validate academic work constitute the framework of power in universities. Dorothy Smith defines ideological practices as 'methods of creating accounts of the world that treat it selectively in terms of a predetermined conceptual framework.' She argues that ideological practices suppress the presence of 'actualities' that do not conform to the established schema. If the accepted precepts and procedures are to be questioned, this process must take place within the established structure without breaking the procedures of the 'ideological circle.' The circle of those who decide policies excludes those who carry out the work of the organization (Smith, 1990: 93, 94–5). Inclusion within the circle, therefore, requires policy-making authority. Authority itself provides the power that makes one's words count. If one's words do not count, then one has no valid authority and thus is not a member of the circle (Smith, 1987: 29–31). Those excluded are subordinated as objects, and their experiences are deemed irrelevant to the exercise of power (Smith, 1990: 18–19).

Smith explains the way in which ideological practices organize status and process in an organization. Professional and bureaucratic procedures are created and rationalized so as to control, and to fit neatly into the system, individual experiences and the realities of the world, which are generally confusing. Professionals and bureaucrats are trained to produce an 'order' out of these realities. The organizational hierarchy inhibits openness to and questioning of these 'actualities' and promotes enforcement of procedures that are relevant to institutional and administrative goals. Bureaucratic goals and objectives implemented by administrators and translated into administrative procedures formalize the procedures as institutional rules. These procedures assign value and legitimacy to certain conditions of work and workers. In the university, administrators have the legitimacy of authority that is entrusted to them by the governing institutions – for example, election or selection procedures, Faculty councils, and the board of governors.

A set of assumptions or ideological practices relating to part-timers underlies the exercise of authority that organizes part-timers' jobs in specific ways. Professional control over the definition of the academic work process downgrades the function of teaching as opposed to research. It precludes the inclusion of 'research' within part-timers' work (Wallace, 1984; Rajagopal and Farr, 1992). According to prevalent gradations of work, research has a higher value than teaching and directing a course is more prestigious than teaching tutorials. Further, part-timer status, itself, is left unranked and categorized as support work. Boundaries between full- and part-time work are rigorously maintained. Thus, academe gets segmented into a dual workforce and part-timers are hired to do only teaching, whereas full-timers are expected both to do research and to make decisions.

Turning now to jobs, we find that institutional goals and administrators' ways of translating these goals into practice are critical in organizing jobs (Kanter, 1979: 8). Administrators' actions in controlling the workplace affect part-timers' jobs and the extent to which these jobs can be creative and self-directed and/or remain routinized, regulated, and orderly. Are part-timers perceived as both teachers and researchers, or only as teachers? If administrators exclude them from committees and other decision-making bodies, part-timers become invisible, their work remains hidden, and their contributions go unrecognized. Are they, formally or informally, denied access to collegial contact and political alliances through peer networks? Part-timers are made irrelevant and powerless when their work is not acknowledged (Rajagopal and Farr, 1989) or not recognized as helping to solve the university's financial problems.[3]

In a segmented workplace, an administration can easily enforce order through a hierarchy. Managing different groups of workers through a line of hierarchical functions is more efficient than centrally administering them. Therefore, the university's central administrators segregate roles and vest full-timers with the power and responsibility of managing part-timers. This situation is analogous to that of other marginalized groups entering and increasing their participation in the workforce, for example, women and ethnic minorities. Intra-occupational segregation occurs as gender inclusion advances in the workplace. A process of job resegregation begins as jobs that were once male-dominated and identified as of higher level get redefined as 'women's jobs' (Blum and Smith, 1988).[4] It is easy in this way to categorize a position as a woman's job and drop it to a lower status (Bielby and Baron, 1986: 776–7, 789; Reskin and Roos, 1987, 1988).[5] Similar to Lowe's (1982) 'degradation of work' of women (also see Rajagopal and Farr, 1992: 320), part-time work becomes labelled as unskilled and routinized and as a result, is poorly paid.

In a bureaucracy, decisions governing the control of personnel may not be conspiratorial, but they may, in fact, be spontaneous or uncoordinated and have unintended consequences: 'Because they can be ideologically legitimated in so many ways, seldom are such decisions or consequences fully understood by those in power' (Scott, 1983: 193). The hiring of part-timers offers the university's central administrators 'flexibility, special expertise, economics, public relations and market conditions' (Leslie, Kellams, and Gunne, 1982: 94).[6] They may save money by not allocating office space or support facilities to part-timers or by withdrawing resources that part-timers may have had and using these savings to meet pressures elsewhere, for example, demands for higher salaries for full-timers (Scott, 1983: 166–70).

Scott remarks that when managers cannot predict business fluctuations, it is more likely that they will hire temporary workers. The central administration can then play one sector of the faculty against the other in their attempts to establish a counterbalancing force to eliminate cost inefficiencies. The part-timers may serve as 'the most important single instrument for such control of middle and upper tiers of the personnel hierarchy' (1993: 193). To survive, the middle tier – full-time junior faculty with tenure-track appointments – would have to be aware of their need to conform via 'muting of critical inquiry,' pursuit of 'politically neutral research,' and avoidance of unionization and collective protests. Senior faculty members live under a veiled threat of retrenchment or mandatory retirement (ibid.). These implied strategies seem to be 'the hidden agenda of management in academic as well as industrial workplaces in the exercise of control over personnel' (ibid.: 192). It is academic administrators, however, not the university's central, bureaucratic administrators, who absorb the costs. Their administrative workload increases as a consequence of an increase in numbers of temporary workers and related management strategies. Their worries about an erosion of educational quality because of the university's temporary hiring also grow. If part-timers are unfamiliar with the pedagogical resources needed for teaching, administrators, with limited finances, have to find the means to bolster their resources. They also face the challenge of integrating the 'temporary' teachers within their departments. Above all, full-timers are beleaguered by the feeling that their numbers are declining (Leslie, Kellams, and Gunne, 1982: 94).

In times of budget reductions, how do administrators view 'downsizing' and its impact? Marcia Dickman et al. suggest that downsizing is a 'complex, multidimensional' process (1996, 457).[7] Women administrators seem to be more opposed than men to staff reductions, perhaps because they themselves are more vulnerable as workers at the margins (ibid.: 465). Schaffer (1992) differentiates the change that the academic world undergoes through budget reductions and downsizing from a comparable situation in business. As he and Newson and Buchbinder (1988) point out, however, universities have increasingly moved in the direction of operating as corporations.[8] Over the years, this trend has increased administrators' powers enormously. There is evidence to show that 'administrators have used the fiscal crisis to become the CEOs of academe' (Slaughter, 1993). Examining seventeen reports on academic freedom and tenure in U.S. universities published in *Academe* from 1980 to 1990, Slaughter found that more than a third of cases (36 per cent) were strongly influenced by financial pressure. This was a steep increase from a tenth of such cases (10 per cent) in 1970. Fiscal crises in U.S. universities also influenced 81 per cent of dismissal cases. The analogy between CEOs in businesses and presidents in U.S. universities became self-evident through the 'managerial discourse' of university presidents, which was identical to corporate parlance. What university administrators call 'strategic planning' and 'restructuring' exactly parallels business decisions made to 'cut inefficiencies' to garner more profits. Once cast in this mode of thinking, academic and non-academic administrators in the university proceed to bolster those programs labelled 'prestigious': business, management, engineering, law, and sciences, which are associated with enriched status and wealthy alumni. Finances are not trimmed so much as they are directed away from certain fields, such as education, nursing, and library science, where female students are in higher proportions, despite the fact that market demand remains high for graduates in these disciplines (Slaughter, 1993). With growing financial crises in higher education in North America since the 1980s, central administrators seem to have gained untrammelled powers over academic matters, including even the curriculum.

In the United States, George Keller (1983) called for a movement to concentrate authority in the hands of the university administration and endow it with 'intrusive leadership.' Bilik and Blum observe that when the euphemism 'strategic management' is uncloaked, it is neither strategic nor managerial: '[It] amounts to rolling out the academic version of the nineteenth century captain of industry: the visionary college president. The scenario dictates that the president and a coterie of strategic planners (commonly known as the "management team") must bypass the cumbersome mechanisms of collegial governance to plot the optimal academic and financial strategy for the institution' (1989: 12–13).[9]

Some commentators urge academic administrators to resist 'biz-speak' so that it will drop out of the 'academic vernacular' and 'return to the patios of specialists in management,' but if those in positions of academic authority continue to employ 'biz-speak,' 'it will in all likelihood increasingly shape administrative perceptions, attitudes, values, and behaviours' (Rollin, 1989: 14). Rollin warns that 'if students are reduced to "customers" and faculty to "employees," it follows that education is a "product"' (ibid.: 17). In order to resist the transformation of academe into business operations, faculty need to act collectively. However, as Julia Ridgely points out: 'Getting faculty to work and act collectively is difficult in part because of faculty culture itself. Faculty do not like to be pulled away from teaching to work, in groups and [to a] deadline, at hammering out policies that may be sketchy and imperfect at first ... When administration solicits the faculty's opinion, deadline counts more than detail ' (1993: 9).

Academic Administrators Surveyed

Of the academic administrators selected for this study (see the appendix), who represent a cross-section of all ranks of administrators, full professors are a majority in each rank (vice-presidents 60 per cent, deans 72 per cent, chairs 59 per cent). They have on average more than five years of experience in their administrative roles. Most have doctorates (84 per cent) and were born in North America or Britain (84 per cent). Only one in six is a woman (17.5 per cent). One of four deans is a woman, but there are very few women vice-presidents (10 per cent) or departmental chairs (16 per cent). The proportion of women administrators in our survey is quite close to figures from the survey of Canadian universities by Berkowitz (1996). She reports that women academic administrators in Canadian universities constitute 20 per cent overall, and 20 per cent of senior and middle management.

Although women have made greater strides in the 1990s, recent studies show that women's entry into, recognition by, and status in academic administration still are quite low. Schwartz (1996) notes that men were historically and still continue to be regarded as pre-eminent in academe and administration: 'The deans of women have been excluded from the story of higher education. Many of the significant accomplishments of the deans of women have been lost or ignored in compilations of modern history of higher education. What remains is an unfortunate caricature of deans of women as "snooping battle axes."[10] The image of the dean of women is one of spinsterly, prudish women whose energies were directed towards the bedevilment of fun-seeking, harmless youth ... The male which has dominated higher education, including the written and oral histories of American colleges and universities, has rarely given much credit to women' (5–6).

Susan Twombly analyses the U.S. literature and finds that negative stereotypes and biases against women administrators in U.S. academe are the major 'deeply ingrained' barriers to women's entry into administration and progress toward gender equality (1993: 207). Johnsrud and Heck confirm this finding for a large U.S public research university: 'Gender stratification within organizations is both pervasive and persistent ... Being female has an initial impact upon the status and responsibility attained from the position held in the organization. The initial gender bias is cumulative ... Being female, therefore, directly affects organizational status and responsibility ... [re first position as administrators] ... and directly as well as indirectly affects status and responsibility [in hierarchical placement – promotion]' (1994: 39).

My survey of administrators reveals that at senior levels more women than men are single. Of the women, 64 per cent (men 90 per cent) are married, and less than 60 per cent (men 95 per cent) are at the level of assistant vice-president or higher. In age, 33 per cent of women (men 14 per cent) are younger than 44, and, on average, ten to twelve years younger than men. In the following sections, I examine interactions between administrators and part-timers.

Hiring

Reasons for Hiring

Academic administrators report that they hire part-timers principally because adequate funds are not available to create full-time positions (61 per cent) (table 6.1). Their secondary reasons are that they require part-timers to replace full-timers on leave (83 per cent), or they need professionals from outside academe (70 per cent), or they must fill sudden vacancies (63 per cent), or they require staffing flexibility to deal with shifting enrolments (54 per cent). A department chairman notes:

TABLE 6.1
Academic administrators' reasons for hiring part-timers

Academic administrators rate importance of reasons (N: 719)	Importance	Total %
No financial resources	Very	61.2
to hire full-time faculty	Somewhat	24.3
	Not	14.5
	Total %	100.0
Need professionals from	Very	29.9
outside	Somewhat	40.5
	Not	29.6
	Total %	100.0
Need teachers to replace	Very	42.6
full-timers on leave	Somewhat	40.0
	Not	17.4
	Total %	100.0
Full-timers need more	Very	6.1
time for research	Somewhat	32.8
	Not	61.1
	Total %	100.0
Shifting enrolments require	Very	17.5
flexibility in hiring	Somewhat	36.9
	Not	45.7
	Total %	100.0
Unable to locate full-time	Very	17.1
candidates	Somewhat	36.2
	Not	46.7
	Total %	100.0
To fill emergency	Very	21.5
vacancies	Somewhat	41.5
	Not	37.0
	Total %	100.0

Source: Rajagopal, Academic Administrators Survey (1991–2)

'We no longer get replacements for faculty members on leave. We may get a part-time person to teach the most enrolled courses which would otherwise be not offered due to the leave. We advertise in such a fashion that we are in a position to hire someone on a limited term or, if funding becomes available, a tenure-track basis. Financial constraints are the worst they have ever been. From 1978 to 1988 course enrolment increased 98 per cent [but] department [faculty] size did not increase. At present the only female faculty member – who is full-time rather than adjunct – is also the only tenure-track appointment.' Another chairman explains how universities hire part-timers to teach large courses even though, ideally, longer-term contract personnel would be preferable: 'You need to be aware that the majority of part-time faculty is employed in our distance-education program stream that has approximately five hundred student course registrations. The ideal would be to hire more full-time or part-time instructors on a 2–3 year contract basis; however, the budget cycle and restrictions currently do not allow this.'

Despite increasing emphasis on research in Canadian universities over the past decade or so, a majority of administrators (61 per cent) report that they do not hire part-timers in order to allow full-timers more time for research. They feel that the full-timers should be able to do both research and teaching. Tang and Chamberlain observe: 'Administrators tend to believe that research and teaching are mutually supportive and that both research and teaching are the mission of their university ... that faculty must be effective teachers ... Faculty members on the other hand, are less inclined to agree with the mission of the university that both teaching and research are essential parts of their jobs ... that they should be required to do either teaching or research, but not both (1997: 223).' In fact, however, in Quebec and in western Canada, a number of university administrations hire part-timers to allow full-timers more time on research. Also, in universities that are research oriented, that are larger, and that offer a full-range of Faculties, four in ten administrators value this form of substitution. A department chair criticizes this trend: 'Poor government funding has led to the trend to get into the "part-time" business to save money. Related to this is the trend for full-time faculty, under research pressure, to unload some teaching on to [those that are on] part-time appointments. My view is that there should be no "full-time" part-time appointments.'

Administrators, particularly in Ontario and western Canada, hire part-timers more often to meet their enrolment crunches. Although inadequate finance is the most common problem, temporarily replacing full-timers who are on leave (rather than creating new full-time positions) is a more important reason for hiring part-timers in the Atlantic provinces. The need to hire professional expertise from outside academe is seen as somewhat more important in Quebec than in other parts of Canada. An assistant dean notes that certain Faculties need full-time secondments from the business world or professional fields: 'In order to maintain contacts with the field in a professional faculty (education), it is necessary to second outstanding teachers to serve in full-time non-tenure track roles. Six of the ten persons in these roles [are] seconded from schools for two years each.' Another administrator looks for professionals who may be interested in teaching part time: 'In today's restrained fiscal climate, part-time faculty members are indispensable to the question of the university. More needs to be done on their selection, development, and assessment. In a professional faculty such as ours (education) we use part-timers principally in [limited areas] ... Most of these people are not looking for full-time positions.'

A departmental chairman cites filling in for full-timers who are on reduced teaching load and securing the expertise of practising professionals as reasons for hiring part-timers: 'As a professional department, we hire two professional engineers each year to teach 1–3 month term courses. The subjects are usually site planning and traffic engineering. This is necessary to provide a professional flavor to the courses (those that are technical electives) and to fill in for the administrators who have a reduced teaching load.' Substantive decisions to use part-timers occur primarily at the departmental level. However, practices vary among universities. Large and research-oriented institutions offering a full range of programs let departments, and in some institutions Faculties, make decisions. In smaller, teaching universities with a limited range of Faculties, decisions involve Faculties and/or university administrations.

Yet there are many administrators who are totally disinclined to hire part-timers. They prefer full-timers, even if they are temporary, contract positions. A department chair feels that it is better not to rely on part-time appointments, even under fluctuating enrolments: 'We have been able to hire more sessional [LTFT] faculty this year, [and] thus have fewer part-time appointments ... Our unit is better off than many others in not having to rely on part-time appointments. [We have] only two [part-timers] in specialized professional areas.' An assistant dean has another strategy: 'Where time does not permit a thorough search, visiting professor positions are established while a further search is conducted. These visiting positions usually obtain the tenure-track position if quality of performance is good.' A department chair explains the policy of his department: 'Our policy is to maintain our coverage of teaching duties with full time appointments. We have an instructor category in the department, which has career advancements and is an entrance type of a position. Instructors can do research and several do, but their main duties are related to teaching.'

Administrators' Objectives for Part-Timers

A majority of administrators (62 per cent) identify meeting enrolment pressures and maintaining lower student-to-faculty ratios as the major reasons for part-time appointments (table 6.2). They (55 per cent) believe in using such appointments mostly for hiring professionals with practical expertise to enrich the academic world. A chairman describes the occasion for part-time appointments: 'Part-time faculty is basically a function of hiring freezes on full-time positions, loss of replacement of a full-time position after a retirement, and the increase in release-time money from Social Science Research Council (SSHRC).' Administrators (58 per cent) take this route only as a temporary solution, if full-time positions cannot be created. They (59 per cent) do not feel that it should be a regular cost-cutting component of staffing policy. In reality, however, vice-presidents and deans who make policies relating to finances and staffing regard the practice as a continuing strategy. They consider such appointments to be money-saving strategies. Department-level administrators would rather have full-time regular appointments than use part-timers except as a temporary measure. A chairman regrets that the part-timers are so financially expedient that they can be hired when needed: 'If part-time faculty were more expensive for the university, then we would have had a better chance of keeping [the department's existing] positions full-time.' Part-timers themselves (73 per cent) are aware of administrators' expediency in employing them. They (57 per cent) feel that they offer the best value for least cost (see chapter 2, above).

The Hiring Process

We now turn to academic administrators' approach to hiring part-timers. In the hiring process, most part-timers are being judged on their academic credentials rather than on any other criteria. Most administrators (74 per cent) rely principally on academic qualifications. In addition, a majority (58 per cent) also require teaching experience. Ser-

TABLE 6.2
Why academic administrators make part-time appointments

Administrators' views		(N: 719) Total %	(N: 161) VP/dean	Administrative rank % (N: 558) chair/ director
To hire practical experts	Agree	55.0	63.8	51.4
	Disagree	20.2	17.4	22.1
	Neither	24.8	18.7	26.5
	Total %	100.0	100.0	100.0
To meet enrolment pressures (n.s.)	Agree	62.0	66.4	60.5
	Disagree	19.5	14.2	21.3
	Neither	17.5	19.3	18.2
	Total %	100.0	100.0	100.0
As temporary solution	Agree	57.6	47.1	61.2
	Disagree	30.7	38.1	28.7
	Neither	11.7	14.8	10.2
	Total %	100.0	100.0	100.0
As regular cost-saving positions***	Agree	18.7	29.0	15.2
	Disagree	58.5	42.6	63.4
	Neither	22.8	28.4	21.3
	Total %	100.0	100.0	100.0
As means of staffing flexibility	Important	47.1	48.7	46.7
	Not important	30.4	30.1	30.5
	Not sure	22.5	21.2	22.9
	Total %	100.0	100.0	100.0

Notes: Significance: p = *<.05, **<.01; ***<.001. All are significant at p = **<.01 unless otherwise indicated. (n.s.): not significant.
Source: See table 6.1.

vice seniority receives lowest priority (24 per cent) and is used relatively more in francophone, high part-timer-intense, wide-range, and unionized universities. Emphasis on seniority clearly differentiates francophone universities from anglophone institutions (table 6.3).

An air of informality permeates the whole hiring process. More

TABLE 6.3
Academic administrators' criteria for hiring part-timers, by university type

Very important criteria[†]	Region %				Unionization %		
	West	Ontario	Quebec	Atlantic	Union	Non-union	Total %
Academic qualifications	78.3	69.1	74.5	72.3	73.2	74.1	73.5
Teaching experience	60.2	56.1	56.3	54.9	55.2	60.1	57.6
Service seniority	10.6***	36.5***	50.0***	9.1***	36.7***	8.3***	24.2
As new scholars, for them to gain experience	9.4	7.2	9.5	10.4	10.0*	7.4*	8.6
Overall total no.	285	244	99	91	379	340	719

Notes: Significance: p = *<.05, **<.01, ***<.001. Differences are not significant unless otherwise indicated.
[†]Respondents could select multiple criteria. The balance of 100 per cent of respondents in each question on criteria did not choose that criterion.
Source: See table 6.1.

administrators (43 per cent) report a very informal process, and fewer hire through competition (35 per cent) or apply the seniority principle (22 per cent) (tables 6.3a, b). A majority of administrators use the informal process in universities in western Canada (62 per cent), in non-union (61 per cent) and small (55 per cent) institutions, and in those with lower part-timer-intensity (54 per cent).[11] In contrast, francophone universities shun informality. Most administrators (69 per cent) in Quebec hire on the basis of service seniority, that is, the number of years a part-timer has continued in a department or university. However, some administrators (28 per cent), primarily in the Atlantic region universities (42 per cent), resort to merit-based competition among part-timers.

Hiring is a departmental affair for a majority of administrators (57 per cent), and the chairs (67 per cent) generally make decisions. Only a minority of Faculty-level (26 per cent) or university-level (13 per cent) administrators control these appointments. Chairs are responsible for the appointments in western, non-unionized, large, and research-oriented universities. Departmental committees participate in some

TABLE 6.3a
Academic administrators' hiring procedures, by university region

		Region %				Total %
		West	Ontario	Quebec	Atlantic	
Hiring process	Open competition	20.7	30.3	22.9	41.7	27.6
	Restricted competition	4.1	11.7	4.2	4.8	7.4
	Informally	62.4	30.3	4.2	48.8	42.9
	Seniority	12.8	27.7	68.8	4.8	22.1
	Total %	100.0	100.0	100.0	100.0	100.0
Appointment decisions made by	Chair	74.2	64.1	45.8	63.1	66.6
	Committee	12.5	25.0	16.7	16.7	18.5
	Full-timers	3.1	0.7	6.3	2.4	2.3
	Dean	10.2	10.1	31.3	17.9	12.6
	Total %	100.0	100.0	100.0	100.0	100.0
Overall total no.		285	244	99	91	719

Notes: All differences are significant at p = ***<.001. Owing to rounding, the numbers may not add up to exactly 100 per cent.
Source: See table 6.1.

small universities and in Ontario. Deans play a more significant role in francophone universities than in anglophone institutions.

Counterbalancing the informality in hiring, most part-timers receive a formal, written contract specifying terms and conditions of work. Most universities also provide them with an oral description of their work and course-related information: curriculum, outlines, and target enrolments. Because of the tentative and last-minute hiring process, however, part-timers remain uncertain about their rehiring and feel insecure. A woman Contemporary explains: 'Job security is the most crucial issue for part-time instructors at both [universities] ... where I have taught. We never know what courses, if any, we will be asked to teach, and despite advances made by [our union] on our behalf, job descriptions can change at the whim of a chairman, allowing for favor-

TABLE 6.3b
Academic administrators' hiring procedures, by university unionization

| | | Union or non-union | | |
		(N: 719) Total %	(N: 379) Union %	(N: 340) Non-union %
Hiring process	Open competition	27.6	27.3	26.9
	Restricted competition	7.4	9.3	4.5
	Informally	42.9	29.9	61.2
	Seniority	22.1	33.5	7.4
	Total %	100.0	100.0	100.0
Appointment deci- sions made by	Chair	66.6	60.8	74.6
	Committee	18.5	22.7	13.1
	Full-time faculty	2.3	2.2	2.1
	Dean	12.6	14.2	10.0
	Total %	100.0	100.0	100.0

Notes: All differences are significant at p = ***<.001. Owing to rounding, the numbers may not add up to exactly 100 per cent.
Source: See table 6.1.

itism of the most patronizing and paternalistic kind. Benefits are the second most important issue.'

Perceptions of Part-timers and Their Work

An Invisible Faculty

After being hired, part-timers tend to languish into obscurity. Institutions lack any centrally or locally accessible data on their numbers and work, since there is no requirement for universities to maintain data on part-timers. By contrast, Statistics Canada regularly collects data on full-timers. Murray and Murray (1996) point out that research on faculty morale identifies administrators' role as a more important factor than other exogenous factors, such as environment or type of institution. Administrators' failure to record a group within the university might make that group feel marginal. Most administrators (76 per cent) do not find it cost efficient to collect data on part-timers, whom they (73 per cent) consider transient. Many (41 per cent), however, do

TABLE 6.4
Why administrators don't maintain data on part-timers

Few universities have data on part-timers because	Importance	Administrative rank		
		(N: 161) VP/dean %	(N: 558) Chair/director %	(N: 719) Total %
Additional spending	Very	13.3	31.6	25.0
would not repay cost***	Some	65.3	44.2	50.7
	Not	21.4	24.2	24.3
	Total %	100.0	100.0	100.0
Part-timers are transient*	Very	12.0	22.9	19.5
	Some	59.8	50.8	53.6
	Not	28.2	26.2	26.9
	Total %	100.0	100.0	100.0
Part-timers are not	Very	16.8	17.2	16.8
interested in an aca-	Some	41.7	42.5	41.6
demic career (n.s.)	Not	40.7	42.5	41.5
	Total %	100.0	100.0	100.0
It is a department's	Very	25.2	33.3	30.9
responsibility**	Some	41.7	48.8	47.4
	Not	33.1	17.8	21.8
	Total %	100.0	100.0	100.0
It is not mandatory to	Very	25.2	39.6	35.0
keep such records*	Some	42.1	32.2	35.3
(e.g., Stats Can)	Not	32.7	28.2	29.7
	Total %	100.0	100.0	100.0

Notes: Significance: $p =$ *<.05, **<.01, ***<.001. All are significant unless otherwise indicated. (n.s.): not significant. Owing to rounding, the numbers may not add up to exactly 100 per cent.
Source: See table 6.1.

not consider part-timers to be casual workers with no career interests in academe. Most (78 per cent) assign record-keeping to departments (table 6.4). Three-quarters of chairs and program directors calculate that the cost of maintaining the data is not worth incurring. They see part-timers as indispensable and agree that data are a departmental responsibility, but they do not collect information. Vice-presidents and deans are vague in responding to the issue. Although they may find the staff resources needed to maintain records, they seem not inclined to do so. Administrators are ambivalent about part-timers' interest in an academic career. Although some administrators (27 per cent) acknowledge these career interests, most (74 per cent) think that they may not remain in teaching for long. This finding is in sharp contrast to the image that part-timers have of themselves.

Although invisible in the corridors of academic power, part-timers are very visible in the classrooms. They (59 per cent) admit that students know whether their teacher is a full-timer or a part-timer. However, only some administrators (40 per cent) think that students would care. Again, only a minority (40 per cent) feel that students may regard full-timers as more credible. Thus, their image of a part-timer is of one who is integrated into classes, but not into the faculty or university.

Teaching

Part-timers are subject to an unspoken, but clearly identified, role of teaching only. Most (73 per cent) administrators either reject the notion that part-timers' academic work includes scholarly research or are oblivious to other things that part-timers do besides teaching. Many (48 per cent) also state that part-timers should only teach: 'Our teaching faculty is all "part-time." Our full-time academics develop programs but do little or no actual teaching.' And, 'We have two types of people in our unit as part-time. One group teaches courses, the others act as faculty associates ... Presently half of our people are faculty associates. They teach courses, supervise students in the field and participate in most parts of the faculty. In addition we have a high percentage of our courses at the undergraduate level taught by sessional [part-time] instructors.' And, 'Part-time employment in many universities is very high in ... summer session periods ... Almost all the graduate teaching ... in Education [Faculty] is done by part-timers during the summer session.'

Part-timers carry a considerable share of undergraduate teaching. Chairs and program directors estimate that part-timers handle at least a fifth of all undergraduate courses, and some teach graduate courses as well. Many administrators (49 per cent) estimate that percentages of students and courses taught by part-timers have increased during the previous five years. Part-timers, therefore, seem to have become an indispensable and regular solution to academic staffing problems, but administrators have planned few, if any, support systems for their teaching. Two-thirds of part-timers (67 per cent) report poor or no training in teaching skills or grading assistance for large classes in their universities. Many (59 per cent) have inadequate or no office space and no telephones (50 per cent).

While neglecting or rejecting the demand for professional development and productive work for part-timers, administrators ignore the implications of this attitude for the quality of this faculty and the students they teach. Bruce Gunn differentiates 'service-oriented' and 'self-oriented' administrators: the 'self-oriented' exert 'hierarchical pressure to squeeze work out of faculty.'[12] Gunn's critique is even more relevant to part-timers: 'The feudal order of the political system [in the university] does not usually prescribe for the use of effective counselling, training, and educational programs to advance the knowledge, skills, and attitudes of faculty over their careers. The subsequent "meat grinder effect" depreciates academicians as human capital which is clearly exemplified in the problem of wage compaction for faculty ... This administrative malpractice can place conscientious faculty under debilitating stress that all too often undermines their family life, health, productivity, and career potential' (1991: 8, 5).

A U.S. survey of higher education asked part-timers to rate their priorities in instruction development (Rhodes, 1991). They rated as highly important: teaching requirements, knowledge of students' special characteristics, and use of strategies for motivating students. Academic administrators rated as important: instructors' skill in evaluating course assignments, their ability to access available tutorial services, and their familiarity with policies and procedures. Part-timers rated these as their lowest needs. While part-timers emphasized their students and teaching, administrators stressed externalities.

Do administrators provide part-timers with necessary information about their work and give them enough time to prepare for their teaching? A majority of administrators (59 per cent) both make part-time appointments and provide information about scheduled courses a few months before classes start. Most administrators, except many from Atlantic universities (58 per cent), report giving necessary lead time to part-timers. But their approach to providing information seems informal. Two-thirds of part-timers report that they do not automatically receive employment statements or contracts, and sometimes they are not even aware of the existence of such documents.

The administrations place clear restrictions on part-timers' work.

Most administrators (86 per cent) limit their course loads to ensure teaching quality, and most (though not so many in Quebec) would also like to limit their class sizes. Part-timers do not have any major curricular input, nor do they have any control over their courses, since course outlines are often preset. Yet most administrators (74 per cent) allow part-timers some freedom in designing course content. A chair acknowledges the limits set for part-timers: 'Part-time positions are used only for sessional appointments and have specific areas of expertise ... They [part-timers] follow course outlines that are established but have a fair degree of flexibility.'

Although administrators annually evaluate part-timers' teaching, there is no plan to reward them with any merit pay. Half the administrators (51 per cent), particularly in those universities with higher part-timer intensity (59 per cent), reject the idea of part-timers' salaries being prorated to those of full-timers. Most, however, would allow some annual salary increments and prorated fringe benefits.

What are part-timers' rights and privileges in the university? Indeed unionized part-timers have more rights and protection than non-unionized ones (table 6.5). Very few administrators (19 per cent) would allow them to move to full-time faculty positions through competitive credentials. Some universities (37 per cent) instead offer pay increases for experience: 60 per cent of administrators in western Canada and 17 per cent of those in Quebec universities so report. Merit pay is quite rare in every region and is awarded by very few administrators in Quebec (2 per cent) and those in the Atlantic provinces (1 per cent).

Fewer Atlantic administrators report that their part-timers have worker rights and privileges. A majority of administrators in all regions (except the Atlantic: 35 per cent) report that part-timers in their universities are entitled to procedural protection against arbitrary termination (57 per cent), fringe benefits (52 per cent), and credit for service seniority in rehiring (56 per cent). Most administrators in Quebec say that part-timers enjoy seniority in hiring (73 per cent versus Atlantic 32 per cent) and protection against arbitrary firing (83 per cent versus Atlantic 35 per cent).[13]

Administrators' responses to two other questions are revealing. First, they report that more than a quarter of part-timers depend completely on their academic income and that for more than a third of them, this income is important for their livelihood. Part-timers, themselves, report that a much larger proportion of them (Contemporaries 65.5 per cent) have no full-time jobs and therefore depend on part-time

TABLE 6.5
Academic administrators report on rights and privileges of part-timers, by university region, size, and unionization

Administrators say part-timers have[†]	Region %				Size %			Union or non-union %		Overall total %
	West	Ontario	Quebec	Atlantic	Large	Middle	small	Union	Non-union	
Procedural protection against arbitrary termination	50.7	66.1	82.6	34.6	58.9	65.8	40.0	71.0	40.8	57.1
Pay increase for experience	59.7	24.2	17.4	20.2	40.7	46.3	14.1	25.4	49.5	36.8
Pay increase for merit	18.0	8.5	2.2	1.2	14.0	10.2	4.9	6.9	15.2	10.8
Upgrade to full-time faculty position based on merit and qualification	17.2 (n.s.)	20.8 (n.s.)	27.7 (n.s.)	14.8 (n.s.)	22.0 (n.s.)	17.5 (n.s.)	16.3 (n.s.)	22.8**	15.4**	19.3
Fringe benefits	52.9	55.7	86.7	20.3	53.2	60.8	35.0	61.7	40.8	51.8
Credit for service seniority in rehiring	51.9	64.1	73.3	32.1	57.7**	60.6**	44.6**	68.8	40.9	55.8
Total no.	285	244	99	91	334	132	153	379	340	719

Notes: Significance: p = *<.05, **<.01, ***<.001. All are significant at p = ***<.001 unless otherwise indicated. (n.s.): not significant.
[†]The response is 'no' for the balance of 100 per cent in each variable (i.e., part-timers do not have the specified rights and benefits).
Source: See table 6.1

income. The average salary of Contemporaries is $14,531 per year according to my survey (1991–2). Yet most administrators (86 per cent) want to restrict a part-timer's total course load. Second, more than half the administrators are either opposed or indifferent to giving part-timers prorated full-timers' salary or merit pay. More than half of vice-presidents, deans, and full professors, rather than chairs/directors and assistant/associate professors, are opposed to such changes. To make these changes, administrators would have to redirect the necessary resources from full-timers. A majority of administrators (55 per cent) find part-timers useful for staffing the required courses and also for lowering full-timers' teaching load, yet they affirm that part-timers should not teach more hours than are deemed to be 'academically sound.' Although administrators do not give part-timers' more autonomy or equitable rewards for their work, they find it indispensable.

Research

Many administrators assume that because of time-intensive teaching duties and minimal access to funding, part-timers who have been scholarly researchers must have fallen inadvertently into that role. Since most administrators see part-timers primarily as teachers, and almost half (48 per cent) would restrict them to teaching, they do not consider it relevant to extend internal research funding to them (tables 6.6 and 6.6a). Very few vice-presidents and deans (19 per cent) would expect part-timers to do scholarly research, much less publish their findings. Fewer vice-presidents and deans (24 per cent) than chairs/directors (41 per cent), fewer full professors (33 per cent) than associate and assistant professors (44 per cent), and fewer male (35 per cent) than female (44 per cent) administrators would extend to part-timers the same rights to internal research funding enjoyed by full-timers (table 6.6a). Whether ranks are aggregated along administrative or academic lines, the higher the rank of full-timers, the lower are their expectations of part-timers to produce scholarly research and their willingness to allow part-timers access to grants. A majority of administrators of all ranks (61 per cent), however, acknowledge that part-timers should have access to research and professional development support. The contradiction between their rhetorical acknowledgement and the reality of their not allowing access to grants becomes evident when we ask about extending grants to part-timers.

Not requiring part-timers to do research appears to be considerate.

TABLE 6.6
Academic administrators' views on part-timers' research and teaching,
by administrative rank

Administrators say part-timers		Administrative rank		
		(N: 161) VP/ dean %	(N: 558) Chair/ director %	(N: 719) Total %
Should also do research and	Agree	18.6	29.1	26.5
scholarship	Disagree	45.2	41.9	42.9
	Neither	36.2	28.9	30.6
	Total %	100.0	100.0	100.0
Get no paid research and time	Agree	78.9	72.0	73.0
from the university	Disagree	7.1	8.4	8.5
	Neither	14.1	19.5	18.5
	Total %	100.0	100.0	100.0
Should have access to research	Agree	51.6**	63.3**	60.8
and professional development	Disagree	21.7**	16.1**	17.4
support	Neither	26.7**	20.6**	21.8
	Total %	100.0	100.0	100.0
Should be allowed access to	Agree	23.5***	41.4***	37.1
internal research grants	Disagree	19.6***	14.5***	15.8
	Neither	56.9***	44.1***	47.1
	Total %	100.0	100.0	100.0

Notes: Significance: p = *<.05, **<.01, ***<.001. All are significant at p = *<.05 unless
otherwise indicated. Owing to rounding, the numbers may not add up to exactly 100 per
cent.
Source: See table 6.1.

As a departmental chairman believes, 'the heavy teaching load for
Senior Instructors [part-timers] would acknowledge that research is
not expected.' The policy excludes them from the more prestigious
part of academic work, however, and prevents them from being recognized as researchers. Tang and Chamberlain report that academic
administrators clearly differed from tenure-track full-timers in their
attitudes towards research and teaching (1997: 223). Full-timers believe
that, since research interferes with teaching, they should be required to
do one or the other. Administrators, in contrast, emphasize that tenure-

TABLE 6.6a
Academic administrators' views on part-timers' research and teaching by academic rank

Administrators say part-timers		(N 442) Professor %	(N 277) Associate/ assistant professor %	(N 719) Total %
			Academic rank of administrators	
Should have access to research	Agree	57.8**	65.8**	60.8
and professional development	Disagree	18.8**	14.2**	17.4
support	Neither	23.4**	20.0**	21.8
	Total %	100.0	100.0	100.0
Should be allowed access to	Agree	32.8	43.6	37.1
internal research grants	Disagree	15.1	17.3	15.8
	Neither	52.1	39.1	47.1
	Total %	100.0	100.0	100.0

Notes: Significance: p = *<.05, **<.01, ***<.001. All are significant at p = ***<.001 unless otherwise indicated. Owing to rounding, the numbers may not add up to exactly 100 per cent.
Source: See table 6.1.

track full-timers must engage in both research and teaching because they are mutually reinforcing. An occasional response to our survey confirms administrators' expectations. A woman chair of department emphasizes how research and teaching go hand in hand: 'There are at least two categories of part-timers. Ninety-five per cent of our part-timers are practising professionals, (earning as much and sometimes much more than full-time teachers). Most of them have no interest in research. Although they are good 'teachers' (most of them are), the content of their teaching leaves much to be desired. Dissociating teaching and research is naïve and counterproductive.' Most academic administrators, however, do not expect a balanced mix of teaching and research from their part-timers; this is quite different from what part-timers, especially Contemporaries, expect of themselves. Administrators' expectations smack of self-fulfilling prophecy. The higher the administrative rank, the smaller is the proportion of administrators who regard part-timers as career academics and attempt to synchronize their role with that of full-timers. Fewer vice-presidents and deans (18 per cent versus chairs 29.1 per cent) expect them to produce scholarly publications and do research. However, more vice-presidents and deans (29 per cent versus chairs 22 per cent) expect part-timers to serve on committees in order to fill them.

Administrators who require part-timers to take part in committee work and provide other non-teaching service make a dubious distinction between part-timers' 'service' and that of full-timers. If part-timers serve on committees, it is only appropriate that they be eligible to participate in all academic councils and committees, but, as most administrators report, part-timers are excluded from almost all decision-making bodies except departmental meetings and some departmental committees. Three in four administrators (73 per cent) concede that part-timers do not get research funding or time off with pay, and they (61 per cent) also acknowledge that part-timers need research and professional support. As a majority of administrators (63 per cent) are either apathetic to or disagree outright with the extension to part-timers of full-timers' privileges to apply for grants, their responses remain, at best, rhetoric.

Aspirations

Administrators and part-timers look differently at part-timers' career aspirations and the barriers to their achieving full-time academic positions. First, administrators seem to know very little about such aspirations (table 6.7). They estimate that some part-timers (37 per cent) may want full-time appointments and report that currently a third (34 per cent) of them meet the required qualifications. Administrators also add that some part-timers (30 per cent), although formally qualified, are not likely to be hired full time even if positions were available. A vice-president comments: 'Part-time and limited term employees fill a need in teaching during the eight-month academic term ... They do not pursue a full-time career in the university. Many "part-time" faculty move to instructional positions in the community college system.' Certain practices in departments, such as hiring retirees rather than filling part-time positions with new applicants from outside, also help to explain why some administrators may have misconceptions: 'Our part-time picture is rather unusual. We have faculty members in our department who have taken early retirement from their own universities. Accordingly they are experienced academics, still very active in research and teaching. We pay them for the courses they teach for us and in this way we supplement their pensions. For all intents and pur-

TABLE 6.7
Academic administrators assess percentage of part-timers
with academic career aspirations

Administrators estimate of part-timers (overall mean %)	Administrative Rank[†]		
	VP/dean	Chair/ director	Total
Interested in full-time appointments	26.8	41.0	37.2
Qualified now for full-time appointment	22.2	37.0	33.5
Qualified but not likely to get full-time (n.s.)	27.8	31.4	30.2
Total no.	161	558	719

Notes: All are significant at $p =$ ***$<.001$ unless otherwise
indicated. (n.s.): not significant.
[†]Each column does not add up to 100%, since each row contains overall means of administrators' rough estimates.
Source: See table 6.1.

poses these people are full-time faculty members in my department.'
Chairs and program directors, in contrast to vice-presidents or deans,
seem to have a slightly better appreciation of their part-timers and of
the plight of the 'lost generation of scholars' because of their familiarity with them. Chairs and directors estimate that 37 per cent of part-timers in their departments are well qualified for full-time positions;
this figure comes closer to the percentage of those part-timers with a
doctorate (39 per cent) who actively search for full-time positions.
However, chairs/directors misunderstand part-timers' own interest in
academic careers. Their estimate of part-timers who want full-time
appointments (41 per cent) is much lower than part-timers themselves
report (53 per cent).

Second, staffing strategies block full-time appointments for part-timers. Both administrators and part-timers agree that the toughest
barrier is the financial constraints in universities. A department chair
explains this acuteness: 'Our department, a language department in
which there has been a 90 per cent increase in student numbers in the
last five years is particularly dependent on part-time faculty to teach

its basic language classes. The university is in a deficit position and so cannot afford new tenure-track positions. We do, in fact, live a hand to mouth existence, never knowing until just before the start of classes exactly how many positions will be available ... Some Sessionals are appointed several months before a term starts, [and] others at the very last moment.' Another chairman of department comments: 'In ... my department ... some [part-timers] are spouses of full-time faculty members, for whom there are no full-time vacancies at this time [in] the only university in town, and who put their marriages ahead of furthering their careers. Since we ... are not provided with sufficient funds to hire enough full-time faculty to teach all the students we are expected to handle, providing part-time employment to these ... individuals is a mutually beneficial arrangement. This does not, however, disguise the fact that they are grossly underpaid.' Part-timers blame administrators' strategies – not lack of funds (57 per cent) – for the dearth of full-time appointments (see chapter two above). Working with financial realities gives most administrators (83 per cent) a heightened awareness of the financial barriers. Many (51 per cent) feel that administrators could create full-time positions instead of hiring more part-timers. Some chairs also agree that not creating regular positions results in a waste of talents: 'My personal wish, as a chairperson, is to have all persons involved in a tenure position, and occasionally in exceptional circumstances, a short-term position. I think it's a waste of time and energy for everybody to have a qualified person for one or three years and let him/her go away after that. In the past, the unit has lost very good candidates for that reason.'

Third, administrators seem to look down at part-timers' academic qualifications. Most (75 per cent) assert that departments prefer those who have most recently completed their doctorates and have research potential (table 6.8). A majority (62 per cent) state that part-timers in their departments are unlikely to get full-time academic jobs because of their poor research productivity. They (54 per cent) also doubt whether part-timers have the potential to do research to get tenure. We have noted from the part-timers' survey, however, that part-timers' (51 per cent) own reporting of their research record and potential is highly positive (see chapter 2, above). In fact, research publications reported by LTFTs and part-timers confirm that their research records are equal to and, in some cases, better than those of some tenured full-timers. A chairman admits: 'Our small department has not been able to promote non-tenured full-time faculty to tenure-track status in spite of excellent

TABLE 6.8
Academic administrators' views on part-timers' barriers to a full-time academic job

(N: 719)	% Administrators				
Administrators say	Agree	Disagree	Not sure	Does not apply	Row total
Part-timers lack research record to get full-time job	61.9	18.1	18.0	12.0	100
If full-time, unlikely to do research to get tenure	54.4	18.0	14.8	12.8	100
Departments prefer new PhDs with research potential	74.8	9.5	6.8	8.9	100
Part-timer label is not a barrier to get full-time job	52.1	22.4	12.0	13.4	100
Being female is not a barrier to get full-time job	60.7	15.1	11.0	13.2	100
No informal barrier against minorities	63.2	9.6	11.6	15.6	100
No barrier against hiring from within	56.4	18.1	10.2	15.2	100
University financial constraints on jobs	82.7	7.6	3.8	5.8	100

Source: See table 6.1.

teaching evaluations and research record (three books in three years, $100,000 in SSHRC grant) and willingness to serve on committees.'

Fourth, a majority of administrators (56 per cent) deny that there is any kind of discrimination against hiring part-timers from within their universities, for full-time positions. Yet a majority of part-timers, particularly Contemporaries, believe that such discrimination exists; only some of them (31 per cent) report that their universities are not influenced by such a discriminatory hiring policy (see chapter 2, above).

Finally, in hiring for full-time positions, influences of gender, ethnicity, and the label and stereotype of having been 'formerly a part-timer,' do not seem significant to part-timers. Fewer of them report gender (15 per cent) or ethnicity (10 per cent) as a negative barrier. More than a third of administrators, however, believe that gender or ethnicity does block part-timers.

Decision-Making

The marginalization of part-timers occurs in two ways: their exclusion from decision-making processes and the discounting of their presence and voice in decision-making bodies. Massengale and Sage suggest that their inclusion would improve the morale of, increase their contributions to, and boost the educational quality of the institution:

> Administrators often claim that decreasing budgets make part-time hiring essential to institutional survival ... Part-timers are painfully aware that administrators and full-time faculty members see them as second-class citizens. However, if educational quality is to be promoted and preserved, an institution's legitimate academic and financial needs must be balanced by the equally legitimate demands of part-time faculty members for improved pay, status, compensation, and benefits ... Most part-time faculty members lack meaningful opportunities to make decisions concerning their professional lives, particularly with regard to curricula, courses, and teaching materials. One of the areas in which improvements are needed is including part-timers in the shared governance of the institution. Erring on the side of inclusion rather than exclusion in faculty governance and departmental deliberations will go a long way in treating part-timers in a more humane, professional, and progressive manner. (1995: 73).

The greater the importance of a body in the university, the greater the percentage of administrators who report part-timers' exclusion from them. Across Canada, most administrators state that part-timers are excluded from the university senate and from its committees (85 per cent and 84 per cent, respectively). Most also report exclusion from Faculty councils and from Faculty committees (74 per cent and 76 per cent, respectively). A majority allow them in department meetings, but not in all committees (61 per cent and 70 per cent, respectively) (tables 6.9 and 6.9a).

In contrast to their anglophone counterparts, most Quebec administrators (74 per cent) report that part-timers are excluded from departmental meetings. More administrators from Quebec (88 per cent versus Atlantic 68 per cent) do not include them in all committees, but more francophone administrators (49 per cent) than anglophone (west 6 per cent, Ontario 24 per cent, Atlantic 4 per cent) allow part-timers to participate in the senate and university-wide committees. Many adminis-

TABLE 6.9
Part-timers' inclusion in and exclusion from decision-making bodies:
academic administrators' report, by university region

Administrators say that part-timers are		Region %				Total %
		West	Ontario	Quebec	Atlantic	
In all committees of	Included	30.6*	30.9*	11.6*	32.5*	29.6
department	Excluded	69.3*	69.1*	88.4*	67.6*	70.4
In some committees	Included	54.1	49.2	48.9	59.2	52.5
of department (n.s.)	Excluded	45.9	50.8	51.1	40.8	47.5
In department	Included	65.6	63.0	26.1	60.7	61.2
meetings	Excluded	34.4	36.9	73.9	39.3	38.8
In Faculty committees	Included	18.0	30.3	33.8	18.7	23.8
	Excluded	81.9	69.7	69.3	81.3	76.2
In Faculty council	Included	21.5	32.4	33.3	17.3	25.9
	Excluded	78.5	67.6	66.6	82.6	74.1
In senate/university	Included	6.4	24.1	48.7	4.1	15.6
committees	Excluded	93.6	75.9	51.2	95.9	84.4
In university senate	Included	5.3	26.0	35.0	4.0	14.8
	Excluded	94.7	74.0	65.0	96.0	85.2
Total no.		285	244	99	91	719

Notes: Significance: $p =$ *<.05, **<.01; ***<.001. All are significant at $p =$ ***<.001 unless otherwise indicated. (n.s.): not significant.
Source: See table 6.1.

trators (56 per cent) report that part-timers have no power to negotiate their salary rate. Most (70 per cent) confirm that part-timers have no influence over their own hiring or rehiring. Part-timers have little say on matters affecting the full-timers or the department in general. The administrators admit that part-timers are isolated and should be more effectively integrated into departments.

Divergent Perceptions and Conflicting Interests

The interests of administrators and those of part-timers display striking differences in three areas: job security and career opportunity, decision-making and employee rights, and unionization. In regard to part-timers' issues, administrators adopt a mainly utilitarian ap-

TABLE 6.9a
Part-timers' inclusion in and exclusion from decision-making bodies: academic administrators' report, by university size and unionization

Administrators say that part-timers are		Size %			Unionization %		Overall total %
		Large	Middle	Small	Union	Non-union	
In all committees of	Included	34.4	20.6	34.6	28.1 (n.s)	32.0 (n.s.)	29.6
department	Excluded	65.6	79.4	65.3	71.8	68.0	70.4
In some committees	Included	57.4	48.8	48.1	52.1(n.s)	53.0 (n.s.)	52.5
of department	Excluded	42.6	51.3	51.9	47.9	47.0	47.5
In department	Included	66.0	53.8	61.5	60.7(n.s)	61.9 (n.s)	61.2
meetings	Excluded	34.0	46.2	37.8	39.4	38.0	38.8
In Faculty committees	Included	31.6	16.0	20.0	29.0	18.2	23.8
	Excluded	68.9	84.0	80.0	71.1	81.8	76.2
In Faculty council	Included	37.1	14.6	17.9	33.0	18.4	25.9
	Excluded	62.9	85.4	82.1	67.0	81.6	74.1
In senate/university	Included	22.7	8.2	12.0	24.1	6.4	15.6
committees	Excluded	77.3	91.8	88.0	75.9	93.6	84.4
In university senate	Included	22.1	7.3	11.1	24.0	5.2	14.8
	Excluded	77.9	92.7	88.9	76.0	94.8	85.2
Total no.		334	132	153	379	340	719

Notes: All are significant at $p = $ ***<.001 unless otherwise indicated. (n.s.): not significant. Each question (included + excluded) totals 100 per cent.
Source: See table 6.1

proach. Their views on the use of part-timers are quite casual. Their staff planning rarely is well thought out. Their strategy, from hiring to managing part-timers, is at best tentative and at worst pragmatic. Most administrators, however, seem to understand 'the phenomenon of part-time faculty' in academe and are personally sympathetic towards the group. A chairwoman finds part-timers a valuable resource and insists that they should be treated more equitably: 'Our part-time faculty is an important resource. They teach a full range of courses (year 1 to year 4) and are experts, not poor alternatives to full-time faculty. Our treatment of them has not so far been fair. The university has been working on treating them more systematically and equitably.' There are also many chairs of departments who condemn excessive use of contract appointments: 'A small number of part-time positions are highly beneficial to the university since it gives short-term flexibility in appointments. It also gives post-doctoral students and mature graduate students an opportunity to gain teaching experience. But the overuse of part-time and limited-term appointments replacing full-time tenure-stream faculty undermines the quality of the university.' Another comment echoes these concerns: 'Part-time and limited term appointments, in my opinion, dangerously affect the quality of education. If possible, the practice of hiring part-time/limited term faculty should be stopped in the interest of the students.' A chairman from a Quebec university, while unappreciative of the quality of part-timers' work in his department, warns that undue emphasis on full-timers' research may affect students: 'The increasing level of recruitment of part-time and term appointments is extremely deleterious to the teaching function of the university. Difficulties for students in lack of faculty continuity in a department or full and free contact with the instructor is a precondition we have to manage if we appoint many part-timers. If full-time professors are too busy with their research and part-timers take over for them, then it leaves the students with a decreasing quality of educational experience.' Another chair compares curricular and academic benefits of the two types of appointments – full and part-time: 'Since its beginning in 1970, this department has always had more students than our full-time faculty could service, so we have always had part-time people. The problem with part-time as I and others see it, is that they are unconnected to the overall curricular goals of the program as a coherent whole, and they cannot contribute to the research output or governance of the department. If the money were available, we would prefer all full-time. Some part-time have taught specific courses for years, and they are very good at it. But many teach a course only once or twice, and never get the chance to develop it.'

First, the interests of administrators and part-timers conflict over job security and careers. Most administrators (78 per cent), particularly men (79 per cent versus women 69 per cent) and those who have served more years as administrators (more than five years 82 per cent versus less than five years 73 per cent), are not interested in any long-term staff planning for use of part-timers. In addition to gender, academic rank seems to play a central role in accentuating the divergence between part-timers and administrators; the higher the rank of the administrators, the greater the divide (table 6.10). They insist that the needs of the department should dictate hiring from year to year to keep staffing flexible (also see table 6.3). Two-thirds of administrators

(67 per cent) reject or do not express an opinion on continuing employ-ment for long-service, qualified part-timers (table 6.10). They express uneasiness about a separate faculty stream – 65 per cent reject the idea of tenure for part-timers. Since temporary hiring allows administrators to make any policy declarations or verbal commitments about part-timers' prospects, they are unwilling to forfeit the opportunity to 'play it by ear' to the tune of financial uncertainties. In contrast, part-timers (52 per cent) argue that the university has an obligation to offer full-time opportunities to part-timers with long service if they are competi-tively qualified. Two-thirds recommend recognition based on their (teaching) course loads, and on whether they have or do not have a full-time non-academic job. Most part-timers (87 per cent) want a dif-ferentiated rank and salary structure that rewards demonstrated qual-ity and length of service. Thus, the survey of part-timers reveals a contrast.

Second, the interests of administrators and of part-timers differ over the power and resources accorded to part-timers. A majority of admin-istrators (56 per cent) do not agree that part-timers should have a role in shaping faculty policies, including those affecting part-timers, via collegial bodies. Many administrators (63 per cent) are indifferent to extending research grants. A majority of part-timers (58 per cent) oppose this position and deplore the fact that research funding invari-ably is not available to them. Nearly two-thirds of part-timers (64 per cent) demand more control over their own hiring and three-quarters (74 per cent) would like to negotiate their own salaries.

Third, administrators' interests and those of part-timers differ on unionization of part-timers. Nearly half of the administrators report that management of part-timers' hiring is quite onerous. More admin-istrators at the rank of associate and assistant professors (53 per cent) as well as women administrators (52 per cent), all directly involved in hiring, find it burdensome. In particular, a majority of women adminis-trators (53 per cent versus men 38 per cent) report that it is also time consuming to supervise part-timers' work. Many (70 per cent) have confronted a situation where part-timers have exercised their influence through their own unions and have experience in dealing with con-straints created by union regulations. Most administrators (82 per cent) generously affirm part-timers' rights to register grievances and com-plaints, however, regardless of the work that these entail. Further, although administrators, in general, do not think that collective agree-ments governing part-timers create constraints that are at odds with

TABLE 6.10
Managing part-timers: academic administrators' views

Administrators say		Sex %		Academic rank %			
		Men	Women	Full professor	Associate/ assistant professor	Total %
Hiring them is onerous	Often	44.7	52.4	41.7	52.8	46.0
	Rarely	1.6	3.4	2.4	1.2	2.1
	Never	53.7	44.3	55.8	46.0	51.9
	Total %	100.0	100.0	100.0	100.0	100.0
Supervising them is time consuming	Often	37.6	52.9	38.5 (n.s.)	43.3 (n.s.)	40.1
	Rarely	2.0	2.5	1.7	2.4	1.8
	Never	60.4	44.6	59.8	54.4	58.1
	Total %	100.0	100.0	100.0	100.0	100.0
They should be hired yearly to suit deptment needs and staffing flexibility	Agree	79.3	69.4	80.3 (n.s.)	72.5 (n.s.)	77.5
	Neither	12.2	14.9	11.8	15.2	13.1
	Disagree	8.5	15.7	7.9	12.4	9.4
	Total %	100.0	100.0	100.0	100.0	100.0
Provide job continuation for long-service part-timers	Agree	30.5	43.9	28.6	38.2	32.9
	Neither	29.7	28.4	30.0	28.5	28.4
	Disagree	39.8	27.7	41.3	33.2	38.7
	Total %	100.0	100.0	100.0	100.0	100.0

TABLE 6.10 (Concluded)

Administrators say		Sex %		Academic rank %		Total %
		Men	Women	Full professor	Associate/ Assistant professor	
Give them access to shape faculty issues	Agree	42.2 (n.s.)	52.5	42.3 (n.s.)	46.5 (n.s.)	44.1
	Neither	26.4	27.8	26.5	26.7	26.1
	Disagree	31.4	19.7	31.2	26.8	29.8
	Total %	100.0	100.0	100.0	100.0	100.0
Give them right to grievance/complaint procedures	Yes	80.3 (n.s.)	83.9 (n.s.)	78.1**	86.4**	81.6
	Not sure	9.4	4.5	9.2	7.5	7.9
	No	10.3	11.6	12.7	6.1	10.5
	Total %	100.0	100.0	100.0	100.0	100.0
Give them access to internal research funding	Yes	35.3	44.1	32.8	43.6	37.1
	Not sure	14.0	27.1	15.1	17.3	15.8
	No	50.7	28.8	52.1	39.1	47.1
	Total %	100.0	100.0	100.0	100.0	100.0
Give them access to tenure in part-time role	Yes	16.3	33.6	16.5**	23.1**	19.2
	Not sure	15.3	20.5	14.4	18.7	16.0
	No	68.4	45.9	69.1	58.2	64.8
	Total %	100.0	100.0	100.0	100.0	100.0
Overall total no.		595	124	442	277	719

Notes: Significance: p = *<.05, **<.01; ***<.001. All are significant at p = ***<.001 unless otherwise indicated. n.s.: not significant.
Source: See table 6.1.

academic quality, many would rather not have the onerous task of implementing collective agreements. A third of all administrators (34 per cent), indeed, argue that collective agreements are troublesome to administer and that they compromise academic quality. A frustrated chairman comments: 'Our part-time faculty has been unionized for just two years (roughly corresponding to my term as chair), and the amount of work and headache that this change has caused is hard to underestimate. In fact, this is a major factor (indirectly) in my decision not to accept a second term as department chair.' A few part-timers agree: 'There is a ... serious problem in our collective agreement which I believe may be working against 'part-timers.' There is a clause which states that after having taught 2 or more full-course equivalents for three years, said lecturer shall have the right of first refusal for which he/she is qualified. The departments at our university are not in favour of being 'locked in' in such a manner. They want to make such decisions themselves. I fear that this is part of the reason for my own uncertain future.' From the response to the survey, however, we find that part-timers seem overwhelmingly to rely on their unions to protect them against arbitrary treatment. Most part-timers (78.2 per cent) regard their unions as the only influential voice they have in the university. They (58 per cent) report that their grievances against administrators have increased during 1987–92. In particular, women part-timers (66.9 per cent) and Contemporaries (61.4 per cent) identify an increase in their conflicts with administrators during this period, and a majority of part-timers (58 per cent), and a higher proportion of part-timers in two Faculties – fine and applied arts (68 per cent) and humanities (71.5 per cent) – see such conflicts are on the rise.

In conclusion, academic administrators seem quite ambivalent about part-timers and their concerns. Although they realize the strengths in academic quality and benefits accruing to universities from part-timers, they seem unsure of longer-term planning needs and of ways to harness part-timers' contributions and enhance their job satisfaction. The universities' managers – the central administrators – seem to augment academic administrators' internal contradictions. The university central administrators' policies and strategies of financial and resource allocations divide the interests of the academic constituencies – academic administrators, full-time faculty, and part-time faculty – against possible 'bonding' among faculty groups. As managers, controllers of finance, and gatekeepers, universities' central bureaucracies act as catalysts that contribute to part-timers' invisibility and marginality: 'Over time managers have increased the number and proportion of part-time faculty, a category of workers over which managers have greater discretion and full-time faculty have little control. The relative lack of standard professional processes and job rights for part-time faculty and their subordinate position, as defined in workforce matters, suggest that this growing category of faculty is less professionalized than full-timers' (Rhoades, 1996: 651). A part-timer sumarizes well: 'Given all this, why do I stick around? Simple, I love the work. I have a great deal of autonomy (once I have secured a course), and flexible work hours. In fact, the feedback from my students is one of my greatest joys. I wish those in power could hear them thanking me for my efforts, for taking the time to speak one on one with them when they need assistance, for trying to make my courses as interesting as possible. Bringing in "ringers" from other institutions or Ph.Ds from the community may raise the profile of our department, but being able to publish, research, or run a successful practice does not guarantee good teaching skills. I wish that there were better evaluation practices and more opportunity for advancement for my position.'

Part Three

THE EMERGENCE OF AN ACADEMIC UNDERCLASS

Chapter Seven

'Sweated Labour'

It would seem that full-time faculty are not really aware of who part-time faculty are. The division of faculty into full-time and part-time status constitutes a class system in which power resides with the group that occupies the higher position in the hierarchy, and the group that occupies the lower position is tacitly assumed to be composed of individuals of inferior quality. Such an assumption is clearly operating in the representation of part-time faculty throughout the Department's academic plan .Part-time academics are the true 'intellectual proletariat.' It is likely that this form of 'sweated labour' will increase for the foreseeable future.

The above comment from a part-time member of the faculty is not an isolated perception. With the introduction of a new type of teacher, the faculty collegium has turned from a rank-privilege structure into an authority-power hierarchy. Although full-time faculty may treat their part-timers with consideration and take them under their wings to protect them from the excesses of university administration, collegiality does not extend to the part-timers. Conceptually, 'sweated labour'[1] describes exploitive production relations in which one section of workers produces a surplus whose use is controlled by other sections that hierarchically control the workers below them (Himmelweit, 1983: 157). These interactions elucidate the class relations between the different groups of workers and between the workers and the owners of the enterprise. The nature of academe and the hierarchically structured (by rank and status) faculty groups within it; the conflicting relations between the tiers, between faculty and university central administrators, and between faculty and governments – all shape the nature of exploitation and the ways in which it occurs. The university is under threat of increasing privatization and integration into business corporations. In the context of such rapid transformation, sweated labour takes the form of extraction of surplus value from temporary workers and part-timers at the lowest tier of the power hierarchy. Internal segmentation, based on work role, status, and gender, divides the faculty into fractions and enables the higher-level class fractions to extract and share in the distribution of surplus value.

In this chapter I examine how the rhetorical academic 'collegium' operates, in reality, as a hierarchy of power and status. Hierarchical relationships based on rank and job status result from four forces that shape the interactions between faculty groups: internal segmentation (managers and workers), degradation of part-timers' work, ideological structures, and stratification (based on power and feminization). Each, in turn, will be considered.

Internal Segmentation: Managers and Workers

The neat division of functions between academic collegium and university administration has become totally blurred now that full-time members of faculty have assumed the role of managing the so-called temporary part-timers. The literature on U.S. higher education includes accounts of how rapid expansion of higher educational institutions in the 1960s created mutual disrespect and distrust between faculty and central administrators. Central administrators increasingly have come under gratuitous pressure from funding agencies and taxpayers to model themselves after chief executive officers (CEOs) of business corporations. The leadership paradigm found to be effective in corporate business hierarchies proves, however, to be disastrous in the academy. Academic administrators fail in their tasks when they create a climate of distrust by emphasizing respect for authority over reliance on the time-honoured ties of collegiality (Kennett, 1996). Karen Thompson, then president of a part-time faculty chapter of the American Association of University Professors (AAUP), explains the dynamic within the hierarchy: 'The larger the low paid stratum, the more economic pressure on those above them. Salary increases are difficult to justify when your courses can be taught by someone working at an academic "minimum wage." An obvious secondary advantage to administrators of faculty stratification is the old "divide and conquer" strategy. Some full-time faculty feel threatened by the presence of a cheap reserve labour force of part-timers. Others find themselves looking down at part-timers from their occasional role as supervisors ... The hierarchical structure naturally benefits short-sighted administrators. It allows them to minimize costs and maximize control. Divided faculties have limited bargaining power and limited effectiveness in faculty governance' (1992: 25).

From the 1970s on, when non-administrative, rank-and-file, full-time faculty began to take on their managerial role, a hierarchical paradigm became operative in academe, accentuating the conflicting interests of full- and part-time members of faculty. In the United States, Cary Nelson[2] suggests, these internal dissensions have become more acute as a result of large, structurally significant disparities in *disciplinary* salaries:

> As higher education moves more deeply into what is at least a long term recession, and perhaps a semi-permanent one, its internal disparities of opportunity and reward – its hierarchies that run from wealth and privilege to impoverishment and exile – are coming under increasing scrutiny. Among faculty there is intellectual celebrity and substantial financial comfort at one end of the spectrum, and marginal part-time employment at the other ... The longstanding *disciplinary* disparities have also helped rationalize campus-wide structural differences between salaries and benefits for tenure-track faculty and part-timers or adjuncts. These in turn have made outsourcing to temporary and part-time employees in maintenance roles more acceptable to campus administrators. But historically the large discipline-based salary differences have laid the groundwork for all 'market-based' forms of campus exploitation. (1997: 38, 40; emphasis added)

Why and how does internal segmentation occur in academe? Catherine Smith and Vivian Hixson,[3] explain how it occurs also within professional occupations as in industrial ones. Stratification of work and the development of a lower, less privileged tier characterize the work conditions in academe. Unlike tenure-stream professors, temporary academics teach a great deal and are given little by way of clearly defined job responsibilities and workers' rights as a group. Lower-tier academics have little access to financial or symbolic rewards and few opportunities to specialize and build a research-based professional career. They are also invisible. 'Administrative rationalities' within the university instigate differential treatment of temporary and tenure-stream faculty members. It is clear that the 'structural underpinnings of emerging labour market segmentation' of the faculty hurt part-timers' career advancement: 'The ivory tower is a sheltered labour market only for certain members of the occupation of university professors, certainly not for the temporary faculty, particularly if they are women' (1987: 179).

Glen Filson (1988) analyses the resulting class stratification.[4] In discussing Ontario teachers' deprofessionalization and proletarianization, he identifies the split among sociologists about 'teachers' class location.' Neither status nor rank explains the proletarianization of professional classes (Pineo and Porter, 1967), because such approaches to socio economic status do not deal with domination or appropriation of surplus labour. Post-industrial theorists (Bell, 1973; Lenski, 1966) hoped to reduce exploitation by encouraging job sharing and leisure time, but the prevalent alienation and domination in advanced capitalist societies dashed such hopes. Weberians (Giddens, 1981) have neglected to explain exploitation – the surplus appropriation of subordinate-class labour by the dominant classes. Although the Marxists are clearer about both domination and exploitation, they are too diversified on the 'class location' of the splits within educated labour (Filson, 1988: 298). Filson believes that professors are professionals who have credentials, have expertise, and are non-managerial. They are not craft artisans controlled by universities in their research and teaching, as Tancred-Sheriff argues, but are 'salaried professionals'[5] inserted into the university, a wing of the state bureaucracy, but increasingly becoming proletarianized (1985: 314).

À la Filson, I suggest that the university, in its process of incorporation into the corporate-capitalist education segment of the society, creates an intensification of both bureaucratization and mutually exclusive work differentiation within the profession. Increasing bureaucratisation pushes routinized and menial tasks to lower-level workers, while the bureaucracy indulges the professoriate by allowing them some control over the definition of their work. As the regular faculty assumes the managerial role for the appointment and regulation of part-timers, it becomes well integrated into the university bureaucracy, albeit camouflaged under the ideology of 'professionalism'. But the facts are different. University bureaucracies are increasingly centralized and hierarchical, and academic ranks are split not only by status and job security but also by the creation of classes of workers – contract faculty groups, such as limited-term full-time faculty and part-timers – within the higher-education profession.

Segmentation in the labour market occurs through a group's use of social closure to restrict access to certain labour markets and social rewards. Martin (1994) notes that both Weberian and Marxist theorists have analysed segmentation in the labour market and its impact on workers (Parkin, 1979; Kreckel, 1980; Wright, 1985).[6] Each social class of workers defines its boundaries in a labour market that is fully separated from or partly closed to other social classes of workers. It practises exclusionary strategies on the basis of what Wright labels 'skill assets' and 'organizational assets.' These strategies create contexts for unequal distribution of social rewards and, more fundamentally, cleavages among the 'middle-class' workers. Thus, three hierarchically arranged classes appear – a working class, a class of experts who have *skill* assets, and a class of managers who have *organizational* assets (Martin, 1994: 358–9). Martin adds that the influence of education, employment sector, gender, labour market experience, unionization, and so on, on earnings or work life are different for 'workers' vis-à-vis 'experts or managers' (ibid.: 357). The characteristics of the segmented academic market are likely to affect the way that instructors in the secondary and tertiary segments serve their clientele (Rosenblum and Rosenblum, 1994). If non-tenure track instructors like part-timers are institutionally disadvantaged in teaching resources that are normally available to regular full-timers, this situation would affect not only their job satisfaction but also the quality of teaching and of the students whom they teach.

Somewhat analogously to this scheme of segmentation, we may identify three classes within academe: an underclass of part-timers, a 'skilled class' of limited-term faculty, and a managerial class of full-time professors and academic administrators. The professoriate defines and closes its boundaries by regulating the terms and conditions solely under which other groups may be allowed to do its type of work – that is, the professorial. A part-timer responding to our survey excerpts from his department's planning document rules that exemplify this practice: 'According to the (department), "the normal role of part-time faculty should not be to staff the same courses year after year but (1) to replace full-time faculty unable to teach particular courses because of leaves or administrative duties, and (2) to allow flexible last-minute expansion of the curriculum to accommodate unexpected additional students."'

In its management role, the professoriate does not attribute any 'skill assets' to part-timers; nor does it want to know what skills the 'workers' have. A part-timer explains: 'A major factor contributing to full-time faculty's lack of awareness of our qualifications and achievements is that we are hired primarily on the basis of blanket application forms which emphasize seniority counts and have almost no space for other information. The Department might find it enlightening to invite part-time faculty members to submit up-to-date CVs, so that they can see exactly who is doing so much of the Department's teaching. A careful scrutiny of the qualifications of part-time faculty members could prove extremely useful to the Department in its ongoing campaign to wrest funding from the Dean.' This segmentation between the 'tenured' and 'contract' faculty further entrenches an inequitable distribution of material and non-material resources within the university. At the 1982 conference of the Canadian Society for the Study of Higher Education, the prominent Canadian labour arbitrator and legal scholar David Beatty (1982) argued that, to date, faculty unionization had realized only in very limited ways the procedural justice and equitable sharing of resources that certification promises. Although better access to procedural justice may have resulted from unionization of various groups of university employees, the hierarchical power structures remain unaffected. Universities use part-timers year after year as a fill–in resource to manage their budget shortfalls. The resulting relationships – particularly those of part-time faculty with full-time faculty and academic administrators – are critically examined in this book.

In the relationship between full- and part-timers, the collegial values, mechanisms, and procedural protections that are central to the full-timers' functioning and are held out as critical to an institution's academic well-being generally do not extend to part-timers. As academic professionals, part-timers have not been admitted to the charmed circle of status that limits membership to full-time faculty. Even where part-timers are unionized, they remain outside the academic decision-making processes. Appointment selection, assignment of courses, access to full-time positions, security of tenure, research funding and support, and effective participation in curricular and academic policy decisions are commonly denied them, *de jure* or *de facto*. Although participation exclusively by full-timers in such matters has been unchallenged, full-timers are reluctant to extend such powers to the part-time faculty. Indeed, full-timers have become managers responsible for hiring, firing, and administering part-timers.

Degradation of Part-Timers' Work: Political Economy

More than one-third of all faculty members in Canadian universities are part-timers; they contribute significantly to academic work, yet they consume only a marginal share of the institutions' economic resources. Myths about their temporariness in the workforce conceal the differing career aspirations and motivations within the group. Two factors render them 'hidden' or 'invisible' academics: the economics of the university system and the ideological structures of academic practices and traditions. In the political economy of universities, the relentless drive to manage enrolments, finances, and teaching costs has resulted in a bureaucratic rationalization of the academic workload and a bifurcated labour force. This workforce is split hierarchically into full- and part-time faculty groups, which have radically different work processes and receive very different treatment. Part-timers are now a permanent and inexpensive source of labour, producing a surplus value that the universities transfer to compensate for the fiscal shortfalls resulting from government underfunding. Universities degrade some work processes by rationalizing and deprofessionalizing selected academic functions. The degradation legitimizes this workforce, split in relative pay and job characteristics, which in turn reinforces the feminization of the part-time faculty.

Authors of several studies in the 1980s have reported on the nature and conditions of part-timers' work in various Canadian universities (Clapp, 1987; Gordon, 1987; Jones, 1987; Weis, n.d.; Professional Women's Association, 1986; Zeytinoglu and Ahmed, 1989; Ahmed et al., 1989). Late in the decade, interest in this group increased sharply, with a major study of chargés de cours in Quebec (Conseil des universités, 1989) and Statistics Canada's early attempts to gather basic, summary data on part-timers.

In the 1990s interest continued. In a study at McGill University Cumming Speirs et al. (1998) report that in 1993 there were more non-tenure track faculty (NTT) – all faculty with job-position titles that did not lead to tenure (total 1,634) – than tenure-track faculty (total 1,320) in the university. About 61 per cent of the NTTs worked more than half the full-time faculty load. There was a greater proportion of women NTTs (47.3 per cent, excluding research assistants), than full-timers (18.3 per cent).

The financial crises in North American higher education since the 1970s spurred rapid expansion in the use of part-timers, in the process creating several problems. Since then, there has been research at micro- and macro-levels[7] on the role and status of part-time faculty, primarily in the United States. It has been found that part-timers receive neither equitable financial rewards nor status. Authors of most macro-level studies propose pluralistic participation and accommodation of the interests of different faculty groups within existing systems of power and status and outline new administrative/managerial policies and standardized practices (for example, Biles and Tuckman, 1986). Those responsible for the micro-level/experiential studies, in contrast, challenge perceived injustices to individuals, and dramatize the human costs involved in the mistreatment of part-timers.

Four Models

Although the authors of the above-mentioned studies have charted the field of research, most have ignored the *system of power* that creates and perpetuates part-timers as marginal academic workers, and the *ideological structures* within academe that legitimate such treatment. I have analysed the development and nature of the relationships most determinative of part-timers' role and status and have examined the internal dynamics between the different hierarchical layers.

In the literature on part-timers, we may identify four major theoretical models: *market, corporate, professional development,* and *political economy.* Although analysts do not treat these models as mutually exclusive or necessarily identify them explicitly, they usually emphasize one or two of them.

In the *market model* relationships between part-timers and their universities are analysed in the context of part-timers' constituting a readily available labour pool (Tuckman, Vogler, and Caldwell, 1978). Their expendability reflects an oversupply in the market where 'the applicant pool consistently outstrips demand.' The part-timers serve 'as buffers against full-timers' retrenchment and to maintain higher full-time salaries' (Leslie, Kellams, and Gunne, 1982: 73, 199).

In the *corporate model* the direction of growth and development in higher education is related to a demand by the public and by the private corporate sector for specialized scientific, technical, and professional training of graduates and for research that serves corporate needs (Bowen and Schuster, 1986: chaps 9, 10). Universities have been reluctant to make long-term personnel and salary commitments to the social sciences and humanities that show weak enrolment or face uncertain funding. Enrolment in graduate schools has continued to rise in those fields, however, resulting in a glut of doctorates in the academic labour market, particularly in fields for which both university and corporate demand is weak.

In the *professional development model* the interests of those 'who see themselves as professional teachers' and require to be treated as such through the establishment of 'just policies' are explained (Wallace (ed.), 1984: xvi). The model applies also to the most numerous subgroup of part-timers: those fully employed outside the university who teach in universities for professional enrichment and intellectual satisfaction (Leslie, Kellams, and Gunne, 1982: 40–6). This school usually argues for policies and support structures that will more fully integrate the part-timers with the full-timers in order to achieve mutual enrichment and effective business/academic 'interfaces.'

In the *political economy model* the relationship between full-timers and part-timers is analysed in the context of the university's power dynamics and political economy. The interrelatedness of power, resource allocation, work processes, and conflicts internal to the university is emphasized.[8] I believe that this comprehensive model is appropriate for my study of the hierarchical interactions studying the university's power structures as well as their ideological justifications. The university is envisioned as a political economy of academic work in the allocation of resources among constituencies, which stratifies power, privilege, and prestige among central administrators, academic administrators, full-timers, limited-term full-timers, and part-timers. According to this model, conflicts between the groups within academe over recruitment and allocation of work and resources create a power dynamic that shapes the relationship between part-timers and other constituencies. The ideology that legitimates the relationship is contained in ideas and images about the academic profession that authorize the power of full-time faculty and academic administrators to regulate and control part-timers.

The conflict itself is latent and invisible – very much like the part-timers themselves. Judith Gappa cautions against literature that reflects the 'myth and bias' built up around part-timers: 'Part-time faculty are as invisible in literature as they are in the faculty club, and attitudinal barriers work to rob the part-timer of professional visibility ... The pretence that they are a fringe group of stateless academics, marginal in capacity and thus exploitable without qualm is grounded in what may fairly be called 'calculated ignorance' (1984: 8–9). Part-timers, left 'unnoticed on the campus green' (Tuckman and Pickerill, 1988: 98), also participate in a labour market separate from that of full-timers and are, in exchange, exploited for their 'low and relatively decreasing salaries' (Gappa, 1984: 75), which create 'an incentive for increasing the use of part-timers within institutions' (Tuckman and Pickerill, 1988: 109). Gappa estimates that part-timers receive 25 to 35 per cent less than full-timers (1984: 75). Excluding part-timers from benefit packages available to full-timers augments savings in salary budgets (Tuckman and Vogler, 1978: 47).

Full-timers, by virtue of their responsibilities and related powers, function as the immediate academic management vis-à-vis part-timers. In university senates, Faculty councils, and departmental committees, the full-timers control academic policies and allocate resources within 'envelopes' defined by the university central administration (senior management). As front-line supervisors in the departments, they hire, terminate, evaluate and direct part-timers. The full-timers' authority role splits academic staff into managerial and subordinate groups, thus fragmenting faculty interests and vitiating the potential for joint action by full- and part-timers to confront their common adversaries: the university's top management and provincial government.

To understand faculty fragmentation and the universities' power structures, we need a comprehensive analysis of class struggle against the hegemonic state in financial crisis (Scott, 1983: chap. 10) and a critique of the corporate state and university management (Newson and Buchbinder, 1988: 15–17, 42–5). These approaches, however, lack the specificity required to explain the complex relations between part- and full-time faculties. Only a differentiated analysis of the constraints, demands, structures, and contexts of the political economy of part-time academic work, within the class struggle against the managerial powers, can explain the contradictions in faculty relations.

According to studies of 'the state in crisis,' when crisis deepens, the state pursues strategies to elicit legitimation and acquiescence from critical groups through 'corporatist arrangements.' These are extra-parliamentary tripartite negotiations among strategic groups: management, organized unions, and business and financial interests, which are eager to press for gains in their corporate interests (Panitch, 1977; Offe, 1980). Other corporate entities, just as complex as the state – for example, universities and business – also trust the strategy of tripartite agreements to manage conflictual interests. Selective inclusion of the only powerful and well-organized sectors leaves out

weaker groups, such as women, minorities, and non-unionized workers, and thus marginalizes them thoroughly. For instance, as more
women and members of minorities begin to enter the professoriate,
salary inequities expand, since salaries tend to vary according to
gender as well as race/ethnicity (Toutkoushian, 1998). The financial
constraints imposed by the state in crisis manifest themselves in
Canadian universities in various forms; for instance, academic employment practices marginalize untenured full-timers and part-timers
in the university. Whichard et al. give an example of part-timers who
felt constrained and marginalized in their work life by the full-timers' expectations of how they – the part-timers – should teach;
because they are in ill-defined and vulnerable positions as temporary
workers, part-timers pursued a 'hidden agenda'[9] in their pedagogy
'in order to show [their] worth and be accepted and rewarded by all
levels of [the academic] hierarchy,' and be protected against firing
(1992: 61). Part-timers experience a gap between the university's rhetoric about its values and rewards and the realities of their situation as
they learn about the limits of the university's vision and the injustice
that it perpetuates (Cayton, 1991).

Notwithstanding the university's and the faculty's zealous advertisement of their progressive image and liberal ethos, their actions to
accommodate these weaker groups fall far too short. Part-timers continue to remain in the 'room at the bottom' within the existing social
and economic hierarchy. Indeed, the full-time faculty collegium,
caught in contradictions based on collegial ideology as opposed to
meritocratic stratification, finds itself further divided within by organizational rifts such as senate versus union and full-timers versus part-
timers. Some faculty members consider these contradictions a reconcil-
able diversity of interests, blocked by the expansion of management's
interventionist power, which is legitimized by the ideology of 'the service university' acting as an arm of the 'high-tech' corporate state
(Newson and Buchbinder, 1988: 25–30, chap. 6).

At a macro level, marginalization of the university as a whole – a
result of the faculty's loss of control over the organization and process
of its work – has been attributed to the financial and resource-allocation functions of the top-level central administrators (Newson and
Buchbinder, 1988: 30). Ironically, however, faculty members themselves appear to contribute to this process by their reluctance to participate in the formal university bodies at the Faculty or university level
(Lennards, 1988). They increasingly leave the decision-making to

union leadership or to those active few who represent them in the senate, thus making it easier for administration to manage conflicts via 'corporatist arrangements.'

Such 'arrangements,' which selectively favour government, university management, and full-time faculty as 'strategic groups,' entirely exclude part-timers from non-formal negotiations. As financial crisis intensifies, full-time faculty become increasingly willing to negotiate their corporate interests with management, whose vested interest, in turn, is to maintain the financial and political stability of the system. Since the organized and more powerful full-time faculty is better able to protect its interests in bargaining over limited resources, it leaves the marginalized groups to fend for themselves. Such tripartite agreements fragment the 'faculty,' stratify it according to power and tenure, divide it into managerial and worker groups, and promote conflictual and adversarial relations between the two groups. The rules and practices of the professoriate, rooted in meritocracy, inform the ideological structures that serve to legitimate social relations between full- and part-time faculty.

Ideological Structures

Studies of the United States' professoriate, from Jencks and Riesman, *The Academic Revolution* (1968), to Bowen and Schuster, *American Professors: A National Resource Imperiled* (1986), have dwelt on the consolidation of professorial power during the heydays of higher education – its period of affluence and expansion. The academic profession's self-image was developed and reinforced by the faculty's role in the university. Eugene Rice describes how the process by which a 'sense of what it is to be an academic professional' became ingrained in the professoriate, as a socially constructed 'powerful fiction,' and how the following elements have shaped the development of the academic profession and its institutions:

- Research is the central professional endeavour and the focus of academic life.
- Quality in the profession is maintained by peer review and professional autonomy.
- The pursuit of knowledge is best organized according to *disciplines* (i.e., according to discipline-based departments).
- Knowledge is to be pursued for its own sake.

- Reputations are established through national and international professional associations.
- Professional rewards and mobility accrue to those who persistently accentuate their specializations. (1987: 11–17; emphasis added)

The professoriate has come to believe fundamentally in these values. By reproducing such ideas and social forms of thought from their dominant position in higher education, they control the issues that enter the discourse of academic 'professionalism.' Analyses of higher education, written from inside academe and purporting to be authoritative, present the ideas as objectively valid. To the extent that these notions govern the profession and socialize its members, they are ideological.

Dorothy Smith, in 'An Analysis of Ideological Structures and How Women Are Excluded,' identifies 'the significance of ideology in the process of ordering ... social relations,' a process whereby the established mechanism of control within higher education is used to exclude women. She defines ideology as 'practices or methods in the use of ideas and images' that 'legitimate and organize social relations' (1975: 356). The ideas and images become social forms of thought, 'a class phenomenon' that originates from the exercise of dominance. Smith identifies institutionalized practices that entrench the existing power structures:

- control of the educational system
- nature and quality of work
- gate-keeping
- status maintenance
- conformity
- exclusivity of membership.

The educational system trains people to absorb and accord significance to knowledge that is legitimized by 'authoritative ideological sources' – authoritative writers and works. Those occupying the positions of power in the system 'constitute a common perspective, set of relevancies, conditions of experience, interests, and objectives.' In higher education, it is tenured faculty who acts as 'gatekeepers,' and in that role 'to a large extent control who shall be admitted to its ranks and what shall be recognized as properly scholarly work' (Smith, 1975: 359, 356, 361).

Smith's analysis focuses on the consequences for women of men's domination of the tenured faculty and of male control of standards and procedures for advancement to influential faculty positions. She finds women concentrated in temporary, non-tenure-track positions, limited largely to teaching, with reappointment conditional on conformity and continual reassessment (1975: 361). Parallels between women's subordination in academe and the marginalization of part-timers are not only striking but also overlapping. Smith's analysis lends itself to an extension – to a study of the way in which the full-time faculty establishes the form and content of an academe where part-timers are vastly underrepresented in status and influence relative to their numbers.

The full-time faculty's perspectives on the academic profession originate from and reinforce its dominant position in academe. Full-timers have power to define the preferences and objectives of the 'collegium,' which orders and legitimizes social relations. Adopting Smith's metaphor of the collegium as an exclusive 'circle' (1975: 364), we find power limited to those in the circle, whose membership is authorized by their full-time status. Part-timers, as a group, are excluded. It is not the work that part-timers do, the academic values to which they subscribe, or the qualifications that they hold that cause them to be labelled differently and treated in a manner categorically different from that accorded to full-timers. Part-timers and full-timers are often indistinguishable in these comparisons. Rather, there is, for whatever reason, a *perception* of part-timers as properly belonging outside the circle of the full-timers. A professional discourse that expresses full-time/part-time relationships and conditions institutional practices reinforces this perception.

Stratification: Power and Feminization

The professoriate and the university have evolved a hierarchical stratification of the academic workforce on the basis of rank, status, and power, all flowing from an ideology grounded in meritocratic principles and legitimized by the corporatist interests of the full-time faculty. The distinction between 'regular' and 'temporary' faculty groups is evident, and the full-time faculty contains further strata, with differentials attributable to rank, service, discipline, and gender. Beneath its system of stratification lies the part-time faculty.

The full-timers help to manage the part-time workforce both collegially and formally. Part-timers, in contrast, are almost entirely excluded from such roles, which can be designated academic management. It would be highly unusual, for example, for a president, vice-president (academic), dean, associate dean, or research director to be selected from outside full-time faculty ranks. At the departmental level, chairs are chosen from among full-timers in accordance with policy or established practice. For example, a proposal by a search committee in a Faculty in an Ontario university to appoint a distinguished, long-service, part-timer as departmental chair prompted a grievance by the full-time faculty union. The union argued that it was contrary to the spirit and intent of its contract to allow a department to be chaired by other than full-time faculty. Such traditions are firmly entrenched and derive from a consensus within the full-time faculty on how academic professional careers should unfold and who should fill positions of influence and authority among them.[10] The full-time faculty's power to make academic decisions seems to flow from its exclusive status as the university's 'real' faculty.

Harry Braverman's historical analysis of the emergence of a new stratum of clerical workers in the early twentieth century provides a theoretical model that is pertinent here. In *Labour Monopoly and Capital*, he shows how certain work processes were degraded by their routinization into lower-skilled jobs in bureaucracies undergoing rationalization (1974: 293–358). The large-scale employment of part-timers represents a similar degradation of work processes in academe. Financial stress pushed the university management and the faculty collegium to rationalize the academic system by degrading teaching to the status of a more routinized, and even less skilled, work process than was originally conceived in the full 'professional' function of teaching, research, and service. In a U.S. study, William Massy and Andrea Wilger,[11] using as a resource interviews with faculty on 'productivity' in academe, report that 'research' is the defining activity': 'Quality teaching may be viewed as the highest priority by those who provide most of higher education's core funding, but almost three times as many episodes in our database deal with centrality of research as with the importance of teaching. We observed a fundamental difference between the philosophy of faculty and the stated goals of mass public education ... Intrinsic motivations and institutional rewards combine to drive the faculty's preoccupation with research ... Faculty ... see [teaching] load escalation as producing decreased not increased productivity ... An increased teaching load reduces faculty discretionary time that otherwise could be devoted to research' (1995: 15, 18).

Although part-timers who are hired for 'teaching only' positions may differ little from full-timers in their professional qualifications and work, they are treated as a bottom-tier payroll workers. The ideology of power and merit exclusive to the full-time collegium structures the university so as to deny that part-timers represent a real addition to their professoriate. Part-timers' exclusion has been further exacerbated by the feminization of the part-time academic workforce. In the United States, Shelley Park notes: 'Educational cutbacks combined with fewer tenure-track positions and more restrictive criteria for tenure and promotion have given rise to a revolving door phenomenon, wherein adjunct and junior faculty are rotated through entry level positions without serious consideration for tenure. This has created a new class of "gypsy scholars," an intellectual "proletariat" who – in order to eke out a living – move from one low paying, dead-end teaching post to another. This proletariat is disproportionately female ... The university as we currently encounter it ... is a hierarchy built on the exploitation of women: the contemporary research university replicates the patriarchal family wherein fathers are breadwinners, mothers are domestic labourers' (1996: 46, 77). An inhabitant describes the resultant world of the part-time faculty: 'Part-time faculty are a problem only if they are relegated to the margins of [academe] ... and treated with the respect usually reserved for skeletons in the collective [university] ... closet' (McGuire, 1993).

In sum, as part-timers become 'permanent temps' and offer a long-term solution to the continuing financial malaise in the university, the political dynamic will reinforce the status and functional split in the academic labour force. The split takes the form not only of differences in status, compensation, career opportunities, and professional development, but also of feminization and occupational segregation.

Epilogue
IvoryTower, Inc.?

What is the future that awaits the contract faculty in Canadian universities? Would they remain part-timers or would they have opportunities to move up to the regular full-time positions that may arise in a number of disciplines in the near future? What are the prospects for faculty members in universities that are clearly expected to perform for the 'bottom line' and increasingly looked upon as business ventures? The Association of Universities and Colleges in Canada (AUCC) in *Trends* reflects on faculty renewal: 'While early retirement packages have achieved savings, they have not allowed universities to reap one of the benefits normally associated with such initiatives – renewal ... Recent hiring restrictions brought about by declining funding threaten our investments in this generation of graduate students. Many of the most highly qualified personnel Canada has trained over the last five to 10 years are likely to be lost to academia ... The return on investment in human capital development ... will be diminished ... hurting our prospects for future economic growth' (1999: 49).

The AUCC projected in the early 1990s that one-third of the university faculty in Canada would need to be replaced by the mid-1990s. Studies of U.S. and British universities also project similar trends based on retirements and mortality, but with a decrease in the supply of qualified academics. In Canada, the demand for higher education has been increasing rapidly. In a review of a report by Statistics Canada and the Council of Ministers of Education, Virginia Galt notes: 'More Canadians than ever before are ... pursuing higher education' (2000: A10). The report identifies the trend of increases in university graduates among 25-to-29-year-old Canadians, from 17 per cent in 1990 to 26 per cent in 1998. In 1996, among selected OECD[1] countries, the proportion of 25-to-64-year-old Canadians (17 per cent) who have completed university education form the second-largest group, next only to that in the United States (26 per cent).[1] A projection of youths (age 18–24) receiving higher education in Ontario shows a steady growth in this decade (figure E.1). The combination of these factors – younger faculty needed to replace retirees and increasing student demand for higher education – underscores the need for increased hiring in universities.

The realities, however, do not accord with this logic. The numbers of full-timers in Canadian universities declined from 37,422 in 1991 to 33,327 in 1998. The academic-salary component of total non-capital expenditures in Canadian universities declined from 34 per cent in 1973 to 27 per cent in 1998. Ron Melchers, in his report, *Not in the Public Interest* (1999), describes how the current funding policies are jeopardizing the quality of university education. His longitudinal analysis of the state of university finances over the past twenty-five years concludes that university administrators' decisions to 'deprioritize' the core functions of teaching and non-sponsored research are bound to cause irreversible harm to higher education.

In U.S. universities, Patricia Gumport 'diagnoses a macro-trend whereby the dominant legitimating idea of public higher education has changed from higher education as a social institution to higher education as an industry.' She continues: 'Three interrelated mechanisms are identified as having advanced this process: academic management, academic consumerism, and academic stratification. This pattern of academic restructuring reflects multiple institutional pressures. While public universities and colleges have increasingly come to rely on market discourse and managerial approaches in order to demonstrate responsiveness to economic exigencies, they may end up losing legitimacy as they move away from their historical character, functions and accumulated heritage as educational institutions. [This would be detrimental to] the longer-term educational legacies and democratic interests that have long characterized American public education' (2000: 67).

Wachman (1994) warns that regulation, litigation, and unionization have helped to dissipate the notion of the university as an 'ivory tower,' cloistered, self-regulated, and self-policed. These forces have also created within the faculty an underclass of cheap labour – a natural outcome of financial and administrative strategies.

First, in 1995 the Progressive Conservative government in Ontario,

FIGURE E.1

Projected percentage of Ontario population age 18–24 attending university, 1998–2010

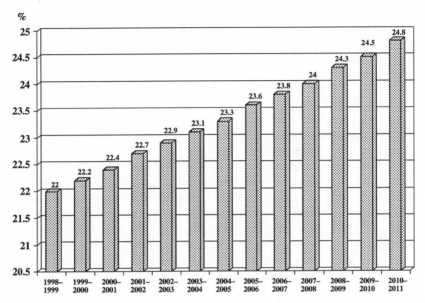

Source: Price Waterhouse Coopers (1999)

in its changes to provincial labour laws targeted part-time workers in order to split them from full-time employees' collective bargaining units and thereby further weakened this class of worker. To quote lawyer James Hayes, 'it's like stepping on weak peoples' heads with steel boots' (Gibb-Clark, 1995: B1). Second, strategies for removing autonomy from the university and for disempowering faculty have taken a deceptively modernizing form: governments and university administrators increase funding for computer technology while reducing funds for faculty renewal. This diversion shows clearly how university administrators faithfully toe the government's policy line and how the issue of faculty shortage is swept under the carpet. Third, the strategy to privatize higher education, apparently to make it 'cost effective' and to free taxpayers from the so-called financial burden, makes it voter friendly.[2] The privatization and commercialization of university has progressed unabatedly turning it into 'University, Inc.,' according to David Harvey: 'A revolution is afoot in higher education ... Those who pay the piper (corporations and governments) will surely call the tune. The relevance of universities is on the line. And a recent flood of books, commentaries, and reports all depict the university as a deeply troubled institution' (1998).

'The Kept University' (Press and Washburn, 2000) is the shape of things that we see in 'the HigherLearning.com.'[3] Press and Washburn capture the milieu in graphic terms when they discuss the situation in U.S. universities:

> Humanities professors at some schools are battling to save their departments from being eliminated, others are discovering, much to their surprise, that university administrators have taken a sudden interest in their course material because of its potential for being marketed online. Seemingly overnight the computer revolution has transformed 'courseware' into a valuable piece of 'content' that can be packaged and sold on the Internet, and online-education companies are racing to collaborate with academic institutions to exploit this burgeoning market ... In a time of budget shortfalls and dwindling public support for education, university administrators and politicians see online education as a way to expand on the cheap. 'Just building campuses is a very expensive proposition,' says E. Jeffrey Livingston, the associate commissioner for the Utah System of Higher Education. 'Governors see [the virtual university] as a way to not spend as much money in the future, to meet growth.' 'Distance learning' is also seen as a promising new teaching tool and as a way to reach nontraditional education markets, such as part-timers and foreign students.

Canadian governments and university administrators are not far behind in pushing for the 'virtual learning' style. Reduced funding for faculty renewal is already a major problem. When the policy permeates further down in the hierarchy, it forebodes a bleak future for part-timers. Jane Hodges writes in the *New York Times* about a surplus of scholars fighting for jobs in U.S. academe; these remarks apply as well to many Canadian academics-in-waiting: 'Scholars ... need to believe in their work, because in one of the hottest employment markets in decades, finding a humanities job in academia remains one of the toughest assignments around. With universities continuing to rely on part-time faculty in their English and foreign-language departments, there is a short supply of jobs that lead to tenured positions ... For scholars who are committed to a traditional academic career, learning to cope with the prolonged uncertainty of part-time or visiting professorships seems, for now, to be just another part of the job' (2000: BU 15).

As we saw above (see chapter four), Contemporaries – the academic part-timers – could provide a reserve pool of highly qualified, well-trained, and readily available workers useful for meeting faculty shortages predicted to occur soon. However, we do not have good data on part-timers, collected periodically on a regular basis, that would help us match supply and demand. Julia Ridgely underscores the significance of data and quotes Jack Schuster: 'The Most important tools are data, data, and data. Data are mightier than rhetoric about beauty, truth, justice, and undercompensated colleagues' (1993: 11; emphasis added). In Canada, part-timers are *hidden*, since their numbers are only estimated (for part-timers after 1990, the year of my first survey) from Statistics Canada reports on university spending on salaries for, rough preliminary numbers on, and estimated workload of part-timers. Currently, no one gathers complete and direct data on this group of academics as Statistics Canada does on full-timers.

The need for reliable data has become more critical because for the past two decades universities have been systematically using part-timers to maintain enrolment flexibility and bridge curricular gaps in staffing. As Kevin Banks (1995) notes, there has been a 'dramatic' change in university employment practices during the last twenty years. Administrations have been increasingly using part- or full-time sessionals to teach the overflow students. This practice has lowered the standard of living of all professors by allowing overall reductions in faculty salaries. Further, the use of part-timers extends the strategies of university central administrators to manipulate all faculty members through their bargaining powers and play one against the other. In Canada, this practice continues, despite a policy of CAUT that restricts use of part-timers to temporary vacancies or to fill specialized areas that would not require a full-time appointment. The U.S. NEA requires that universities give the same salary and benefits to full- and part-time sessionals as they do to tenure-track faculty, though prorated according to workload. The NEA also advocates limiting such appointments to two years and expects that, if the need should continue in the field, then the position would be placed in the tenure track. All such parity requirements, however, are honoured more in the breach than in the observance (Banks, 1995).

Elizabeth Wallace notes that Bowen (and Sosa), in *Prospects for Faculty in Arts and Sciences* (1989), ignore the backlog of underemployed PhDs, many of whom continued for a number of years as part-timers or sessionals. Further, she warns that in the next ten years there was no guarantee that tenure-track appointments would replace retiring professors, and therefore these positions might be permanently lost, especially in the humanities (1991: 353). The present Conservative government in Ontario would use universities as places to train youth for jobs in technology and science, rather than to provide a well-rounded general education that includes humanities and social sciences.

In a preset, government-engineered milieu, the role of academic administrators becomes even more important. They do have the power to shape academe, and, as academics themselves, if they do not insist on the public good as the end product of learning in the university and on the liberal arts and general education, the university mill could well start churning out graduates with only 'digital diplomas' (Noble, 1998) and become a training ground of labour for industry. Martin, Samuels, and Assoc. (1997) entrust the responsibility for making these significant but difficult changes to the chief academic officers. Many administrators now earnestly promote 'partnerships' between academe and industry with an almost missionary zeal. Teresa Campbell and Sheila Slaughter warn: 'If university-industry activity is strongly promoted ... involved faculty are likely to devote more time to university-industry activity, perhaps reluctantly leaving a greater share of teaching to temporary faculty or lecturers ... Once begun, this cycle will serve to reproduce and reinforce non-involved faculty's diminished status by progressively reducing their opportunities to gain autonomy, income, and prestige. Increased interaction with industry may also contribute to a trend in which public service becomes service for fee rather than for free, and only the service that generates external revenue may be encouraged. If such differentiation between involved and non-involved faculty continues, faculty members are likely to lose their identity as a collegium, undermining their collective strength and further eroding their professional status' (1999: 346–7).

Not only do academic administrators have an obligation to protect the university from business's 'largesse' as well as from political ideologues and their sharp financial cuts, they must also nurture their faculties. Administrators can see the needs of their faculty members and should provide mentoring, open communications, and peer support. They must not become overzealous – 'mothering' their faculty and 'bed-checking' – but through careful efforts contribute to the professional development of their faculty (Miller, 1996). Faculty members, especially part-timers, clearly show disenchantment and apathy vis-à-vis university affairs because of non-recognition of their work. Academic administrators, claims Welch (1996), should provide vision and motivation and should display vigour, foresight, and will in creating and sustaining an institutional milieu capable of nurturing faculty vitality.

Such a vision must include an emphasis on teaching, not merely on excellence in research. Joan North argues: 'Because diverting attention to scholarship is so seductive ... where a Dean visibly spends her time (and money) sends signals through [out the university] ... about priorities' (1996: 26). This situation is particularly harmful to part-timers who are hired as teaching-only workers. Further, if part-timers themselves continue to increase their workloads to make up for low pay, lack of time for research and professional development would handicap them, in their competition with new doctorates. As more experienced teachers, part-timers would become a lost resource at a time when the public is criticizing what it perceives as universities' neglect of the teaching function. Canadian universities would gain more credibility if they supported part-timers who are heavily involved in teaching. Karen Thompson writes as the president of the Part-Time Lecturer Faculty Chapter of the Rutgers Council of AAUP: 'Interchange between different groups is almost non-existent. In fact, contact within groups is often limited. The gap is easily filled by an aggressive administration ready to control what the faculty has yet to discuss. The students see all this from the bottom of the pyramid where they are more likely to come in contact with part-timers than senior professors ... Teachers without tenure and academic freedom may appear to students as fearful and circumscribed instructors, carrying out orders from on high. This may not present the profession in an attractive way but it does prepare students for the corporate managerial model they may encounter in their careers ... As the top of the pyramid moves farther away from the students and the educational encounter, so does academic freedom and tenure' (1992: 25).

In the United States, Gappa and Leslie urge university administrators and full-timers to respond quickly to the rumblings of public discontent over their current priorities (1993: 230). They point out that the tenured faculty would be underestimating public dissatisfaction if it continued to expect to be subsidized by part-timers who perform the most intensive teaching functions under conditions the least conducive to good work. Similarly, we could surmise that if Canadians feel that publicly funded higher education undervalues teaching, their disdain for ivory towers and antipathy towards institutions of higher learning will become more acute. As taxpayers, most Canadians would become only more disillusioned with the purpose of the university and more entrenched in their recalcitrance towards higher education funding if universities were to continue to downplay teaching. It will not take long for them to see how the teaching function is degraded through deliberate bifurcation of the professoriate. Warnings in United States clearly echo these sentiments. Berube and Nelson comment on U.S. 'academy bashing': 'The university's critics are now trying to convince the American public that their tax dollars are being misspent on faculty whose only concerns are research and professional advancement' (1995: 6).

Based on their understanding of academic workplace realities and their dependence on Contemporaries' contributions, universities may consider two options. First, they could hire only Classics as their part-timers. This move is unlikely, since universities have found Contemporaries well qualified and able to teach any session at any time. Second, they could recognize Contemporaries as an integral workforce and treat them as such. Universities' ad hoc approach to part-timers has short-changed these institutions. If universities consider a full complement of academic motivations and professional competence as necessary preconditions for joining the faculty, then they must recognize Contemporaries' need for equitable salaries, benefits, job security, and opportunities for professional development and career enrichment. In these times of rapid changes in knowledge related to academic fields – for instance, in science, in technology and in ideas – an added bonus for universities in hiring their well-qualified, long-term part-timers will be faculty renewal at much shorter periods. Those part-timers who have been teaching since the 1980s, if hired now for a full-time position, are likely to retire sooner than a freshly minted younger graduate hired today.

So far, however, universities have not recognized and addressed such issues through their planning. A senior administrator in a university where part-timers are unionized complained whenever contract negotiations with part-timers were under way: 'Why don't part-timers want a contract that would describe and safeguard their own work conditions? Why do they always want a contract that is analogous to full-time faculty contract with parallel provisions?' Gary Rhoades answers these questions by explaining that part-timers are not considered professionals; they want a contract that would define their conditions of employment in professional terms and recognize their status as professionals. He finds that in U.S. universities their work conditions are mostly undefined: 'The work of part-timers is for the most part delimited to instruction. This delimitation is a major dimension of deprofessionalization, and it is augmented by managers' extensive discretion in whether and how to evaluate part-timers. Professional processes of evaluating quality and rewarding merit and professional control of such processes are lacking' (1996: 652).

Not only do part-timers want to be treated as professionals, but they also want to be a force to be reckoned with so that they can get out of situations such as the one that Cary Nelson describes: 'One of our recent Ph.D.s lives with his wife in a tin cowshed on the Texas border. Unemployed, they live off the land. Though they still have the dreams, their main ambition at the moment is running water' (1995: 20). To become a force within the university, part-timers must overcome the fragmentation in the hierarchy. Kathy Newman suggests a strategy of unifying all contract faculty – LTFTs, and temporary faculty of all stripes – who should then push for increasing the total percentage of tenure-stream faculty (1999: 33). There seems to be an element of sympathy for this strategy even among full-time professors. About the career crisis dispiriting graduates in higher education, Sandra Gilbert quotes George Levine, a professor of English at Rutgers University. While attending a meeting of the Modern Language Association's Committee on Professional Employment, Levine observed: 'I am here because not long ago I saw a car parked on my street with a bumper sticker that said 'Friends Don't Let Friends Go to Graduate School' (1996: 12).

We have found that women are more numerous among part-time and LTFT faculty than among tenure-stream full-timers. Lesley Bellamy (1994) urges that universities and analysts should address the conclusions of Caplan (1993), Hackman (1991), and Altbach and Lomotey (1991), instead of waiting for time and perseverance to rectify the low proportion of women. Caplan (1993) suggests that active measures are necessary and that responsibility for correcting the imbalance rests with the university. Universities must find ways to include more women rather than merely announcing new policies. Others (for example, Hackman, 1991) call for networks of connections for women, analogous to 'old-boys' networks,' as a necessary pre-condition for allowing more women to enter higher education. Further, to include marginalized groups, such as minorities and women, it is essential to change the curriculum and programs, which would draw in certain areas and methods of study – for instance, those relating to minorities and women – hitherto deemed marginal (Altbach and Lomotey, 1991). The push for more women full-timers must also come from public policy and from the society at large. It is often emphasized that state policy and social expectations of gender roles can remove or create impediments to labour-market gender equality (Lane, 1993). In addition, women's increasing political awareness and the influence of unions, political parties, and pressure groups could advance the demand for women workers.

Women in academe also may be working part time for reasons other than non-availability of full-time jobs or their not being hired as full-timers. Their situations also tend to marginalize them as people who are not professional or career oriented. If we discover why their behaviour is different from that of men in similar situations, we can explode the myths that degrade their résumés. One category of such women academics includes those who have paused in their search for a full-time position for family reasons. Some women in my surveys had to give up or turn down a tenure-stream position and become either part time or LTFT in a location where family or child-care support was not available or not affordable. Creating opportunities for women in these situations would keep them out of the large part-timer group and allow them time for research. Certain forms of professional activity allow greater flexibility and freedom to accommodate additional activities. Certain variations are supposedly more acceptable in women's résumés: 'negotiated strategies' such as post-doctoral appointments, guest lecturing, visiting positions, fellowships, or special academic appointments.

Creating shared academic positions for academic couples could be a major breakthrough in dealing with shortages of full-time openings, as well as in catering to couples wishing to be parents while maintaining professional careers (Didion, 1996). Such couples experience various pressures: commuting, unequal career paths, part-time positions. Although policy-makers are beginning to understand the urgent need to shift their attention to what Herbert Gans calls a 'post-work society,' they have not yet made the effort to examine its implications; he predicts that in the post-work society 'full-time work eventually would no longer be the major determinant of personal identity, prestige, and that all-important feeling of social usefulness' (1993: B3) or workers' basic source of income, status, and self-respect. Given the rigidities within the university administration, however, sensitizing administrators to the needs of women and families and establishing a faculty structure of time-sharing positions would be quite difficult (Didion, 1996; Norrell and Norrell, 1996).

Gender also plays a role in differentials between men and women academics' positions and pay. We saw above that, of the women in academe, large numbers are part-timers and LTFTs, and far fewer are full-timers. Beyond the low-paying jobs, they experience pay differentials based simply on gender. Since women are entering the workplace in greater numbers, it is imperative that they receive equitable retirement earnings based on years of service. In particular, women academics with long service in part-time positions, even if they eventually obtain full-time positions, cannot make up for the shortfall in their pension contributions. As part-timers, they have not had the right to contribute to any retirement benefits. After perhaps a decade or more as part-timers, with the long period of service common among 1980s graduates of the 'lost generation of scholars,' they have missed out on making a third or more of their likely pension contributions. What Ornstein and Stewart (1996)[4] argue for women full-timers applies equally for both sexes:

> In recent years universities in Canada have come under considerable pressure to institute equity measures and this pressure may have resulted in more women entering the academic profession, and in what appears to be a decline in the difference in male and female pay. This is encouraging, but these changes will not assist senior women faculty, who are relatively worse off than their junior colleagues. Furthermore, since pensions are usually based on individuals' earnings in the few years before retirement, discrimination against women will be perpetuated into their retirement. Finally, the bureaucratic character of pay differences suggests that structural changes, particularly a serious effort to prevent discrimination at the time of hiring, are key to changing patterns of discrimination.

In conclusion, it has become clear in the past three decades that an appropriate complement of part-timers is essential to accomplish the university's mission of excellence in teaching, research, and service. Under increasing strains in funding for higher education and facing political agendas to privatize public institutions, numbers of tenure-stream full-timers in the publicly funded institutions already are shrinking. Under this duress, without part-timers to share the workload, universities will fail in their mission. As Michael Parsons wrote more than a decade ago, contract faculty are vital to higher education: 'A commitment to excellence requires a comprehensive systematic design for part-time faculty recruitment, development, assessment, and integration into the institution's delivery system. Careful attention to recruitment recognizes that [the] part-time teacher often personifies the institution for the student' (1985: abstract).

Appendix
Survey and Methodology

The lack of information on and knowledge about part-timers represents a critical missing piece in a comprehensive description of the Canadian academic workforce. Some universities or groups of universities (see Rajagopal and Farr, 1992: 319) from time to time had studied part-timers for various ad hoc reasons (for example, Status of Women Committee of the Council of Ontario Universities), but there had been no assembling of national data. My survey of part-timers is an attempt to fill this gap. My national data may throw light on the numbers, characteristics, roles, and working conditions of part-timers in Canadian universities. I selected twenty-two representative universities using critical variables for Canadian higher education: geographical location (east/west), language groups (francophone/anglophone), size (large/small) of student population, range (multi-faculty/single or fewer) of Faculties, research intensity (high/low),[1] collectivization (unionized/non-unionized), and use of part-timers (high intensity/low intensity).[2] From lists of part-timers' names supplied by universities, I corrected for errors such as names/status that were inconsistent with my definition or were duplicated in several departments.

I randomly chose every four out of five part-timers in each selected university (4,900 part-timers from a total of 6,100 part-timers) as my sample. The part-timers in the selected universities represent 61 per cent of the all part-timers in Canadian universities. I developed a detailed, eleven-page questionnaire on various attitudinal and interactive aspects of part-timers' work and life in academe and administered it to members of this faculty across Canada. The total response rate was 45 per cent. Unlike full-time faculty on university campuses, contract (part-timers and LTFTs) faculties are temporary and mobile, which suggests the difficulties in gathering information from them. Therefore, I had to design special methods to reach them, which demanded the goodwill not only of the respondents but also of central administrations in universities across Canada.

I developed surveys on the basis of an extensive review of literature on part-timers in other parts of the world. I found that the phenomena of part-timers and LTFTs are a result of actions by other parts of the university, such as budget administration, personnel administration, full-timers' teaching loads, Faculty structures, and academic administrators' policies. Therefore, from the beginning, I viewed the part-timers' issues from a number of perspectives, which led me to design six different surveys: two institutional and four direct surveys addressed to individual respondents:

- National Institutional Pre-Survey (1990); a survey of definitions of part-timers and LTFTs
- National Institutional Survey (1990–1); a survey of part-time and LTFT faculty
- Part-Time Faculty Survey (1991–2)
- LTFT Faculty Survey (1991–2)
- Academic Administrators Survey (1991–2); views on part-timers and LTFTs
- Full-Time Faculty Survey (1991–2); views on part-timers and LTFTs

National Institutional Pre-Survey

The survey on definitions of part-timers and LTFTs constituted my National Institutional Pre-Survey, 1990. It collected the definitions and concepts in usage relating to part-timers in universities across Canada. Universities use different terminologies in referring to their part-timers, such as sessional faculty, contract faculty, and teaching assistant other than graduate assistant. I needed a standardized and consistent terminology that could be understood across universities that were using different parameters in reference to pay periods, terms of appointment, salary and benefits, and so on. Therefore, I sent a pre-survey questionnaire to forty-five English-speaking, degree-granting Canadian institutions, introducing the project and seeking information on their definitions and the best local sources of data and information on part-timers. I addressed similar questions directly (in a personal interview) to the director-general of the Conference of Vice-Rectors of Universities of Quebec, who provided useful information and documentary sources. I received detailed responses from sixteen of the anglophone universities. To avoid any further delay, I undertook informal phone discussions with other university administrators in various provinces. These steps enabled me to feel confident about developing definitions and questions to collect quantitative data and information about institutional practices that would be set out in the institutional survey. The pre-survey and informal discussions also helped me to identify key contacts in respondent universities and gave them early notice of the more extensive requests for information to follow.

Most important, the information allowed me to learn more about the different usages of 'part-timers' and to work out an operational definition of 'part-time faculty.' After further consultations with selected universities, I concluded that respondent universities would be able precisely to recognize this term unambiguously. The exclusion from my definition of part-timers of graduate assistants (GAs) and of full-time faculty performing overload work or moonlighting constituted two key decisions. The work characteristics and academic status of these two groups differ from those of part-timers. Further, I decided to seek information on medical Faculty part-timers separately, in order not to 'contaminate' my main data on otherwise consistently understood 'part-timers.' Part-timers in other Faculties – arts, science, fine arts, and so on – have types of employment contracts and remuneration that differ from those common in medical faculties, where 'part-time faculty' has a radically dissimilar connotation.

Using the explanations given by various universities, I developed a definition of part-timers – those members of an institution's instructional staff who are employed part time and who do not hold appointments with full-time status. Included are those part-time appointees with teaching responsibilities (for instance, as course director, tutorial/seminar leader, laboratory demonstrator/supervisor). I excluded five categories: part-time academic staff who do not have teaching duties (for example, those doing only marking/grading; research assistant/associate) or who have only occasional duties (such as guest lecturers); people holding appointments as full-timers but teaching only part time or carrying a partial load; full-time students (graduate or undergraduate) performing teaching duties; full-timers teaching overload, with or without additional remuneration; and medical part-timers.

National Institutional Survey

This survey covered part-timers and LTFTs in all universities in Canada. Specifically, I sent the survey to central administrations, requesting information on their definitions of part-timers and their faculty's basic demographic characteristics. This was an important stage, since there were no extant data on the identity and location of part-timers. I mailed the survey directly to eighty-seven institutions identified in the handbook of the Association of Universities and Colleges of Canada (AUCC). Sixty-one universities responded: thirteen of the sixteen in Quebec, and forty-eight of the seventy-one in the rest of Canada. Information was requested on numbers, workloads, salaries and benefits, support services, policies regarding part-timers and level of unionization.

The survey established a primary database of part-timers in 1990–1 on their numbers, teaching loads, disciplinary distributions, unionization, support services, and universities' budgets for paying part-timers. I developed ratios of intensity in using part-timers relative to full-timers, proportions of teaching done by part-timers, and proportions of instructional budget allocated to pay part-timers in reference to other standardized databases publicly available to Canadian universities. For instance, I collected details on full-time faculty from Statistics Canada, *Information on University Expenditures, Salaries, and Research Budgets*. I obtained undergraduate and graduate enrolments directly from the AUCC. For details not available through other sources on Quebec universities, I turned to the Conference of Rectors and/or the Conseil des universités du Québec. Various individuals within universities, from part-timers to vice-presidents, kindly provided crucial information supplementing and clarifying the survey data, and I progressively gained confidence in the representativeness of the university samples. Thus, my second survey formed the basis for a further selection of universities, where I would carry out a set of four major surveys designed to address the individual members of different constituencies that I planned to study.

Of those who responded to my National Institutional Survey, fifty-six universities provided sufficient details to allow me to build my data on various institutional aspects of part-timers' situation: their numbers, salaries, policies, and so on. The respondent universities represented 86 per cent of total full-time student enrolments in Canada, as well as a very substantial portion of all the degree-granting institutions. Where gaps or anomalies occurred in the responses, I pursued them through informal discussions with contact persons to ensure completeness of the information and consistency in my understanding of terminologies.

Surveys of Individual Respondents, 1991–2

Design of Instrument and Distribution of Questionnaires

Using the information provided by the two institutional surveys as well as the literature, I developed my questions, all related to and about the part-time and limited-term full-time faculty. I designed the surveys as parts of an integrated study in order to establish, for the first time, a national database on the part-timers and LTFTs in Canadian universities. I received encouragement and cooperation from contacts with university administrators and staff, which convinced me that it was feasible to gather information on the many issues raised in these questions. I felt that I could go beyond the level of information collected in U.S. surveys on part-timers and gather more detailed, qualitative, and attitudinal responses. Developing and finalizing the questions took a considerable time, since there were no earlier surveys for guidance.

Finally, I developed four surveys to collect the required information from the segments of the university the shape the activities of part-timers that concern me – part-timers, LTFTs, full-timers, and academic administrators.

Selection of Sample Universities

Canadian universities have certain distinctive characteristics that have to be represented in any selection of samples in order to be comprehensive. I selected twenty-two universities to constitute a representative sample covering seven critical variables of Canadian higher education: geographical location (east/west/north/south), language groups (francophone/anglophone), size of student population (large/mid/small), range of Faculties (many/fewer), orientation (research or teaching oriented), collectivization (union/non-union), and intensity of part-timer use (high/low).[3]

- **Geography**: Across Canada's geographically diverse and vast expanse, universities are established in four major regions: the Atlantic provinces, Quebec, Ontario, and the west.[4]
- **Language**: I chose all my francophone institutions from Quebec regions that have similar external, political, financial, and regional characteristics. I decided not to include the few non-Quebec francophone universities and colleges. It would have been helpful to include an anglophone institution from Quebec, but none would participate.
- **Size**:[5] As measures of size, both student enrolments and numbers of full-timers are critical in any study of part-timers. Growing enrolment in higher education over the past thirty years has not led to the opening of new universities in Canada. Once-small universities, such as Trent or Laurentian, now have more than 200 full-timers. I selected twenty-two universities to cover three sizes: ten large universities with more than 1,000 full-timers, four small universities with fewer than 300 full-timers, and eight mid-sized universities with 300–1,000 full-timers. Two universities, however, early on decided not to participate. In one, an anglophone mid-sized university, the central administration declined. In the other, a large Quebec institution, the part-timers' union denied access to its members. A Quebec translator of sur-

veys translated all my surveys into French, but the union leadership declared the translation inappropriate. Although all surveys in French were already printed, I acceded to their request to do the translation themselves. The union leadership came back with a proposal to control the style of language and design of the survey, which would have made their survey unique and incomparable even within Quebec.

- **Range**: To ensure diversity and variety in program levels, I selected universities that were representative of three ranges: full, wide, and limited. Full-range included all three levels and programs: undergraduate, graduate, and professional programs. Wide-range universities are those with graduate programs but only limited professional programs. Limited-range universities focus largely on undergraduate arts and science programs with only a limited range of graduate programs.

- **Research orientation**: In order to determine whether part-timers would be hired and viewed differently according to the university's primary function, I differentiated teaching-oriented from research-oriented universities. The distinguishing measure was fiscal: the ratio in 1988–89 of research expenses to operating expenses by universities (CAUBO). The average was 0.21 for the fifty-six universities on which data were compiled. Very few universities had ratios well above that level, of which I included a few in my sample: Université de Montréal, Waterloo, Queen's, and McMaster. In Canada, in contrast to the United States, such a distinction is, at best, relative, since Canada does not have tiers of universities with a standard classification differentiating research from teaching universities.[6]

- **Collective organization**: I selected universities according to whether or not their part-timers are represented by unions. In 1991 in eight universities part-timers had their own unions, in five they were represented by full-timers' unions, and in seven they were not unionized.

- **Intensity of part-timer use**: From the data on full-timers and part-timers gathered through my main institutional survey, I developed a ratio of 'part-time intensity' for these four surveys. The intensity is the ratio of part-timers to all faculty, both part-timers and full-timers. I could have used the ratio of part-timers to full-timers, but my method of calculation would make it easy to determine how many part-timers there are out of 10 or 100 of all faculty members in the university. The selected universities represented both intensities: nine higher and eleven lower intensity than the average, 0.385, for all Canadian universities.

- **Disciplinary areas**: My classification follows Statistics Canada's disciplinary codes and titles in both the surveys and the analyses. The major fields of study are social sciences, humanities, fine and applied arts, pure sciences, applied sciences/engineering, health sciences, education, business/administration, law, and 'other' to be specified. The surveys asked respondents simply to record the academic discipline(s) of their highest degree.[8]

A final list of twenty universities were selected according to the above detailed characteristics: Alberta, Lakehead, Laurentian, Laval, Manitoba, McMaster, Memorial, Montréal, Mount St Vincent, New Brunswick, Ottawa, Queen's, Regina, Saskatchewan, Sherbrooke, Simon Fraser, Trent, Victoria, Windsor, and York.

Part-Timers: From lists of part-timers' names sent by universities, I avoided duplication of part-timers who might be teaching simultaneously in different departments. I chose as my sample every four from out of five part-timers in each of the selected universities (4,900 part-timers from a total of 6,100). I administered to this sample an eleven-page survey on part-timers' work and life in academe. The response rate was 45.3 per cent.

LTFTs: From my institutional survey, I found some 1,700 full-timers who held single or multi-year contracts, and I decided to survey all of them. The response rate was 47.5 per cent.

Academic administrators: Seven types of positions – academic vice-presidents, associate and assistant vice-presidents, deans, associate and assistant deans, research unit directors, department chairs, and program directors – constitute academic administrators for this survey. These administrators are members of the faculty who perform administrative functions at various levels and ranks. I surveyed these officials in each selected university to find out their views on part-timers. The universities supplied the lists of names of academic administrators in all non-medical Faculties and their campus addresses; 41.2 per cent of the administrators responded.

Full-timers: I directed this survey at samples of full-time members of faculty, other than those serving as academic administrators. This survey gathered their views on part-timers. I designed the sample from each university to include a greater percentage of full-timers from those disciplinary fields that employed greater proportions of part-timers and to include smaller percentages from disciplines that had fewer or no part-timers. I describe this procedure next.

Methodology

Before establishing faculty proportions in different disciplines, I ensured that the discipline areas of full-timers and part-timers coincided. Then, using numbers of part-timers and full-timers in each discipline area, I calculated a ratio of part-timers to full-timers. The next step was ordering the discipline data in the descending order of this ratio. In dividing this ratio-list into three groups, I ensured that each group contained approximately one-third of the total number of part-timers employed in all disciplines – *high*: ratios of part-time to full-timers 29.5 and above; *medium*: ratios of 17.1 to 29.4; *low*: ratios of 17.0 and below. I surveyed one out of three full-timers in high ratio disciplines; one in five in medium ratio areas; and one in ten in disciplines with a low ratio or with no part-timers. This procedure resulted in an overall sample of 1 in 4.75 full-timers in the universities surveyed.

I used information from Statistics Canada (1989) on faculty numbers in different disciplines to select the sample in anglophone universities. For Quebec universities, I relied on reports of the Conférence des Recteurs (1991)[9] for full-time faculty and of the Conseil des universités (1989) for part-timers because Statistics Canada reports do not provide the necessary data. The universities sent me their lists of names of current tenure-stream full-timers broken down by department/academic specialization. I checked these lists to remove names of academic administrators, non-academics, persons on leave, and LTFTs. I then grouped the names into discipline areas and drew an appropriate sample according to the ascertained ratio. The response rate from full-timers as a group was 45.4 per cent.

Rather than mailing individual packages directly from the Institute for Social Research, York University (which was responsible for administering the whole project), I made arrangements with a reliable facilitator at each participating university to receive a box with individually addressed survey packages and 'reminder' cards. These facilitators then distributed the survey packages by means of the internal mailing system within each university.

Part-timers often do not have a mailing address in a department or university, a facility that is normally available for all full-timers. Also, part-timers may not be located on the campus that houses their department office(s), since they may teach on several campuses. Further, in many departments, part-timers do not have mailboxes or offices. Therefore, sending the survey personally addressed to them directly to their departments or universities would not have guaranteed delivery. Therefore, with the advice and help of local university administrators and staff, I devised the above delivery procedure. It ensured that the surveys not only reached part-timers with certainty but also that they were individually and directly addressed to them. To assure uniformity, I followed the same system of internal delivery for each of the other surveys.

Personal Narratives and Oral History

In writing the text, I have combined the personal narratives and stories that many of my respondents – from part-timers to full-timers – have generously found the time and patience to provide and send along with their survey responses. Patricia Gumport stresses the need to combine both data analysis and personal narratives, since this technique allows investigators to see the institutions or the processes being examined through respondents' eyes and thereby opens the path to the 'unanticipated.' This method is more open and flexible than the predictive and generalizing approaches used for studying academic organizations. The combination of data and people's own experiences reveals individuals' multiple views within organizations (1989: 187).

In some cases, clarifications of definitions and explanations emerged through personal interviews, based on respondents' narratives. Stacy Wenzel and Carol Hollenshead (1994) and Rita Karwacki Bode (1996) have used the narratives to discuss their populations' feelings about their universities. Bode has explored the various characteristics of collegiality based on what the new faculty have defined as collegiality in their responses to open-ended questions. Miles and Haberman (1994) elaborate on the traditional qualitative research and the invaluable resource of respondents' comments. David Northrup (1997) has emphasized validating survey research further by checking quantitative interpretations against the respondents' 'voices,' as well as by comparing the results with other surveys conducted on the population.

Notes

Introduction: 'Changing Times and Changing Mission'

1 For instance, Michael Taube writes in the *Globe and Mail*: 'Valuable university funds are spent on unnecessary programs and irrelevant research grants. For example, certain Canadian universities run inefficient doctorate programs, especially in the Humanities.' He adds that universities should not be spending wastefully by offering PhD in such areas as political science, sociology, and so on, which do not have market demand, but should privatize universities and cater to the marketplace demand for jobs (1999: B2).
2 Bill Graham was the president of the University of Toronto Faculty Association (UTFA).
3 Deborah Flynn was then president of the Ontario Confederation of University Faculty Associations (OCUFA).
4 Ron Melchers analyses changes in faculty salaries, academic budgets, and university operating budgets from 1994 to 1997. He teaches criminology at the University of Ottawa.
5 Janice Newson (professor of sociology, York University) acknowledges, however, that 'there can be no meaningful intervention [of changes from outside] without [academics'] understanding that, as privileged and influential professional workers, academics themselves have played a significant role in the shaping of their workplaces ... Moreover, processes interior to the university recruit faculty and students alike in adopting practices that help to implement objectives and values for their work that they may not consciously intend but which nevertheless advance neo-liberal and neo-conservative visions' (2000: 9).
6 Philip G. Altbach and Lionel S. Lewis surveyed academics in fourteen

countries in Europe, Asia, Latin America, the Middle East, and North America. The Carnegie Foundation for the Advancement of Teaching initiated the survey, which was carried out in 1991 and 1992 by research teams in each participating country. Respondents numbered between 1,000 and 3,500 per country, and the total sample was about 20,000. This survey established data comparable not only on the demographic facts of academe but, more important, for the first time on the attitudes and activities of the academic profession in those countries.

7 The Treaty of Versailles entrenched Workers' Clauses (or the Labour Charter) that included the articles pertaining to workers' freedoms, eight-hour workday, regulations governing equal wages for work of equal value, weekly rest day, prohibition of child labour, and labour not to be deemed a commodity. Member Countries who subscribed to the ILO constitution and who were members of that institution were expected to adopt these labour regulations, which formed the variously numbered conventions of the ILO. See Vosko (2000: 67–70).

8 Non-standard and contingent workforces are terms that describe workers who do not hold regular positions and whose jobs are deemed temporary. Because full-time jobs are considered 'regular,' part-time work becomes non-standard.

9 International Labour Office figures are quoted in Thurman and Trah (1990). This article was adapted from the introduction to their original report (ILO, 1989). Please see the report for a more elaborate discussion on this topic.

10 Bernard H. Levin et al. examine the changes in state funding over a decade (1981–91) in a large college system (Virginia community colleges). Marvin Wachman discusses the reduction in institutional autonomy and therefore the end of the 'Ivory Tower' – universities are increasingly drawn into litigation over issues such as grading, admission, tenure, harassment, and racial discrimination.

11 Cynthia Hardy compares the strategies of two universities in British Columbia – Simon Fraser University (SFU) and the University of British Columbia (UBC) – in dealing with financial constraints. She argues that political contexts structured cutbacks in the universities. UBC retrenched the faculty and closed programs because of the position of the board of governors, powerful deans, and an active Senate. At SFU, faculty's voluntary pay cut and central administrators' strategies of engaging collegial and professorial representatives in the process substantially reduced opposition from the affected groups.

12 I call those part-timers who do not hold any full-time job but work only

part time 'Contemporaries' in this book. See chapter 4 for a fuller explanation of this term.

13 Robert N. Bellah is Elliott Professor of Sociology, emeritus, at the University of California, Berkeley. He has edited *Habits of the Heart* (Berkeley: University of California Press, 1985) and co-authored *The Good Society* (New York: Knopf; distributed by Random House, 1991).

14 This was an advertisement paid for by the University of Toronto Faculty Association under the banner 'Our Shame: Another Long-Service Faculty Member Fired' (*UTFA Bulletin*, 1991).

15 According to the *CAUT Bulletin*, unionization (with Thomas Hood leading the organizing campaign) at Bishop's university in Lennoxville, Quebec, was initiated by a group of part-time faculty who had long been frustrated with low wages, job insecurity, and lack of resources.

16 Full-time equivalent (FTE) in workload is a 'standard' measure arrived at by dividing the total number of hours that part-timers teach in an institution by the number of hours in full-timers' average workload. It may also be used as an indicator of how many full-time appointments would be needed to replace part-timers' total teaching hours.

17 Bill Farr's responsibilities involved advising me on the design and implementation of surveys, contacting university central administrators and enlisting their cooperation to participate in collecting data, and ensuring the distribution of surveys. After administering the surveys, he left the project. As the principal investigator, I take responsibility for surveys, responses, and their analysis. For purposes of clarity and consistency, the term 'I' appears instead of 'we' throughout this book; but due credit goes to Bill Farr, my associate at the survey stage.

18 A few universities, for instance, York, began (in the year 2000) to accommodate the demands of the part-timer union that their long-service part-timers receive longer-term contracts – called special renewable contracts (SRCs) – of five to ten years at salary rates regulated by the York University Faculty Union (YUFA). This position, however, is neither that of contract nor that of full-time regular faculty. Another way of accommodating part-timers' demands emerged at York in the late 1980s. A few long-term part-timers who had doctorates and had been teaching for a decade or two at York University won the right to apply for competitions for a few tenure-stream full-time positions advertised within the university. Based on competitive merit, with all the accompanying credentials and references, approximately three such 'conversions' took place during each year of the term of the collective agreement. At the end of every contract, the university attempted to

take this clause back, which was cause for a long strike that lasted seventy-six days in 2000–1. Finally, the university administration agreed to continue 'conversions.' A part-timer comments: 'The big "gain" from the strike was that we resisted their attempts to scale back these programs, and got two more tenure-stream [conversions].' Currently, the part-timer union reports that under the new contract, the university administration has agreed to allow two tenure-stream 'conversions,' four limited-term full-timers (LTFTs), and five SRCs in 2000–1, and four tenure-stream conversions, and six SRCs in 2001–2. Very few universities if any, have such a formalized process, through bargaining, that recognizes part-timers' long service.

19 Arnita Jones (1990) notes that David Riesman compared the 'lost generation of scholars' (those who left their search for jobs in academe due to the severe faculty job shortages of the 1970s and 1980s) with the victims of the Chinese Cultural Revolution.

Chapter One: Permanent 'Temps' and Surplus Value

1 Although my part-time faculty survey itself was quite lengthy (eleven printed pages), numerous respondents added rich comments, sometimes of several typed pages.

2 Although William G. Bowen and Julie Ann Sosa refer to the U.S. situation, the comment is also appropriate for Canada because of the strong financial and political support for higher education during that period. Newson and Buchbinder sum up the 1950s and 1960s as a period of expansion in institution-building, public support, student accessibility, and faculty control over their professional status (1988: 14).

3 However, see Premier William Davis's warning to the universities that greater accountability would be required in their use of public funds.

4 Neatby quotes Frank Underhill (Whalley, 1964).

5 Paul Axelrod (1982: 185) analyses a survey by Clark and Zsigmond (1981: 7).

6 Arnita Jones (1990) refers to Riesman's interview with *Esquire* magazine.

7 In 1988 in Ontario, eight universities encompassed the highest numbers of part-timers and highest proportions of part-timers; four of these institutions had both the highest numbers and highest proportions of part-timers.

8 Rajagopal and Farr collected data for 1987–8 on use of part-timers, salaries, and terms and conditions of employment in Ontario universities. The Council of Ontario Universities (COU) initiated the study. The resultant report by Rajagopal and Farr (1990) was endorsed and included in the COU report (1991).

9 Although the statistical and scientific validity of the ranking of universities by Maclean's has been open to debate (Page, 1996), the budget data and faculty information are derived from public records or from the universities themselves.

10 Although universities believed that seasoned professors must teach entrant students to enrich their first-year experience, fewer professors seem to teach these classes, which are usually larger than those at upper-levels.

11 When the New Democratic party (NDP) was in power in Ontario (1990–5), the government established a 'Social Contract,' which, among other things, suspended income increments at most Ontario universities between 1993–6. Further, the government implemented wage freezes and 'days without pay' (Rae days, named after the premier) across the entire public sector. Melcher convincingly argues that when Social Contract policies ended and collective bargaining resumed, university administrators captured the largest chunk of these savings and diverted them to non-academic and other expenditures instead of restoring faculty numbers and academic payrolls (Melchers, 1998).

12 Twelve unionized (CUPE) universities (August 1999) were Athabasca, British Columbia, Carleton, Guelph, McMaster, Manitoba, Ottawa, Ryerson, Saskatchewan, Trent, Victoria, and York.

13 UBC and Athabasca University are among the few universities that did not report numbers of part-timers in response to our institutional survey.

14 See the appendix for a definition of 'part-time faculty' used in my surveys.

15 We cannot compare my survey numbers with those of Statistics Canada because of differences in methodologies and in definitions of 'part-timers.' Statistics Canada's definition of part-timers (Teresa Omiecinski@statcan.ca, e-mail note to the author, 2 May 2001) includes short-term, full-time appointments and regular faculty teaching overload.

16 Statistics Canada reports that Quebec's part-timers' figures are not available but that the numbers have increased, while full-timers have shrunk by 8.7 per cent between 1993–9.

17 For instance, some universities have reduced the numbers of non-prerequisite courses offered and increased the class lengths from one-hour tutorial to two-hour tutorial by changing first year credit-course requirements. Further, student numbers in these classes have doubled. This allowed the universities to assign more students per instructor and to manage workloads without increasing the number of instructors.

18 This research report is based on in-depth survey responses from a stratified random sample of 517 professors in Ontario colleges. As a result of provincial funding cuts from 1992 to 1998, colleges had 21 per cent less funding,

and the axe was wielded at a time when their enrolments were increasing over 9 per cent, in 1991–2 and 1995–6 (*York Gazette*, 2000).

19 *The Work Roles of Academics in Australian Universities*, which elaborates on job satisfaction, can be found at www.detya.gov.au/highered/eippubs.htm#00-5.

20 Fosh and Husbands (1993) attribute the information on British universities' passivity to Keep and Sisson (1992).

21 The 1990 data on part-timers from our Institutional Survey exemplify this effect. Generally speaking, where university spending per student is low as a result of underfunding, the use of part-timers is high in order to reduce student-faculty ratios.

Chapter Two: Hidden Academics

1 I requested information on all faculty members for 1989–90 – their status, discipline, pay, and so on – from all universities in Canada I received data from sixty institutions (see the appendix), of which ten reported their total part-time faculty without giving either a disciplinary or a gender break-down. The National Institutional Survey asked for the actual numbers from all universities, not from a representative sample of universities presented in table 2.2.

2 This was not an institutional survey, but a direct survey of part-timers from a representative sample of universities.

3 Throughout this book I refer to all part-timers who *teach* in francophone universities as francophone part-timers and those part-timers in anglophone universities as anglophones. These terms are *not* restricted to those whose mother tongue is French or English.

4 Pucel et al. (1992) studied different groups of instructors in Minnesota's training colleges, enquiring about their job needs that attracted them to vocational education. They found differences in the reasons why groups stayed or left the colleges. The experienced teachers who stayed in teaching highly rated the extrinsic aspects of teaching, such as salary, fringe benefits, work environment, working with students, and job security. On the other hand, beginning instructors highly rated the intrinsic aspects, such as sharing knowledge, career advancement, and association with co-workers.

5 Lundy and Warme's (1985) survey of Canadian part-timers concludes that part-timers' official status as part time, not full time instructors, does not affect students' learning or their rating of their instructors' efficiency. In most cases, the students may not even be aware of their teachers' status.

6 Jos Lennards's survey (carried out in 1986) is the first and only comprehen-

sive all-Canada survey of full-timers. The results of the study were
reported in 1988.

7 Trent University Study, 1985–6; figures reported by Bill Farr, then vice-
   president of finance and administration, York University.

8 As reported by Bill Farr, then vice-president of finance and administration,
   York University.

9 Sandy Bottiani reports that when women part-timers who are mothers consider relocation for jobs, they take into account their family obligations and
   the low pay they can expect as part-timers. However, 'the prejudice against
   women with children is deep-seated in the profession. From graduate
   school onward, women are not taken seriously as professional teachers and
   scholars' (1994: Abstract).

10 COU refers to holders of short-term appointments in Ontario universities
    as 'Gypsy Scholars' (1976: 16). Shelly Park (1996: 46) credits use of the term
    to E.L. Boyer (1986). As the term may be considered politically incorrect, I
    use an alternative, 'Freeway Fliers,' in this book.

11 All data in this section on the full-timers are taken from Lennards (1988).

12 Biles and Tuckman, (1986) elaborate on the part-timers' contract and the
    resources that are needed for integrating them into academe. Lampignano
    (1990) argues that incentives to part-timers and input from them are two
    major ingredients for professional development. Hall and Atnip argue that
    'administrators must consider the individual needs and situations of part-
    time faculty in order to structure a satisfying environment (1992: 27).'
    Gappa and Leslie (1993), through an interview of part-timers on various
    North American campuses, find out that this faculty group is keen on pro-
    fessional development. Lankard (1993) emphasizes that, since part-timers
    are hired for their professional competence, they could benefit from train-
    ing in teaching. Professional development programs focusing on teaching
    could enhance their pedagogy. McGuire (1993) points out that part-timers
    receive the same ratings and achieve the same student outcomes as the full-
    timers.

13 According to Stanley and Lumpkins, 'much of the difficulty with develop-
    ing professional development programs for part-time faculty is the result of
    institutional passiveness' (1992: 65).

14 The authors present 'majority and minority faculty perceptions,' from
    which we could draw an analogy to describe the part-timers' status. As
    they do in the labour market, segmented contexts exist in academe for
    minority faculty members – participation in minority affairs (as distinct
    from non-minority affairs, which are central to the university). These seg-
    mented contexts separate and isolate minority faculty from mainstream

activities – a critical exclusion, since mainstream activities shape the ideological character of the institution. The minority faculty are included in and visible for affirmative action counts, but otherwise are invisible.

15 Mary Cayton writes about why part-timers feel like outsiders and have marginalized status: 'It took me nine years to publish the dissertation because somewhere along the way, I became convinced ... that I was incapable of speaking and being heard by those who counted ... [We] as marginalized outsiders, are silenced, and silence ourselves in the face of the cultural expectation that the speech of others is powerful and privileged. From years of living with the professional understanding that I was not an equal participant in the life of the profession, my university, or my department, I internalized the notion that I did not yet know enough to be able to speak with any authority about any subject' (1991: 649).

16 Newson elaborates on the decline of faculty influence in dealing with the effects of the corporate agenda.

17 From the mid-1990s on, however, in Canadian provinces where right-wing governments have unleashed 'common sense revolutions,' unions and their rights are often called into question, and, wherever possible, corporations and governments try to thwart union formation and truncate workers' rights.

Chapter Three: Invisible Women

1 Women's share of the professoriate in Canada shows a trend of growth in the 1990s, for example, from 21 per cent in 1994 (Statistics Canada, 1994a: 182) to 26.2 per cent in 1998–9 (*CAUT Bulletin* Insert, April 2000).

2 No gender breakdown was available from the following universities/campuses: Alberta, Carleton, Chicoutimi, Concordia, École Polytechnique, École des Haute Études, Hull, Laval, McGill, Nova Scotia, OISE, Rimouski, Temiskaming, Trent, Trois Rivières. Brock University did not respond to my institutional survey.

3 The arguments of Veltmeyer and Sacouman support my position that the 'involuntary' nature of part-time work has often been exaggerated. Since the mid-1970s 'involuntary part-time work' has increased in the structure of employment. The highest rate of increase in 'involuntary part-time workers' is among men age 25–44, fewer of whom would wish to work part time.

4 The 'glass box' is a metaphor for the rise of segregated employment sectors for women. Dawn Walton (1999) reports on *Shattering the Glass Box? Women*

Entrepreneurs and the Knowledge-Based Economy, Report of Industry Canada, 1999. It is pointed out in the report that the entrepreneurial women might rightly feel that they could crash the 'glass ceiling' by starting their own businesses. Research has shown, however, that these women are 'clustered in sectors' where the financial returns are quite low compared with those of male entrepreneurs, which are more remunerative sectors. Women entrepreneurs also invariably confront situations where they are unable to acquire the required skills and know-how for business expansion and advancement. Therefore, they may find themselves trapped in a 'glass box' as difficult to penetrate as the 'glass ceiling' documented in the literature (Morrison, White, and Van Velsor, 1987a; Morrison and Van Glinow, 1990; Cannings, 1991; Burke and McKeen, 1992; Melamed, 1995).

5 Tolbert and Oberfield ask: 'what are the forces that produce the unequal distribution of women among college and university faculties?' They show that in universities there is organizational-level segregation of women. Women are also segregated across departments and other divisions within higher educational institutions along organizational lines. 'Organizations play a major role in the creation and preservation of patterns of social inequality in contemporary society.' The decisive factors are 'resources' and 'student body gender ratios.' First, women faculty members are fewer in institutions that have a relatively higher level of critical resources. Second, universities and colleges with higher enrolments of female students are more likely to have more female faculty members. However, curricular emphases or other structural characteristics, such as types of programs, may help to explain the clustering of female faculty (1991: 313, 310–11).

6 Bagilhole discusses the patterns of discrimination and their impact on women faculty: 'Discrimination was described as subtle ... Whether it was intentional or deliberate ... it was present, and had an effect. There seems to be an undervaluing and stereotyping of women as part of the male organization. Subtle behaviour is both prevalent, and more problematic than overtly discriminatory behaviour. Often inadvertent, sometimes well-intentioned, it often seems so normal as to be virtually invisible, yet creates an environment that wastes women's resources, takes time and energy to ignore or deal with, undermines self-esteem, and damages professional morale' (1993: 270).

7 Kulis and Miller-Loessi examine the extent to which academic ranks in sociology are gendered. They also explore the level of concentration of men and women in different academic ranks. 'High institutional prestige, research orientation, large size, public auspices, non-urban setting, and

faculty growth are major predictors of higher representation of women' (1992a: 157). Also see Kulis and Miller-Loessi (1992b).

8 Mabel Hayes (1990) refers to Lindsay's (1988) study, which indicates that research undertaken by members of minorities or women is sometimes questioned as to its rigour and validity. Also, their research publications in journals may be demeaned as low, questionable, and spurious scholarship that could appear only in secondary or peripheral venues (Hayes, 1990: 14).

9 Finkel and Olswang note that the system of tenure is too antiquated to accommodate the current problems that women face, such as finding time for children. The tenure system is 'an exclusionary model designed for males. Men were professors, and their wives were at home caring for their children' (1996: 136).

10 Explaining what 'chilly climate' means, Sandra Pyke quotes Adrienne Rich (1970): 'What we have at present is a man-centred university, a breeding ground not of humanism, but of masculine privilege. As women have gradually and reluctantly been admitted into the mainstream of higher education, they have been made participants in a system that prepares men to take up roles of power in a man-centred society, that asks questions and teaches 'facts' generated by a male intellectual tradition, and that both subtly and openly confirms men as the leaders and shapers of human destiny both within and outside academia.' Pyke continues: 'In somewhat the same vein, Hall and Sandler (1982, 1984; Sandler and Hall, 1986) contend that universities can be inhospitable, unwelcoming, even hostile to women. Systemic discriminatory practices and micro-inequities that may chill the climate include expressions of sexist humour and stereotypical views of women; the use of sexist language; neglect of women in the curriculum; more attention given to male students, from more frequent calls on them in class to invitations to them to participate in papers or articles; use of an argumentative, competitive, abstract, and impersonal approach to learning combined with a discounting of experiential knowledge; the paucity of women faculty as role models and mentors; gender-based differential attributions; and the not-infrequent spectre of sexual harassment' (1997: 156).

11 'At universities across Canada these days, there is occurring what the media usually describe as "a gender war." They portray women faculty members threatening what were once male bastions within the various faculties, while a few male faculty members of dinosaurian inclinations resist this "inevitable" transformation. That a controversy is raging is undeniable, but it is not a "gender war" – a war between men and women. It is a war between two factions. One sees the university as it has traditionally seen

itself, as a kind of marketplace of ideologies where all views can be expressed and examined, and can compete freely to win adherents. The other faction sees the university as an "agency for social change," in which any philosophy that appears to resist or challenge such change must be eradicated' (*Western Report*, 1994).

12 Professor John Fekete, cultural studies and English, at Trent University is quoted. Fekete is the author of *Moral Panic: Biopolitics Rising* (1994), in which he documents gender harassment cases in universities. He argues: 'The complaints are starting to focus on the theoretical treatment of feminism, rather than the treatment of real women, so the crimes have become ideological.'

13 Under the heading 'Joining the Old Boy's Club,' Linda E. Taylor discusses how difficult it is for women to attain positions of 'real' power. It is not easy to break through the glass ceiling. 'Judy Rebick, former president of the National Action Committee on the Status of Women, complains that companies are run like old boys' networks, where top jobs go to those who fit the mould of the people already in power. Women are rarely fast-tracked into senior jobs or encouraged to take on leadership roles, as is often done with men ... While there has been progress, family leave and pay equity policies still are seen as innovative. Even Canadian unions and their U.S. counterparts have a long way to go in promoting women to executive positions. That's the opinion of the International Labour Organization (ILO). The ILO is concerned with internal union practices that are intimidating or offensive to potential women leaders. In a 1993 report, it said that, if women are ever going to achieve equality, they have to be essential partners in trade unions' (Taylor, 1995: 50).

14 Pay inequity and insecurity in their jobs were not reported as often as the heavy workload and its demanding nature, which precluded reasonable amounts of time for family, friends, relaxation, and recreation (Tsai and Schwindt, 1996: 104).

15 John Goyder helps to explain the role of professorial rank in Canadian universities. He argues that in the late 1960s a debate developed over university hiring on the basis of ascriptive characteristics after concern arose over filling too many academic positions with foreigners. This debate continued when gender became central to questioning male-female pay differentials. In the United States pay is the more commonly used yardstick between sexes because of the variation in institutional prestige between universities. Top-ranking universities in the United States can pay the highest salaries. In Canada, it is more appropriate to link sex ascription than institutional

prestige to rank based professorial prestige. As a result, rank may reveal sex inequalities if we look at the percentage of women and men at different ranks of the professoriate (1992: 334).

16 Clark and Corcoran explain the term 'Matthew effect' as an 'allusion to Christ's description of accumulating faith: "For whosoever hath, to him shall be given, and he shall have more abundance; but whosoever hath not, from him shall be taken away even that he hath" (King James version, Matt. 25: 29).' Many writers – Merton, Zuckerman, Cole, Lorber, and others – identify social status advantages and disadvantages using this allusion: the rich get richer, and the poor get poorer. Vis-à-vis women in academe, we are referring to the 'accumulated' disadvantages. If women do not work guided by the best professors, work in the best departments, and receive the top scholarships, they begin with an initial disadvantage that grows with time. With regard to their hiring, tenure, or promotion, they might be more disadvantaged than men who have been in more established circles of academic power as protégés of renowned, mostly male, professoriate. These processes that disadvantage women are not easy to quantify or keep track of, but they are real (1993: 401).

17 Clark and Corcoran refer to the 'Salieri phenomenon,' Lorber's adaptation of the 'Matthew effect'; Lorber (1983) alludes to Salieri in Peter Schaffer's play *Amadeus*. Antonio Salieri, as the 'gatekeeper' of royal patronage in music in Emperor Joseph's court, prevents Mozart from achieving due recognition for his extraordinary accomplishments in music during the latter's lifetime. 'Functionally irrelevant characteristics,' for instance, Mozart's 'lack of social graces' disturbed Salieri so much that, although he recommends him to be appointed to the court, he ensures that the salary is low. He pretends to be a benefactor to Mozart, but Mozart, although unhappy with his poor salary at the royal court (owing to Salieri's intervention), does not know that his career is blocked rather than advanced. Lorber uses this term to identify academic women's behaviour and performance deemed as not up to par because of their assigned social status – the gatekeepers and inner circle of powerful male professoriate dominant in academe judge it as such. The women may still be formally in place and not totally 'blocked out,' but their advancement and progress would be restricted in a pre-eminently male profession and in societies under the predominance of men (Clark and Corcoran 1993: 401–2).

18 Some argue that women's presence and participation in academe will increase incrementally. Smith questions the validity of this argument.

Chapter Four: Contemporaries and Classics: Segmented Interests

1 *Work situations*: part-timer employment status: non-academic full-time,
   retired, or part-time only, used in U.S. surveys (Tuckman, 1978: 305–15;
   Leslie, Kellams, and Gunne, 1982: 36–41; Kuchera and Miller, 1988; Gappa
   and Leslie, 1993: 45–9). *Employment expectations*: hope to get academic full-
   time employment, pre-retirees expecting to teach after retirement, and students pursuing degrees who are planning to teach (Biles and Tuckman,
   1986: 11; Gappa and Leslie, 1993: 47–9). *Reasons and motivations*: love of
   teaching, career interests, economic need, caregivers' responsibilities
   (Leslie, Kellams, and Gunne, 1982: 36–41; Wallace, 1984: 30–7; Abel, 1984:
   80–111). *Preferences and constraints*: voluntary or involuntary part-timing,
   prefer academic part-time / want full-time, willing or unwilling part-
   timing, academic disciplines, ethnicity or gender (Yang and Zak, 1981: 48;
   Scott, 1983: 188–93; Abel, 1984: 90–9; Tuckman and Pickerill, 1988: 99;
   Lundy and Warme, 1990: 216–17; Rajagopal and Farr, 1990 and 1992; Gappa
   and Leslie, 1993: 57)

2 Of U.S. studies, Tuckman's (1978) classification is the most elaborate. He
   identifies several groups: Hopeful full-timers (who want, but could not
   find, a full-time academic position), Part-mooners (who hold two or more
   part-time jobs), Homeworkers (caregivers), Full-mooners (who hold a full-
   time job elsewhere), and part-unknowners (whose motives for becoming
   part-timers are not classified). Although 'Hopeful full-timers' will be a suitable label for those whom our hypothesis seeks to identify as academically
   career-oriented part-timers, to examine part-timers' motivations we must
   include all of those in Tuckman's categories who are not holding a full-time
   non-academic job.

3 Yang and Zak (1981) identify differences in job satisfaction between those
   who 'choose' to teach part-time in academe, and those 'unwillingly confined.' They find that the latter are likely to be less satisfied than the former.
   Consistent with these findings, Lundy and Warme (1988) confirm that part-
   timers' dissatisfaction is related more to their status than to their teaching
   function. In this study they differentiate between voluntary and involuntary part-timers in terms of their satisfaction with their 'teaching' role as
   distinct from their part-time 'job-status.'

4 I report only those differences between Classics and Contemporaries that
   are statistically significant.

5 A logistic regression is considered appropriate when the dependent variable has two levels, as it does in Classic and Contemporary (see p. 282).

Operational definition of variables used in logistic regression (parameter coding)

Variable	Description				
Models	Dependent variable	0 = classic model 1 = contemporaries			
			Coding		
	Value	Freq	(1)	(2)	(3)
Age					
Under 30	1	137	1	0	0
Under 40	2	709	0	1	0
Under 50	3	763	0	0	1
50 and over	4	496	−1	−1	−1
Education (Q59)			(1)	(2)	
Less than Master's degree	1	459	1	0	
Master's less than Doctorate	2	1086	0	1	
Doctorate	3	560	−1	−1	
Birthplace (Q51)					
West	1	1889	1		
Other	2	216	−1		
Number of children (Q55)					
No child	1	919	1		
One or more	2	1186	−1		
Gender (Q50)					
Male	1	1148	1		
Female	2	957	−1		

6 Further, job responsibility profiles of most Classics suggest that universities hire Classics from administrative or technical areas, rather than from the community service or clinical fields, perhaps because of curricular needs in universities.

7 Forty-two per cent of all part-timers want academic full-time positions. The comparable U.S. figure is 16 per cent.

Chapter Five: Conflicts That Divide: Full-Timers versus Part-Timers

1 Newson notes that in Canada, the university's affluent and expansion years during the 1950s and 1960s, created structures and situations that extended the faculty's collective influence in decision-making processes. Faculty members had to face the reversal of this trend when financial cutbacks in the 1970s constrained their powers and autonomy. This change forced the

seeds of the 'corporate agenda' on academe where they began to take root (1990: 4).

2 Tien and Blackburn point out that although rank and productivity are linked, higher rank alone does not increase productivity: 'Institutions promote productive faculty. Consequently, higher rank members are academic "winners" ... full-professors publish significantly more research than do assistant professors and associate professors. However, no difference in publication exists between assistant professors and associate professors ... Institutional policies as well as market conditions can influence the promotion interval' (1996: 7, 9, 19). Shelly Park notes that emphasis on research leads to the use of low-paid women to teach classes, so that others, mostly male professors, can continue their research – a form of 'economic exploitation.' Further, a decrease in external funding, combined with greater emphasis on research 'productivity,' has made tenure and promotion more difficult to obtain, particularly for women.

3 Sandra Acker explains that faculty women's responsibilities of mentoring, nurturing, and providing role models have become quite onerous because two-thirds of the students, but only one-third of the faculty are women. She studied 200 academics in four professional fields for her piece in the *Forum*. The interviews took place during 1995–8 in five Canadian universities in four provinces. Each lasted more than an hour. Acker points out that workload and work expectations from women were central to the burden that women academics face. She quotes many passages from her interviews: Moira says: 'I write ... at 10.00 at night till three in the morning ... Sometimes I have breakfast meetings with students at 8 in the morning. I don't have another life; my life when I get home is my children.' Penny explains her situation: 'I have to wait till the kids are in bed before I do my admin[istrative] stuff. I am the only driver in the family ... I have to do the running around, pay bills, and get groceries. Sometimes you can see me at A & P if it's open till midnight getting groceries.' Lucille referred to herself as 'a departmental resource, like the fire extinguisher.' Acker notes that women academics report that they are expected to work harder than their male colleagues, and have disproportionately heavier responsibilities for service work in their departments (1999: 7, 6–7). This article has many excellent references to Acker's other works.

4 Abel argues effectively: 'The pursuit of sex discrimination grievances by faculty women ... involves a conflict between two competing images of society: the individualism that underlies both the legal and educational systems, and the collectivism inherent in any political protest ... If their protest is waged collectively ... [it] is inconsistent with the educational selection

system, according to which rewards are distributed solely on the basis of individual talent and effort. Women who have derived real benefits from the system are often reluctant to question its basic tenets' (1981: 505). Abel adds that the grievance process itself undermines women's collective aims. Although women know that collective protest against systemic discrimination is far more powerful at breaking down barriers, they are required to file their complaints in individualistic terms, highlighting their own personal and professional qualities.

5 In analysing the survey data on the two groups of LTFTs, I found statistically significant differences between the two in most issues that are sensitive to contract faculty experiences in the university.

6 Questions are listed in table 5.1 and detailed here: B1 = Q17a; B2 = Q17b; B3 = Q17c; B4 = Q 17d; B5 = Q 18a; B6 = Q 18b.

7 *Webster's Dictionary* (Springfield, Mass.: Merriam-Webster, 1977: 168).

8 The survey question provided a scale: 'all part-timers,' 'most,' 'about half,' 'some,' 'few,' 'none,' or 'not sure' of part-timers

9 Iadevaia collected data for the past five years from Pima College Computer Center student information files. He selected those students who got a grade C or better and divided them into those taking courses taught by full-timers and those taught by part-timers. He analysed the data using frequency distributions for each variable combination (teaching effectiveness measures, gender, age, course level, and job status of course teachers) and performed a chi-square analysis for each variable. He then regrouped the data by reading level, gender, and age. A comparison followed between courses taught by part-timers and those taught by full-timers and also between successful and unsuccessful students in each type of course. These courses were randomly selected using a random number generator. The comparison did not yield any significant difference ($p = 0.05$) between the two faculty groups.

Chapter Six: Interests That Diverge: Administrators versus Part-Timers

1 Ideological perspectives are delineated in Wallace (1984); Abel (1979, 1984), and Scott (1983); the 'institutional' perspectives are given in Biles and Tuckman (1986); and Gappa and Leslie (1993).

2 For Kanter, 'power is accumultated in two ways: one is through the organization of jobs, and the other is through political alliances.' Power is defined as 'value neutral,' not as domination, tyranny, or control. My purpose in using Kanter's discussion of 'power' is to locate it and describe its characteristics in an organization – university administrations. However, I

extend the meaning of 'power' to identify control or dominance within a hierarchy.

3 The discussion here follows Kanter's explanation of how power is structured in organizations, and it identifies several organizational criteria for allowing workers to gain power.

4 As Linda Blum and Vicki Smith have combined two divergent ideological perspectives, I also find it useful to incorporate Kanter's 'organizational perspective,' and 'the occupational segmentation and labour-market structure analysis.' Blum and Smith write that Kanter's 'framework simply assumes the capitalist relations of the firm's environment rather than examining the connection between capitalism and corporate structures ... Kanter talks about "empowering" individuals, but she fails to acknowledge that most American organizations are structured on a division of labour, authority, and expertise that excludes most employees from genuine control in the workplace ... The notion of empowerment individualizes the responsibility for change, directing attention from the larger questions of ownership and control, as well as from the examination of institutionalized work arrangements and personnel practices' (1988: 543–4). Instead of a notional 'empowerment,' collective awareness and threats of collective action are the genuine alternatives for women and the workers whom they manage in their search for real control over their workplace.

5 Many who study matters such as 'labour force,' 'management,' and 'organizational or functional stratification within administration' in relation to gender segregation find women clustered in lower levels, with less occupational mobility and lower salaries than men. According to William Bielby and James Baron, within the wide range of jobs in the management hierarchy, there is clearly an intra-occupational stratificaiton based on gender, which camouflages sex-segregation under the notion of occupational integration, for example, recruiting women into 'management' positions. They report that, as soon as women enter a set of positions once dominated by males, these jobs are deemed inappropriate for men. Examining intra-occupational segregation patterns, with men in higher-skilled and better paid jobs and women in clericalized or deskilled ones, Barbara Reskin and Patricia Roos found that when women gained access to male-dominated jobs, the work became lower skilled and lower paid.

6 These administrators are not academics who are elected or selected from within the Faculty; they are hired as part of the non-academic bureaucracy.

7 Dickman et al. conclude: ' The budget reduction choices were more similar than dissimilar on most dimensions ... Moreover, the finding of some reasonable dimensionality and rational differences on some dimensions (but

not others) confirms the authors' suspicion that the human interests in downsizing are multidimensional and complex' (1996: 466). Constituencies opted for different strategies to achieve 'effectiveness, efficiency, and satisfaction' in budget reductions. These options added to the repertoire of useful dimensions for solving the problem. The multidimensionality helped people to comprehend the differences as well as the similarities in strategies.

8 Newson and Buchbinder summarize: 'Universities were made vulnerable to the ... new corporate agenda in the years of contraction following expansion of funding and universities. To accommodate budgetary shortfalls, academic work was reorganized in ways that now facilitate implementation of the service university model. Changes in administrative structures and the shift of control to full-time managers to deal with the fiscal crisis are being consolidated in order to develop relations with corporate clients and to exercise strong leadership in the new "Indusversity" marketplace.' Corporatization of the university has created a 'managerial change': 'The corporate-university agenda intensifies the managerial expansion within universities.' Expanding on how this occurred, the authors add: 'The focus on efficiency and spending accountability contributed to the idea that better management would provide a solution to the university's financial woes ... Administration acquired a new place within university governing structures – a place "of their own" ... "Management" has assumed a presence within the decision-making structures, so that even academics with full-time or partial administrative tasks are directed by management, rather than by academic bodies such as senates, faculty councils, and college committees ... To the average faculty member, deans are increasingly perceived as managers and less as academic leaders. They are seen as representing not the will of the collegium but the decisions of management' (1988: 93, 84, 16–17).

9 Bilik and Blum briefly trace the history of U.S. higher education management: 'Intrusive management is not new to higher education. The AAUP was created in 1915 in large part to shield the professoriate from the arbitrary exercise of managerial authority ... Two decades of explosive growth of higher education after 1955 brought new threats to collegial governance. The unprecedented increase in the size and number of state colleges and universities ushered in a new stratum of administrators oriented less to the traditions of the academy as articulated by the AAUP and more to the culture of public bureaucracy with its hierarchical structure and tendency to proliferation.' The authors note why academic administrators also embrace this managerial approach: 'The attraction of academic administrators to

management styles that exalt their own role is comprehensible, yet – in relation to the traditions and values of higher education – it is highly ironic ... The professoriate has long recognized that shared authority and joint responsibility are essential to the nurture of creative thought and expression in the academy. Corporate leadership has only in recent years begun to appreciate that these same principles apply equally to successful management of business organizations. As long as academic leaders resist implementation of these principles in their own institutions, they threaten to drag higher education into the corporate past' (1989: 12–13).

10 Schwartz attributes this term to Rhatigan (1978).

11 Canadian universities selected for this study fall into groups based on region, size, range, unionization of faculty, research/teaching orientation, and lower or higher ratio of part-timers. See the appendix.

12 Bruce Gunn defines those 'who have strong character which motivates them to build self-respect by making significant contributions to their university as "service-oriented" administrators ... "Self-oriented" administrators usually employ authoritative leadership styles with a shift from productivity to the maintenance of the status quo in the dominance order of the organization ... These patterns create pressure to squeeze work out of faculty and put academicians into a position of compromising long term productivity for short term gains in salary and rank ... They use "mushroom" management to mask administrative malpractice' (1991: abstract, 5).

13 All figures in this paragraph are expressed as a percentage of administrators in their regions, respectively.

Chapter Seven: 'Sweated Labour'

1 'Sweated labour' is derived from the term 'sweating system' prevalent in the early industrialization during the nineteenth and early twentieth centuries, which historically connotes exploitation. In the modern era, the marginalized labour force is pressed into this kind of work the characteristics of which are piecemeal work, long hours (fifteen to eighteen hour days), very low wages, and working conditions harmful to workers' health. Typically, women, children, and the elderly constitute such a workforce. Another manifestation of 'sweated labour' thrives under the subcontracting of work to an intermediary who hires workers and presses them into production in an unregulated workplace.

2 Cary Nelson is Jubilee Professor of Liberal Arts and Sciences at the University of Illinois at Urbana-Champaign.

3 'The Work of University Professor' by Smith and Hixson (1997) is an

important contribution on theoretical and empirical aspects of the segmented labour market within academe.

4 The discussion in this paragraph follows Filson's (1988) analysis of stratification and also derives from his citations.

5 Filson notes that professionals are 'credentialized' workers vis-à-vis wage workers or proletarians, who are unable to gain the advantages of owning or controlling credential assets and means of production.

6 The discussion here follows and summarizes Bill Martin's (1994) conceptual analysis. For a rich literature and elaboration on these issues, refer to Martin's paper.

7 I have classified the more specific area- or issue-oriented studies as well as the experiential or anecdotal studies, as micro-level, for instance, Chell (1982); Kantrowitz (1981); Yang and Zak (1981); and Lundy and Warme (1985). I refer to national-level studies and to research on the fiscal, work, or other broad-based themes in higher education as macro level – for instance, Tuckman, Vogler, and Caldwell (1978); Leslie, Kellams, and Gunne (1982); Scott (1983); Abel (1979); Abel (1984); Bowen and Schuster (1986); and Wallace (1984).

8 Authors of many works on the faculty and on the academic profession fully discuss these differentials, for example, Finkelstein (1984) and Simeone (1987).

9 Whichard et al. use the concept 'hidden agenda' to explain 'the unstated purpose behind pedagogy' (1992: 63). Although in their teaching of writing classes, part-timers were conscious that they must encourage their English composition students not to consider writing to fit an ideal pattern, as subordinates within the academic hierarchy they invariably found themselves using a pedagogy that met the expectations of their superiors and that served to protect their own jobs.

10 York University Faculty Association, Grievance Files, Office of the Vice-President (Finance and Administration), York University.

11 Massy is professor of education, and director of Stanford Institute for Higher Education Research (SIHER), Stanford, California. Wilger is assistant director of SIHER.

Epilogue: IvoryTower, Inc.?

1 On average, university graduates constitute 13 per cent of the population age 25 to 64 in OECD countries (Galt, 2000).

2 'Statistics compiled by CAUT reveal that since 1992, federal cash transfers, when adjusted for inflation, have declined from $2.9 billion to $1.6 billion – a walloping 44 per cent. On a constant per capita basis, cash transfers fell

from $102 in 1992 to ... $54 in 1998. The biggest declines came in 1996 with the introduction of the Canada Health and Social Transfer (CHST), which slashed $7 billion from health, post-secondary education and social services ... [James L.] Turk noted that recent statistics show that as a share of all university operating funds, government funding fell from 74 per cent in 1980 to ... 58 per cent in 1997. Meanwhile, private funding doubled over the same period. "What's troubling about this reliance on private funding is the impact on the type of research conducted," added [Bill] Graham. "Basic research is a very hard sell in the boardrooms of Canada's biggest corporations"' (*CAUT Bulletin*, Sept. 1999: 1, 7).

3 TheHigherLearning.com (Press and Washburn): University of California at Berkeley recently signed a deal with America Online, the University of Colorado has teamed up with Real Education, and the (U.S.) Western Governors' Association has founded a 'virtual university' linking more than thirty schools in twenty-two states. Michael Milken, the convicted junk-bond trader, is investing heavily in an Internet education company known as UNext.com, which recently signed deals with Columbia University and the University of Chicago.

4 Ornstein and Stewart (1996) believe that faculty unions should get involved in establishing equity for women: 'As a minority, women may be neglected by unions and faculty associations reluctant to actively advocate on their behalf, but Bridges and Nelson see hope when they argue that "when agencies and unions get involved in claims for female and mixed jobs, the results are just as good as they are for male jobs" (1989: 651).'

Appendix: Survey and Methodology

1 Research intensity was measured in fiscal terms: the ratio of 1988–9 institutional total of research expenses to operating expenses (from CAUBO reports).

2 The intensity of part-timers is measured as a ratio between the two populations: the ratio of part-timers' total (reported by universities to my institutional survey) to all faculty numbers (for instance, part-timers *plus* full-timers) in *each* of the universities.

3 Penni Stewart and Janice Drakich (1995) elaborate on the factors related to organizational change and equity for women faculty in Ontario universities. In accounting for organizational differentiation, various characteristics – size, growth, region, language, research versus teaching orientation, range of programs, and unionization – have been found to influence the nature and functioning of Canadian universities.

4 Regionalism colours Canadian politics and society. Regional contexts and

their unique features also shape universities. David Nock explains the role of universities' regional contexts in acceptance of scholarship fit for publication in academic journals; regional factor affects how universities are viewed, for example, in the quality of doctorates produced (1992: 348). Curtis and Tepperman (1990) and Hiller (1986) have provided a clear focus on the various facets of regionalism in Canada.

5 Stewart and Drakich point out that university's size would affect adoption of equity policies in relation to women faculty. They found that larger institutions are less likely to change. Thus 'size' is significantly related to internal organizational policies (1995: 429).

6 On research versus teaching orientation, Henderson and Kane (1991) discuss the differences between the roles of research universities and teaching universities in U.S., and what they are 'expected' to do. These 'expected roles' create a situation where comprehensive universities with a wide range of programs become 'caught in the middle.' Their faculty are expected to do research as well as carry heavy teaching loads, mostly without graduate students to assist in their research. They therefore face problems different from those of large research-oriented universities or small teaching universities. In Canada, although such demarcations between universities are not so clear, if we apply the measure of research funding, we can identify universities that have been drawn heavily into research. It then becomes feasible to find the relationship between universities' 'research orientation' and their 'intensity of use of part-time faculty,' and we can compare 'research' and 'teaching' institutions in their use of part-timers. Also see Mireille Brochu (1997).

7 In a study on faculty members, the reasons for differentiating universities on the basis of their faculty unionization are clear. For more on the issue, see Annunziato and Johnson (1994), where Don Savage describes Canada's higher education system; see also Kevin Banks (1995), who explains the differences between the United States and Canada in collective bargaining. Frank Annunziato discusses how collective bargaining, as a model of conflict resolution, is a necessary component in the life of unionized universities. Collective bargaining agreements could be used as an instrument of resolving conflicts over a range of disputes, both academic and financial. In U.S. public colleges and universities, 'Yeshiva decision's indicia of managerial authority' (1995a: 56) to resolve disputes does not apply, and conflicts are regularly resolved through collective bargaining by administrators, faculty, and where relevant, also by students.

8 There are many sources that emphasize the need to make differences based on faculty members' disciplinary area in their work. Hargens and Kelly-

Wilson, (1994) argue that the 'disciplinary field' level variables are strong determinants of how a 'discipline' is perceived in scholarly quality. The analysis by Paechter and Head (1996) reveals how certain areas or disciplines of study become gendered. They argue that lower-status school subjects – for example, physical education or design and technology – become more 'masculine' in orientation. Certain subjects or areas of study are historically gendered because of the importance of the physical body in the process of learning in these areas. We also notice increasingly that women have marginal numbers and significance in science fields. Science versus arts creates contradictory status positions for pursuers of the two areas, if they are women. If more women enter a sub-field within an area of science, it might become devalued or turned marginal, for example, data-entry/programming within computer science.

9 See, especially, 'Caractéristiques et remuneration des professeurs de carrière des universités québécoises.'

References

AAUP (American Association of University Professors). (1992). 'Report on the Status of Non-tenure Track Faculty.' *Academe* 78 no. 6: 39–48.
– (1995). 'A Ray of Sunshine? Annual Report of the Economic Status of the Profession (ARESP) 1994–95.' *Academe* 81 no. 2: 1, 8–106.
– (1996). Not So Bad: Annual Report of the Economic Status of the Profession (ARESP) 1995–96. *Academe* 82 no. 2: 14–108.
– (1999) 'Ups and Downs: Annual Report of the Economic Status of the Profession (ARESP) 1998–99.' *Academe* 85 no. 2: 1, 12–97.
Abel, Emily M. (1979). 'The View from the Bottom: The Impact of Proposition 13 on Part-Time Faculty.' Paper presented at the Annual Conference of the Modern Languages Association, San Francisco, Calif., 1979. *ERIC*. CD-ROM. SilverPlatter.
– (1981). 'Collective Protest and the Meritocracy: Faculty Women and Sex Discrimination Lawsuits.' *Feminist Studies* 7: 505–38.
– (1984). *Terminal Degrees: The Job Crisis in Higher Education*. New York: Praeger.
Acker, Sandra. (1999). 'Equity with Strings Attached: Experiences and Concerns of Women Academics in Faculties of Education.' *Forum* Fall: 6–9.
Aguirre, Adalberto, Jr, Ruben Martinez, and Anthony Hernandez. (1993). ' Majority and Minority Faculty Perceptions in Academe.' *Research in Higher Education* 34: 371–85.
Ahmed, Maroussia. (1989). 'Status of Women Column – Part-Time Faculty: A Challenge for the Faculty Association.' *CAUT Bulletin* 36 no. 6: 10.
Ahmed, Maroussia, et al. (1989). 'Integration of Female Faculty at McMaster.' Status of Women Committee. McMaster University Faculty Association, Hamilton.
Akyeampong, Ernest B. (1986). '"Involuntary" Part-time Employment in Can-

ada, 1975–1985.' Reprint 11, originally published in *The Labour Force* (71-001). Ottawa: Canadian Government Publishing Centre.

– (1987). 'Persons on the Margins of the Labour Force.' Reprint 14, originally published in *The Labour Force* (71-001). Ottawa: Canadian Government Publishing Centre.

Albert, Louis S., and Rollin J. Watson. (1980). 'Mainstreaming Part-time Faculty: Issue or Imperative?' In Michael Parsons, ed., *Using Part-time Faculty Effectively. New Directions for Community Colleges 39*. San Francisco: Jossey-Bass.

Altbach, Philip G., and Lionel S. Lewis. (1995). 'Professorial Attitudes – an International Survey.' *Change* 27 no. 6: 51–7.

Altbach, Philip G., and K. Lomotey. (1991). *The Racial Crisis in American Higher Education*. Albany: State University of New York Press.

Althusser, L. (1971). *Lenin and Philosophy and Other Essays*. London: New Left.

Annunziato, Frank R. (1995a). 'From Conflict to Accord: Collective Bargaining at the Academy.' *New Directions for Higher Education* 92 Fall: 51–7.

– (1995b). 'Unionization among College Faculty – 1995.' *Newsletter: National Centre for the Study of Collective Bargaining in Higher Education and the Professions* 23 no. 1: 1–13. *ERIC*. CD-ROM. SilverPlatter.

Annunziato, Frank R., and Beth H. Johnson, eds. (1994). *Higher Education Collective Bargaining during a Period of Change*. Proceedings of the Annual Conference, City University of New York, April New York: NCSCBHEP. *ERIC*. CD-ROM. SilverPlatter.

Armstrong, Pat. (1996). 'The Feminization of the Labour Force: Harmonizing Down in a Global Economy.' In I. Bakker, ed., *Rethinking Restructuring: Gender and Change in Canada*. Toronto: University of Toronto Press.

Armstrong, Pat, and Hugh Armstrong. (1983). *A Working Majority: What Women Must Do for Pay*. Ottawa: Supply and Services Canada for the Canadian Advisory Council on the Status of Women.

– (1988). 'Taking Women into Account: Redefining and Intensifying Employment in Canada.' In Jane Jenson, Elisabeth Hagen, and Ceallaigh Reddy, eds, *Feminization of the Labour Force: Paradoxes and Promises*. New York: Oxford University.

AUCC (Association of Universities and Colleges of Canada). (1998). Data sent to the author.

– (1999). Publications and Communications Division. *Trends: The Canadian University in Profile*. Ottawa, 1999.

AUT (Association of University Teachers). UK. (1993). 'Part-Time Poor Deal.' *AUT Report*. London: AUT.

Axelrod, Paul. (1982). *Scholars and Dollars*. Toronto: University of Toronto Press.

- (1999) 'The Uncertain Future of the Liberal Education.' *CAUT Bulletin* 46 no. 8: 5.
Backhouse, C., R. Harris, G. Mitchell, and A. Wylie. (1989). *The Chilly Climate for Faculty Women at the University of Western Ontario: Postscript to the Backhouse Report*. London: University of Western Ontario.
Bagilhole, Barbara. (1993). 'How to Keep a Good Woman Down: An Investigation of the Role of Institutional Factors in the Process of Discrimination against Women Academics.' *British Journal of Sociology of Education* 14: 261–71.
Baldwin, Roger G. (1982). 'Fostering Faculty Vitality: Options for Institutions and Administrators.' *Administrator's Update* 4 no. 1: 1–5.
- (1988). *Faculty Vitality in 'Different Worlds': The View from Three Academic Areas*. Paper presented to the Nov. 1988 Annual Meeting of the ASHE. St Louis, Miss.: American Society for Higher Education. *ERIC*. CD-ROM. SilverPlatter.
Banks, Kevin. (1995). 'Weakening the Tenure System: The Misuse and Abuse of Sessional Appointments.' *CAUT Bulletin* 42 no. 5: 3.
Beatty, David M. (1982). 'Decision Making in Universities: The Impact of Collective Bargaining.' Unpublished paper presented to the Canadian Society for the Study of Higher Education, Ottawa.
Beck, Nuala. (1993). 'The New Economy: Education Is an Industry in Itself.' *Globe and Mail* 2 March.
Bell, D. (1973). *The Coming of Post-Industrial Society: A Venture in Social Forecasting*. New York: Basic Books.
Bellah, Robert N. (1997). 'Class Wars and Culture Wars in the University Today: Why We Can't Defend Ourselves.' *Academe* 83 no. 4: 22–6.
- (1999). 'Freedom, Coercion, Authority.' *Academe* 85 no. 1: 16–21.
Bellamy, Lesley A. (1994). 'Review of Alexander D. Gregor and Jasmin Gilles, eds, *Higher Education in Canada*.' *Canadian Journal of Higher Education* 24 no. 1: 110–12.
Bellas, Marcia L. (1993). 'Faculty Salaries: Still a Cost of Being Female?' *Social Science Quarterly* 74: 62–75.
- (1997). 'Disciplinary Differences in Faculty Salaries: Does Gender Bias Play a Role?' *Journal of Higher Education* 68: 299–321.
Benjamin, Ernst. (1998). 'On the Eccessive Reliance on Part-Time Faculty Appointments.' *Academe* 84 no. 1: 26.
- (1999). 'Disparities in the Salaries and Appointments of Academic Women and Men: An Update of a 1998 Report of Committee W on the Status of Women in the Academic Profession.' *Academe*, 85 no. 1: 60–2.
Berkowitz, Peggy. (1996). 'More Alike than Different: A Look at Male and

Female Experiences in University Administration.' *University Affairs* (Jan.): 12–13.

Berube, Michael, and Cary Nelson, eds. (1995). *Higher Education under Fire: Politics, Economics, and the Crisis of the Humanities*. New York: Routledge.

Bess, James L. (1998). 'Contract Systems, Bureaucracies, and Faculty Motivation: The Probable Effects of a No Tenure Policy.' *Journal of Higher Education* 69 no. 1: 1–22.

Best, Pamela. (1995). *Canadian Social Trends: Women, Men, and Work*. Ottawa: Statistics Canada.

Bielby, William, and James Baron. (1986). 'Men and Women at Work: Sex Segregation and Statistical Discrimination.' *American Journal of Sociology* 91: 759–99.

Bielby, D.D., and W.T. Bielby. (1988). 'She Works Hard for the Money: Household Responsibilities and the Allocation of Work Effort.' *American Journal of Sociology* 93: 1031–59.

Biles, George E., and Howard P. Tuckman. (1986). *Part-Time Faculty Personnel Management Policies*. New York: Macmillan.

Bilik, Laurie J., and Mark C. Blum. (1989). '"Déjà Vu All Over Again": Initiatives in Academic Management.' *Academe* 75 no. 1: 10–13.

Blakely, John H. (1989). 'What Should the Goals Be? Employment Equity for Female Faculty in Canada.' *Canadian Journal of Higher Education* 19 no. 1: 29–48.

Blum, Linda, and Vicky Smith. (1988). 'Women's Mobility in the Corporation: A Critique of the Politics of Optimism.' *Signs: Journal of Women and Culture in Society* 13 no. 3: 528–45.

Bode, Rita Karwacki. (1996). 'A Collegiality Encountered by New Faculty.' Paper presented at the Annual meeting of the American Society for Higher Education, Nov. *ERIC*. CD-ROM. SilverPlatter.

Bottiani, Sandy. (1994). 'Part-Time Teaching/Full-Time Parenting/Full-Time Consequences.' Paper presented at the Forty-Fifth Annual Meeting of the Conference on College Composition and Communication, March. Nashville, Tenn. *ERIC*. CD-ROM. SilverPlatter.

Bowen, Howard R., and Jack H. Schuster. (1986). *American Professors: A National Resource Imperilled*. New York: Oxford University Press.

Bowen, William.G., and Julie Ann Sosa. (1989). *Prospects for Faculty in the Arts and Sciences* Princeton, N.J.: Princeton University Press.

Boyer, Ernest L. (1986). *College: The Undergraduate Experience in America*. New York: Oxford University Press.

Braverman, Harry. (1974). *Labour and Monopoly Capital: The Degradation of Work in the Twentieth Century*. New York: Monthly Review Press.

Breslauer, Helen. (1985). 'Women in the Professoriate.' In *The Professoriate –
Occupation in Crisis*. Toronto: Ontario Institute for Studies in Education.

Bridges, William, and Robert Nelson. (1989). 'Markets in Hierarchies: Organizational and Market Influences on Gender Inequality in a State Pay System.'
American Journal of Sociology 95 no. 3: 616–58.

Brochu, Mireille. (1997). *The Impact of Provincial Policies on Universiy Research: A
Comparative View of Selected Canadian Provinces: A Report*. Toronto: Council of
Ontario Universities. ERIC. CD-ROM. SilverPlatter.

Brown, Corrine M. (1992). 'Evaluating Part-Time Faculty.' In Susan L. Faulkner,
ed., *Community College Professional Development: Sharing What Works*. Proceedings of a National Conference, 18–19 Oct. Berkeley, Calif. *ERIC*. CD-
ROM. SilverPlatter.

Burke, Ronald J., and Carol A. McKeen. (1990). 'Mentoring in Organizations:
Implications for Women.' *Journal of Business Ethics* 9: 317–32.

– (1992). 'Women in Management.' In Cary L. Cooper and Ivan T. Robertson,
eds, *International Review of Industrial and Organizational Psychology* Special
Issue 7. Chichester: John Wiley.

– (1993). 'Career Priority Patterns among Managerial and Professional
Women.' *Applied Psychology: An International Review* 42: 341–52.

Butrica, James L.P. (1999). Letter. *Globe and Mail* 11 Aug.: A11.

California State Postsecondary Education Commission. (1994). *Faculty Salaries
in California's Community Colleges, 1993–94: A Report to the Legislature and the
Governor in Response to Supplemental Report Language for the 1979 Budget Act*
(July). Sacramento, Calif.: ERIC. CD-ROM. SilverPlatter.

Campbell, Teresa I.D., and Sheila Slaughter. (1999). 'Faculty and Administrators' Attitudes toward Potential Conflict of Interest, Commitment and
Equity in University–Industry Relationships.' *Journal of Higher Education* 70
no. 3: 309–52.

Canadian Association of University Business Officers (CAUBO). (1988–9). The
Financial Report of Ontario Universitites. Toronto: Council of Ontario Universities (Research Division).

Cannings, K. (1991). 'An Interdisciplinary Approach to Analyzing the Gender
Gap.' *Human Relations* 7: 679–95.

Caplan, Paula J. (1993). *Lifting a Ton of Feathers: A Women's Guide to Surviving in
the Academic World*. Toronto: University of Toronto Press.

Carlyle, Cathy. (2000). 'York Study Shows Impact of Funding Cuts on Ontario
Colleges.' *York Gazette* 30 no. 17: 3.

CAUBO (Canadian Association of University Business Officers). (1988–9). *The
Financial Report of Ontario Universities*. Toronto: Council of Ontario Universities (Research Division).

CAUT (Canadian Association of University Teachers). (1986). *Handbook of Policy Statements and Model Clauses*. Ottawa: CAUT.
- (Sept. 1999). 'CAUT Begins Campaign to Shore Up Funding.' *CAUT Bulletin* 46 no. 7: 1, 7.
- (Dec. 1999). 'Canadian Universities Face Creeping Privatization.' *CAUT Bulletin* 46 no. 10: 5.
- (March 2000). *CAUT Bulletin* 47 no. 3: 1.
- (April 2000). *2000 Status of Women Supplement*. *CAUT Bulletin* Insert 47 no. 4: 1–8.
- (June 2000). 'Ontario Universities Continue to Lose Ground.' *CAUT Bulletin* 47 no. 6: 4.
- (Sept. 2000). 'Study Finds Job Satisfaction Dropping for Australian Faculty.' *CAUT Bulletin*, 47 no. 7: A9
- (Oct. 2000a). 'Nipissing's Drive to Organize Contract Staff.' *CAUT Bulletin* 47 no. 8: A1.
- (Oct. 2000b). 'Job Security for Temps in BC.' *CAUT Bulletin* 47 no. 8: A4.
- (Feb. 2001) 'Exploitation of Contract Staff, Topic of San Jose Conference.' *CAUT Bulletin* 48 no. 2: A5.
Cayton, Mary K. (1991). 'Writing as Outsiders: Academic Discourse and Marginalized Faculty.' *College English* 53: 647–60.
Cemer, Brett. (1998). 'Academics Cut Too Deeply in the '90s – OCUFA.' *Active Voice, YUFA (York University Faculty Association)* 9 no. 4: 3–4.
Chaffins, Stephanie, Mary Forbes, Harold E. Fuqua, Jr, and Joseph P. Cangemi. (1995). 'The Glass Ceiling: Are Women Where They Should Be?' *Education* 115 no. 3: 380–6.
Chell, Cara. (1982). 'Memoirs and Confessions of a Part-Time Lecturer.' *College English* 44: 35–40.
Chow, Clement, et al. (1996). 'Gaining on the Goals? Affirmative Action Policies, Practices and Outcomes in Media Communication Education.' Paper presented at the 41st Annual Meeting of the Broadcast Education Association, 12–15 April. Las Vegas. *ERIC*. CD-ROM. SilverPlatter.
Clapp, P. (1987). 'Part-Time Teaching as Career Development.' Unpublished paper, University of Calgary.
Clark, Shirley M., and Mary Corcoran. (1993). 'Perspectives on the Professional Socialization of Women Faculty: A Case of Accumulative Disadvantage?' In Judith S. Glazer, Estela M. Bensimon, and Barbara K. Townsend, eds, *Women in Higher Education: A Feminist Perspective*. ASHE Reader Series. Needham Heights, Mass.: Ginn Press.
Clark, W., and Z. Zsigmond. (1981). *Job Market Reality for Post-Secondary Gradu-*

ates: Employment Outcome by 1978. Two Years after Graduation. Ottawa: Statistics Canada.

Cole, Jonathan R. (1979). *Fair Science: Women in Scientific Community.* New York: Free Press.

Cole, J.R., and S. Cole. (1973). *Social Stratification in Science.* Chicago: University of Chicago Press.

Cole, Stephen. (1979). 'Age and Scientific Performance.' *American Journal of Sociology* 84: 958–77.

College of the Canyons, Calif. (1993). *Survey of Part-Time Faculty, Fall 1992. ERIC.* CD-ROM. SilverPlatter.

Conférence des recteurs et des principaux des universités du Québec (CREPUQ). (1991). *Rapport de l'Enquête sur le personnel enseignant, Années 1988/89 et 1989/90.* Montreal: CREPUQ.

Conseil des universités. (1989). *Les chargés de cours dans les universités québécoises* (à vis au ministre de l'Enseignement supérieur et de la Science Code 2310-0145). Sainte-Foy, Que: Gouvernement du Québec.

Costello, Cynthia. (1984). 'Women's Work in the Office.' *Social Science Journal* 21: 116–21.

COU (Council of Ontario Universities). (1976). *Academic Career Planning: The Ivory Tower and the Crystal Ball.* Toronto: COU.

– (1985). *Bottoming Out: Review 1982–83 to 1985–86.* Toronto: COU.

– (1990). *Financial Reports, Ontario Universities 1977–1990.* Toronto: COU.

– (1991). *Non-Regular Instruction Personnel in Ontario Universities.* Toronto: COU.

Creamer, Elizabeth G. (1996). 'The Perceived Contribution of Academic Partners to Women's Publishing Productivity.' ASHE Annual Meeting Paper. Paper Presented at the 21st Annual Meeting of the Association for the Study of Higher Education, 31 Oct.–3 Nov. 1996. Memphis, Tenn. *ERIC.* CD-ROM. SilverPlatter.

CUEW (Canadian Union of Education Workers). (1976–87). Local 3 Grievance Files. York University, Toronto.

– (1985–7). Local 3 Collective Agreement. York University, Toronto.

Cumming Speirs, Carol, Rhonda Amsel, Malcolm G. Baines, and Jo-Anne Pickel. (1998). 'Off the Track: A Profile of Non-Tenure Track Faculty at McGill University.' *Canadian Journal of Higher Education* 28 no. 2/3: 1–19.

Curtis, James, and Lorne Tepperman. (1990). *Images of Canada: The Sociological Tradition.* Toronto: Prentice-Hall.

Cutright, Marc. (2000). 'A Review of P.G. Taylor 1999. *Making Sense of Academic Life: Academics, Universities, and Change.* Buckingham: Society for Research into Higher Education and Open University. *Higher Education* 40: 489–91.

Cyr, D., and B. Horner Reich, eds. (1996). *Scaling the Ivory Tower: Stories from Women in Business School Faculties*. Westport, Conn.: Praeger.

Dagg, Anne Innis. (1993). 'Academic Faculty Wives and Systematic Discrimination – Antinepotism and "Inbreeding."' *Canadian Journal of Higher Education* 23 no. 1: 1–18.

Dassas, Veronique. (1990). 'The Thorny Problem of Sessionals.' *CAUT Bulletin* 37 no. 2: 11.

Davies, John. (1994). 'Perspective: An Unlevel Playing Field.' *Times Higher Education* 19 (Aug.): 15–16.

Davis, William G. (1966). 'The Government of Ontario and the Universities of the Province.' In William Mansfield Cooper, ed., *Governments and the University*. Toronto: Macmillan.

Dean, Misao. (1995). 'Shock Troops on Campus.' *Canadian Forum* 74 no. 841: 14–19.

Dickman, Marcia M., Dale R. Fuqua, William T. Coombs, and James M. Seals. (1996). 'Downsizing in Higher Education: Institutional Budget Reduction Priorities and Strategies.' *Journal of College Student Development*, 37 no. 4: 457–67.

Didion, Catherine Jay. (1996). 'Dual Careers and Shared Positions.' *Journal of College Science Teaching* 26: 123–4.

Dugger, Ronnie. (2000). 'The Struggle That Matters the Most.' In Geoffry D. White and Flannery C. Hauck, eds, *Campus, Inc*. Amherst, NY, Prometheus Books.

Economic Council of Canada. (1965). *Second Annual Review*. Ottawa.

Economist. (1999). 'Employment: Part-Time Workers' 26 June–2 July: 118.

– (2000) 'Employment: Part-time Workers' 22 June. http://www.economist.com/

– (2001) 'Part-time Workers' 26 June. http://www.eonomist.com/

Eggers, Patricia. (1990). 'Part-Time, Off-Campus Instructors: A Support Program for Improving Teaching Effectiveness.' Paper presented at the Seventieth Annual Convention of the American Association of Community and Junior Colleges, 22–25 April, Seattle. *ERIC*. CD-ROM. SilverPlatter.

Eisenmann, Linda. (1996). 'Review of Patricia Ann Palmieri, *In Adamless Eden: The Community of Women Faculty at Wellesley*, and Margaret W. Rossiter, *Women Scientists in America: Before Affirmative Action, 1940–1972*.' *Harvard Educational Review* 66: 858–73.

Erskin, Bruce. (1997). 'Professors "Ripped Off": Part-Time Faculty at Poverty Level, Union Says.' *Mail-Star-Halifax Chronicle Herald*, 23 Dec.: A9. *Canadian Index*. CD-ROM. SilverPlatter.

Faulkner, Susan L., et al. (1992). 'Community College Professional Development: Sharing What Works.' In Proceedings of a National Conference, 18–19 Oct. 1991. San Antonio, Texas *ERIC*. CD-ROM. SilverPlatter.

Fekete, John. (1994). *Moral Panic: Biopolitics Rising*. Montreal: R. Davies.

Feldthusen, Bruce. (1995). 'Gender Wars: Where the Boys Are.' In Chilly Collective, eds, *Breaking Anonymity: The Chilly Climate for Women Faculty*. Waterloo, Ont.: Wilfrid Laurier University Press.

Filson, Glen. (1988). 'Ontario Teachers' Deprofessionalization and Proletarianization.' *Comparative Education Review* 32: 298–317.

Finkel, Susan K., and Steven G, Olswang. (1996). 'Child Rearing as a Career Impediment to Women Assistant Professors.' *Review of Higher Education* 19: 123–39.

Finkelstein, Martin. J. (1984). *The American Academic Profession: A Synthesis of Social Scientific Inquiry Since World War II*. Columbus: Ohio State University Press.

Flynn, Deborah. (1998). 'The "New Design" for Universities.' *OCUFA Forum* Spring: 9.

FNEEQ (Fédération nationale des enseignants et enseignantes du Québec). (1990). *Réplique à l'avis du Conseil des Universités sur les chargées de cours dans les universités québécoises*. Montreal: FNEEQ-CSN.

Foley, Duncan. (1983). 'Labour Power.' In Tom Bottomore, ed., *A Dictionary of Marxist Thought*. Cambridge, Mass.: Harvard University Press.

Fosh, Patricia, and Christopher T. Husbands. (1993). 'Part-Time Teaching and Auxiliaries and the Assurance of Teaching Quality in Higher Education.' Paper prepared for the 15th Annual EAIR Forum on Higher Education in a Changing Environment: Regional, National, and Transnational Issues. University of Turku, Turku, Finland, 15–18 Aug.

Fox, Mary F., and Catherine A. Faver. (1985). 'Men, Women, and Publication Productivity: Patterns among Social Work Academics.' *Sociological Quarterly* 26: 537–49.

Freeman, Bonnie Cook. (1977). 'Faculty Women in the American University: Up the Down Staircase.' *Higher Education* 6: 165–88.

French, Wendell L., Edward Gross, and Herman Resnick. (1986). 'Effects of a Budget Cut Crisis on Faculty at a Large State University.' *Sociology and Social Research* 70 no. 4: 272–5.

Galt, Virginia. (2000). 'Canadians Pursuing Higher Education in Record Numbers.' *Globe and Mail* 22 Feb.: A10.

Gannon, Martin J. (1971) 'The Management of Peripheral Employees.' *Proceedings of the Academy of Management* Aug.: 254–63.

Gans, Herbert J. (1993). 'A Scholars' Role in Planning a Post-Work Society.' *Chronicle of Higher Education* 9 June: B3.

Gappa, Judith M. (1984). Part-Time Faculty: Higher Education at a Crossroads. Higher Education Research Report, No. 3. Washington, DC.: ASHE–ERIC.

– (1987). 'The Stress-Producing Working Conditions of Part-Time Faculty.' In Peter Seldin, ed., *Coping with Faculty Stress*. San Francisco: Jossey-Bass.

Gappa, Judith M., and David W. Leslie (1993) *The Invisible Faculty*. San Francisco: Jossey-Bass.

Gibb-Clark, Margot (1995) 'Ontario Part-Time Workers Targeted.' *Globe and Mail* 8 Aug.: B1–B2.

Giddens, Anthony. (1981). *The Class Structure of Advanced Societies*. 2nd ed. London: Hutchinson.

Gilbert, Sandra M. (1996). 'The (Academic) Job System and the Economy, Stupid: or Should a Friend Let a Friend Get a Ph.D.?' *Academe* 82 no. 5: 12–15.

Gilbert, Sid. (1999). 'Performance Indicators for Universities: Ogres or Opportunities?' *OCUFA Forum* Spring: 19–21.

Gordon, J. (1987). 'We Tried: A Case Study of Ideology and Inertia.' Paper presented at the Conference on Part-Time Teaching in the University, York University, Toronto.

Gordon, Jane. (1997). 'Breaking Anonymity: The Chilly Climate for Women Faculty. Review of *The Chilly Collective*.' *Atlantis: A Women's Studies Journal* 21 no. 2: 121–3.

Goyder, John. (1992). 'Gender Inequalities in Academic Rank.' *Canadian Journal of Sociology* 17 no. 3: 333–43.

Graham, Bill. (1998a). *Toronto Star* 17 May: F6: quoted in Gilbert (1999: 19).

– (1998b). 'The Corporate University.' *OCUFA Forum* Spring: 4–6.

– (1999a). 'Reinvestment Needed To Avert Looming Crisis.' *CAUT Bulletin* 46 no. 8: 3.

– (1999b). 'Fighting for the Freedom of Inquiry.' *CAUT Bulletin* 46 no. 9: 36.

Greenwood, Richard D. (1980). 'Making "What's-His-Face" Feel at Home: Integrating Part-Time Faculty.' In Michael Parsons, ed., *Using Part-Time Faculty Effectively. New Directions for Community Colleges* 8 no. 2: 55–60.

Gumport, J. Patricia. (1989). 'Postsecondary Organization as Settings for Life History: A Rationale and Illustration of Research Methods.' *Current Perspectives on Aging and Life Cycle* 3: 175–90.

– (2000). 'Academic Restructuring: Organizational Change and Institutional Imperatives.' *Higher Education* 39 no. 1: 67–91.

Gunn, Bruce. (1991). 'The Dysfunctional Nature of Political Systems in University Administration.' ERIC. CD-ROM. SilverPlatter.

Hackman, J. Dozier. (1991). 'What Is Going On in Higher Education? Is It Time for a Change?' *Review of Higher Education* 16 no. 1: 1–17.

Hall, Christine, and Carol Atnip. (1992). 'The Senior Lecturer Program:

Rewarding Part-Time/Adjunct Faculty.' In Barbara Gallow Lyman, and
Emily Miller Payne, eds, *National Association for Development Education Six-
teenth Annual Conference Proceedings, 26 Feb.–1 March 1992*. San Antonio,
Texas. *ERIC*. CD-ROM. SilverPlatter.

Hall, R.M., and B.R. Sandler (1982). *The Classroom Climate: A Chilly One for
Women?* Washington, DC: Project on the Status and Education of Women,
Association of American Colleges.

– (1983). *Academic Mentoring for Women Students and Faculty: A New Look at an
Old Way to Get Ahead*. Washington, DC: Project on the Status and Education
of Women, Association of American Colleges.

– (1984). *Out of the Classroom: A Chilly Campus Climate for Women?* Washington,
DC: Project on the Status and Education of Women, Association of American
Colleges.

Hardy, Cynthia. (1992). 'Retrenchment Strategies in Two Canadian Universities: A Political Analysis.' *Canadian Journal of Administrative Sciences* 9: 180–
91.

Hargens, Lowell L., and Lisa Kelly-Wilson. (1994). 'Determinants of Disciplinary Discontent.' *Social Forces* 72 no. 4: 1177–95.

Hart, A. (1993). *Part-Time, Poor Deal: A Survey of Part-Time Staff in Traditional
Universities*. London: Association of University Teachers Research Depart-
ment, January. Quoted in 'Perspective: An Unlevel Playing Field.' *The Times
Higher Education* 19 Aug. 1994. *Canadian Index*. CD-ROM. SilverPlatter.

Harvey, David. (1998). 'University, Inc.' *Atlantic Monthly Online*. Oct. http://
www.theatlantic.com.

Hauser, Deborah. (1992). 'The Budget Crisis and Women's Experience: Part-
Time Faculty at California State University.' Paper presented at the Sixty-
Third Annual Meeting of the Western States Communication Association,
21–5 Feb. Boise, Idaho. *ERIC*. CD-ROM. SilverPlatter.

Hayes, Mabel E. (1990). 'Minority Women in Higher Education: Status and
Challenges.' Paper presented at the Annual Meeting of the Comparative and
International Educational Society. Anaheim, Calif. *ERIC*. CD-ROM. Silver-
Platter.

Heller, Agnes. (1976). *The Theory of Need in Marx*. New York: St Martin's
Press.

Heller, Scott. (1990). 'The Expected Turnaround in the Faculty Job Market May
Come Too Late for 'Lost Generation' of Scholars.' *Chronicle of Higher Education* 23 May: A1.

Henderson, Bruce B., and William D. Kane. (1991). 'Caught in the Middle: Faculty and Institutional Status and Quality in State Comprehensive Universities.' *Higher Education* 22 no. 4: 339–50.

Henry, Mary. (1990). 'Voices of Academic Women on Feminine Gender Scripts.' *British Journal of Sociology of Education* 11: 121–35.

Hiller, Harry H. (1986). *Canadian Society: A Macro Analysis.* Scarborough, Ont: Prentice-Hall.

Himmelweit, Susan. (1983). 'Exploitation.' In Tom Bottomore, ed., *A Dictionary of Marxist Thought,* Cambridge, Mass.: Harvard University Press.

Hodges, Jane. (2000). 'A Surplus of Scholars Fight for Jobs in Academia.' *New York Times* 16 Jan.: BU 15.

Huber, Sonya. (2000). 'Faculty Workers: Tenure on the Corporate Assembly Line.' In Geoffry D. White and Flannery C. Hauck, eds, *Campus, Inc.* Amherst, NY: Prometheus Books.

Iadevaia, David G. (1991). 'A Comparison of Full-Time to Part-Time Faculty and Full-Time to Part-Time Science Faculty in Terms of Student Success at Pima Community College, Tucson.' Doctoral (EdD) diss., Nova University, Arizona. *ERIC.* CD-ROM. SilverPlatter.

ILO (International Labour Office). (1987). *World Labour Reports.* Oxford: Oxford University Press.

– (1989). *Conditions of Work Digest: Part-Time Work,* 8 no. 1. Geneva.

Jencks, Christopher, and David Riesman. (1968). *The Academic Revolution.* Garden City, NY: Doubleday.

Johnson, Beth Hillman, ed. (1992). *The Impact of Collective Bargaining on Higher Education: A Twenty Year Retrospective. Proceedings of the Twentieth Annual Conference, 13–14 April.* New York. *ERIC.* CD-ROM. SilverPlatter.

Johnson, Candice. (1993). 'Professional Sense of Community.' In Jim Fullen, ed., *OATYC Journal* 18 no. 1–2: 47. *ERIC.* CD-ROM. SilverPlatter.

Johnsrud, Linda K., and Ronald H. Heck. (1994). 'Administrative Promotion within a University: The Cumulative Impact of Gender.' *Journal of Higher Education* 65 no. 1: 23–44.

Johnsrud, Linda K., Ronald H. Heck, and Vicki J. Rosser. (2000). 'Morale Matters: Midlevel Administrators and Their Intent to Leave.' *Journal of Higher Education* 71: 34–59.

Jones, Arnita. (1990). 'Colleges Must Help Some of Their Humanities Ph.D.s to Pursue Career outside Academe.' *Chronicle of Higher Education* 1 Aug.: B2.

Jones, Glen, and Michael Skolnik. (1992). 'A Comparative Analysis of Arrangements for State Coordination of Higher Education in Canada and the United States.' *Journal of Higher Education* 63:121–42.

Jones, Paul. (1987). 'The Situation of Chargées de Cours in Quebec.' Fédération nationale des enseignants et des enseignantes du Québec (FNEEQ). Paper presented at the International Conference on Part-Time Faculty, Glendon College, York University.

Kamps, Don. (1996). *Continuous Quality Improvement in the Employment of Adjunct Faculty: A NIACC Plan. ERIC.* CD-ROM. Silverplatter.

Kanter, Rosabeth Moss. (1977). 'Some Effects of Proportions on Group Life: Skewed Sex Ratios and Responses to Token Women.' *American Journal of Sociology* 82: 965–90.

– (1979). 'Changing the Shape of Work: Reform in Academe.' In Rosabeth Moss Kanter, Morton Darrow, and Michael Maccoby, eds, *Perspectives on Leadership.* Current Issues in Higher Education Series 1. Washington, DC: American Association of Higher Education.

Kantrowitz, Joanne S. (1981). 'Paying Your Dues, Part-Time.' In Gloria DeSole and Leonore Hoffman, eds, *Rocking the Boat: Academic Women and Academic Processes.* New York: MLA.

Keep, E., and K. Sisson. (1992). 'Owning the Problem: Staffing the System in the 1990s.' In David Finegold et al., eds, *Higher Education: Expansion and Reform.* London: Institute for Public Policy Research.

Keller, George. (1983). *Academic Strategy: The Management Revolution in Higher Education.* Baltimore: Johns Hopkins University Press. Quoted in Laurie J. Bilik, and Mark C. Blum, 'Déjà Vu All Over Again: Initiatives in Academic Management.' *Academe* 75, no. 1 (1989): 10–13.

Kelley, Kathryn, et al. (1996). 'Resilient Older Academic Women: Stories Told in Their Own Voices.' Paper presented at the Eighty-Second Annual Meeting of the Speech Communication Association, 23–6 Nov. 1996. San Diego. *ERIC.* CD-ROM. SilverPlatter.

Kelly, Diana K. (1992). *Part-Time and Evening Faculty: Promoting Teaching Excellence for Adult Evening College Students. 1991/92 Fund for Instructional Improvement Grant Project. Final Report.* Fullerton College, Calif. *ERIC.* CD-ROM. SilverPlatter.

Kennett, Joyce A. (1996). 'Faculty/Administration Relations in Community Colleges.' In *Issues of Education at Community Colleges: Essays by Fellows in the Mid-Career Fellowship Program at Princeton University.* Princeton, NJ. *ERIC.* CD-ROM. SilverPlatter.

Kirk, Stuart A., and Aaron Rosenblatt. (1984). 'The Contribution of Women Faculty to Social Work Journals.' *Social Work* Jan./Feb.: 67–9.

Kirshstein, Rita J., et al. (1996). *Institutional Policies and Practices Regarding Faculty in Higher Education. 1993 National Study of Postsecondary Faculty (NSOPF-93). Statistical Analysis Report.* Washington, DC. *ERIC.* CD-ROM. SilverPlatter.

Kivinen, Osmo, and Sakari Ahola. (1999). 'Higher Education as Human Risk Capital: Reflections on Changing Labour Markets.' *Higher Education* 38: 191–208.

Klein, Waldo C., Dan Weisman, and Thomas Edward Smith. (1996). 'The Use of Adjunct Faculty: An Exploratory Study of Eight Social Work Programs.' *Journal of Social Work Education* 32 no. 2: 253–63.

Knutson, Peter. (1995). 'An Academic Peddler.' *Academe* 81 no. 1: 16–18.

Kolodny, Annette. (1998). *Failing the Future: A Dean Looks at Higher Education in the Twenty-First Century.* Durham, NC: Duke University Press.

Konrad, Alison M., Susan Winter, and Barbara A. Gutek. (1992). 'Diversity in Work Group Sex Composition: Implications for Majority and Minority Members.' *Research in the Sociology of Organizations* 10: 115–40.

Krahn, Harvey. (1992). *Quality of Work In the Service Sector.* Cat. 11-612E, no. 6, March. Ottawa: Statistics Canada.

Krahn, Harvey J., and Graham S. Lowe. (1998). *Work Industry and Canadian Society.* Scarborough, Ont.: International Thomson Publishing.

Kreckel, R. (1980). 'Unequal Opportunity Structure and Labour Market Segmentation.' *Sociology,* 14: 525–50.

Krefting, Linda A., and Philip K. Berger. (1979). 'Masculinity-Femininity Perceptions of Job Requirements and Their Relationship to Job-Sex Stereotypes.' *Journal of Vocational Behavior* 15: 164–274.

Kubursi, A.A. (1994). *The Economic Impact of University Expenditures. Discussion Series, Issue 2.* A report commissioned by the Alliance for Ontario Universities. Toronto: Council of Ontario Universities. *ERIC.* CD-ROM. SilverPlatter.

Kuchera, Michael E., and Steven I. Miller. (1988). 'The Effects of Perceptions of the Academic Job Market on Adjunct Faculty: An Identity Theory Analysis.' *Sociology of Education* 61: 240–54.

Kulis, Stephen, and Karen A. Miller-Loessi. (1992a). 'Organizational Dynamics and Gender Equity: The Case of Sociology Departments in the Pacific Region.' *Work and Occupations* 19 no. 2: 157–83.

– (1992b). 'Organizations, Labor Markets, and Gender Integration in Academic Sociology.' *Sociological Perspectives* 35 no. 1: 93–117.

Kyvik, S. (1990). 'Motherhood and Scientific Productivity.' *Social Studies of Science* 20: 149–60.

Lampignano, John. (1990). 'Increasing the Effectiveness of Part-Time Faculty.' *Vision '90: The Maricopa Community Colleges Journal of Teaching and Learning* 2 nos. 1–2: 30–4.

Lane, Christel (1989). 'From Welfare Capitalism to Market Capitalism: A Comparative Review of Trends toward Employment Flexibility in the Labour Markets of Three Major European Societies.' *Sociology* 23 no. 4: 583–610.

– (1993). 'Gender and the Labour Market in Europe: Britain, Germany and France Compared.' *Sociological Review* 41 no. 2: 274–301.

Lankard, Bettina A. (1993). *Part-Time Faculty in Adult and Vocational Education.* *ERIC Digest.* ERIC. CD-ROM. SilverPlatter.

Lee, Barbara A. (1991). 'Improving Faculty employment decisions.' *Thought and Action* 7 no. 1: 73–87.

Lee, Barbara A., David W. Leslie, and Steven G. Olswang. (1987). 'Implications of Comparable Worth for Academe.' *Journal of Higher Education* 58 no. 6: 609–28.

Lee, John. (1997). 'Part-Time Employment in Academe.' *NEA Higher Education Research Center Update* 3 no. 1: 1–6.

Lee, Stewart. (1990). *'It's Up to You': Women at UBC in the Early Years.* Vancouver: University of British Columbia Press.

Lemon, Hallie S., et al., comps. (1994). *Redefining the Role of 'Permanent Temps': Proving Ourselves Professionals.* Proceedings of a Roundtable Sessions at the Forty-Fifth Annual Conference on College Composition and Communication, March 16–19. Nashville, Tenn. ERIC. CD-ROM. SilverPlatter.

Lennards, Joseph L. (1988). 'The Academic Profession in Canada.' Unpublished data and summary report.

Lenski, G. (1966). *Power and Privilege: A Theory of Social Stratification.* New York: McGraw-Hill.

Leslie, David. W. (1984). 'Policies for Part-Time Faculty: Developments in Law and Collective Bargaining.' Paper presented at the Annual Conference of the American Association for Higher Education. Chicago.

– ed. (1998). *The Growing Use of Part-Time Faculty: Understanding Causes and Effects.* San Francisco: Jossey-Bass.

Leslie, David W., Samuel E. Kellams, and Manny G. Gunne. (1982). *Part-Time Faculty in American Higher Education.* New York: Praeger.

Levin, Bernard H., James R. Perkins, and Darrel A. Clowes. (1992). 'Changing Times, Changing Missions?' Paper presented at the Twenty-First Annual Conference of the Southeastern Association for Community Colleges, Aug. 1992. Orlando, Fla.. ERIC. CD-ROM. SilverPlatter.

Lewington, Jennifer. (1997). 'Cash Strapped Canadian Universities Seek New Ways to Bring in Money.' *Chronicle of Higher Education* 2 May: A47–8.

Lewis, Lionel S., and Philip G. Altbach. (1996). 'The Professoriate in International Perspective: Who They Are and What They Do.' *Academe* 82 no. 3: 29–33.

– (1997). 'The Dilemma of Higher Education.' *Academe* 83 no. 4: 28–9.

Lie, Suzanne Stiver, and Virginia E. O'Leary. (1990). *Storming the Tower: Women in the Academic World.* London: Kogan Page.

Lie, Suzanne, Lynda Malik, and Duncan Harris, eds. (1994). *World Yearbook of Education, 1994. The Gender Gap in Higher Education.* London: Kogan Page.

Limerick, Patricia N. (1998). Review of Annette Kolodny, *Failing the Future.* 'The Dean's List.' *New York Times Book Review* 26 April: 35.

Lindsay, Beverly. (1988). 'Public and Higher Education Policies Influencing African-American Women.' *Higher Education.* 17: 563–80.

Little, Bruce. (1993). 'Full-Time Work on the Decline.' *Globe and Mail* 19 July: A1–A2.

Lombardi, John. (1973). *Managing Finances in Community Colleges.* San Francisco, Calif.: Jossey-Bass.

– (1992). 'The Ambiguity of the Part-Time Faculty.' In John Lombardi, and Arthur M. Cohen, eds, *Perspectives on the Community College: Essays.* ERIC. CD-ROM. SilverPlatter.

Looker, E. Dianne. (1993). 'Gender Issues in University: The University as Employer of Academic and Non-Academic Women and Men.' *Canadian Journal of Higher Education* 23 no. 2: 19–43.

Lorber, Judith. (1983). 'Women as Colleagues: The Matthew Effect and the Salieri Phenomenon.' Paper presented at American Sociological Association Meetings, Detroit. *Sociological Abstracts.* CD-ROM. SilverPlatter.

Lowe, Graham S. (1982). 'Class, Job, and Gender in the Canadian Office.' *Labour / Le Travailleur* 10 Autumn: 11–37.

Lundy, Katherina L.P., and Barbara D. Warme. (1985). 'Part-Time Faculty: Institutional Needs and Career Dilemmas.' Paper presented at the 1985 ASHE Annual Meeting, Chicago, Ill.

– (1989). 'Part-Time Faculty: Student Perceptions and Experiences.' *Canadian Journal of Higher Education* 19 no. 2: 73–85.

– (1990). 'Gender and Career Trajectory: The Case of Part-Time Faculty.' *Studies in Higher Education* 15 no. 2: 207–22.

McGuire, John. (1993). 'Part-Time Faculty: Partners in Excellence.' *Leadership Abstracts* 6 no. 6 (1993): 2–3. ERIC. CD-ROM. SilverPlatter.

Maclean's. (1997). 'Ranking Road Map: *Maclean's* Takes the Measure of Canadian Universities.' Toronto ed., 24 Nov.: 31. *Infotrac: Expanded Academic ASAP.* CD-ROM. Information Access.

Martin, Bill. (1994). 'Understanding Class Segmentation in the Labour Market: An Empirical Study of Earnings Determination in Australia.' *Work, Employment and Society* 8 no. 3: 357–85.

Martin, James E., James E. Samels, and Associates. (1997). *First among Equals: The Role of the Chief Academic Officer.* Baltimore: Johns Hopkins University Press.

Maslen, Geoffrey. (1998). 'The End of Contract Teaching? Australia's Campuses to End Contract Employment.' Originally published in *Chronicle of Higher Education* (1998). Reported in *YUFA Active Voice* 9 no. 4: 8–10.

Massengale, John D., and George H. Sage. (1995). 'Shared Power through Negotiation in Higher Education.' *Quest* 47: 64–75.

Massy, William F., and Andrea K. Wilger. (1995). 'Improving Productivity: What Faculty Think about It, and Its Effect on Quality.' *Change* 27 no. 4: 10–20.

Mattice, Nancy J., and Russell C. Richardson. (1993). *College of the Canyons Survey of Teaching Practices*, Spring. Valencia, Calif. *ERIC*. CD-ROM. SilverPlatter.

Melamed, Tuvia. (1995). 'Barriers to Women's Career Success: Human Capital, Career Choices, Structural Determinants, or Simply Sex Discrimination.' *Applied Psychology* 44 no. 4: 295–314.

Melchers, Ron. (1998). 'Ontario Universities: The Collective Bargaining Context for 1998–99.' *OCUFA Forum* Spring: 10–11.

– (1999). *Not in the Public Interest: CAUT Report*, quoted in *CAUT Bulletin*, 46 no. 10: 5.

Merton, R.K. (1968). 'The Matthew Effect in Science.' *Science* 199 (5 Jan.): 55–63.

Meyer-Renschhausen, Elisabeth. (1990). 'Feminist Research at German Universities? Nearly Impossible! Taking Stock after Ten Years.' *Critical Sociology* 18 no. 3: 61–73.

Mignault, Louis B (1991). 'Our Shame: Another Long-Service Faculty Member Fired.' *University of Toronto Bulletin* 1 April: 12.

Miles, M.B., and A.M. Haberman. (1994). *Qualitative Data Analysis: An Expanded Sourcebook*. Thousand Oaks, Calif.: Sage.

Miller, Michael T. (1996). *Research Agenda Development by New Faculty: A Case Study. ERIC*. CD-ROM. SilverPlatter.

Mitchell, Alanna. (1995). 'Aging Professors Target of Study.' *Globe and Mail* 2 Sept.: A1, A10.

Moffat, Linda K. (1980). *Room at the Bottom*. Toronto: Ontario Ministry of Colleges and Universities.

Mooney, Carolyn J. (1993). 'Tenured Faculty Members Are Spared in the Latest Round of Belt Tightening.' *Chronicle of Higher Education* 13 Jan.: A17.

Morrison, Ann M., and Mary Ann Von Glinow. (1990). 'Women and Minorities in Management.' *American Psychologist* 45: 200–8.

Morrison, Ann M., Randall P. White, and Ellen Van Velsor. (1987a). *Breaking the Glass Ceiling. Reading*. Mass.: Addison-Wesley.

– (1987b). 'The Narrow Band.' *Issues and Observations* 7: 1–7.

Muller, Carol B. (1990). 'Hidden Passages to Success in the Academic Labour Market.' Paper presented at the Annual Meeting of the American Educational Research Association, 16–20 April. Boston: *ERIC*. CD-ROM. SilverPlatter.

Murry, John, and Judy Murry. (1996). 'Job Dissatisfaction and Turnover among

Two Year College Department/Division Chairpersons.' *Proceedings of the Fifth Annual International Conference of the National Community College Chair Academy, 14–17 Feb. 1996. Phoenix, AZ. ERIC.* CD-ROM. SilverPlatter.

Mwenifumbo, Lorraine, and K. Edward Renner. (1998). 'Institutional Variations in Faculty Demographic Profiles.' *Canadian Journal of Higher Education* 28: 21–46.

Nakamura, Alice. (1990). 'Gender Differences in Earnings: A Comment.' *Canadian Journal of Sociology* 15: 463–9.

NATFHE (National Association of Teachers in Further and Higher Education). (1993). *Losing Out: A Report of NATFHE 1993.* Quoted in John Davies, 'Perspective: An Unlevel Playing Field.' *Times Higher Education* 19 Aug. 1994: 15–16.

NCES (National Center for Education Statistics). (1990a). *Survey Report: A Descriptive Report of Academic Departments in Higher Education Institutions.* Jan. NCES 90-339. Washington, DC: U.S. Department of Education, Office of Educational Research and Improvement.

– (1990b). *1988 National Survey of Post-Secondary Faculty: Faculty in Higher Education Institutions.* March. NCES 90-365. Washington, DC: U.S. Department of Education.

(1999). NCES Online. *Digest of Education Statistics, 1998.* NCES 1999-036. U.S. Department of Education, National Center for Education Statistics. March. Tables 223, 225, 227, 228, 230. http://nces.ed.gov/1999036/usreport.pdf/

Neatby, Blair. (1985). 'The Academic Profession.' In Higher Education Group, ed., *The Professoriate: Occupation in Crisis.* Toronto: Ontario Institute for Studies in Education.

Nelson, Cary. (1995). 'Lessons from the Job Wars: What Is to Be Done?' *Academe* 81 no. 6: 18–25.

– (1997). 'Superstars.' *Academe* 83 no. 1: 38–43, 54.

New York Times. (2000). 16 Jan.: BU 15.

Newman, Kathy. (1999). 'Nice Work If We Can Keep It: Confessions of a Junior Professor.' *Academe* 85 no. 3: 28–33.

Newson, Janice A. (1990). 'The Decline of Faculty Influence: Confronting the Effects of the Corporate Agenda.' Paper presented at the Canadian Association of Sociology and Anthropology Meetings, 26 May–1 June.

– (2000). 'Essays Explore Evolution of U.S. Academic Workplace.' Review of Randy Martin, ed., *Chalk Lines: The Politics of Work in the Managed University, CAUT Bulletin* 47 no. 3: 9.

Newson, Janice A., and Howard Buchbinder. (1988). *The University Means Business: Universities. Corporations and Academic Work.* Toronto: Garmond Press.

NLRB v. Yeshiva University (1981). 444 U.S. 672.

Noble, David F. (1998). 'Digital Diploma Mills: The Automation of Higher Education – Part Two.' *OCUFA Forum* Fall: 18–21.

Nock, David A. (1992). 'Star Wars: Aspects of Social Construction of Citations in Anglo-Canadian Sociology.' *Canadian Review of Sociology and Anthropology* 23 no. 3: 346–60.

Norrell, J. Elizabeth, and Thomas H. Norrell. (1996). 'Faculty and Family Policies in Higher Education.' *Journal of Family Issues* 17: 204–25.

North, Joan DeGuire. (1996). 'Read My Lips: The Academic Administrator's Role in the Campus Focus on Teaching.' In Theodore J. Marchese, ed., *AAHE Bulletin* 48 nos 1–10 (1995–6): 25–33. *ERIC*. CD-ROM. SilverPlatter.

Northrup, David A. (1997). 'The Problem of the Self Report in Survey Research.' *Institute of Social Research Newsletter* 12 no. 1: 1–2.

Offe, Claus. (1980). 'The Separation of Form and Content in Liberal Democratic Politics.' *Studies in Political Economy* 3: 5–16.

Ogbonna, Emmanuel, and Mike Noon. (1995). 'Experience Inequality: Ethnic Minorities and the Employment Training Scheme.' *Work, Employment and Society* 9: 537–58.

Olsen, Deborah. (1992). 'Interviews with Exiting Faculty: Why Do They Leave?' In Donald H. Wulff and Jody D. Nyquist. eds, *Resources for Faculty, Instructional, and Organizational Development: To Improve the Academy* 11: 35–47. Stillwater, Okla. *ERIC*. CD-ROM. SilverPlatter.

Olsen, Deborah, and Janet P. Near. (1994). 'Role Conflict and Faculty Life Satisfaction.' *Review of Higher Education* 17: 179–95.

Olsen, Deborah, Sue A. Maple, and Frances K. Stage. (1995). 'Women and Minority Faculty Job Satisfaction.' *Journal of Higher Education* 66 no. 3: 265–93.

OECD (Organization of Economic Cooperation and Development). (1986). *OECD Employment Outlook*. Paris: OECD.

Ornstein, Michael, and Penni Stewart. (1996). 'Gender and Faculty Pay in Canada.' *Canadian Journal of Sociology* 21 no. 4: 461–81. *Canadian Index*. CD-ROM. SilverPlatter.

Paechter, Carrie, and John Head. (1996). 'Gender, Identity, Status and the Body: Life in a Marginal Subject.' *Gender and Education* 8: 21–9.

Page, Stewart. (1996). 'Ranking of Canadian Universities, 1995: More Problems in Interpretation.' *Canadian Journal of Higher Education* 26 no. 2: 47–58.

Panitch, Leo. (1977). 'The Development of Corporatism in Liberal Democracies.' *Comparative Political Studies* 10: 61–90.

Park, Shelly, M. (1996). 'Research, Teaching, and Service: Why Shouldn't Women's Work Count?' *The Journal of Higher Education* 67 no. 1: 46–84.

Parkin, F. (1979). *Marxism and Class Theory: A Bourgeoise Critique*. London: Tavistock.

Parliament, Jo-Anne B. (1990). 'Labour Force Trends: Two Decades in Review.' In *Canadian Social Trends*. Ottawa: Statistics Canada.

Parsons, Michael H. (1980). 'Future Directions: Eight Steps to Parity of Part-Time Faculty.' In Michael Parsons, ed., *Using Part-Time faculty Effectively. New Directions for Community Colleges 39*. San Francisco: Jossey-Bass.

– (1985). *Part-Time Occupational Faculty: A Contribution to Excellence*. Information Series no. 300. *ERIC*. CD-ROM. SilverPlatter.

Parsons, Talcott, and Gerald M. Platt. (1973). *The American University*. Cambridge, Mass.: Harvard University Press.

Pineo, P. and J. Porter. (1967). 'Occupational Prestige in Canada.' *Canadian Review of Anthropology and Sociology* 4 no. 1: 24–40.

Pleck, Elizabeth. (1990). 'The Unfulfilled Promise: Women and Academe.' *Sociological Forum* 5: 515–24.

Polishook, Irwin H. (1992). 'The State of the Union in Higher Education: Unions in a Battered Academy.' In Beth Hillman Johnson, ed., *The Impact of Collective Bargaining on Higher Education: A Twenty Year Retrospective. Proceedings of the Twentieth Annual Conference, 13–14 April 1992*. New York, 1992. *ERIC*. CD-ROM. SilverPlatter.

Pollington, M. (1991). 'Part-Time Teachers or Teachers Who Work Part-Time?' ED331083. *ERIC*. CD-ROM. SilverPlatter.

Pratt, Linda Ray. (1993). Quoted in Julia Ridgely, 'Faculty Senates and the Fiscal Crisis.' *Academe* 79 no. 6: 8.

Press, Eyal, and Jennifer Washburn. (2000). 'The Kept University.' *Atlantic Monthly* 285 no. 3: 39–54. Online: http://www.theatlantic.com.

Price Waterhouse Coopers. (1999). *Will There Be Room for Me?* Report on Capacity and Related Issues in Ontario's Universities in the Face of Record Student Demand for University Education over the Next Decade. Toronto: Price Waterhouse Coopers.

Professional Women's Association. (1986). *Report of a Study on Part-Time Faculty and Staff*. Waterloo, Ont.: University of Waterloo.

Pucel, David, et al. (1992). *A Comparison of Factors Related to the Job Satisfaction and Professional Development of Beginning and Experienced Technical College Instructors*. St Paul: University of Minnesota: *ERIC*. CD-ROM. SilverPlatter.

Pyke, Sandra W. (1997). 'Education and the "Woman Question."' (1997) *Canadian Psychology* 38 no. 3: 154–63.

Rajagopal, Indhu, and William D. Farr. (1988). 'A Preliminary Report to the Committee on the Status of Women, Council of Ontario Universities: Part-Time Faculty in Ontario Universities.' Unpublished paper.

– (1989). 'The Political Economy of Part-Time Academic Work in Canada.' *Higher Education* 18: 267–85.

– (1991a). *Part-Time Faculty in Ontario Universities: 1987–88. Institutional Survey Report*. Prepared for the Committee on the Status of Women, Council of Ontario Universities, 1990. In *Non-Regular Instruction Personnel in Ontario Universities*. Toronto: COU.

– (1991b). 'Unpacking the Notion of Part-Time faculty.' *University Affairs*, April: 40.

– (1992). 'Hidden Academics: The Part-Time Faculty in Canada.' *Higher Education* 24: 317–31.

Rajagopal, Indhu, and Zeng Lin. (1996). 'Hidden Careerists in Canadian Universities.' *Higher Education* 32: 247–66.

Renner, K. Edward. (1988). 'The Dark and Light Side of the Crisis in Higher Education.' *CAUT Bulletin* 35 no. 9: 16.

– (1995). *The New Agenda for Higher Education: Choices Universities Can Make to Ensure a Brighter Future*. Calgary, Alta: Detselig Enterprises.

Report of the Royal Commission on National Development of the Arts, Letters and Sciences (Massey Report). (1951). Ottawa: Queen's Printer.

Report of the Senate Committee on Part-Time Faculty. (1976). 25 March. Archives of the Senate of York University.

Reskin, Barbara, and Patricia A. Roos. (1987). 'Status Hierarchies and Sex Segregation.' In C. Bose and G. Spitz, eds, *Ingredients for Women's Employment Policy*. New York: State University of New York Press.

– (1988). 'Sex Differentiation and Devaluation of Women's Work: Implications for Women's Occupational Progress and Comparable Worth.' (Paper delivered at the University of Illinois at Urbana-Champaign, June 1987.) Quoted in Linda Blum and Vicky Smith, 'Women's Mobility in the Corporation: A Critique of the Politics of Optimism.' *Signs: Journal of Women and Culture in Society* 13 no. 3: 541.

Rhatigan, James J. (1978). 'A Corrective Lookback.' In James Appleton, Channing Briggs, and James J. Rhatigan, eds, *Pieces of Eight: The Rites, Roles, and Styles of the Dean by Eight Who Have Been There*. Portland, Oreg: NASPA, Institute of Research and Development.

Rhoades, Gary. (1996). 'Reorganizing the Faculty Workforce for Flexibility: Part-Time Professional Labor.' *Journal of Higher Education* 67: 626–59.

Rhodes, Jean. (1991). 'A Study of Instruction Needs of Part-Time Faculty at Northwestern Michigan College.' Master's diss., Ferris State University, Michigan. *ERIC*. CD-ROM. SilverPlatter.

Rice, Eugene. (1987). 'The American Professoriate: Rewards and Satisfactions.' In Joel M. Douglas, ed. *The Faculty Life Cycle: A Legal Perspective*. New York: National Center for the Study of Collective Bargaining in Higher Education and the Professions.

Rich, Adrienne. (1979). *On Lies, Secrets and Silence*. New York: Norton.

Ridgely, Julia. (1993). 'Faculty, Senate and the Fiscal Crisis.' *Academe*, 79 no. 6: 7–11.

Roderer, Larry, and Betty Weissbecker. (1990). 'Perspectives on Part-Time Teaching in Community Colleges: Pressures, Politics, and Prospects.' *VCCA [Virginia Community Colleges Asso.] Journal* 5: 28–33.

Rogow, Robert, and Daniel R. Birch. (1984). 'Teaching Assistant Unionization: Origins and Implications.' *Canadian Journal of Higher Education* 14: 11–29.

Rollin, Roger. 1989. 'There's No Business Like Education.' *Academe* 75 no. 1: 14–17.

Rose, Phyllis. (1984). *Parallel Lives: Five Victorian Marriages*. New York: Knopf.

Rosenblum, Gerald, and Barbara Rubin Rosenblum. (1994). 'Academic Labour Markets: Perspectives from Ontario.' *Canadian Journal of Higher Education* 24 no. 1: 49–71.

Rossiter, Margaret W. (1995). *Women Scientists in America: Before Affirmative Action, 1940–1972*. Baltimore: Johns Hopkins University Press.

Rothblum, Esther D. (1988). 'Leaving the Ivory Tower: Factors Contributing to Women's Voluntary Resignation from Academia.' *Frontiers* 10 no. 2: 14–17.

Sandler, Bernice Resnick, ed. (1996). *About Women on Campus* 5 nos 1–4: 3–80. Center for Women Policy Studies, Washington, DC. *ERIC*. CD-ROM. Silver-Platter.

Sandler, Bernice R., and Roberta M. Hall. (1986). *The Campus Climate Revisited: Chilly for Women Faculty, Administrators, and Graduate Students*. Washington, DC: Project on the Status and Education of Women.

Saul, John Ralston. (1995). *The Unconscious Civilization*. Concord, Ont.: Anansi Press.

Schaffer, S.M. (1992). 'Reformation Comes to the University. ' *Journal of Higher Education Management* 8: 7–12.

Schwartz, Robert A. (1996). 'Reconceptualizing the Leadership Roles of Women in Higher Education: A Brief History on the Importance of Deans of Women.' Paper presented at the Annual Meeting of the American Educational Research Association, April 1996. New York. *ERIC*. CD-ROM. Silver-Platter.

Scott, Barbara Ann. (1983). *Crisis Management in American Higher Education*. New York: Praeger.

Shannon, David M., et al. (1998). 'TA Teaching Effectiveness: The Impact of Training and Teaching Experience.' *Journal of Higher Education* 69: 440–66.

Shapiro, James. (1998). 'Beyond the Culture Wars: Three Books Look at the Crisis American Colleges Face in the Age of Superprofs and Research Grants.'

Review of Donald Kennedy, *Academic Duty*; George Dennis O'Brien, *All the Essential Half-Truths about Higher Education*; and Martha C. Nussbaum, *Cultivating Humanity. New York Times Book Review* 4 Jan.: 18.

Shattering the Glass Box? Women Entrepreneurs and the Knowledge-Based Economy, Report of Industry Canada, 1999. (1999). Ottawa: Government Publications.

Shattock, Michael. (1989). 'Thatcherism and British Higher Education.' *Change* 21 no. 5: 30–9.

Shegda, Iris. (1996). 'Status Quo Holding Fast in Universities, Study Says (Edward Renner).' Canadian Press Newswire, 24 July. *Canadian Index*. CD-ROM. SilverPlatter.

Sherwood, J. (1993). 'The Tenuous State of Part-Time Faculty.' *CAUT Bulletin* 40 no. 1: 11.

Shostak, Arthur B. (1992). 'The State of Unions in Higher Education: Robust Unionism and Unions in Higher Education.' In Beth Hillman Johnson, ed., *The Impact of Collective Bargaining on Higher Education: A Twenty Year Retrospective. Proceedings of the Twentieth Annual Conference, 13–14 April.* New York. ERIC. CD-ROM. SilverPlatter.

Simeone, Angela. (1987). *Academic Women: Working towards Equality.* South Hadley, Mass.: Bergin and Garvin.

Skolnik, Michael L. (1988). 'The Evolution of Relations between Management and Faculty in Ontario Colleges of Applied Arts and Technology.' *Canadian Journal of Higher Education* 18 no. 3: 83–112.

– (1990). 'Lipset's "Continental Divide" and the Ideological Basis for Differences in Higher Education between Canada and the United States.' *Canadian Journal of Higher Education* 20 no. 2: 81–93.

Slaughter, Sheila. (1993). 'Retrenchment in the 1980s.' *Journal of Higher Education* 64 no. 3: 250–82.

Slaughter, Sheila, and Larry L. Leslie. (1997). *Academic Capitalism: Politics, Policies, and the Entrepreneurial University.* Baltimore and London: Johns Hopkins University Press.

Smith, Catherine Begnoche, and Vivian Scott Hixson. (1987). 'The Work of University Professor: Evidence of Segmented Labor Markets inside the Academy.' *Current Research on Occupations and Professions* 4: 159–80.

Smith, Dorothy E. (1975). 'An Analysis of Ideological Structures and How Women Are Excluded: Considerations for Academic Women.' *Canadian Review of Sociology and Anthropology* 12 no. 4: 353–69.

– (1987). *The Everyday World as Problematic: A Feminist Sociology.* Toronto: University of Toronto Press.

– (1990). *The Conceptual Practices of Power: A Feminist Sociology of Knowledge.* Toronto: University of Toronto Press.

– (1997). Review of Patricia M. Marchak, *Racism, Sexism and the University: The Political Science Affair at the University of British Columbia. Canadian Journal of Higher Education* 27 nos. 2–3: 252–6.

– (1999). *Writing the Social: Critique, Theory, and Investigations.* Toronto: University of Toronto Press.

Smith, Myrna J., Steve Goling, and Enid Friedman. (1992). 'Cosmopolitan Communities for Faculty Developers.' *To Improve the Academy* 11: 167–74.

Sowers-Hoag, Karen M. and Dianne F. Harrison. (1991). 'Women in Social Work Education: Progress or Promise?' *Journal of Social Work Education* 27 no. 3: 320–8.

Speer, Tom. (1992). 'Part-Time Instructors: Strategies to Survive in the 90s.' *Teaching English in the Two Year College* 19: 266–73.

Standing, Guy. (1989). 'Global Feminization through Flexible Labour.' *World Development* 17 no. 7: 1077–95.

– (1999). 'Global Feminization through Flexible Labour: A Theme Revisited.' *World Development* 27 no. 3: 583–602.

Stanley, Christine A., and Terrence D. Lumpkins. (1992). 'Instructional Needs of Part-Time Faculty: Implications for Faculty Development.' Donald H. Wulff and Jody D. Nyquist. Stillwater, eds (1992). *Resources for Faculty, Instructional, and Organizational Development, To Improve the Academy* 11: 59–70. *ERIC.* CD-ROM. SilverPlatter.

'Statement from the Conference on the Growing Use of Part-Time and Adjunct Faculty, Washington DC. 26–8 Sept. 1997.' (1998). *Academe* 84 no. 1: 54–60.

Statistics Canada. (1975–95) *Information on University Expenditures, Salaries, and Research Budgets.* Ottawa: Statistics Canada.

– (1989) *University Staff by Institution and Principal Subject Taught.* Ottawa: Statistics Canada.

– (1991a). Education, Culture and Tourism Division. *Proposed University Part-Time Teaching Staff System Manual 1991–92.* Ottawa: Statistics Canada.

– (1991b). Education Division. *A Report on Part-Time University Faculty.* Comp. Ahmad Consultants Inc. Ottawa: Statistics Canada.

– (1994a). *Education in Canada.* Ottawa Statistics Canada.

– (1994b). *Women in the Labour Force.* Cat. no. 75-507E. Ottawa Statistics Canada.

– (1996). *Labour Force* 52 no. 12: B33, B34, B41.

– (1997). *Perspectives* Autumn: 21–31. Cat. no. 75-001-XPE. Ottawa: Statistics Canada.

– (1998). *University Full-Time Teaching Staff by Sex, by Type of Appointment, by Province, for 1996–97.* 24 June. Data sent to the author.

– (1999a). *Labour Force Update* 3 no. 1: 5–15. Cat. no. 71-005-XPB.

- (1999b) *Labour Force Information* 17 April. Cat. no. 71-001-PPB.
- (1999c) *Labour Force Update* 3 no. 2: 16–33. Cat. no. 71-005-XPB.
- (1999d). *Labour Force Information* 19 June. Cat. no. 71-001-PPB.
- (2000a). 'Part-Time University Faculty, 1992-93 to 1997–98.' *Education Quarterly Review* 7 no. 1: 51–2. Cat. no. 81-003. Ottawa: Statistics Canada.
- (2000b). *Women in Canada 2000*. Cat. no. 89-503-xpe. Ottawa: Statistics Canada.

Stewart, Penni, and Janice Drakich. (1995). 'Factors Related to Organizational Change and Equity for Women Faculty in Ontario Universities.' *Canadian Public Policy* 21: 429–48.

Stookey, Lorena. (1994). 'Beyond the Classroom: The Professional Work of Permanent Temps.' In Hallie S. Lemon et al., comps, *Redefining the Role of 'Permanent Temps': Proving Ourselves Professionals. Proceedings of a Roundtable Session at the Forty-fifth Annual Conference on College Composition and Communication*, March 16–19. Nashville, Tenn. ERIC. CD-ROM. SilverPlatter.

Strauss, Stephen. (1993). 'Citing the Citations.' *Globe and Mail* 6 March: D8.

Strong, David. (1992). 'UVic Profs: Many Outstanding, but Salaries Lag Behind.' *Monday Magazine* 30 April–6 May.

Tafler. Sid. (1992a). 'The UVic trick: Money for Nothing and Hard Times for Hard Work.' *Monday Magazine* 16–22 April.

- (1992b). 'More UVic Tricks: Exploiting and Demeaning the "Illegal Immigrants."' *Monday Magazine* 23–29 April.

Tancred-Sheriff, P. (1985). 'Craft Hierarchy and Bureaucracy: Modes of Control of Academic Labour Process.' *Canadian Journal of Sociology* 10 no. 4: 369–90.

Tang, Thomas Li-Ping, and Mitchell Chamberlin. (1997). 'Attitudes toward Research and Teaching: Differences between Administrators and Faculty Members.' *Journal of Higher Education* 68 no. 2: 212–27.

Taube, Michael. (1999). 'Private Universities Would Be a Credit.' *Globe and Mail* 23 Aug.: B2.

Taylor, Linda E. (1995). 'Joining the Old Boy's Club: It Is Extremely Difficult for Women to Attain Positions of real power.' Canada and the World Backgrounder 60 no. 4: 12–15. *Canadian Index*. CD-ROM. SilverPlatter.

Teevan, James T., Susan Pepper, and Joseph R. Pellizzari. (1992). 'Academic Employment Decisions and Gender.' *Research in Higher Education* 33: 141–60.

Thompson, Karen. (1992). 'Recognizing Mutual Interests.' *Academe* 78 no. 6: 22–6.

Thurman, Joseph E., and Gabriele Trah. (1990). 'Part-Time Work in International Perspective.' *International Labour Review* 129: 23–40.

Tien, Flora F., and Robert T. Blackburn. (1996). 'Faculty Rank System, Research Motivation, and Faculty Research Productivity.' *Journal of Higher Education* 67 no. 1: 2–22.

Times Higher Education. (1994). 'Perspective: An Unlevel Playing Field.' 19 August: 15–16.

Tolbert, Pamela S., and Alice A. Oberfield. (1991). 'Sources of Organizational Demography: Faculty Sex Ratios in Colleges and Universities.' *Sociology of Education* 64 Oct.: 305–15.

Toren, Nina. (1987). 'The Status of Women in Academia.' *Israel Social Science Research* 5: 138–46.

– (1991). 'The Nexus between Family and Work Roles of Academic Women in Israel: Reality and Representation.' *Sex Roles* 24: 651–67.

Toren, Nina, and Vered Kraus. (1987). 'The Effects of Minority Size on Women's Position in Academia.' *Social Forces* 65: 1090–1107.

Toronto Star. (1998). 17 May: F6. Quoted in *OCUFA Forum* (1999) Spring: 19.

Toutkoushian, Robert K. (1998). 'Racial and Marital Status Differences in Faculty Pay.' *Journal of Higher Education* 69: 513–41.

Tsai, Chin-Fen, and Robert C. Schwindt. (1996). 'Career Development and Stress of Female Faculty Members at Pittsburg State University.' *Rethinking Diversity. Proceedings of the Academy of Human Resource Development Conference, 29 Feb.–3 March 1996*. Minneapolis, Minn. ERIC. CD-ROM. SilverPlatter.

Tuckman, Howard P. (1978). 'Who Is Part-Time in Academe?' *AAUP Bulletin* 64: 305–15.

– (1983). 'Part-Time Faculty: Some Suggestions of Policy.' *OATYC [Ohio Association of Two-Year Colleges] Journal* 8 nos 1–2: 23–8. ERIC. CD-ROM. SilverPlatter.

Tuckman, Howard P., and K.L. Pickerill. (1988). 'Part-Time Faculty and Part-Time Academic Careers.' In D.W. Breneman and T.I.K. Youn, eds, *Academic Labour Markets and Careers*. Philadelphia: Falmer Press.

Tuckman, Howard P., and William Vogler. (1978). 'The "Part" in Part-Time Wages.' *AAUP Bulletin* 64: 70–7.

Tuckman, Howard P., Jamie Caldwell, and William Vogler. (1978). 'Part-Timers and the Academic Labor Market of the Eighties.' *American Sociologist* 13: 184–95.

Tuckman, Howard P., William D. Vogler, and Jamie Caldwell. (1978). *Part-Time Faculty Series*. Washington, DC: AAUP.

Twombly, Susan B. (1993). 'What We Know about Women in Community Colleges: An Examination of the Literature Using Feminist Phase Theory.' *Journal of Higher Education* 64 no. 2: 186–210.

UTFA (University of Toronto Faculty Association). (1991). 'Our Shame.' *University of Toronto Bulletin* 1 April: 12.

Van Arsdale, G. (1978). 'De-Professionalizing a Part-Time Teaching Faculty:

How Many, Feeling Small, Seeming Few, Getting Less, Dream of More?'
American Sociologist 13: 195–201.

Van Steijn, Frans. (1985). 'Part-Time Professors in the Netherlands: Old Wine in
New Bottles?' *European Journal of Education* 20: 57–65.

Veltmeyer, Henry, and James Sacouman. (1998). 'Political Economy of Part-
Time Work.' *Studies in Political Economy.* 56: 115–43.

Vosko, Leah F. (2000). *Temporary Work: The Gendered Rise of a Precarious Employment Relationship.* Toronto: University of Toronto Press.

Wachman, Marvin (1994). 'The End of the Ivory Tower: Students, Administration, and Community.' Paper presented at the American Association for
Higher Education, 24 March, Chicago. *ERIC.* CD-ROM. SilverPlatter.

Walker, Henry A. (1980). 'A Reevaluation of a Test of Kanter's Hypothesis.'
American Journal of Sociology 85: 1226–9.

Wallace, Elizabeth M. (1984). 'Women, Part-Time Teaching, and Affirmative
Action.' In Elizabeth Wallace, ed., *Part-Time Academic Employment in the
Humanities.* New York: MLA.

– (1991). 'A One-Time Part-Timer's Response to the CCCC Statement of
Professional Standards.' *College Composition and Communication* 42 no. 3:
350–5.

– ed. (1984). *Part-Time Academic Employment in the Humanities.* New York:
MLA.

Walton, Dawn. (1999). 'Women Take to Self-Employment.' *Globe and Mail* 14
January: B7.

Ward Kathryn B., and Linda Grant. (1996). 'Gender and Academic Publishing.
In J. Smart, ed., *Higher Education: Handbook of Theory and Research.* Edison, NJ:
Agathon.

Watkins, Regina M., et al. (1996). 'The University Community Where Equity
Can Happen: Getting Past the Rhetoric.' Paper presented at the Forty-Eighth
Annual Meeting of the American Association of Colleges for Teacher Educa-
tion, 21–24 February, Chicago. *ERIC.* CD-ROM. SilverPlatter.

Weis, L. (n.d.)' Falling through the Cracks: Sessionals in Alberta.' Unpublished
paper, University of Alberta.

Welch, Gerry. (1996). 'Seasoned Chairs and Deans Can Learn New Tricks.'
*Olympics of Leadership: Overcoming Obstacles, Balancing Skills, Taking Risks.
Proceedings of the Fifth Annual International Conference of the National Commu-
nity College Chair Academy, 14–17 Feb.* Phoenix, Ariz. *ERIC.* CD-ROM. Silver-
Platter.

Wenzel, Stacy A., and Carol Hollenshead. (1994). 'Tenured Women Faculty:
Reasons for Leaving One Research University.' Paper presented at the
Nineteenth Annual Meeting of the Association for the Study of Higher

Education, 10–13 Nov. Tucson, Ariz. ED 375713. *ERIC*. CD-ROM. Silver-Platter.

Western Report. (1994). 'A Woman Academic Pins Down Exactly What Is at Stake in the Campus "Gender War."' *Western Report* 9 no. 4: 44. *Canadian Index*. CD-ROM. SilverPlatter.

Whalley, George. (1964). *A Place of Liberty*. Toronto: Clarke Irwin.

Whichard, Nancy Winggardner, Cayo Gamber, Valerie Lester, Gordon Leighton, Judith Carlberg, and William Whitaker. (1992). 'Life in the Margin: The Hidden Agenda in Commenting on Student Writing.' *Journal of Teaching Writing* 11: 51–64.

White, Geoffry D., and Flannery C. Hauck, eds. (2000). *Campus, Inc*. Amherst, NY: Prometheus Books.

Woodard, Joseph K. (1995). 'Ivory Towers under Siege: Fembos, Pleasant and Otherwise, Bid for Control of the West's Universities.' *Western Report* 10 nos. 25 and 26: 28–31. *Canadian Index*. CD-ROM. SilverPlatter.

The Work Roles of Academics in Australian Universities. (2000). www.detya. gov.au/highered/eippubs.htm#00-5.

Wright, Eric O. (1985). *Classes*. London: Verso.

Wright, Eric O., and D. Cho. (1992). 'State Employment, Class Location, and Ideological Orientation: A Comparative Analysis of the United States and Sweden.' *Politics and Society* 20 no. 2: 167-96

Yang, Shu O. Wu, and Michele Wender Zak. (1981). *Part-Time Faculty Employment in Ohio: A Statewide Study*. Kent, Ohio: Kent State University.

Yantz, Patricia M., and Charles Brechtold. (1994). 'Part-Time Faculty: Here Today, Not Gone Tomorrow, or Professional Development of Part-Time Faculty and the Changing Role of Division Chairperson.' Paper presented at the Third International Conference for Community College Chairs, Deans, and Other Instructional Leaders, 23–26 February 1994, Phoenix, Ariz. *ERIC*. CD-ROM. SilverPlatter.

York Gazette (2000). 30 no. 17: 3.

Youn, T.I.K. (1988). 'Studies of Academic Markets and Careers: An Historical Review.' In D.W. Breneman and T.I.K. Youn, eds, *Academic Labour Markets and Careers* Philadelphia: Falmer Press.

Young, Carlotta Joyner, Doris Layton MacKenzie, and Carolyn Wood Sherif. (1980). 'In Search of Token Women in Academia.' *Psychology of Women Quarterly* 4: 508–25.

YUFA (York University Faculty Association). (2000). 'Ontario Budget 2000.' Online posting to members. 4 May. yufa@yorku.ca.

Zeytinoglu, Isik Urla. (1989). *Part-Time Workers in Unionized Organizations: Results of a Survey of Employers and Unions*. Report. McMaster University, Hamilton, Ont.

Zeytinoglu, Isik Urla, and Maroussia Ahmed. (1989). 'Results of a Survey on Part-Time Faculty at McMaster University.' Report of the Committee on the Status of Women to the McMaster University Faculty Association, Hamilton, Ont.

Zuckerman, H.A. (1977) *Scientific Elite*. New York: Free Press.

Index